The St. Louis Cardinals—
the First Century

The St. Louis Cardinals— the First Century

A Short History of the National League's Greatest Team

Mario Vricella

VANTAGE PRESS
New York

Published by Vantage Press, Inc.
516 West 34th Street, New York, New York 10001

Manufactured in the United States of America
ISBN: 0-533-10163-8

Library of Congress Catalog Card No.: 91-91504

0 9 8 7 6 5 4 3 2 1

To my mother, whose support made this book possible

Contents

Preface

The St. Louis Cardinals. The name evokes memories of great teams, players, and pennant races. Who could forget the 1934 Gashouse Gang? Or Stan Musial lashing out base hits in Brooklyn's Ebbets Field in many key September series there? Or the capturing of the 1964 pennant after getting off to a bad start? Many of the all-time great players began their careers as a Cardinal: Hornsby and Haines, Hafey and Bottomley, Medwick and Mize, Musial and Slaughter, Flood and Gibson. Branch Rickey, probably the game's greatest innovator, first proved himself as a baseball genius while with the Cardinals. The Cardinals under Rickey did not invent the minor leagues or even the farm system, but they did show the way to better build a ball club from the minors on up. Today mentioning the Cardinals brings to mind fabulous success and wealth—after all, the Cardinals have won fifteen pennants and nine world championships in their National League history and they have also drawn 3 million fans in a season while playing in a small market—but such prosperity wasn't always the case. Indeed, the Cardinals suffered through some mighty hard times early in their National League life.

Did you know that the Cardinals were first called the Browns and played in the then major league American Association from 1882 to 1891? No, the Cardinals were not a part of the National League in its first year of 1876 (only the Chicago Cubs remain from the circuit's first season), although St. Louis did have a team in the league in its first two years of life. Today's Cardinals were quite successful as the Browns in the association and were owned by the colorful Chris Von Der Ahe (who brought the hot dog to baseball as one of his long-lasting ideas), who was a combination Charlie Finley, George Steinbrenner, and Bill Veeck, and people took either a strong liking or hating of him to heart. The Browns also gave St. Louis its first popular athlete in infielder Arlie Latham, who was called "the Freshest Man on Earth." Latham was much like a later St. Louis infielder named Leo Durocher, playing hard-nosed ball and tormenting opposing teams with vicious bench jockeying. In Latham's day, baseball was not for the genteel, and ladies rarely attended games because of the rampant cursing, drinking, and fighting that went on at them, so the male fans delighted in Latham's style of play. The "Freshest Man" never had to worry about offending anyone because the fans came to expect their idol to insult and belittle the enemy, and Latham never disappointed the crowd. Had Latham been born a few decades later, he would have fit in quite nicely on the 1934 Cardinals.

The association's Browns were much like the National League's Cardinals of the 1940s, but once they switched circuits, disaster struck. The Cardinals joined the Baltimore Orioles and two other association clubs in merging with the National League in 1892, but only the Orioles made a mark in the older circuit. Although the Cardinals were actually born in 1882, their official history goes back to 1892, when they joined the National League. Thus 1992 is the centennial of the St. Louis Cardinals.

Once the Cardinals switched circuits, thirty years of failure struck. Bad ownership, crumbling stadiums, debts, competition from other leagues, lack of good players, and poor attendance all put the Cardinals on the edge of extinction several times. In the late 1890s, the Cardinals nearly went bankrupt after Chris Von Der Ahe spent the team into the ground. In 1902 the American League put the Browns into St. Louis, and the new team in town stole the top players from the old team. In the 1910s the Cardinals were run by another inept owner and faced further competition from a Federal League club and came close to moving out of town. Even after getting on track in the late 1920s, the Cardinals faced hardship. The Depression of the 1930s caused such a steep decline in attendance that the Cardinals considered moving out of town, even though they were one of the best teams in baseball. As recently as 1953 there was the possibility of the Cardinals leaving town, but somehow they overcame the odds and survived.

Despite their humble National League beginnings as a poor laughingstock, the St. Louis Cardinals have not only survived, but have flourished, and they outlasted seven out of the other eleven teams that comprised the National League in 1892. The Brooklyn Dodgers, New York Giants, Boston Braves, Cleveland Spiders, Louisville Colonels, Baltimore Orioles (the National League version), and Washington Nationals have all been swept into the trash can of history since 1892, and the Cardinals, despite their early problems, managed to avoid the fate that befell these aforementioned clubs. No National League club has won as many pennants and world championships as the Cardinals have since 1892, and if one discounts the Cardinals' first thirty-four years in the N.L., their feats concerning postseason play look even more impressive.

What has made the Cardinals last for a century despite all of the fiscal insanity that has gripped baseball from time to time? Financial prudence is the answer. Branch Rickey and Sam Breadon took over a team that was a hopeless mess, and through fiscal acumen the Cardinals finally stabilized. Both men were considered tightwads, but in the end they were proven right: their tightness with a dollar kept the Cardinals in town, while the free-spending Browns of Phil Ball no longer exist. Even after Rickey and Breadon left the Cardinal scene, their successors maintained their financial policy. During the 1970s and 1980s the Cardinals stood basically on the sidelines, while other teams foolishly threw away millions of dollars on free agents who ended up getting seriously hurt or underachieving. Even though the Cardinals passed on most big-name free agents, they still managed to claim three pennants in the 1980s, more than any other team in that decade. Although they play in one of the smallest markets, the Cardinals are considered one of baseball's richest teams and are able to compete against such large market teams as the Chicago Cubs, the New York Mets, and the Los Angeles Dodgers. Today's struggling smaller teams would do well to study the past history of the Cardinals and follow their precedent to get to the top, rather than always cry foul.

On the field, the Cardinals have been successful mainly with the speed game. Other teams, like the Yankees, have gotten to the top primarily by hitting plenty of homers, but the Cardinals have usually achieved greatness via speed. Yes, the Cardinals have led the league in homers over the years from time to time, but speed has been the main weapon for scoring runs. Looking at Appendix F shows how important speed has been for the Cardinals, since many of the seasonal leaders in stolen bases and triples played for St. Louis. Some of the Cardinals who led the league in triples may baffle the reader. While Garry Templeton leading the league in triples is not a surprise, Tim McCarver doing so is (he wasn't a leadfoot, but then again he wasn't Mercury either) and *Johnny Mize* is even more shocking, so that proves that speed has always been a Cardinal weapon. Triples and steals are speed-generated statistics that show up in a box score, while going from first to third on a single does not show up in a box score, but you can be sure the Cardinals have excelled in this act for a lot longer than the 1980s, when Whitey Herzog was praised for having his team play "Whiteyball." Herzog did not bring the speed game to St. Louis for the first time ever; he simply revived it after it died out in the 1970s. Speed has always been an important weapon for St. Louis, and as long as they play in spacious Busch Stadium, the Cardinals will always have to stress speed in order to be successful.

Being a Cardinals fan is to expect the unexpected. Many times in their history the Cardinals were expected to do well going into a season but ended doing nothing instead, like in 1932, after winning two straight pennants. Many more times the Cardinals went into a season expected to do nothing and instead captured glory, like in 1985 after losing relief ace Bruce Sutter. More often than not the Cardinals have come through with exciting seasons and have left many memories in the minds of fans, even if the team did not win the flag in that particular year. Many people remember Stan Musial getting his 3,000th career hit in 1958, Lou Brock's 105th stolen base of 1974, and Brock's 3,000th career hit in 1979. Some older fans will recall the 1922 trade the Cardinals and Cubs made right after the first game of a doubleheader between the two teams. In 1951 the Cardinals played a twin bill with two different teams for an opponent (the Giants and Braves), and that is certainly something not to be forgotten. And nobody who saw it will forget the Cardinals' 4–3 win over the Mets in a 1974 game that lasted 25 innings and ended at 3:30 A.M., the longest-lasting game that produced a winner in National League history. Of course, pennant clinchings are always memorable, and the Cardinals have given their fans many memories of these as well.

As long as the Cardinals keep coming up with speedsters like

Vince Coleman, bat masters like Stan Musial, fierce competitors like Bob Gibson, brainy players like Tim McCarver, and sluggers like Ducky Medwick, while pulling off a shrewd trade like the one for Lou Brock, they will continue to be the National League's finest team. These and hundreds of other players have thrilled and excited Cardinals' fans throughout their first century, and millions of people have their own memories and their own favorite Cardinal players in the last one hundred years. Nineteen-ninety-two marks the second century of the St. Louis Cardinals, and the future looks great. Here's to their next century!

The St. Louis Cardinals—
the First Century

Part I

The Origins of the Cardinals
(1875–91)

I

Baseball was already being played in St. Louis on the amateur level when the Cincinnati Redlegs became the first professional team in 1869. The Redlegs traveled around the nation, playing mostly amateur teams, and compiled fifty-six wins in over a year. The success of the Redlegs on the field and at the gate prompted the founding of the first professional baseball organization, the National Association, in 1871. Nine clubs formed the association in its first season, and none came from St. Louis. In 1875 St. Louis finally joined the association, entering with two teams. One, called the Reds, was managed by Charles Sweasy and posted a 4–14 record before dropping out. The other St. Louis team (whose name is yet to be uncovered) was 39–29 under manager Dickey Pearce. These two clubs were the first professional ones St. Louis ever fielded.

By the end of the 1875 season, it was apparent that the National Association was in trouble. The Boston club had just won the pennant by fifteen games and had won the previous three flags as well, causing a lack of interest in games played outside of Boston. Several clubs had financial troubles and dropped out or simply would fail to appear for scheduled games. Players moved from team to team at ease, causing a lack of fan loyalty. Gambling, fighting, and drunkenness were rampant. The lack of a schedule prepared before Opening Day caused confusion for teams and fans alike. Obviously something needed to be done.

On February 2, 1876, representatives from Boston, Chicago, New York, Philadelphia, Cincinnati, Louisville, Hartford, and St. Louis met at New York's Grand Central Hotel and hammered out an agreement to create the National League, which was to operate more strictly than the National Association and eliminate all of the association's ills. William Hulbert, the man who gathered the new league's representatives together (despite animosities between the eastern and western clubs' leaders in the past) declined the league's presidency and instead endorsed Morgan Bulkeley for the job. The clubs agreed and Bulkeley became the first president of the National League.

April 22, 1876, marked the start of the National League when Boston defeated Philadelphia 6–5 at Philadelphia. The National League's debut in St. Louis was happier for the home team, as St. Louis shut out Chicago 1–0 on May 5. The first National Leaguer to win a game for St. Louis was George Bradley, who went on to toss the league's first no-hitter (July 15 against Hartford) en route to a 45–19 record.

That 45–19 record by Bradley was the final record of the entire St. Louis club. In those days, pitchers completed what they started and usually one man did all the pitching for his team. Despite Bradley's heroics, he was not the league's top hurler. Chicago's Al Spalding went 47–13 as his club's only pitcher, and that was good enough to give Chicago the first pennant in National League history. As it turned out, St. Louis finished in a second-place tie with Hartford, both teams being six games behind the team that is now called the Cubs.

The 1876 season proved to be a tough one for the new league. Founded to eliminate the wrongs of the old association, the league quickly suffered many of the same problems as its predecessor. Philadelphia and New York failed to complete their last trips west, citing fiscal trouble, and were suspended. Club heads began feuding over past grievances, gambling and rowdyism continued, and disputes over allowing beer at parks made the league's pledge to repudiate the association look like a bad joke.

Despite the turmoil of 1876, the National League returned for business in 1877, minus the suspended Philadelphia and New York clubs. St. Louis entered the season without George Bradley, who moved on to Chicago. In 1877, St. Louis got its pitching from Tricky Nichols and Joe Blong, who combined for a 28–32 mark. With Nichols and Blong not pitching consistently, St. Louis sank to fourth in the six-team National League with a lackluster 28–32 mark, fourteen games behind pennant-winning Boston.

Without moneymaking teams in New York and Philadelphia, the National League suffered financially. Club heads begged for

4

reinstatement of the two suspended clubs, but to no avail. William Hulbert, the man who had gathered the heads of the league's current teams together to create it, was dead set against returning violators to his creation. Morgan Bulkeley, the weak figurehead president of the National League, left after 1876, and Hulbert assumed the job. Hulbert was iron-fisted and was determined to run the National League the right way—his own way. As a result, almost all of the teams lost money in 1877, including St. Louis. In fact, the St. Louis club lost so heavily that it had to drop out of the league. As a result, St. Louis went without major league baseball until 1882.

II

By 1882, the National League looked like it was ready to fold. Clubs came and went, bankruptcy had stricken many clubs, and Hulbert's iron fist was angering enough wealthy men who wanted to own a club that the time was ripe to create a rival league.

In 1881, Cincinnati fought the National League to allow beer in its ballpark. The righteous National League refused, and the Cincinnati club either dropped out or was thrown out of the league, depending on what each side said. The Cincinnati club then called on other cities that were at odds with the National League to join them in forming a new league. Eager rich men, including one named Chris Von Der Ahe, jumped at the chance to own a ball club. On November 2, 1881, the American Association was created and awarded franchises to Cincinnati, Brooklyn, Louisville, Pittsburgh, and St. Louis. The St. Louis club was called the Browns and was owned by Chris Von Der Ahe and is the direct ancestor of the current Cardinals.

Chris Von Der Ahe turned out to be the first of a long line of offbeat, colorful owners in baseball history. Born on November 7, 1851, in Hille, Germany, Von Der Ahe spoke with a thick German accent and by age thirty had made a fortune in St. Louis as a beer brewer. Von Der Ahe was notoriously cheap with his ball players (despite living a lavish life himself), delivered tirades to his team when the spirit moved him, turned his park into something like

"Six Flags over Busch Stadium," and even managed the team himself for several brief spells. By the time he died broke on June 7, 1913, his ball club (by then in the National League and called the Cardinals) still hadn't recovered.

Von Der Ahe's antics, though, were in the future. Already before the 1882 season began, the American Association was in flux. Brooklyn dropped out and was replaced by Baltimore, and Philadelphia also decided to join. The new league decided to allow the "evils" that the National League had abhorred: Sunday games, booze, and quarter admissions (the National League charged fifty-cent admissions for its games). Also, the association decided that the team with the highest winning percentage rather than the most wins would be the pennant winner.

The A.A. had no pennant race that first year as Cincinnati, a perennial cellar dweller in the N.L., breezed by second-place Philadelphia by 11 ½ games. St. Louis, playing at the Grand Avenue Grounds, ended up fifth in a six-team league with a measly 37–43 record. Von Der Ahe was already showing how impatient he was with failure by firing manager Ned Cuthbert 59 games into the 80-game season. The only other noteworthy thing about the 1882 Browns is that their first baseman, Charles Comiskey, would later end up as owner of the Chicago White Sox.

The Browns, along with the rest of the association and new teams in New York and Columbus, returned for 1883. The Browns got off to a good start under new manager Ted Sullivan (the team's third since Opening Day, 1882) but Von Der Ahe found him lacking and fired him despite the club's 53–27 record under him. Charles Comiskey then took over as manager number four in two seasons. Tony Mullane and Jumbo McGinnis were the workhorses (by this time, a two-man pitching staff was the norm), Mullane going 35–15 and McGinnis going 28–16. Despite this one-two punch, though, the Browns finished second to Philadelphia, just one game out at 65–33. The 1883 A.A. race was the closest in major league history up to that time.

In 1884, the American Association again expanded, this time from eight clubs to thirteen. The expansion proved a disaster, as the new Washington and Richmond clubs failed to complete the season and came at a time when a third major league, the Union

6

Association, had been created for the season. The Union Association refused to recognize the reserve clause (a clause in every player's contract that, in effect, bound him to his team unless he was sold, traded, or released—even after a contract expired, that same team had the rights to that player forever) of contracted players in the A.A. and N.L. The U.A. raided the other two leagues and placed teams in cities already serviced by the other leagues, causing a financial strain to all concerned.

The Browns, playing in one of the smaller cities already served by the big leagues, suffered as the U.A. put a team called the Maroons in St. Louis. Although the Browns were competitive at 67–40, they finished fourth, 8 games behind New York. The Maroons, a novelty in town, went 94–19 and won many fans as well as the Union pennant. Von Der Ahe was less than pleased at the sight of an upstart winning the first flag of any kind for St. Louis. Even more distressing for "Der Boss" (as some people began calling Chris Von Der Ahe, long before George Steinbrenner was even born) was the way the Maroons were flaunting themselves under the direction of their twenty-seven-year-old owner-manager, Henry Lucas. Lucas called his park, which was larger than the Browns', "the palace park of America." Ironically, Lucas's park would serve as the home of the Browns in 1920, when they were the National League's Cardinals, but of course Von Der Ahe didn't know that.

After 1884, though, the Union Association called it quits. Several clubs failed to complete the season; oddly, the ones that failed were located in cities not in either established league. Also, the U.A. placed teams in such strange towns as Altoona and Wilmington, tiny even by the standards of the 1880s. The three leagues then decided that it was time to settle things for the good of the game. All players pirated by the U.A. would return to their old clubs, some U.A. owners would stay in organized ball (mostly in the minors), and Henry Lucas's Maroons would be transferred to the N.L. Chris Von Der Ahe was furious that the N.L. would allow a team stronger than his own and aggressive in promoting itself to stay in town to compete with him, which was a violation of the uneasy peace between the A.A. and the N.L. This and the return of players blacklisted for talking with the Union Association were to cause headaches for Chris Von Der Ahe and his Browns.

Many players who had contact with the Union Association were barred by each of the established leagues. Under the agreement made between the National League and American Association in 1882 (in which the National League recognized the American Association as a major league) neither league could remove barred players from its blacklist without the approval of the other league. The National League moved to reinstate players from its blacklist without the consent of the A.A. right after the U.A. disbanded, causing suspicion in the A.A. camp. The N.L. also allowed some of its teams to make some rather shady deals with one another, and Henry Lucas, the leader of the U.A. (as well as the St. Louis Maroons), had his hand in that as well. Chris Von Der Ahe was already irked that Lucas was allowed to stay in his town, even though Lucas agreed to run his team under the stricter rules of the N.L. (namely, no booze at the park and fifty-cent admission prices), when the Tony Mullane episode occurred.

In 1883, Tony Mullane went 35–15 for the Browns. After the season, Henry Lucas approached Mullane and offered him a contract to play for the Maroons in 1884. Von Der Ahe got wind of this deal and quickly moved to keep Mullane out of the clutches of his intracity rival. Technically, Mullane violated the reserve clause by signing with the Maroons and that made him, in the eyes of many, a player who should be blacklisted. Evidently, Mullane thought likewise and jumped the Maroons before they even played a game. Von Der Ahe then decided to ship his ace pitcher to the A.A.'s new (and weak) Toledo club of the 1884 season. Mullane won another 35 games in 1884, and when the Toledo club hit the skids financially, its owners tried to sell their top hurler in an attempt to recover some of their cash. Toledo tried selling Mullane and some other players to Cincinnati, but when Cincinnati did not quickly act on the deal, Toledo offered Mullane back to the Browns. Von Der Ahe was happy to get his old ace back but then, to his horror, discovered that during the mandatory ten-day waiting period before signing with a new team after his "release" (this term had little truth to it at the time, since the Toledo players were released only because the club owners were assured that they would get paid money for letting their players sign with the Browns free of any other club's claim to them—in effect, the A.A. saw to it that the players in question would go directly to the Browns and only to them, even though they were technically free agents) Mullane had signed with Cincinnati! The A.A.'s "back-scratching" method concerning "free agents" had been dealt a big blow, as both Cincinnati and St. Louis claimed Mullane was theirs. Von Der Ahe ranted and raved over this affair, and the A.A. then decided that Mullane had to return some of the money Cincinnati had advanced him, while also suspending him for 1885. In 1886 Mullane returned to the A.A. for Cincinnati and he went on to win 285 games in his career. The fact that Mullane was not blacklisted for signing a U.A. contract like other players, even though he never honored it, shows the hypocrisy of both the N.L. and A.A. concerning blacklisting "bad boys." Practically all players blacklisted for contact with the Union Association returned to the majors.

III

Despite the presence of Henry Lucas's National League Maroons in town, Chris Von Der Ahe's Browns were now ready to battle for the American Association flag. At the start of 1885, Von Der Ahe named Charles Comiskey to manage the Browns, the sixth managerial change Von Der Ahe made since the start of the 1882 season. The 1885 Browns came up with a new pitcher in Bob Caruthers to go with holdover Jumbo McGinnis and another newcomer, of the previous season, Dave Foutz. The Browns got off to a hot start under Comiskey (who also played first base) and captured the A.A. title with a 79–33 record, sixteen games ahead of Chris Von Der Ahe's new enemy, Cincinnati. Foutz posted a 33–14 mark, and Caruthers became the ace at 40–13. The Browns were the only association team to have two pitchers with at least 20 wins and also led the league with the fewest errors at 380!

During the 1880s both major leagues held a primitive World Series between the pennant winners as part of the peace agreement they signed in 1882. The 1885 series pitted the Browns against Chicago, the N.L. champs who won eighty-seven games while losing just twenty-five. The World Series of this time was sort of a barnstorming one, where the two teams would play some games in their own cities as well as playing some games in others. As can be imagined, this type of series drew rather poorly in towns whose teams were not in it and would lead to little money being made. Still, in the 1880s players played for pride as well as money, and both the Browns and the Chicago club were happy to be in the series.

As ancient series went, this one really was wild. The first game was played on October 14 in Chicago, and after eight innings it was called because of darkness with the score tied at five. Game 2 was played in St. Louis the next day, and things got out of control in the sixth inning. Umpire Dan Sullivan (there was only one in each game back then) made a bad call against the Browns with Chicago leading 5–4. Browns manager Charles Comiskey was so angered by the call that he pulled the Browns off the field, triggering a near riot at the Grand Avenue Grounds. Sullivan had little choice but to forfeit the game to Chicago, which upset the always excitable Chris Von Der Ahe. Game 3 was more sedate, as the hometown Browns downed Chicago 7–4. Game 4, also at St. Louis, saw the Browns score twice in the eighth to shade Chicago 3–2. Game 5 was played at Pittsburgh before a less than enthusiastic crowd of five hundred and saw Chicago pound the Browns 9–2. The next day saw the same score favoring Chicago, although game 6 was played in Cincinnati. The local crowd cheered for Chicago while the fans and Browns engaged in shouting matches against each other, all of this the fallout from the Tony Mullane mess. The seventh and last game of the series came on October 24 in front of another pro-Chicago crowd of Cincinnatians. This game was truly not out of a textbook on how to play baseball correctly, as an incredible total of 27 errors were made in this game, 17 by Chicago alone. The errors certainly helped the Browns, who won this travesty 13–4. Who won this series (and the $1,000 coming with the win) is left up to the reader, since the forfeit in the second game was controversial. Strangely, the Browns were the home team in all but the first game.

There was no doubt in Chris Von Der Ahe's mind who had won the 1885 series, and he was ready for 1886. Von Der Ahe was pleased to see that the Maroons in 1885 plunged into the N.L. cellar and were already in financial trouble entering 1886. In fact, the Maroons just avoided being dropped by the league and Henry Lucas quit managing the team so he could concentrate on keeping the struggling club afloat.

The 1886 season saw the Browns move to a three-man pitching staff with Nat Hudson (going 16–10 in his rookie season) in the rotation. Third baseman Arlie Latham, fast becoming the most popular man in town, hit .301 and was joined by second baseman Yank Robinson (.274) and center fielder Curt Welch (.281) in forming the heart of an improving Browns lineup. St. Louis, in fact, hit .273 as a team in 1886, good enough to lead the association in club hitting, and that high average was quite a feat in the days when pitching received all of the help from the rules of the day. Again the Browns got off to a good start, and they easily won the pennant by twelve games over Pittsburgh.

The Browns' opponent in the 1886 series was again Chicago. As usual, series rules concerning its format were drawn up by the contestants after winning their respective flags, and in 1886 the teams agreed to seven games in seven days, with the final game, if needed, to be played in Cincinnati. This time, the first six games would be split evenly in the home parks of the contestants. The seven games in seven days was forced upon the teams because Chris Von Der Ahe wanted to put the final nails into the coffin of the Maroons by playing (and humiliating) them in a postseason series. This was strange thinking on Von Der Ahe's part, since the Maroons were nearly dead by the end of 1886. The Maroons were so bad that they finished ahead of only Kansas City and Washington, the National League's two new teams for the season. Still, the Chicago club agreed to this strange series arrangement.

Chicago and the Browns were both claiming to be the series champs of the previous year when the 1886 series began. The Browns entered the series confident of victory after beating the Maroons in the first four games of their intracity series. Chicago and the Browns split the first four games, which were marked by heavy bench jockeying. (Charles Comiskey was the Browns' best at this now lost art.) The fourth game saw Chicago's Fred Pfeffer drop an infield fly on purpose to try for a double play (this was common before the infield fly rule was passed decades later), but

11

instead he booted it for an error, triggering a game-winning Browns rally in the process. Fans thought a fix was on after this game, though none can be proved. Chicago manager Cap Anson denied a fix was on in order to stretch the series (and thereby the profits), and he and his teammates were determined to play harder than ever.

The Browns won the fifth game 10–3 in a seven-inning, darkness-stopped game. The sixth game, played at St. Louis, showed how brazen the Browns could be when it came to winning games. Chicago held a 3–0 lead entering the last of the eighth when Arlie Latham tripled home 2 runs, tying the score in the process. In the bottom of the tenth, Curt Welch tried hard and succeeded in getting hit by a pitch. When Chicago catcher King Kelly argued that Welch was trying to get hit deliberately, the umpire sent Welch back to bat. John Clarkson then gave up a single to Welch, and after one out the Brown center fielder was at third. The bench jockeying continued as Welch tried to distract the Chicago ace. Finally, Clarkson was so flustered he threw a wild pitch, and Welch scored the winning run. The Browns had won the 1886 World Series four games to two.

Chris Von Der Ahe should have been happy that he now owned baseball's undisputed champion. The day after the series ended, the Browns beat the Maroons in the fifth and final game of the intracity series, sealing the doom of the N.L. club in St. Louis. Despite all of this, Von Der Ahe wanted still more. Von Der Ahe wanted to play the unneeded seventh game of the series in Cincinnati against Chicago, but Cap Anson refused. Von Der Ahe sulked over the loss of extra money he might have made had Chicago agreed to play the game, but he finally got over it.

Eighteen-eighty-seven loomed as a happy year for Von Der Ahe. The N.L. decided to drop the St. Louis Maroons from their roster, so the Browns had St. Louis to themselves. The Browns were also coming off of two straight pennants and, in the mind of "Der Boss," two straight world championships. As usual, the Browns got off to a good start, led by veterans Dave Foutz (25–12) and Bob Caruthers (19–9) and newcomer Silver King (34–11). Foutz and Caruthers must have been quite durable, since they had formed two-thirds of the St. Louis rotation for the last few seasons, while the number three man tended to get a sore arm after one year of use. The Browns lineup continued to improve, as everyone but Curt Welch, shortstop Bill Gleason, and catcher Jack Boyle hit over .300 in 1887. Overall, the Browns led the A.A. with a .307 team average and scored 1,131 runs, also tops. It should be noted, however, that all of this hitting was due to the fact that walks counted as hits in 1887 (the only year that this was allowed under the always-changing rules of the time), so that explains how Charles Comiskey went from hitting .254 in 1886 to hitting .335 a year later, among other hitting anomalies of 1887.

The Browns clinched their third straight pennant with a 95–40 mark, fourteen games ahead of Cincinnati, and this time faced a new opponent in the World Series, Detroit. The 1887 series, it was decided by the contestants, was to be more of a barnstorming event than a contest to see which team was best. The series was slated to go to fifteen games and would be played in ten different cities. As was the case in the 1885 series, interest in cities without a representative would be cool, and following such a large, drawn-out series would tire even the biggest baseball fans. The Browns lost their world championship to Detroit ten games to five, attendance and gate receipts were poor, and it was becoming obvious that some sort of permanent rules governing the series were needed to make it a success.

In 1888, the Browns won their fourth straight flag, but this time there was a race for the flag in the A.A., as the Browns did not get off to their usual fast start. Bob Caruthers and Dave Foutz were no longer factors for the Browns, as Silver King (45–21), Nat Hudson (15–10 after missing most of the previous year with an injury), and Icebox Chamberlain (11–2 in half a season) provided most of the pitching. Batting averages were more or less back to their 1886 levels after walks were no longer counted as hits in 1888. The Browns held title to the league's batting champ in left fielder Tip O'Neill (.336), even though the Browns no longer posted the highest team average (though at .250 they were only one point behind). The Browns battled with Brooklyn for the flag all year (Philadelphia was tough as well), and had they not traded for Icebox (or Iceberg) Chamberlain of the weak Louisville team, it's likely that Brooklyn would have won the pennant.

Serving as the Browns' opponents for the 1888 series was New York, a club that was owned by the same man who had owned the New York team in the A.A. as well before it expired. Chris Von Der Ahe spared no expense at showing the New Yorkers that his Browns could be as lavish as the team from the big city. Von Der Ahe had a special train take his team to New York and bought each of his players a new suit as they partied hard. Evidently, the Browns were so smashed from the partying that they went out and lost six games out of the ten-game series to New York. Von Der Ahe probably was well stewed himself, since he didn't worry too much about the defeat. Hardly anyone could blame Chris Von Der Ahe for taking the loss seriously; after all, the Browns were baseball's first dynasty, winning four straight pennants. Unfortunately for Von Der Ahe and the Browns, there would be no fifth straight flag. The next time another team would win four straight flags would be 1921–24, when the team that had defeated the Browns in the '88 series, the Giants of New York, would do it under John McGraw.

IV

By 1889, baseball was again undergoing rumblings. The players of most teams, sick of being treated like property rather than people, were hinting at starting an early form of players' union, maybe their own league run by the players, for the players (rather than by and for the owners). The American Association itself was having problems. The Browns had long been the class of the A.A., and as a result, the other teams had trouble making money when facing each other rather than the Browns. Clubs entered, then left the association quickly. A disturbing trend was begun by the association's Pittsburgh club, which finished second to the Browns in 1886, when it moved into the National League in 1887. Although the agreement between the two leagues allowed teams to switch leagues, the A.A. feared that some of its teams would try to flee to the more prestigious N.L., and the shift by Pittsburgh (now the current Pirates club) seemed to confirm those fears.

Naturally, the Browns were hated by other teams in the A.A.

because they won every year (just like the hatred of the Yankees in this century) and Von Der Ahe himself was less than loved by his fellow owners. The Tony Mullane mess showed what a whiner and complainer "Der Boss" could be, and his antics were not appreciated at all. Von Der Ahe was cheap with his players most of the time, tried to dominate the association whenever the club heads met, and tried several promotions at his park. (Fireworks and hot dogs are two that have lasted to the present.) In short, Von Der Ahe was the Charlie Finley of his time, and like Finley, his demise in baseball would not be lamented by his cohorts, nor would it be pretty to watch.

Despite the problems off the field, the Browns were ready for another pennant. Icebox Chamberlain (32–15) and Silver King (33–17) got some help from new arrival Jack Stivetts (13–7 and a league-leading 2.25 ERA) as the pitching did its usual good job for the Browns. On the hitting side, Tip O'Neill hit .335 and drove in 110 runs while Charles Comiskey (still managing the club in a sign of Brownie stability) had 102 RBIs himself. Right fielder Tommy McCarthy (a future Hall of Famer, like Comiskey) added a .291 average to an offense that socked a league-high fifty-eight homers. Much to the regret of the St. Louis fans, Arlie Latham hit only .246, as he was declining, and after the season, the popular third baseman was shipped to Chicago of a new major league, although it was Latham who shipped himself by jumping the Browns.

Despite these good performances, the Browns failed to bag the pennant, losing out to Brooklyn by just two games. One man prominent in Brooklyn's first flag ever was Bob Caruthers, the former ace of the Browns. Von Der Ahe sent Caruthers to Brooklyn after the 1887 season, and now, two years later, he posted a league-leading 40 wins. It would not be the last time that Von Der Ahe would make a costly miscalculation. Still, the Browns had a solid team that was gradually in need of some fresh blood to keep it well.

Instead of getting fresh blood, the Browns lost the old blood that made them baseball's top team, thanks to the creation of the Players League in 1890. The threats of the players to form a union and maybe their own league were finally carried out and had disastrous consequences for both the Browns and the American

15

Association. Players from both the American Association and the National League jumped their teams and quickly formed an eight-team league in protest of their treatment at the hands of their former bosses. The Players League placed teams in Boston, Brooklyn, New York, Chicago, Philadelphia, Pittsburgh, Cleveland, and Buffalo. The Chicago team of the P.L. consisted mostly of former St. Louis Browns and finished in fourth place in the P.L.

With most of the established veterans and the superstars now playing in the P.L., the other two leagues elevated their spare players to regular status, went after minor league players harder than ever (weakening the minors more than ever in the process), and even looked at college players in an attempt to keep their organizations going. What the N.L. and A.A. did in 1890 was similar to what the National Football League did in 1987 when their players went on strike. These "scab" games in 1890 turned off the fans, who decided to see their favorite stars perform in the P.L. The season was a total disaster for all three leagues, as attendance was down in the N.L. and A.A. and the P.L. was not able to promote itself properly, nor were they able to acquire suitable ballparks.

The scabs performing in Browns uniforms did well enough to finish third in the A.A., but they were hardly in the race and ended up twelve games behind the suddenly good Louisville club. The American Association itself was fatally wounded by the players it lost. The association was suffering from declining attendance in the last few years, and now things were worse than ever. Chris Von Der Ahe tried all kinds of giveaways and promotions, but they did little to increase attendance in 1890. Even though the Players League didn't place a team in St. Louis, the effect of taking the 1889 Browns away was worse than the appearance of the St. Louis Maroons in the Union Association in 1884.

After the 1890 season ended, the three leagues sat down and tried to set things right. The resulting agreements had some Players League clubs merge with their National League opponents in some cities both leagues serviced. The American Association was allowed to run some Players League outfits in cities that were not in the A.A. in 1890. Things would more or less be the way they had been prior to the formation of the Players League. On the surface, things looked calm and peaceful in baseball again.

16

The peace did not last long. The association's club in Philadelphia was now owned by two backers of the Players League (who owned that league's Philadelphia club also) and they wanted to keep twenty-six players that they had taken from the association before 1890. However, when the time came under the peace agreement between the three leagues to reserve players that had been in the P.L., the Philadelphia owners failed to reserve those two players. The National League's Pittsburgh club then claimed the two players. One player, Louis Bierbauer, signed with the Pittsburgh club (which were called the Pirates from then on), while the other, Harry Stovey, balked at Pittsburgh's offer and instead signed with the National League club in Boston.

The A.A.'s Philadelphia club was upset over the loss of two players they intended to send to the A.A.'s Boston club. The Philadelphia A.A. club appealed to the board governing relations between the two leagues, and the board ruled in favor of the N.L. Other players had been in the same boat as Bierbauer and Stovey, but these two players were stars that the A.A. no longer had. Naturally, the association was angered and accused the league of not living up to the peace agreement. Depending on the point of view, the association either withdrew from or was thrown out of the old agreement governing relations between the two leagues, and the league declared that association players were now fair game for league teams. Lawsuits followed, and one involved Chris Von Der Ahe. When Mark Baldwin jumped from the Columbus club of the A.A. to Pittsburgh in the N.L., he tried to get other players in the A.A. to join him in defecting to the other league. Von Der Ahe, assigned by the association to uphold its honor, had Baldwin arrested for "conspiracy." Baldwin sued Von Der Ahe for $20,000 in retaliation and ended up winning $2,500.

On the field, the 1891 season turned out to be almost as bad as the 1890 season, at least in the association. Most of the 1889 Browns returned to St. Louis after a year as the Chicago club of the Players League, and the Browns ended up second to the A.A.'s new Boston team. Jack Stivetts was 33–22 as the ace, Willie McGill went 18–10 after coming from Cincinnati in a deal, and rookie Clark Griffith went 14–6 before going to Boston in a trade. New third baseman Denny Lyons hit .315, Tommy McCarthy hit .310 as the

17

right fielder, and left fielder Tip O'Neill batted .321 to lead the Brownie attack. Still, the Browns ended up eight and a half games behind Boston, and the only thing that could be said about the 1891 Browns was that they had two future owners playing for them (Comiskey and Griffith).

For the rest of the American Association, the season was a wreck. The Cincinnati team went broke, then moved to Milwaukee in midseason. Most of the clubs, especially the newer ones, lost money. Even the Browns suffered, as their owner spent more and more time trying to keep the association going while neglecting his own team. Boston won the pennant, but there was no series, as the two leagues were at each other's throats. The association still had to pay off people who had lost teams in the A.A. during the life of the Players League and the settlement afterward. Obviously something had to be done concerning the failing American Association.

Both leagues were already discussing the future of the game of baseball during the season. Some A.A. owners were ready for some sort of merger with the N.L. while others wanted out of the sport completely, but with some cash as compensation. The N.L. was receptive and meetings took place. Chris Von Der Ahe, one of the A.A.'s founding fathers, was reluctant to have the association simply disappear from sight. Those wanting peace between both leagues knew that Von Der Ahe was going to have to be placated if real peace was to be achieved. The league sent three men to convince "Der Boss" to go along with a possible merger, since Von Der Ahe would lose even more money in trying to subsidize such association weaklings as Columbus and Louisville. Money was something that Von Der Ahe had lost plenty of just running his own club the last two seasons, and "Der Boss" was now heading toward bankruptcy. Given a choice between trying to hold up a rickety American Association and joining a prestigious National League, he would join the latter. After all, the Browns were still a good team and it looked like they would make more money than ever in the more profitable National League.

On December 15, 1891, both leagues met at Indianapolis and hammered out an agreement. The National League would change its official name to the National League and American Association of Professional Base Ball Clubs, bring in Baltimore, Washington, Louisville, and St. Louis to join the N.L.'s eight existing clubs, and buy out the other four old association clubs and dispose of the leftover players from the dead teams. Sunday ball was allowed, fifty-cent admissions were the norm (with provision for quarter seats), and a split season for 1892 was approved, the winner of each half facing each other in a "World Series." The owners of the newly enlarged league were allowed to keep players under contract to them (so there would not be "free agents" around to cause teams to try to outrob one another like in the past), and all teams shared the expense of buying out the dropped clubs. Chris Von Der Ahe was happy, but he was soon not to be, for his club was now embarking on a three-decade voyage into the desert.

Part II

Three Decades in the Desert
(1892–1920)

I

After the 1891 season, Chris Von Der Ahe set out to rebuild his ball club. True, it was an aging ball club and some changes were needed, especially since the Browns had not finished first since 1888. The first order of business was to dispatch Charles Comiskey, the manager and first baseman of the Browns since 1882, to Cincinnati. Comiskey was followed by several of his Browns teammates, and by the time the 1892 season began, it looked like the Browns franchise had simply packed up and moved en masse. The transfusion of the Browns players had made Cincinnati jump from a 56–81 record in 1891 to an 82–68 mark in 1892 under the managing of Comiskey. Disaster was starting to engulf the St. Louis Browns.

With most of his veteran (and relatively expensive) stars now at Cincinnati, Chris Von Der Ahe next replaced his stars with cheaply paid rookies and second-string players in a cost-cutting move. Also, to save a few bucks more, Von Der Ahe decided to name himself as the manager of the team. After all, without a league to try to keep afloat Von Der Ahe now had plenty of time on his hands, so he might as well do something with it, he probably figured. In fairness to Von Der Ahe, it should be noted that all the other teams were also busy cutting salaries, which had gone up during the life of the Players League, but at least most of the teams kept a nucleus of players to build their futures around.

The Browns got off to a poor start in 1892, playing at a miserable .425 clip in the first half of the season. The attendance figures at St. Louis were up initially as fans got to see National League stars for the first time, but as the Browns limped around with a team of rejects the novelty wore off and the fans began staying home. Von Der Ahe then resorted to issuing promises that the team wouldn't be the same in the second half. He was right. The Browns played at an even more dismal .325 clip in the second half, beating out the even more pathetic Washington club for eleventh place by one game. The 1892 season was a total disaster for the Browns, who compiled a 56–94 record over the course of the entire season. Only Baltimore's 46–101 mark was worse in the league. Things were so bad that Bob Caruthers, once the Browns' ace pitcher, returned to the team as an outfielder and led the team with a .277 average. The once hard-hitting Browns found National League pitching tough to hit, as their league-low .226 average shows, and their pitching was nearly as bad, with the second highest ERA, 4.20. Kid Gleason, a future big league manager, was the ace pitcher with a 16–24 record and a 3.33 ERA.

In 1892 the split season format didn't attract much fan interest, nor did the series between first-half winner Boston and second-half winner Cleveland, so the idea was dropped for 1893. For bad teams like the Browns the loss of the split season format was making a bad situation worse. In 1893, once a team got off to a bad start and fell out of the race early, the attendance would fall off very noticeably in a twelve-team league. In 1893 the Browns were one such team.

After making a fool of himself on the field as manager (as well as a target for fan abuse), Von Der Ahe named Bill Watkins as manager. Watkins had little to work with, especially on the mound, where Ted Breitenstein was the ace at 19–20, with a league-leading 3.18 ERA. The offense improved as the team hit .264, but then the league's hitting improved all around as its composite average jumped from .245 to .280. Moving the mound to sixty feet, six inches may have had something to do with that. More telling was the Browns' team scoring just 745 runs, next to last in the league.

Von Der Ahe, the promoter, was busy thinking of how to pack his ballpark. Prior to Opening Day in 1893 he gave St. Louis a new park, naming it Sportsman's Park. The new park was nicer to be in than the old park by the same name (previously known as the Grand Avenue Grounds), but by itself it didn't do much to attract fans to see the Browns post a 57–75 mark, bad enough for tenth in the N.L.

If you can't give the fans a winning team, then give them circuses. Von Der Ahe couldn't give the fans the former, so he worked on the latter. "Der Boss" poured more of his money into his new park in an attempt to turn it into "Coney Island West," complete with beer gardens, horse races, and boat rides, among other things. The other owners rolled their eyes in amazement and were waiting for the chance to dump Von Der Ahe.

The only reason the National League accepted Von Der Ahe in 1891 was because they (the other owners) were afraid of his potential to cause trouble outside of their racket. Most of the National League owners always viewed the American Association with disdain for allowing Sunday games, booze, and quarter games. The A.A. owners were more of a slap-you-on-the-back, have-a-beer type group (which is why they formed their own league anyway), while the N.L. bosses were "stuffed shirts." The worst of the "common" owners, in everyone's view, was Von Der Ahe. The N.L. fully expected that he would conform to their "high" standards and when he wouldn't, they couldn't wait to get rid of him. Von Der Ahe was busy furnishing his enemies with the rope needed for his hanging. Soon a lynching would take place.

On the ball field itself, the Browns continued to play poorly. In 1894 George Miller was the victim picked to manage the Browns. The club soared to ninth place despite an ERA of 5.29 (the league's was 5.32). Ted Breitenstein again was the ace at 27–25, 4.79, and got help from Pink Hawley (19–26, 4.90) and Dad Clarkson (8–17, 6.36), if that's what it can be called. The hitting was good, but then again, all teams were still crushing the ball at a .309 clip. At 56–76, the Browns posted their best mark since joining the league.

By 1895 the whole bloated league was having problems with its size. Every year the same teams would contend, while other teams could always be expected to finish in the outhouse. (St. Louis qualifies here.) The owners tried to boost attendance with talk of splitting into two divisions, implementing a designated hitter rule, and maybe dropping some of the biggest losers. Despite all of this talk, the owners did nothing to improve the situation and, in fact, took steps to worsen things. It was common in the 1890s to have losing teams transfer some home games to their opponents' parks if more money could be made that way. Most of the time, the National League would either look the other way or even approve of such transfers. Some teams would fiddle with turnstiles just to have an excuse to do some transferring. Such transferring of games certainly did little to inspire fan loyalty to the home team. The Washington club was notorious for trying to play its home games elsewhere.

The year 1895 turned out to be the beginning of the end for Chris Von Der Ahe. When Von Der Ahe was caught fooling around with another woman, his wife sued for divorce. Von Der Ahe also was sued for property by his son in 1895, and all of this made Von Der Ahe more intolerant of failure on the field. On the field, players came and went with amazing speed as the team got off to its patented slow start. Al Buckenberger was the opening manager, but he was sacked for winning only sixteen of forty-eight games. Next on the list was second baseman Joe Quinn, who lasted for forty games at the helm before he was found lacking. Victim number three was Lew Phelan, who was put out of his misery after just twenty-nine games. Finally, the architect of the disaster called the Browns, Chris Von Der Ahe himself, took the reins and guided the team to a 2–12 finish. Von Der Ahe was now having trouble finding masochists who could stand both his tirades and the dismal play on the field.

The other owners were also tired of coming to St. Louis and seeing their teams play second fiddle to boat races and drinking marathons. Von Der Ahe was deeply in hock for everything he owned, and now there was the possibility that a bankruptcy court might seize control of the Browns. At league meetings Von Der Ahe was asked to sell his team, but such pleas only enraged him. Von Der Ahe delivered tirades to fellow owners who called him incompetent, and all the arguing made him more determined to hang onto the club at all costs.

If 1895's Browns team was a mess at 39–92 (and four managers guiding them to eleventh place), then the 1896 version wasn't much better. Not only did the Browns post a 40–90 record in finishing eleventh (again); they actually increased the number of managers to five and the offense had begun to resemble the pitching in ineptness. The Browns finished last in ERA, batting average, and runs scored. These two teams, however, were world beaters compared to St. Louis's 1897 squad. By the time Chris Von Der Ahe had guided the team to a 1–2 finish, three managers had come and gone, the club ERA soared to 6.21 (Red Donohue was the ace in '97 with 11–33, 6.13 marks), the pitchers allowed 1,083 runs, and the team compiled a horrendous 29–102 mark for a disgusting .221 winning percentage. Needless to say, the Browns ended up 63½ games out of first place. After this debacle, the National League finally moved to do something.

By 1898, Von Der Ahe, strapped for cash, was finally shopping the Browns around, but he found no buyers for his decrepit ball club. A court appointed someone to take control of the ball club, but Von Der Ahe fought against this move. The National League recognized the court-appointed trustee instead of Von Der Ahe and was prepared to expel the Browns if the court forced an owner on the Browns that the league would not approve. Meanwhile, with the club's future up in the air, the Browns (who were now also being called the Maroons by some fans for the color of their uniforms) took the field in 1898 and did their usual thing, which was losing badly and often. At least Tim Hurst got through the entire season as the manager, but he probably wished he didn't. The pitching started coming around (a 4.53 ERA), but due to the continuing poor offense that saw only Lave Cross (.317) and Jake Stenzel (.282) do well, the Browns posted another last-place finish with a 39–111 record.

After the 1898 season ended, the National League was again undergoing turmoil. Cleveland, a perennial contender and 81–68 in the just-ended season, was having increasing trouble drawing fans, thanks to its inability to play Sunday ball (banned by the local "Blue Laws"). Late in the season, the Cleveland owners, Frank and Stanley Robison, put their team on the road for the rest of the season, angering the fans in Cleveland. The Robisons then had ideas of moving their club to Detroit, which allowed Sunday ball. The league, however, had other ideas. The other owners didn't want to see the Cleveland Spiders move to a smaller city (cutting into gate receipts), and the Robisons were forced to stay put for the time being. The Robisons were understandably angry, since the Spiders drew fewer fans than even the dreadful Browns, despite the wide disparity in records.

Meanwhile, the legal mess that was known as the Browns was still unresolved. It was determined that the league and not the court-appointed trustee had real control over the franchise and so the National League could put whoever it wanted in charge of

27

the Browns. The Browns were already suspended for failure to pay their bills, and it was highly unlikely that an outsider would want to buy a debt-ridden, suspended ball club that was a laughingstock on the field as well. Without someone to properly run the club, the Browns were in danger of simply being dropped. The league then came up with a bizarre scheme to solve two of its problems.

Syndicate baseball was the practice by which one man would own two ball clubs and would be able to transfer players from one of his teams to the other. Naturally, an owner could pack one team with superstars while turning the other one into a corpse. Syndicates were already being set up between the Brooklyn and Baltimore teams and the Pittsburgh and Louisville clubs, both of which had the apparent blessing of the league. While Brooklyn and Pittsburgh were getting ready to build powerhouses at the expense of Baltimore and Louisville, the National League decided to marry the Cleveland and St. Louis clubs together.

The Cleveland–St. Louis deal was consummated to save the Browns in St. Louis. St. Louis was larger than Cleveland and allowed Sunday ball, so sacrificing Cleveland made economic sense for the owners. Before 1899 began, the Robisons were allowed to buy into the St. Louis team while keeping their interest in the Spiders. Quickly the new Browns owners swapped players between the two clubs, giving St. Louis a silk purse and Cleveland a sow's ear. Patsy Tebeau, who had played first base and managed the Spiders, filled both roles for the Browns. The stage was now set for a historic event at Cleveland and a new era for the Browns. The days of Chris Von Der Ahe, who had been a big force in St. Louis baseball for over fifteen years, were at an end.

II

Baseball history has been filled with many instances where one team virtually turned another into a farm team for itself. In the 1920s the Yankees and Giants basically bought every player of value from the two Boston clubs. In the 1950s, the Yankees were always making one-sided deals with the Kansas City Athletics, always sending leftovers to the Athletics in exchange for front-line

28

players that Kansas City had in its possession. But these blatant attempts at robbing the poor to sustain the rich were nothing compared to what was to take place in 1899 between St. Louis and Cleveland.

Prior to opening the new season, the Robisons decided to give their new team a new name. The name Browns disappeared in favor of the name least likely to be connected to that team's success over the last few years. The St. Louis team was now to be called the Perfectos. Matthew Stanley Robison named himself to head the Cleveland Spiders (dubbed the Exiles by the local papers for what happened late in the '98 season) while brother Frank was now the president of the Perfectos.

On April 15, the Perfectos went out and beat the Spiders 10–1 behind Cy Young. Already the madness was under way, since this was supposed to be Cleveland's home opener, but for profit's sake the game was played in St. Louis instead. St. Louis's fans must have been mighty pleased to see the formerly weak-hitting hometown team score ten runs in the first game under new ownership. The Perfectos got off to a good start but still weren't in the pennant race, because another club that benefitted from syndication, Brooklyn, jumped out to a commanding lead, with only Boston and Philadelphia giving chase.

Although the Perfectos were not battling for the flag, the Robisons wanted their new fans to be happy and any time a Spider was doing well he would be sent to St. Louis for a struggling Perfecto. Evidently, Willie Sudhoff was too good for Cleveland with his 3–8 record and 6.98 ERA, so he was rewarded, along with player-manager Lave Cross (batting .286), with a trade to the Perfectos. Sudhoff's marks for Cleveland may look bad, but his 3 wins were the second highest total on the club, even though he was traded in early June! Ossee Schreckengost, one of the players the Perfectos sent to the Spiders in the Sudhoff deal, was doing so well for his new team that the Robisons sent him right back to St. Louis as a result. The press cried long and loud over this shuttling of players, and even Cincinnati owner John Brush complained that the league was looking bad by allowing such blatant trading of players on the mere whim of the owners of both clubs. The Robisons had managed to turn the Cleveland Spiders into a virtual farm team of the St. Louis Perfectos. Needless to say, nobody in Cleveland was amused by the complete destruction of their once fine team.

When the 1899 season ended, the Perfectos finished fifth with a nice 84–67 record. Cy Young posted a 26–15 record with a 2.58 ERA and was backed by Jack Powell at 23–21, 3.52, and Willie Sudhoff (13–10, 3.61 at St. Louis). The offense improved markedly as shortstop Bobby Wallace hit .302 with 12 homers and 108 RBIs, left fielder Jesse Burkett cracked the ball at a .402 clip (no batting title, though, as Ed Delahanty hit .408 for Philly), and Emmet Heidrick hit .328 while playing right field. Lave Cross chipped in with a .303 mark after returning from the "minor" league team at Cleveland. As for the Spiders, they truly were reduced to minor status by serving as a farm club for the Perfectos years before a farm system was even thought of. Cleveland finished the season with a record safe for the ages: 20–134, bad enough for a .130 winning percentage. The Spiders also finished eighty-four games out of first.

After the 1899 season, the owners decided that a twelve-team league was too bulky to operate and decided to drop four teams. Cleveland, which was expected to be dropped even before the Robisons hatched their scheme, was the first team to go. Baltimore and Louisville, two other clubs that suffered the effects of syndication, were also dropped. Washington, long a doormat, was the fourth team to die. The Perfectos took the lion's share of what few good players were left in Cleveland. Brooklyn and Pittsburgh did likewise with Baltimore and Louisville, respectively. Boston got first crack at Washington's players. The owners of the dropped clubs also got some money for their troubles. The Robisons, owners of the now dead Cleveland club, also got some money for their lost interests there. In effect, the league rewarded the Robisons for destroying the Cleveland franchise. For 1900, the league would now have eight teams: New York, Brooklyn, Philadelphia, and Boston in the east and Chicago, Pittsburgh, Cincinnati, and St. Louis in the west. This was to remain the National League's lineup until 1953.

For 1900, the Perfectos got a little bonus when it came to disposing of players from the disbanded teams. John McGraw and

Wilbert Robinson had both been with Baltimore the previous season and were slated to go to Brooklyn (as part of the syndicate deal between those two clubs). The two players balked, citing business interests in Baltimore that they wanted to stay near. It didn't matter to the two players that they would not be playing for Brooklyn even though the team won the pennant and their balking at going to Brooklyn didn't matter to that team's president, Ned Hanlon. Ned turned around and sold McGraw and Robinson to the Perfectos, but still they didn't want to go away from Baltimore. The Robisons met with the players in person to convince them to go west. The Robisons then offered two nice contracts to the men and even removed the reserve clause from their contracts. McGraw and Robinson signed the deals and went west.

After the success of 1899, it was expected that the Perfectos would improve in 1900, especially if two players from the former powerhouse Baltimore Orioles were to join the team. McGraw managed a depleted Oriole team to a good 86–62 mark in '99 and was considered to be one of the most intelligent of players and managers. Instead of success, though, the 1900 Perfectos regressed to a 65–75 mark. Patsy Tebeau, tired of the rigors of managing, quit the job with the team mired in a slump. Louis Heilbronner, the team secretary, was then named manager, even though he lacked baseball know-how. John McGraw, batting .344 as the team's third baseman, advised Heilbronner on the bench, but the team just couldn't overcome weak pitching. Cy Young posted a 20–18 record but was the only reliable hurler on the Perfectos. Despite a .291 team average, the Perfectos ended up in sixth place. To make matters worse, McGraw and Wilbert Robinson then left the team at the end of their contracts and headed for the Baltimore team in the newly created American League.

As things were shaping up, 1901 was a pivotal year in baseball history. Ban Johnson declared that his once minor league outfit was now ready for major league status. Johnson's once minor outfit was, of course, the American League, and for the 1901 season he announced that his league would go head-to-head with the National League in Boston, Chicago, and Philadelphia. Other teams were placed in Baltimore, Cleveland, Washington, Detroit, and Milwaukee. The A.L. also announced that it would go after any

National League player still unsigned to an N.L. contract. Secretly, the A.L. hoped to lure signed players as well and did manage to pluck some N.L. stars for itself. Unfortunately for the Perfectos, one of those stars was their ace pitcher, Cy Young, who returned to Boston as a member of that city's A.L. club. The Perfectos were understandably upset at losing their ace to the new league, but they were relieved that the A.L. didn't put a team in St. Louis—at least for the time being.

Patsy Donovan, the Perfecto right fielder, was named as manager for 1901, and he did a good job after losing his ace. Jesse Burkett won the batting title with a .382 average, Emmet Heidrick hit .339, and the increasingly popular shortstop, Bobby Wallace, hit .322 with 91 RBIs. Jack Powell went 19–19 and got help from Willie Sudhoff (17–11) and Jack Harper (23–13) as the Perfectos improved to a fourth-place finish and a 76–64 record. Attendance was good, and it looked like the Perfectos were finally on the road to a solid future. Unfortunately for the Perfectos, things would not be so "Perfect" after all.

III

After the 1901 season, the war between the two leagues began heating up. The American League drew extremely well in its first year as a big league, and that included the three cities that also had National League teams. What seemingly irked the N.L. as much as the pirating of its players was the fact that the A.L. had placed a team in the "holy" city of Boston. In the past, when a rival to the N.L. was created, it would be sure to incur the wrath of the older league if it invaded Boston. The American Association was content in avoiding Boston during most of its life, which is why that league got along relatively well with the N.L. After the Players League folded, the N.L. allowed the A.A. to run a weak team in Boston, but right after that happened the two leagues merged and the Boston issue was at an end.

Ban Johnson, though, was not about to bow to the older league and see his own creation die quickly. Not only did Johnson put a team in Boston, but he secured several stars of that city's

N.L. team as well. The results were amazing. Boston's N.L. club finished fifth in 1901 with a mediocre 69–69 record and drew 146,502 fans. Johnson's Bostons finished second with a 79–57 record and drew 289,448. Already the days of National League baseball in Boston were being numbered. The A.L. team in Chicago also outdrew its rival, and even though the N.L. won the attendance war in Philadelphia, the A.L. team there wasn't far behind.

It was obvious that the American League was here to stay. The N.L. tried raiding the new league itself but had only some success. Peace feelers put out by the older league suggested that the two leagues try some sort of merger where all the players would in effect be thrown into a common pot. Johnson would have none of this, saying the A.L. must and would remain a separate and independent operation. The A.L. would not go the way of other leagues, in Ban Johnson's mind, and it was now time to make the A.L. even stronger. However, Johnson's next move proved to be a near disaster.

One of the American League teams in 1901 was located in Milwaukee, one of the smallest cities in the big leagues. The Milwaukee team drew poorly, finished last, and was low on funds. Johnson decided that moving the sickly Milwaukee club to a larger city would bring it around to profitability. The largest city in the west (the west being east of the Mississippi River in baseball's geography of the time) that had fewer than two teams and a ballpark that could quickly be upgraded was St. Louis. In 1902, the Milwaukee Brewers would become the St. Louis American League baseball club.

The Robisons were frightened at the prospect of the new league invading their town. Not only would the Perfectos have to fight to keep their fan base, but it could be expected that the new team would try to steal as many stars off the older team as possible. The Robisons were right. The new team came to town and quickly plucked shortstop Bobby Wallace, second baseman Dick Padden, left fielder Jesse Burkett, center fielder Emmet Heidrick, and pitchers Jack Powell, Willie Sudhoff, and Jack Harper, as well as a few players of lesser note. The results for 1902 were very predictable. The Perfectos staggered to a sixth-place finish on a 56–78 record. The new team in town battled for the A.L. flag and finished second at 78–58. A grand total of 272,283 people saw the new team perform well with the former stars of the Perfectos, while 226,417 fans paid to see the Perfectos sink into the second division.

Robert Hedges, owner of the new St. Louis team, not only grabbed many of the older club's players, but he also grabbed their old name and made it his own. The St. Louis Browns of the American League also took over an old park, namely, the one that Henry Lucas had built for his Union Association Maroons. Hedges fixed up the crumbling park, and it managed to stay in use into 1966. The Browns had arrived in town with much fanfare and looked like a team that would be in far better shape than the Perfectos. After all, the Browns had taken the most popular players away from the Perfectos, players like Wallace and Burkett, so it was expected that Perfecto fans would flock to the Browns' park. Cleveland fans must have been pleased, as many former Spiders that the Perfectos had stolen were in turn stolen from them by the Browns. Despite the euphoria of the Browns' success in their first year in town, there was one problem that would haunt both St. Louis clubs for decades. The 1900 census showed that St. Louis had about 500,000 people, and in 1902 this meant that St. Louis was the smallest city hosting two teams. As a result of the small population base, both clubs would have to cut down on as many expenses as they could. Naturally, when a team cuts too deeply on expenses, mistakes are made, and growth can be stunted. In St. Louis the question would be which team would make the fewest mistakes and get to a pennant first.

As 1903 opened, it looked a lot more certain that the Browns would bring home a pennant rather than the Perfectos. The Robisons were starting to experience financial trouble even before the Browns arrived and had accepted money from other N.L. owners (a common occurrence in those days). As a result, the residue of syndication had touched the Perfectos, since some of the club's stock was in the hands of other club owners. Unlike the syndicate deals of 1899, though, these "foreign" shareholders did not shuttle any players around in droves, since that would show the A.L. how weak the N.L. could be.

On the field, the Robisons put out a team of cheaply paid ball players and the team suffered. Jim Hackett, Dave Brain, George Barclay, Chappie McFarland, and Clarence Currie are members of the 1903 Perfectos that will not easily come to mind when one thinks of who appeared in a St. Louis National League uniform over the decades. These players were members of the '03 Perfecto squad that hit the cellar at 43–94. Needless to say, manager Patsy Donovan was given a pink slip after the season.

For 1904, Kid Nichols was hired to manage a team that began to look more and more like it did ten years before. Nichols was one of the few well-known players the Perfectos employed after losing their stars to the Browns, and by 1904 the Kid was thirty-five and had won 328 games for Boston's National League team. Nichols was thinking of retiring as a player, but after seeing the lack of talent in St. Louis he figured he'd better keep on pitching. Nichols (who's in the Hall of Fame) coaxed a decent 75–79 record out of his new team (and went 21–13 himself) and moved the Perfectos up to fifth. Nichols did such a nice job that the Robisons brought him back for 1905.

Nichols didn't last long in '05, though. The Kid's arm was shot and the team had gotten off to a 19–29 start under him when the Robisons got some well-needed cash by selling their manager-pitcher to the Phillies. Jimmy Burke then took the helm, but his 17–32 record was hardly an improvement and Matthew Robison left his office to manage personally the mess he owned. By season's end, the considerably less than perfect Perfectos dropped a notch to sixth and posted a poor 58–96 record.

These were tough times to be a baseball fan in St. Louis. After their promising debut in 1902, the Browns had begun to rival the Perfectos in tightfistedness with money and ineptitude on the field. While the Perfectos were busy fighting to stay out of last place in 1905, the Browns got there. Browns owner Robert Hedges watched as the stars he took from the Perfectos got old and retired and did next to nothing to replace them. As for the Perfectos, there were problems off the field to torment them as well. The ballpark was already falling apart, and people stayed away from it not just to avoid watching bad baseball, but for reasons of safety as well. Matthew Robison, who by now was the sole man in charge of running the club, couldn't even afford to make the necessary repairs on the park. As is often the case, Robison tried to raise cash by selling his players, but most of them were so bad that there was little interest in them.

John McCloskey took the helm of a crumbling Perfecto team that was now being dressed in reddish uniforms (done probably to match the players' faces as the anger and embarrassment increased with each loss) and called them Maroons and even Cardinals as a result. The 1906 team went out and barely beat out the even worse Boston team for seventh place. En route to their 52–98 mark, the St. Louis club had no pitcher win as many as 10 games (last-place Boston at least had three), hit a league-low 10 homers (double their total of three years earlier, which should last as the club record for futility forever), and pitched a league-low four shutouts. (This was the dead ball era, it should be noted.) Luckily for St. Louis, the Boston team had a record-setting pitching staff that featured four 20-game losers; otherwise St. Louis would have easily captured the cellar spot. A year later, though, Mc-Closkey did have his team in the basement, as St. Louis posted 100 losses for the fist time since the last days of Chris Von Der Ahe.

Matthew Robison continued to preside over the disaster that once was called the Perfectos and now was being called the Cardinals. Every now and then a fire would break out in the wooden ballpark, and repairs were slow in coming. Robison for some perverse reason kept John McCloskey on as manager despite the team's worsening performance. The bills continued to pile up as attendance declined. The 1907 club drew just 185,377 fans, and even though the Browns were little better, they drew an amazing total of 419,000 people to see their sixth-place team.

In 1908, the Cardinals (henceforth the St. Louis N.L. club will be called by this name) were finally able to pay off several bills that had been accumulated under the Von Der Ahe mess of the previous decade, despite another last-place finish. Attendance improved to just above the 200,000 mark, as most teams were finally doing well financially. Still, the Cardinals were hurting for attention in town, as the Browns were engaged in a hot four-team pennant race that saw them end up 6½ games out of first.

After the dismal 49–105 record of 1908 was compiled (which remains the worst mark the Cardinals have compiled in this century), John McCloskey was finally fired as Matthew Robison jumped at the chance to grab a big name for his team. For some time the New York press speculated that Giants catcher Roger Bresnahan would become manager of that team, replacing the highly successful John McGraw. Bresnahan, credited with inventing shin guards, was the most highly regarded catcher in baseball, and many felt he should manage the Giants. The Giants, though, were happy with McGraw at the helm, and McGraw decided he no longer needed Bresnahan's services. On December 12, 1908, the Giants sent Bresnahan to the Cardinals in exchange for Bugs Raymond, Red Murray, and Admiral Schlei. The reaction in St. Louis was elation. Before he even arrived in town, Bresnahan was being hailed as the miracle man who would transform the Cardinals into a contender.

One look at the Cardinals' roster in 1909 shows that Bresnahan would have to perform a miracle of epic proportions to have his team in contention. For openers, Bresnahan was without the ace pitcher of the '08 team, Bugs Raymond (at 15–25, he looks less than an ace, but his 324 innings pitched and 2.03 ERA show his true value) because he had gone east in the trade that brought Bresnahan to St. Louis. Also, many of the 1909 Cardinals were just plain mediocre, guys like Bobby Byrne (whose .191 average the year before was the league's worst for a batter with at least 400 at bats), Chappy Charles (a .219 lifetime hitter), and Joe Delahanty (whose .238 lifetime mark makes one wonder if he's really the brother of Hall of Famer Ed Delahanty, with his lifetime average of .345), so it was obvious that Bresnahan had his hands full.

The Cardinals performed much like the mediocrity that had finished last the year before. The 1909 Cardinals ended the season out of the cellar, but at 54–98 the season would hardly qualify as a success. Bresnahan's managing may not have improved the team on the field, but his appearance in a Cardinal uniform boosted attendance up almost by 100,000. Bresnahan was popular with the fans and press, so the failures on the field were forgotten, at least for now.

For 1910, the Cardinals replaced weak-hitting Chappy Charles at second base with Miller Huggins, the future manager of the Cardinals. Huggins and several other players (mostly mediocre) were brought in to improve the team, but the result was nearly the same. Another stop in seventh place, this time with a slightly better mark of 63–90, was the fruit of Bresnahan's labors. Prospects for a brighter 1911 season didn't look too good when on March 24 of that year the news came down that at first looked good but turned out to be terrible. Matthew Robison was dead.

IV

Matthew Robison was just short of turning fifty-two when he died in 1911. Both Matthew and brother Frank quite possibly saved National League baseball in St. Louis by transferring the Cleveland Spiders' top players to their new team and agreeing to keep the club going against the A.L. by accepting money from both the N.L. and other owners of N.L. teams. But by 1911, the Cardinals were run on a shoestring budget and were playing in a tiny firetrap while still facing stiff competition from the crosstown Browns. The Cardinals were doing better financially in recent years, but still were not doing as well as a lot of other clubs. As long as the Cardinals were losers on the field, little money would come in via gate receipts and the budget would have to remain tight.

Control of the Cardinals now passed to Matthew Robison's niece (and Frank's daughter), Mrs. Schuyler Britton. Britton became one of the first women to own a big league ball club and was also a suffragette. Nobody knew what to expect with a woman owning the club, even though Britton made it clear that things would be run in the same way as before. In other words, more penny-pinching off the field and more losing on it.

The change of ownership seemed to have a positive effect on the Cardinals. Bresnahan got 23 wins out of Bob Harmon, 18 out of Bill Steele, and a nifty 15–9, 2.76 season from Slim Sallee as the pitching staff finally got some help from Ed Konetchy (.289 and 88 RBIs), Steve Evans (.294), brainy Miller Huggins (.261), and even a .278 mark from the part-time catcher Bresnahan himself. The Cardinals captured fifth place with a 75–74 record, the first time that the Cardinals finished above .500 since 1901. A total of 447,768 people packed themselves into the Cardinals' park, more than double the crowd that went to see the last-place Browns. Britton was so pleased with the results of her first year as owner that she gave Bresnahan a five-year contract, a raise in salary, and a share of the earnings in a season that Cardinal fans celebrated gloriously.

The next year, though, brought the Cardinals crashing back to reality. After the 1911 season, the Cardinals made virtually no changes in their lineup, and when the pitchers began struggling (despite good hitting) St. Louis found itself back at the depths of the league standings. The club reverted to a 63–90 record, and the attendance also reverted to low levels. Roger Bresnahan grew frustrated at the team's failures and began having problems with owner Britton. When Bresnahan first came to St. Louis, he insisted that he have a free hand both on the field and when it came to making roster adjustments. Matthew Robison had agreed to the request, and never was a roster move made without Bresnahan's approval. Britton, however, felt that as owner she should be able to do as she pleased and without having to ask an employee for an okay. Britton herself was not too involved with the day-to-day operation of the team, but she instructed her subordinates not to take any guff from the manager. Now, in 1912, Bresnahan was griping about the lack of trades to improve the team and front office infighting was getting out of control. Britton was determined not to spend a penny on the team unless it was absolutely, positively necessary. At the end of 1912, the inevitable happened when Bresnahan was given a pink slip.

The unpleasant task of managing the Cardinals for 1913 fell to Miller Huggins. At under five feet, seven inches tall Huggins was dubbed "Mighty Mite" for his hard play at second base and his demeanor in approaching trouble whenever it arose. Huggins was also considered by many one of the smartest players in the league, and it was only natural that he would be selected to manage. Huggins's amazing patience was sorely tested as his pitching staff crumbled and the offense began to fall off (even though the manager batted .286 himself). The 1913 Cardinals were dead last at 51–99. If Huggins found his patience exhausted after this season, it was nothing compared to what was to happen next.

V

The year 1913 saw a new minor league appear called the Federal League. Most of the F.L. owners were wealthy and had a desire to own their own big league teams. When none of the sixteen big league owners wanted to sell, eight disappointed men simply formed their own league, even if it was a minor one. The F.L. owners had the same idea that Ban Johnson had when he first ran his minor Western League—declare it a major league and then try to grab as many big names from the older leagues as possible. After the 1913 season the Federal League turned major and began raiding the other leagues. For St. Louis, a near catastrophe was about to engulf its baseball life.

The Federal League placed teams in eight cities, four of them already major, and that included St. Louis. St. Louis, which couldn't even support two teams, now had three to deal with. The St. Louis Federals (called Sloufeds) did what other Federal teams did, which was sign stars who were clearly fading. The Sloufeds, owned by Phil Ball, hired Three Finger Brown to manage a collection of old-timers and youngsters who would be hard pressed to do well in the other two leagues. The Cardinals and Browns, seeing their existence threatened, joined together to combat the Sloufeds, but it did little good. Both established teams had finished last in 1913, so they were left unscathed by the Sloufed attempt to stock its team.

The Sloufeds got off to a weak start and began wallowing near the bottom of the standings. Still, the Sloufeds drew well at first, attracting curious fans who wanted to see if Three Finger Brown could still bring it (he couldn't). While the Sloufeds were heading for the cellar, the Browns and Cardinals escaped their home of the previous season. The Browns climbed to fifth with a 71–82 record under a man who was in his first full season as manager—Branch Rickey. The Cardinals, under Miller Huggins, were actually involved in their first pennant race since joining the National League over twenty years before. After the Giants got off to a good start, they began to fade and the Cardinals saw first place for the fist time ever (or at least since they were in the American Association). However, the breath of fresh air was not to last, as the Boston

Braves, another longtime laughingstock that had shared the netherworld with the Cardinals, rose from last place on July 4 to capture the pennant by 10½ games over the Giants and 13 over the Cardinals. It was the first time the Cardinals had ended up in the first division since 1901.

Despite Huggins's brilliant job of managing, the Cardinals saw their attendance increase by only about fifty thousand. The Browns actually saw their attendance drop despite their improvement. The arrival of the Sloufeds did enough damage that both established teams lost money. Now for 1915, all teams in the two older leagues had to increase salaries to keep players from the F.L. This was the case in 1914 as well, and that's why the two St. Louis teams lost money despite dramatic improvements on the field. More salary raises for 1915 meant even more losses for the two St. Louis clubs unless they won their respective flags. And the chances of either St. Louis team winning a pennant were rather small.

Neither established team in St. Louis had to worry about going for the pennant. The Browns promptly went 63–91 and finished 39½ games out. The Cardinals, plagued by faulty hitting, dropped back to 72–81, 18½ games out. After the 1915 season ended, it looked as if the Federal League might still operate for the next season. The Sloufeds finished in a first-place tie and wanted to play the other two local teams in a postseason series, but both declined. After watching the Sloufeds tie for first, the Cardinals' officials were convinced that St. Louis would not be big enough for two teams, much less three. The Federal League expressed interest in buying the Cardinals, stripping the team down, and sending the best players of the team to Baltimore's F.L. team, which was about the same as simply moving the team from St. Louis to Baltimore. Cardinals officials mulled the offer over, but the National League stated that it would not allow the Cardinals to be moved or stripped by the Federal League. The Cardinals would have to stay put, and Baltimore would have to wait a few more decades before acquiring a St. Louis team.

Before the 1916 season opened, the three leagues sat down and signed an agreement that brought the war between the leagues to an end. Part of the agreement gave two Federal League owners, Charles Weeghman and Phil Ball, the right to buy into the established leagues. The former bought the Chicago Cubs and moved his new team into the park he had built for his Federal League team. The latter bought the St. Louis Browns, a team that former Brownie Jimmy Austin said years later owned St. Louis at the time. Ball, unlike previous Browns owner Robert Hedges, had the money and willingness to build the Browns into a contender. The Cardinals sat around and watched as they expected Ball, the newcomer, to make their lives even more miserable. The Browns and their fans were now looking forward to a new era.

Nineteen-sixteen looked like it was indeed going to be a good year for the Browns. Ball moved his best Sloufed players to the Browns, and they finished 79–76. The Cardinals went out and posted a 60–93 record, sharing the basement with the Cincinnati Reds. Miller Huggins, who once was considered a genius manager, was now being criticized. Still, the Cardinals stuck by him as Huggins searched wide and far for players to improve his bad club. Huggins had some success when he tried out a nineteen-year-old infielder at shortstop late in the 1915 season. The kid's fielding was a bit bad, but he did hit .246 (not bad by Cardinal standards). The kid's name was Rogers Hornsby.

Huggins also was busy looking for pitching (at this time it was common for managers to double as scouts) and came up with some gems in Bill Doak and Lee Meadows, two guys who would give the Cardinals some steady hurling for the next few years. Red Ames also contributed nicely. Still, Huggins chafed under the tightfistedness under which the Cardinals were operated. With little money available, the Cardinals could not compete with the rich teams like the Giants and Cubs when it came to buying (or even finding) young players that could build up the team.

Nineteen-seventeen opened with the Cardinals getting off to a good start and staying in the race for the first half of the season. Hornsby, now the regular shortstop, hit .327 as the Cardinals' top hitter. Walt Cruise hit .295 and Jack Smith chipped in at .297. Hard-luck Bill Doak lost 20, but Lee Meadows, Red Ames, and Wilt Watson all chipped in with good years. Although the Cardinals faded in the second half, they ended the season in third place with an 82–70 record.

After the 1917 season ended, important events were unfolding. The New York Yankees were looking for a new manager to lead that then terrible team to its first flag, and the Cardinals allowed Miller Huggins to talk to the Yankees. After the Yankees assured Huggins that he would be fully backed by a checkbook the size of New York, the Mighty Mite took the job. Huggins went on to manage the first part of the mighty Yankees dynasty and was named to the Hall of Fame in 1964.

The next important development was the dispute between Phil Ball and Branch Rickey on the Browns. Evidently, Ball wanted to spend lavishly to turn his team into a power in the A.L. (as well as St. Louis) while Rickey liked to save nickels and dimes whenever possible. Besides, Rickey had an idea on how to build up a club cheaply, compared to simply throwing money at minor league owners. Ball decided that he would build his team up his own way, and when Rickey's contract with him expired, he let him go. The Cardinals, hearing that Rickey, the eccentric, had some good ideas (especially on how to save money), offered him stock in the club if he would work for them. Rickey agreed.

Finally, Mrs. Schuyler Britton, weary of running a club that looked like it would never realize a profit or win a pennant, decided to sell the club. No one person dared buy all or most of the stock in the rickety Cardinal club, so shares of stock were offered to whoever had the cash to buy it. In time, literally hundreds of people would be owners of Cardinal stock. Branch Rickey was one who bought in, and another was Sam Breadon, a car dealer.

By 1918, Branch Rickey held enough stock in the club to be labeled as its president. Unfortunately, World War I was under way and Rickey was called by the military to serve as an adviser. While Rickey was away, Breadon kept buying up stock in the club, so he was soon the largest stockholder. On the field, the Cardinals had a new boss in Jack Hendricks, who promptly managed the club back to its familiar home in the second division. The 1918 club finished last with a 51–78 record that would have been worse had the season not been cut due to wartime restriction. The only player of note to newly arrive on the Cardinals was pitcher Bill Sherdel, who went 6–12 with a 2.71 ERA. Sherdel would become a key pitcher for the team in the future, although he didn't seem to indicate that in 1918.

After the 1918 season Breadon had become the president of the Cardinals, which probably surprised Branch Rickey when he returned from the military. Rickey didn't seem to mind as long as he would be left alone to do what he thought was best to improve his new club. Breadon in general was a hands-off owner (*president* and *owner* were two terms that basically were interchangeable in those days) who would be satisfied with Rickey as long as he could get the Cardinals moving in the right direction.

For 1919, Rickey decided the best way to acquaint himself with his new team was to manage it on the field. He fired Jack Hendricks and managed his second team ever (the first being the Browns). Rickey decided to shift Rogers Hornsby from shortstop to third base in an attempt to improve the club's fielding. Overall, Rickey probably didn't like what he saw, as the club was filled with average and below-average players. The pitching staff had some good arms in Doak and Sherdel, but Lee Meadows was sent to the Phillies as he went on to lose 20 games. Rickey's first season as Cardinal manager ended with a seventh-place finish and a 54–83 record. After surveying his team's less than stellar performance, Rickey decided to have a little chat with boss Sam Breadon.

VI

If one looks at Branch Rickey's success (or lack of) as a manager through 1919, one would guess that Rickey must have been a masochist. First, Rickey piloted the usually woeful Browns for two full seasons and compiled a less than great 134–173 record. Then Rickey guided the 1919 Cardinals to 54–83. Why would somebody even think of going to work for two such hapless teams in any capacity, much less in the role of manager?

Branch Rickey was born on December 20, 1881, in Lucasville, Ohio. Farm life was not to Rickey's liking, so he decided to become a great student. Rickey succeeded in getting a college education (a rarity for anyone other than owners in baseball in those days), and after he graduated from college he signed with a minor league team to play baseball, a sport he had taken up and liked in college. In 1905 Rickey appeared in one game as a catcher for the Browns, going 0 for 3. The next year, Rickey became a platooned catcher for the Browns and showed he could hit by hitting .284. The Browns, however, were puzzled that Rickey would not play on Sundays. Rickey said he had promised his mother he would not go to the ballpark on Sundays and he intended to keep that promise. In December 1906 the already impoverished Browns sold Rickey to the New York Highlanders (later called Yankees) in their never-ending quest for making a buck.

Rickey went from one lackluster club to another. The Highlanders finished in the race in 1906, but in 1907 they dropped under the .500 mark. Rickey struggled like the rest of his New York teammates, hitting just .182. If Rickey thought he had trouble hitting the ball, he was even more baffled behind the plate. On June 28, Rickey was behind the plate when thirteen runners stole bases against him, a record that seems safe for some time. After this dismal season was over, Rickey retired to pursue a law degree, which he gained in 1911. Despite leaving the game as a player, Rickey still recommended possible players to interested teams in an effort to pick up some money.

Rickey returned to the big league scene in 1913 when Browns owner Robert Hedges offered him a job as his assistant in building the Browns up. Luckily for Hedges, Rickey was also a coach at the University of Michigan, a job that enabled Rickey to keep his eyes open for some possibly useful bodies to fill out Browns uniforms. Rickey also had contacts with some minor league operators, and any time Rickey found a prospect he'd send him to one of the minor league teams to gain a little seasoning.

Later in the 1913 season, the Browns were stung by the Sloufeds when they lured the Brownie manager, George Stovall, to their team. Hedges asked Rickey to manage the team, and he did, going 5–6 with the last-place Browns. Although Rickey was regarded by many as a fine manager, others thought he was "too scientific," as he expounded all kinds of seemingly bizarre theories on how the game should be played. When he wasn't busy managing, Rickey kept looking for prospects, and his first big find at the University of Michigan was a hard-hitting pitcher named George Sisler.

Rickey seemed to be enjoying the challenges of finding new

talent and piloting the Browns when Phil Ball bought the club in 1916. Ball had no use for his employee who would not drink, not go the park on Sundays, and babble on about just about anything that came to mind. It also didn't help matters that despite his theories, Rickey couldn't apply them well enough to his dismal team and turn it around. Ball kept Rickey around for 1916 but fired him as manager and replaced him with his Sloufed skipper, Fielder Jones. Jones did little better as the Brownie manager than did Rickey.

The free-spending Ball and the tightfisted Rickey did not see eye to eye on how to build the Browns, and by 1917 Rickey realized that he would not be back with the Browns. As soon as the Cardinals made it known that its stock was up for grabs, Rickey decided to buy some and get a job with the crosstown team. Rickey certainly knew what he was getting himself into. He had heard how the Cardinals were almost packed away in a coffin to Baltimore and how run-down the ballpark was. Rickey also knew that if there was any team run on a budget even tighter than the Browns, it was the Cardinals. Rickey loved a challenge and he certainly had a big one on his hands with the Cardinals.

Unlike on the Browns, Rickey was offered free rein to run the Cardinals any way he liked, as long as he could stick to the budget. Sam Breadon was no spendthrift himself, but he would open his wallet a bit wider than the previous ownership ever was willing to do. The old ownership had left some debts behind and that matter had to be dealt with, just like about a couple of hundred problems concerning the roster and other areas.

The mess confronting Rickey and Breadon was formidable. The leagues both had to cut their seasons short in 1918 due to restrictions on manpower caused by World War I. Everyone lost money in 1918. After that miserable season was over, the owners didn't know what to do concerning the 1919 season. The war was still going on and it looked like it would last into the next year, and the owners, fearing a possible ban on baseball due to need for more manpower, voted to play only 140 games for 1919. The owners had miscalculated the whole thing, and when the war ended before 1918 did, the owners still decided to keep the short-ened schedule rather than lengthen it to the usual 154 games. As a result, 1919 yielded small profits for teams that should have cashed in big. Babe Ruth began a home run craze in the American League by hitting a then record twenty-nine. The A.L. obviously benefitted from Ruth mania, but the game in general did well for 1919. Except the Cardinals. In 1918 the Cardinals drew just over 110,000 fans, their worst ever, and in 1919 they did little better by having 167,000 people show up. Money wasn't exactly pouring into Cardinal coffers via gate receipts, but the fans couldn't be blamed. Previous ownerships had made the team an unwatchable farce.

VII

By January 1, 1920, the St. Louis Cardinals had been a National League club for twenty-eight years. They had contributed virtually nothing to the city that housed it in its three decades of National League life. Still, this wretched ball club had a loyal following (after all, they did draw over 100,000 to see a last-place team in 1918), albeit a small one. From 1892 through 1919 the Cardinals posted just five seasons in which they won more than they lost. In none of those five winning seasons did the Cardinals stay in a pennant race from start to finish. Just twice (1914 and 1917) did the Cardinals play as much as half a season of baseball worthy of a contender. In twenty-eight years, the Cardinals finished in the first division (sixth or better from 1892 to 1899, fourth or better from 1900 to 1919) a mere four times, lost 100 games four times, lost 90 or more games fifteen times, and came no closer to first place than 13 games. In short, the Cardinals gave St. Louis twenty-eight years of some of the worst baseball ever seen by one team over a prolonged period. The early Cardinals were so consistently dismal that they must be compared to some other benchmarks of failure that illustrate just how awful these Cardinals were.

People lament over the Chicago Cubs of the post–World War II era. True, the Cubs have won just two divisional titles since 1946, but at least they finished first in two instances. Take any twenty-eight-year period in Cubs history from 1946 to the present and one would still see more .500 seasons by the Cubs during such a stretch than the Cardinals put together from 1892 to 1919.

The Cleveland Indians are also ridiculed, since they haven't won a thing since 1954. Still, from 1955 to 1983 the Indians climbed over the .500 mark nine times. If one includes the 1966 Indians, who finished right on the .500 mark, that would give the Indians twice as many winning seasons as the Cardinals.

Even older benchmarks of failure can't measure up to the awful Cardinals of 1892–1919. Sixty years of the first Washington Senators team never included a twenty-eight-year stretch as bad as the Cardinals'. The closest the Senators come to rivaling the Cardinals was from 1932 to 1960 (the last year this awful team lived before it turned into the Minnesota Twins), when the Senators posted seven .500 marks and contended for the flag wire to wire in 1945. The Philadelphia Athletics never had twenty-eight straight years of abject futility as bad as the Cardinals', even if they produced some of the all-time single-season disasters. Even the St. Louis Browns just can't compare to the Cardinals. From 1903 to 1931 the Browns had eight .500 seasons and were in two pennant races (1908 and 1922) from start to finish. The Boston Braves of 1903–31 come close with only four .500 records, but at least they won a world championship and contended two out of the other three seasons. Only the Philadelphia Phillies (which has rung up a major league record of nearly 9,000 losses since 1883) can top the performance of the early Cardinal teams. From 1918 to 1946 the Phillies posted the incredible total of *one* .500 season (in 1932), a record the Phils were just starting to work on and one that will probably last as long as there are cities looking for bad teams to buy and move. As 1920 dawned, the Phillies were just two years along on their streak to surpass the Cardinals for utter failure.

Besides offering plenty of losing baseball to the fans, the Cardinals also offered their fans a cramped, run-down, ancient stadium to see their favorite team get their brains beat out as 1920 arrived. The Cardinals' park had already been hit by fires in the grandstand on a few occasions, and even if no fires took place, the stadium was a crumbling wreck. Built by Chris Von Der Ahe and the site of horse racing and other strange things for a baseball field, the Cardinals' park was twenty-seven years old and certainly wasn't built to last that long, since it was made primarily of wood. The Cardinal players must have marvelled over the nice new steel and concrete stadiums that rivals had put up in New York and Pittsburgh and other cities, while home for them was little more than a shack. The Cardinals were so poor that painting the stadium qualified as a massive renovation of the park. At least this miserable situation was to be resolved before the 1920 season began when Sam Breadon convinced Phil Ball to take in the Cardinals as tenants of the Browns. Ball didn't mind too much, since his was the dominant team in town. Breadon was relieved that he no longer had to worry about maintaining a ballpark and sold the land the old one was on. Breadon then put the money into fixing up his team.

Branch Rickey was shrewd enough to realize that people would not become Cardinal fans on a permanent basis as long as they kept losing ballgames, so Rickey racked his brain trying to come up with an idea to get new fans. In 1918 he came up with an idea to let kids see games free (from less than good vantage points, of course), and in 1919 the "Knothole Gang" was created. Hundreds of kids got to see games and became hooked on the Cardinals. Soon this became a regular feature, and thousands of kids over the years became Cardinal fans through this idea. Later, when Rickey tried to end it because it was becoming costly (a loss of gate receipts, that is), the city put up such a fuss that Rickey let the program continue.

The Cardinals also had plenty of bills left over from the past that had to be paid. Things were better than some twenty years earlier, when the league and some of its owners put money into the team to keep it afloat. Many of the bills were taken care of with the cash Breadon got in the sale of the Cardinals' old park. At least the club didn't have any stock in the hands of other owners.

The Cardinals entered 1920 still in the city with the smallest population that had at least two teams (the others were Chicago, Philadelphia, New York, and Boston) and were facing the big checkbook of their new landlord, Phil Ball. After looking back on twenty-eight years of enduring failure, it was quite an accomplishment that the Cardinals were still around and still in St. Louis. Rickey and Breadon still had to run the team on a shoestring, but at least their stewardship gave the fans some hope.

Nineteen-twenty also saw Branch Rickey setting out in force

to implement his idea on how to cheaply bring players to the big leagues. In the past, owners would send their managers to the minors to look around for some help. Shrewd minor league owners, like Jack Dunn of Baltimore, would hold out for the highest possible price for the player wanted. The minor leagues in those days were not affiliated with the majors as they now are. Minor leagues operated on their own and made much of their profit by selling players to the majors. Some minor leagues, like the Pacific Coast League, were considered so strong that they could almost pass as a major league.

In the late 1910s the minors were in big trouble. First the Federal League placed teams in some of the bigger minor league cities, such as Baltimore (of the International League). The Federal League move into the minor league cities brought on even worse hardships to the teams involved there than the F.L.'s move on big league towns had done to the big league teams. Since the minors were independent from the majors, they could expect no help from the big leagues when the F.L. raided teams and invaded cities. Some minor leagues went bankrupt; others came close. The majors (excluding the Federal League) were worried that a prime source of players was drying up, but there was little they could do about it.

Once the Federal League went out of business, the minors were ready for good times, but World War I hit. Players were drafted en masse, and by 1918 only one minor league was able to complete its season. The minors were now in danger of total extinction.

Branch Rickey had connections in the minors and came up with an idea while still with the Browns. The idea was to have a major league team subsidize a minor league one, and in return the major league team could send prospects to that minor league team for seasoning. When the player was needed, the major league team could dip down to its minor league club and get the player, while no other big league team would be allowed to get that player. The farm system concept was born.

Rickey didn't get the chance to implement his plan for the Browns, but when he came back from the military in late 1918 he was ready to try it for the Cardinals. By the time of Rickey's return, a farm system was needed more than ever, and not just by the Cardinals. For a three-year period starting in 1919 the majors had to suspend their draft of minor leaguers so that the minors could be replenished. Getting new players thereafter would cost more money, and during the draft suspension it was hard to find new players to add to major league rosters. Rickey looked around the country to see which minor league teams, or even leagues, were available to be affiliated with the Cardinals. Rickey had seen several players he found in the past get away when the player's minor league team would notify a rich big league team and that team would fork over more money to get that player. Now Rickey found himself two minor leagues (the Nebraska State and Arkansas State leagues) ready to sign deals with him. Both leagues agreed to keep and develop players for the Cardinals and not get rid of them unless St. Louis agreed. The Cardinals would then be able to call up or send down a player without the fear that a minor league operator would call a rich big league club and sell the player to the other big league team. In return the Cardinals would subsidize the two leagues.

In 1919 these two minor leagues began operations as Cardinal farm units. The Cardinals found little use for the players in the two farm leagues, and at first the idea in practice looked a bit disappointing. After the 1919 season was over the Cardinals were in need of a starting pitcher and they went out and bought Jesse Haines from Kansas City of the minor league American Association. "Pop" Haines had pitched very briefly for the Reds in 1918 but was found lacking and sent back to the minors. Pop Haines was the last player bought from the minors by the Cardinals, and he would go on to have a Hall of Fame career. It would be a long time before the Cardinals would have to buy a minor leaguer.

VIII

The 1920 season on the field looked much like all the other ones endured by the Cardinals and their fans. Rickey had made some trades after the 1919 season, and they seemed to pan out. Jack Fournier was picked up from the Yankees and hit .306 while playing well at first base. Hal Janvrin hit .274 as a utilityman, and Pop Haines had a 2.98 ERA despite losing 20 games. Rogers Hornsby continued to improve at bat as he led the league with 94 RBIs and won his first batting title at .370. Bill Doak went 20–12, and Ferdie Schupp posted a 16–13 mark. All in all, 1920 was another lost year on the field for the Cardinals. At 75–79 they improved to within sight of respectability, but they still finished sixth, tied with the Cubs and 18 games out.

Manager Branch Rickey was happy to see some improvement on the field, but Rickey the businessman was not happy, as another losing record was not the way to draw fans. In the Cardinals first season at Sportsman's Park (former home of the Union Association's Maroons) attendance improved to almost 327,000 (up from 167,000 in 1919), but it still trailed the attendance of the landlord Browns by about 90,000. Rogers Hornsby (now a second baseman) was now the Cardinals' star and most popular player, and the time would come when he would have to be paid accordingly. This was something Rickey probably had in the back of his mind as he looked back on the season just concluded.

Off the field, the Cardinals continued to sign up minor league teams and leagues to its farm system. The Cardinals were actually starting to show a little profit, as they began selling off players who they didn't think would make it to other big league clubs. Rickey checked the stats daily to see who was hot and might be ready to be recalled. As far as Rickey was concerned, nobody was quite ready for a recall just yet, but players were moving along.

Naturally, the teams that did not understand the nature of both the Cardinals' problems and the farm team concept ridiculed and criticized the Cardinals' blatant use of the minors as a farm. Even though teams condemned the Cardinal farm system, they gladly took players from it for cash. Breadon and Rickey took most of that money and poured it right back into the farm system. Not only was the farm system producing a deep supply of guaranteed players, but it was also now supplying the Cardinals with plenty of cash as well. Now, for the first time since joining the National League, the St. Louis Cardinals had the potential to take on the rich teams from bigger cities like the New York Giants and Chicago Cubs and build a possible dynasty of their own. Previously only teams like the Cubs and Giants were able to build a long-running contender because of the large fan bases that those two teams could draw on. Of course, a rich owner willing to spend the money to get new players to keep the team in contention and bring in the fans was necessary, as nobody in any city would pay to see a loser on the field. That was a lesson the Giants of the turn of the century and the Red Sox of the 1920s found out the hard way. With the farm system doubling as a cash cow, the Cardinals now had the financial resources to challenge the big boys. Still, the Cardinals had to spend more wisely because of their small, shared market. Reckless spending in New York could be overcome, but reckless spending in St. Louis would land the Cardinals right back into the fiscal position of the past three decades. The St. Louis Browns would show what such spending in a small, shared market would lead to.

Thus as the 1921 season approached the Cardinals were ready to enter a new age after thirty years of aimless wandering. Branch Rickey and Sam Breadon had purchased enough stock in the team to make them the undisputed bosses (although Breadon held more than Rickey). The prudence and patience of these two men were now about to pay off, as the Cardinals were prepared to launch themselves into the upper echelons of the National League and baseball at large. The St. Louis Cardinals were now ready to claim the title as the finest club in National League history.

Part III

The House That Rickey Built
(1921–49)

I

Going into the 1921 season, the so-called experts were predicting that the pennant race would involve the defending champion Brooklyn Robins (named after their skipper, former Cardinal Wilbert Robinson), the always tough New York Giants of John McGraw, and the up-and-coming Pittsburgh Pirates. The Boston Braves and Philadelphia Phillies, two impoverished teams that just a few years earlier had been the cream of the league, were expected to battle for the cellar. That left the last first-division slot open to the Chicago Cubs, the Cincinnati Reds, and the St. Louis Cardinals. As usual, the Cardinals were expected by most to join the Phillies and Braves at the bottom of the heap.

The experts were wrong. As the season commenced, the Giants and Pirates did contend, but instead of being joined by the Robins in the race, they had to contend with birds of a different color. The Giants and Pirates spent the year trading first place between each other while the Cardinals waited for a shot at the top themselves. The Cardinals drew close to the top spot on several occasions, but the experienced Giants were just too much for either the Cardinals or the Pirates to overcome. At season's end, the Cardinals finished third with a club-best record of 87–66. At 7 games back, it was by far the closest the Cardinals had ever come to first place.

The Cardinals were certainly pleased with the 1921 season. Rogers Hornsby was now the league's most dominating hitter, as he won the batting title with a sizzling .397 average, led the league in RBIs with 126, doubles with 44, hits with 235, triples with 18, and runs scored with 131, placing second in homers with 21. The Cardinal batting attack in general was devastating, as four other regulars topped the .300 mark and several platoon players came through with averages above that level as well. The Cardinals as a club led the league with a nifty .308 mark and finished second in homers with 83 in a year that saw offense explode in both leagues. On the hill, the club could have used a little help, as Pop Haines led the team in wins with 18 and Bill Doak led the league with a 2.59 ERA. Rickey's farm system also yielded its first big star in Jim Bottomley, who wasn't quite ready yet for the majors but was definitely in Rickey's plans, despite a .227 average in the minors.

Attendance continued to rise as almost 385,000 went to see the suddenly good Cardinals. Rickey was also looking good as a trader, as he picked up catcher Eddie Ainsmith from Detroit and pitcher Jeff Pfeffer from the fading Robins. Ainsmith brought years of experience to the team, and Pfeffer ended up going 9–3 for the Cardinals after a poor start in Brooklyn. Branch Rickey and Sam Breadon were now in the unfamiliar but happy position of being considered the bosses of a contender.

Nineteen-twenty-two was a year of great joy for baseball fans in St. Louis. The Browns got off to a great start and were in first place in the American League, as Phil Ball's method of building a club seemed to be paying off. The Cardinals also started off well and found themselves in a five-team battle with the Giants, Pirates, Reds, and Cubs.

The Cardinals looked better than they did the previous year, as Rogers Hornsby was en route to a Triple Crown year (leading the league with a .401 average, 42 homers, and 152 RBIs). In early July, the Giants came to town and Sportsman's Park was packed with delirious fans. The Giants were nice guests, as they lost 3 out of 4 to the locals, keeping the Cardinals in the race. With Hornsby leading the way, it looked like the Cardinals might get their first pennant ever, and with the Browns in first place in the other league an all St. Louis World Series looked like a good possibility.

The Cardinals had their way of improving themselves, and the Giants had their own way as well. As a matter of fact, both New York teams built up their clubs by simply buying veterans from other big league clubs struggling to keep going. The Yankees had a virtual farm club of their own up in Boston called the Red Sox. The Red Sox, owned by Broadway producer Harry Frazee, had sold virtually every quality player they had (including Babe Ruth) to the Yankees in the last few years so Frazee could get money to put on his Broadway shows. The results were amazing. The Red Sox, long an American League power, plunged into the second division while the perennially bad Yankees rose to contention. Other clubs complained loudly over the way the Yankees had procured players at the expense of poor clubs like Boston, but little could be done.

On July 23, 1922, the Yankees sent four players they had little use for and $50,000 to their Boston "farm team." This deal, coming so late in the season, angered Browns fans, who felt the Yankees were unfairly "buying" a pennant. Phil Ball wasn't exactly a pauper, but there was no way he could afford the prices the Yankees were willing to pay to get big league veterans. It didn't help matters that the Yanks also got veteran Elmer Smith in the deal as more or less a throw-in.

A week later, the Cardinals and their fans were really seeing red when the Giants sent two bodies and $100,000 to *its* Boston "farm club," known as the Braves, for pitcher Hugh "Red" McQuillan. For some time the Giants, like the Yankees, had used cash to get veteran big leaguers, and the Braves were in the same condition that the Cardinals had been in just a few years earlier. Actually, the Giants were blessed with two "farm teams," since the Phillies were also in constant need of money infusions. Just the previous year the Giants had picked up Casey Stengel from the Phillies in a one-sided deal that didn't involve cash, but it clearly was a deal that favored the Giants.

Branch Rickey was furious. "How can we compete when rich clubs can simply buy players in the heat of a pennant race?" he asked. The Cardinals appealed to Commissioner Kenesaw Landis for help, but Landis did nothing at the time. Once the season was over, though, Landis instituted a rule that made June 15 the trading deadline. Any deals made after that date would have to involve putting traded players on waivers before they could go to a new club. The rule lasted into the 1980s and in time was useless, as the owners always scratched one another's back when it came to waiver deals.

The actions of the two New York clubs to deprive the St. Louis teams of their respective pennants were not forgotten by the fans. The newly acquired players gave the New York teams some needed shots in their arms as they moved into first place. When the Yankees arrived in St. Louis for a pivotal September series, the fans got even. Throughout the series, the fans yelled and screamed louder than ever at the Yankees and threw things at them from time to time. In one game, center fielder Whitey Witt was about to catch a fly ball when a flying soda bottle smashed into his head, knocking him cold. Witt was taken out on a stretcher, and the umpires threatened to forfeit the game to the Yankees if the fans didn't stop throwing things at the Yankees. As things turned out, Witt played a key role later in the series, as his team won it and knocked the Browns out of first place. The Browns went on to post a 93–61 record, the best mark the club would ever attain. Unfortunately for the Browns, the Yankees won the flag by just 1 game.

Cardinal fans were somewhat more sedate when the Giants came to town, but by then their team was fading down the stretch. The Cardinals, though, figured in a bizarre incident that involved the Giants. Giant pitcher Phil Douglas, a noted drinker, had been having trouble with his manager, the volatile John McGraw, all season long. The arrival of Red McQuillan of Boston probably upset Douglas more than ever. After losing to the Pirates in late July, Douglas disappeared and got drunk. McGraw found him a few days later and had him "dry out" at a hospital. After being released, Douglas became mad over the fact that he had to pay the hospital and blamed McGraw for this. A few days later the depressed Douglas, who had been the Giants' top pitcher in the first half of the season, wrote a letter to Cardinal outfielder Les Mann, a former teammate of Douglas on the Cubs. The letter indicated that, for the right price, Douglas would not bear down on the Cardinals the next time he faced them, because he didn't want McGraw to win the pennant. In fact, for the right price Douglas said he would simply jump the Giants.

Mann passed the letter over to Branch Rickey, who then sent it to Commissioner Landis. After the scandal of the 1919 World Series, this Douglas affair was a serious matter. Landis then did what most people figured he would do, banishing Douglas from the majors for life. McGraw was now without one of his top starters, but the effect wasn't too great.

The Cardinal fade continued and in late September the Giants clinched the pennant at their expense. Still, the season was a good one. The Cardinals slipped back to fourth place with an 85–69 record (tied with the Pirates, so it can be said that the Cardinals still ended up third). Attendance skyrocketed to over the 500,000 mark, easily a club record up to that time. Hornsby was now the undisputed top slugger in the league, as he led a powerful attack to 107 homers, second only to the Phillies in that category. Jim Bottomley came up from the farm late in the season, and he looked like a sure bet when he drove in 35 runs in 37 games. Rickey's farm system was clearly working now.

For 1923, Rickey decided to make Bottomley his first baseman, and made room for him by shipping hard-hitting incumbent Jack Fournier to Brooklyn for center fielder Hi Myers. Aside from this deal, though, Rickey was unable to do much to improve the Cardinals with proven major leaguers. Cardinal fans, no longer expecting a mediocre team hoping to get to the first division but a possible champion instead, were less than happy to see a known quantity like Fournier be replaced by the unknown Bottomley and little else.

The Cardinals were a competitive club in 1923, but they were not much of a factor in the race. Bottomley hit .371 and drove in 94 runs in a great first full season. Myers made the Fournier deal look even better by hitting .300, Hornsby won another batting title with a .384 mark, and longtime Cardinal Jack Smith chipped in with a .310 mark himself. Despite these performances and a league-leading total of 274 doubles, the Cardinal lineup was not all that great in this time of heavy hitting. Specs Toporcer and Ray Blades were farm products getting more time in the starting lineup as Rickey tried to rebuild his lineup with more home-grown players. Pop Haines was now the ace of the pitching staff, as he went 20–13 with a 3.11 ERA. In this age of four-man rotations, though, the Cardinals did not have depth on the mound. Bill Doak was fading at 8–13, as was Jeff Pfeffer (8–9, 4.02), and Fred Toney was mediocre at 11–12. Only Bill Sherdel at 15–13 gave Haines some help, but his 4.32 ERA was not too helpful.

A fifth-place finish at 79–74 was certainly not what the Cardinal fans had expected for 1923, and Rickey had some explaining to do. Attendance dipped by about 200,000 and now Sam Breadon was also getting impatient, as Rickey tried to assure him that players coming up from the farm would turn the team into a champ if given time. Nineteen-twenty-four turned out to be a really bad season as the Cardinals tried to make the transition from an aging team of veterans to a team of youngsters that would lead to a contender. More farm products were arriving and getting part-time playing jobs that the fading veterans were having trouble keeping. Some youngsters, like Wattie Holm, would have good seasons for St. Louis but never would be stars. Others, like Chick Hafey, would join Bottomley in being superstars and going to the Hall of Fame. Still, 1924 was one of those years of transition, and the team plunged to a dismal 65–89 record, bad enough for sixth place just ahead of the always awful Phillies and Braves. Things were so bad that Pop Haines went from 20 wins to 19 losses in one year. Attendance dropped further.

At this point it looked like Branch Rickey's vision of building a contender by developing one's own players in the minors was becoming a nightmare. After reaching the 87-win level in 1921, the Cardinals were looking at an increasingly worsening team that now owned 22 fewer wins and a not too cheap minor league system. True, the farm system was producing more major leaguers, but the record showed regress, not progress. Sam Breadon was now ready to sack Rickey as manager, but Rickey finagled another year of commitment from Breadon as manager of the club.

Nineteen-twenty-five got off to a poor start, and it looked like yet another year of regression when Breadon fired Rickey as the team's pilot. Rickey was angered over this, even though his record as the skipper at that point was 13–25. As a result of the firing, Rickey sold most of his stock to the new manager, Rogers Hornsby, which would be a problem a few years later. Despite his anger over being canned as manager, Rickey stayed with the team as its general manager in the never-ending quest to right the Cardinals.

Breadon's hiring of Hornsby as manager was a great idea. Hornsby had become the darling of the Cardinal fans, and they figured he would turn the team around. Hornsby was having yet another brilliant year, as he captured another Triple Crown in 1925, batting .403 in the process. At Hornsby's urging, Rickey began getting rid of veterans, getting the roster cleared for farm products to make good. Rickey picked up a few veterans from other teams to give Hornsby help in the leadership department.

Bob O'Farrell was a valuable pickup from the Cubs, costing only the seldom used Mike Gonzalez and Howard Freigau. Ralph Shinners was picked up for next to nothing, bringing some needed class that he had picked up on the pennant-winning Giants. These two players helped to break in youngsters such as Chick Hafey, Tommy Thevenow, and Ray Blades into the lineup so that they gained some always needed confidence. Specs Toporcer and Jim Bottomley were already proving their value to the club. Bottomley was already a feared hitter who had driven in a record-setting 12 runs in one game the previous year. Bottomley posted a .367 average with 21 homers and 128 RBIs in 1925, making him and Hornsby one of the best 1-2 punches in the majors. Toporcer, the first infielder to wear glasses while playing in the field, hit .284 and was a solid shortstop, although he would later be relegated to backup status by Thevenow. Although Pop Haines struggled in 1925, Bill Sherdel did well at 15–6, 3.11, and the farm finally yielded a pitcher in hard-drinking Flint Rhem, who went only 8–13 with a 4.92 ERA in his first full big league season.

Despite the poor start under Rickey, Hornsby whipped the team into a 64–51 unit under his stewardship as the Cardinals overall went 77–76, good enough for a fourth-place finish. Hornsby's presence as manager boosted the gate to past the 400,000 mark. Rickey had gotten over the fact that Breadon didn't think much of his managing ability after seeing the profits that Hornsby brought the team as its top player and new manager. Imagine what a pennant winner would do for profits.

II

Few people would pick the Cardinals to win the flag in 1926. After all, the Cardinals entered that season with no first-place finishes in their thirty-four year National League life. Nineteen-twenty-five certainly didn't offer any indication that the team would do much in 1926. At best, a third-place finish might be all the Cardinals could hope for. Besides, Rogers Hornsby was not the easiest manager in the world to get along with, and his abrasive style might be detrimental to the young players who were hoped to bring better things for St. Louis's National League fans.

Hornsby may have been one of the finest hitters in the history of baseball, but as a human being he was often found wanting. Born in Winters, Texas, in 1896, Hornsby was hitting a paltry (for him) .277 for Denison in the Western Association in 1915 when the Cardinals signed him. Later that year, the Cardinals recalled him and stuck him at shortstop. As a shortstop, Hornsby was no Honus Wagner, the man all shortstops were measured against in those days, and his .246 average was less than stellar. Still, the Cardinals kept him, and in 1916 he hit .313 as he shuttled from one infield position to another. Hornsby had lots of promise as a hitter, but his glove was a problem even in the days of small gloves and rocky, poorly kept fields. When Branch Rickey arrived in 1919, he had Hornsby play third base but found him wanting and decided to try him at second. Second base would be Hornsby's home for the rest of his time in the majors, and although he would not look graceful playing that position, he did an acceptable job around the bag.

One thing that could not be denied was Hornsby's ability to hit a ball. In 1920, the "Rajah" won the first of six straight batting titles and seven overall. Hornsby also smacked the long ball, as he hit 301 in his career, including 42 in 1922, a record for second basemen that was tied by Davey Johnson of the 1973 Atlanta Braves. Nine times Hornsby led the league in slugging percentage, and he also won four RBI titles. Rajah's biggest accomplishments took place between 1921 and 1925, when he won two Triple Crowns and hit the ball for a .401 average.

All of these batting feats had made Rogers Hornsby a popular man with the fans and brought him acclaim from opponents. Unfortunately for Branch Rickey, he had to deal with Hornsby on two levels. As manager, Rickey had to keep the clubhouse some-what harmonious, which was not easy with Hornsby around. Hornsby would get a swelled head when praised, and much of the time he expected his teammates to do as well as he did. Naturally, many players were turned off by this attitude, since they *were* doing the best that they could. After all, how many Rogers Hornsbys were out there anyhow? Hornsby figured if others put out effort at 100 percent, they too could be like him. Hornsby would have a few arguments on this point with his teammates over the years, poisoning the clubhouse attitude in the process. Teammates who needled Hornsby about his not reading or seeing a movie in order to save his eyesight would often feel the effects of his tongue-lashings.

On another level, Rickey had to deal with Hornsby when it came to money. As the league's best hitter, Hornsby expected to be paid accordingly, and fans would usually support him in his battle with the penny-pinching Rickey. One couldn't blame Hornsby for battling for every penny, since he was the man who put "fannies in the seats" with his great hitting. After being fired as manager, Rickey decided to sell Hornsby his stock in the club, probably to show him what it was like to have to be an owner and pay out salaries. It's doubtful if Hornsby minded much.

As 1926 arrived, it was expected that defending champ Pittsburgh would battle with the Giants for the flag. The Cardinals were dismissed as a .500 team by most people. After all, the Cardinals had done virtually nothing to improve the team after the mediocre 1925 season.

The Giants got off to their usual good start and were battling the Pirates for the flag. The Reds, led by former Cardinal pilot Jack Hendricks, also were doing a nice job staying near the top. The Cardinals, plagued by the usual problem of lack of pitching depth, got off to a rocky start. Soon the Cubs made their move and joined the pennant race. Despite the shaky start, Hornsby and his charges were getting along well, much to the surprise of Cardinal watchers. Then, on June 22, the Cubs finally solved the Cardinals' problem of little pitching by sending Grover Cleveland Alexander to St. Louis via waivers. Alexander was one of the most notorious drinkers in an age when many players drank themselves right out of the game (like Phil Douglas). Alexander was thirty-nine years old in 1926 and the Cubs were sure he was through, despite his having given over seven years of good pitching to them. Old Grover had indeed been around for some time, breaking in with the Phillies in 1911 and posting 28 wins as a rookie and three straight years of 30 wins before the foolish Phillies shipped him to the Cubs.

Now the Cardinals had a thirty-nine-year-old alcoholic pitcher owning a 3–3 record for the season on a staff that needed a boost. The waiver deal between the Cubs and Cardinals was hardly noticed and one wonders that if Commissioner Landis didn't institute the trading deadline of June 15 a few years earlier what would have happened in the 1926 pennant race. It's possible that the Cubs would have held onto Alexander a little longer, then sold him right to the Giants, as was so often the case in the past concerning the Braves and Phillies when they dealt with the Giants. Still, the Giants could have claimed Alexander on waivers, which either would have bagged the hurler for them or at least would have kept him out of the Cardinals' clutches. It seems that the Giants also thought Alexander was washed up and that the Cardinals were not to be taken seriously as a contender.

Whatever the reasons, Alexander was now a Cardinal, and he joined an improving staff led by the developing Flint Rhem, Bill Sherdel, and Pop Haines. Hornsby was not hitting as well as he had in the past, as he concentrated on managing the team, but he still was a tough out. Jim Bottomley began driving in runs after a slow start, and other farm products also began making great contributions. To show how lightly the Giants were taking the Cardinals, they shipped outfielder Billy Southworth to them on June 14 for fading Heinie Mueller. All Southworth would do was hit .317 in St. Louis.

Bolstered by the Alexander and Southworth deals, the Cardinals began to make their move. The Giants, plagued by dissension, began to lose their lead. The Pirates and Reds began to struggle as well, as the Cardinals moved into the first division. The Cubs, probably wishing they had held onto the "washed-up" Alexander, dropped out of the race altogether. As August came around, the Pirates were in first place, with the Cardinals, Reds, and Giants right behind them.

In late August the Giants arrived in St. Louis for a key three-game series. The Cardinals won the first two games rather easily, which made Giant manager John McGraw less than thrilled. The third game, played on August 20, turned out to be pivotal for both clubs and their second basemen. In the seventh inning that day, the Giants were already en route to another loss when second baseman Frankie Frisch missed a pickoff sign with Cardinal runners on first and third. Tommy Thevenow then singled home a run as a result, aiding the Cardinal sweep and adding to the dissension on the Giants. After this game, and being berated by McGraw for the missed pickoff sign, Frisch demanded to be traded. After the season, Frisch would get his wish.

The three-game sweep of the Giants boosted Cardinal spirits and sent the Giants reeling out of the race. The Pirates were having their own internal troubles, involving a player revolt against manager Bill McKechnie, and they also began to fade. The Reds were the only team able to stay with the Cardinals in the race, but Alexander was now hitting his stride as Hornsby tried to dry him out, and the Cardinals could not be denied. The hitting was good as Hornsby hit .317 with 93 RBIs, Bottomley drove in a league-leading 120 runs, Les Bell came up with 100 RBIs on a .325 average, Southworth hit .317, and Taylor Douthit hit .308. Defensively, Douthit was turning into a brilliant center fielder, Thevenow showed a strong arm and range at short, and Bob O'Farrell did a great job behind the plate while also hitting .293. On the hill, Flint Rhem posted a 20–7, 3.21 season while Sherdel went 16–12 and Haines went 13–4 despite injuries. Alexander went 9–7 with a 2.91 ERA as the number-four starter.

The pennant was clearly in sight in September as the Reds began struggling. Still, despite the Reds' struggle, they kept on winning enough games to stay close to the Cardinals. People in St. Louis began to worry about the Cardinals possibly blowing the pennant, but Hornsby made sure that wouldn't happen by getting on his team whenever needed. The journey through the desert that the St. Louis Cardinals had embarked upon thirty-four years earlier finally came to an end when ex-Giant Billy Southworth slammed a homer against his former teammates in New York on September 24, 1926. The Cardinals had finally claimed their first pennant of any kind, which St. Louis had lacked since the American Association's Browns won their fourth in a row in 1888. Needless to say, wild celebrating of a type never before seen in St. Louis had engulfed the town. The long wait for glory was finally over.

The next order of business on the Cardinals' agenda was the World Series. The New York Yankees were already in their dynasty mode by this time and were managed by former Cardinal skipper

Miller Huggins. The Yankees were similar to the Cardinals in that the Yankees had been at the bottom of the heap the previous year and had survived a tough pennant race themselves. The Yankees of Ruth, Gehrig, Meusel, Combs, and the rest were heavily favored to take the series, since most of these stars had already been to postseason play. The series was slated to open in New York on October 2.

Game 1 was a pitching duel, pitting Sherdel against 23-game winner Herb Pennock, one of the players acquired from the Boston "farm" club. In the first inning Jim Bottomley singled home Taylor Douthit, giving the Cardinals a quick lead. The Yankees then tied the score when Lou Gehrig drove in Earle Combs with an RBI single to score Babe Ruth in the sixth, and that was all of the scoring in the game, as the Yankees won 2–1.

The second game featured a 12-hit Cardinal attack that knocked Urban Shocker out of the box. Thevenow and Southworth both homered as the Cardinals overcame a 2–0 deficit to win the game 6–2. Grover Alexander fanned ten en route to the victory. Game 3 was played in St. Louis on October 5, and it saw Pop Haines scatter 5 hits in shutting out the hard-hitting New Yorkers 4–0. The fans could hardly believe that the locals had a 2–1 lead in the series.

Game 4 saw plenty of scoring, as each team collected fourteen hits. The Cardinals overcame a 3–1 deficit in the fourth by scoring 3 runs, but the game was all Babe Ruth, as he slammed 3 homers, the first time in series history that the feat was accomplished. The Yanks went on to tie the series by winning 10–5. Sherdel and Pennock then hooked up in another pitching duel in the fifth game that went 10 innings before the Cardinals eked out a 3–2 loss.

The series shifted back to New York on October 9, and after the tough loss in the fifth game many expected the Cardinals to fold. Instead, they bombed 3 pitchers for 13 hits and 10 runs as the Cardinals tied the series in game 6 by a 10–2 score. That set the stage for the climactic seventh game.

After the Yankees scored once in the third, the Cardinals scored thrice in the top of the fourth on a 2-run single by Thevenow and an RBI single by O'Farrell. After allowing a run in the sixth, starter Pop Haines got into a bases-loaded jam with two out in the seventh. Hornsby summoned Alexander to the mound, even though Alex had pitched a complete game the day before. After he got Lazzeri to hit a foul that almost was an extra-base hit, Alex proceeded to fan the rookie slugger and get the Cardinals out of the mess. In the ninth, Alexander walked Babe Ruth, but then the series ended quickly as O'Farrell (who was named the N.L.'s most valuable player for that year) threw out Ruth when he tried to steal second. The Cardinals had completed the remarkable season on October 10, shocking almost everyone by winning the World Series.

After the World Series, the Cardinals were feted with a parade through town. The Cardinals had drawn over 668,000 fans during the season, while the seventh-place Browns had drawn just 284,000. The Cardinals were still tenants of the Browns, but they were now the richer team and from this point on the Cardinals would be the dominant team in town. Branch Rickey was proven right when he said he had a cheap way to build up a big league ball club. Soon other teams would set up their own farm systems and would turn the minor leagues into a virtual ocean of players from where all teams would get their players. The day of the independent minor league operator and the independent minor leagues was coming to an end.

While everything on the surface looked rosy in St. Louis, Sam Breadon and Branch Rickey were ready to deliver another surprise to the fans before the year was over. Rogers Hornsby the player-manager was well liked by the Cardinal bosses, but Rogers Hornsby the person out of uniform was another story. Hornsby liked placing bets on the horses, and he had lost plenty of money. Now Hornsby wanted a nice multiyear contract, something few owners would even consider in those days. Rajah figured a three-year deal would be just about right, especially at around $50,000 per year. Breadon and Rickey thought otherwise. Rickey, probably the most religious man ever to work in baseball, simply could not understand gambling and why his star-manager would indulge in it. Rickey hated to see money go to waste, and Hornsby had done plenty of "wasting" in the last few years. The hardheaded Hornsby was insistent on getting a three-year deal. The Cardinal bosses pointed out that there had been some player grumbling going on in the clubhouse during the just-concluded season and that indicated that maybe the manager was losing control. That claim doesn't seem to be true, at least as far as 1926 went. Years later Bob O'Farrell claimed that "he never bothered any of us," the "he" being Hornsby. Still, Breadon was anxious about having Rajah around and in a position of possible decline while under a three-year contract, so he decided to trade him. Rickey agreed.

At the same time that the Cardinal bosses were wondering what to do with Hornsby, the New York Giants had their own headaches. Frankie Frisch was once the darling of pilot John McGraw and was named captain of the team, quite an honor in those days and one that had a few more bucks attached to it. After his blowup with McGraw on August 20 on the blown pickoff play in St. Louis, Frisch wanted out of New York. Now, four months later, Frisch was still intent on being traded. John McGraw was in a bind, since Frisch was highly popular in New York and still had some good years left. If he traded Frisch, who would fill his shoes?

On December 20, 1926, the Giants sent Frankie Frisch and pitcher Jimmy Ring to the Cardinals in exchange for Rogers Hornsby. The trade made huge headlines in both cities and is quite possibly the biggest trade in the history of baseball. Both players had already had several fine years, both were the best at their position, both were highly popular in their home cities, and both had good years left. Usually, when two players with big names are swapped at least one of them is fading, but this wasn't the case in the Frisch-Hornsby swap. Besides, who would swap a manager who had just taken his team to its first ever pennant? Fans in New York and St. Louis were outraged.

As soon as the shocking trade was announced, commissioner Kenesaw Landis got involved. Landis did not like the fact that Hornsby, now a Giant, held over 1,000 shares of stock in the Cardinals. Landis ordered Hornsby to sell the stock at once, or else Hornsby could not play for the Giants. Hornsby was intrigued at the possibility of playing in New York, where the team also had plenty of money that it would be willing to pay him. Rajah said the stock was for sale, the same stock that Rickey had sold him less than two years earlier. Breadon was willing to buy the stock, but when Hornsby got an appraisal on it, Breadon balked at paying

Hornsby's price. John McGraw was, meanwhile, fuming that he had gotten a player who would not be allowed to play for him. McGraw threatened to sue the National League if Hornsby was not available for Opening Day. Finally, the whole mess was resolved when Hornsby lowered his price and all of the National League owners bought shares in the Cardinals. Although other owners had some shares in the Cardinals, the specter of syndication did not appear. After the stock was sold, the big leagues passed a rule barring the sale of team stock to players.

III

Now that the Cardinals were at the top of the baseball world there was nowhere to go but down. The Cardinals were determined to keep the championship in St. Louis, and the man selected to lead in the defense of the flag was the league's MVP, catcher Bob O'Farrell. Except for the trade for Frisch and the signing of catcher Frank Snyder, the Cardinals of 1927 were almost identical to the 1926 squad. After the festivities of Opening Day were dispensed with (complete with boos for Frankie Frisch), the Cardinals went off to a great start, staying in a four-team race with the Pirates, Giants, and Cubs. The Cardinals got a .337 average out of Frisch that season and Bottomley was now the big RBI man (he had 124), but the hitting was spotty and some good pitching by the "washed-up" 40-year-old Grover Alexander (24–10, 2.72) was wasted as a result. Still, O'Farrell did a great job in his year as a major league manager, going 92–61 in his rookie year. Unfortunately, although the record was a club record, it was only good enough for a second-place finish behind Pittsburgh, 1½ games out. For his efforts, Bob O'Farrell was fired after the season. Second place was no longer good enough for Breadon and Rickey.

Despite record-setting attendance (over 749,000), the bosses decided to replace O'Farrell with Bill McKechnie. McKechnie was no novice to the managing game. In 1915 he had piloted the Newark team of the Federal League, and he had led the Pirates from 1922 to 1926, when a group of players tried hard to get him fired. The Pirates did fire McKechnie after the season, and the Cardinals picked him as a coach. McKechnie had managed the Pirates from mediocrity to a World Series win in 1925 and was a likable man. To aid McKechnie in his quest for a pennant, Rickey picked up Andy High from the Braves in one of the few deals Rickey tended to make at this time. High was a good-hitting third baseman and cost only the fading Les Bell. In a weird note to the trade, the always cash-poor Braves threw in $25,000 to the rich Cardinals. Perhaps the Braves were desperate to get rid of the .300 hitter.

Nineteen-twenty-eight proved to be a year for hot pennant races. The American League saw the Yankees fighting off the now resurgent Philadelphia Athletics and just nipping them late in the season. That was nothing compared to the race in the National League, where the Cardinals, Giants, and Cubs were in a life-and-death struggle all year long. First off, the Giants got off to a sluggish start, leaving the race to the Cardinals and Cubs and, for a time, the Pirates. At this time, fans of the Cardinals would journey to Chicago to see their favorite team play and risked life and limb by doing so (the same could be said for Cubs fans who went to St. Louis), but it was all in the fun of a pennant race. Both teams traded first place, with the Pirates lurking nearby. In May, the Giants came to town and were handled easily, since they were still undergoing a slow start. Even in July, when the Giants were finally really getting started, the Cardinals were able to handle them.

The Cardinals were clicking well. Bottomley led the league in homers and RBIs with 31 and 136 respectively, while Chick Hafey became a regular and batted .337 with 27 homers and 111 RBIs. Frisch, Douthit, Bottomley, and part-timer George Harper all topped the .300 mark. Rabbit Maranville, who had missed all of the previous season due to illness, gave the team solid defense at short. On the hill, Sherdel went 21–10, Haines went 20–8, and Alexander went 16–9. Rhem, bothered by a "slight" drinking problem, went only 11–8, with a 4.14 ERA. As a group, the Cardinals yielded the fewest walks, hit the most doubles, stole the most bases, and logged the most complete games. Only the Cubs made fewer errors, and only the Giants hit more homers. Rickey's farm was producing quality goods.

In late September, the Cardinals went to New York for a doubleheader. George Harper popped three homers in the opener, the first time a Cardinals player had done that since Frank Shugart did it on May 10, 1894, and that game gave the Cardinals a 3-game lead on the Giants. The Giants then won the second game, to cut the lead to 2. A few days later the Cardinal lead shrank to half a game as the Giants kept winning. Still there was hope, as the Giants were slated to face the Cubs, who were still in the hunt themselves, while the Cardinals faced the dismal Braves. The Cardinals won at Boston while the Giants and Cubs split a doubleheader in New York, the first game of which angered McGraw so much that he kept a picture of the game's most controversial play in his office (the Cub catcher held onto a Giant trying to score, and the runner was then tagged out) as a monument to injustice. The next day the Cubs beat the Giants while the Cardinals won as well. On September 29, the Cubs defeated the Giants again while the Cardinals again downed Boston, giving St. Louis its second pennant in three years.

The Cardinals' opponent in the 1928 World Series was New York, winner of its third straight pennant. The Yankees had most of the 1926 squad around for the rematch of the '26 Series, while St. Louis had made some changes. The Yanks had swept Pittsburgh in 4 straight in the 1927 series and were again favored to win.

Game 1 took place in New York on October 4. Bill Sherdel faced Waite Hoyt, and Sherdel allowed 1 run in the first and 2 in the fourth as the Cardinals went down to a 4–1 defeat. The next day Alexander went out and he probably wished he was loaded, as the Yankees scored nine runs in the game, eight in the first three frames, en route to a 9–3 win. On October 7 the Series moved to St. Louis and saw the Yankees turn a 2–0 deficit into a 7–3 win. Two days later the series came to a crashing end when Babe Ruth slammed 3 homers, leading the Yankees to a 7–3 win and a 4-game sweep of the postseason. The Cardinals batted just .206 in the series and posted a 6.09 ERA in being totally destroyed.

Cardinal fans were shocked, not so much that their team lost, but by the way it lost. Sam Breadon was irate and decided to banish manager Bill McKechnie to the minors and elevate Billy South-worth to club manager. As usual, the Cardinals did little trading to upgrade the club, the major move being the sale of Maranville to the Braves. Breadon was criticized for not making any trades year after year, but he stuck by his guns and continued to place his faith in the farm system.

By 1929 the Cardinals were considered one of the top teams in baseball. Two pennants in three seasons and a close second-place finish in-between had certainly proved that. The Cardinals were also being imitated by other teams that were poor, and even the rich teams had been shown the way. The Cardinals also now had the attitude of a winner. In previous years the Cardinals would always enter a game and expect to get their brains beat out, and they usually did. The fans were now expecting at least a contender, and the attitude in the front office mirrored those expectations. The firing of O'Farrell after a fine rookie season and the removal of McKechnie showed just how high the expectations were in the front office. The success that both managers had would have brought delirium in town ten years earlier, but now those successes were looked at as failures. The Cardinals were now resembling the Yankees and Giants in attitude and expectations.

The expectations in 1929 were for another pennant. Unfortunately for the Cardinals, the Cubs got off to a blazing start and nobody was able to catch them. The Cardinals started sluggishly under new manager Billy Southworth as the pitching staff crumbled under injury, age, and other afflictions. Grover Alexander was now really at the end of the line at age 42, and his drinking was not helping him any either. Flint Rhem missed the whole year due to booze-related problems himself. Bill Sherdel was suddenly very hittable, as his 10–15, 5.93 numbers show. Pop Haines was nagged by injury and posted a dismal 5.71 ERA. The offense kept up with the rest of the league as Bottomley, Frisch, Douthit, and Hafey all hit over .300. Earl Smith and Jimmie Wilson both hit over .300 as the platoon catchers. Andy High hit .295. Bottomley and Hafey both crossed the 100-RBIs barrier again. Still, the hitting was not enough to offset the pitching, and as a result Southworth was fired with the team at 43–45. The new manager turned out to be the old one, as Bill McKechnie was recalled from the minors to take over the team. Under McKechnie, the Cardinals went 33–29, and overall they ended in fourth place with a 78–74 record (2 wins coming under interim pilot Gabby Street).

The season was a financial disaster. Attendance went from a

74

club high of over 761,000 to under 400,000. It didn't help that the Browns had a good year at 79–73 as that team continued to be a source of financial trouble. Even though the Browns were now basically playing second fiddle to their tenants, they still represented a threat to the Cardinals. Phil Ball was trying hard throughout the 1920s to turn his dismal team around, and in 1922 he came close to grabbing the first pennant for St. Louis before the Cardinals did. After the heartbreaking '22 season, though, the Browns reverted back to second-division status. In 1924, in an attempt to stimulate interest in the team, Ball hired his superstar hitter as manager. George Sisler proved to be a far better hitter than manager, as the team languished around the .500 mark under him. Whatever Ball tried, it failed. Most trades were flops and Ball was starting to feel the pinch in his wallet. The Cardinals were contenders and the Browns were not, and the fans, knowing that the bottom line is winning a pennant, were bound to favor the Cardinals.

Despite the small size of the market, St. Louis was definitely a good baseball town. In 1928 the two teams combined to draw over a million people. The problem was that only one team would be able to survive economically while the other would suffer. The Cardinals were better at marketing themselves, with things like the Knothole Gang, than were the Browns, who could offer only the hitting of George Sisler as an inducement to lure fans. Once Sisler began to fade, attendance followed. The Browns had nobody to replace him, and they still got players the old way, a way that was costly to Ball. With all the money Ball poured into his team, he had little to show for it. As a result, the Browns were doomed to enduring failure.

The Cardinals made sure their days of failure would not return anytime soon. Branch Rickey continued to scout around for new talent and new teams to add to his farm system. Although some teams had plans to develop their own farm system, other teams persisted in attacking the Cardinals and their way of procuring players. As is always the case concerning successful teams, there was jealousy of the Cardinals' success. The complaining continued unabated, and it was so loud and persistent that Commissioner Landis began looking into the matter.

The commissioner was not just the boss of the big leagues, but of all of organized baseball, which included the minor leagues. Landis kept an eye out for any instances where a minor league player or owner was being unfairly taken advantage of. Landis feared that the Cardinal way of creating farms would destroy the whole minor league system, even though the minors had made a strong comeback in the 1920s after the lean times of the 1910s. With all the commotion over the Cardinals and their success at exploiting young talent in their rise from worst to first, Landis kept a very close watch on them. In most instances, though, Landis found no wrongdoing at this time. As a matter of fact, he probably was pleased when he saw that Cardinal farm teams were making money themselves.

One case that Landis did beef about was the case of Gus Mancuso. Mancuso played in 11 games for the Cardinals in 1928 after starting the season in the minors. After the season, the Cardinals decided to send him back down for more seasoning. In those days, a player could be sent up and down almost indefinitely, a situation that certainly did little for the player's confidence. Mancuso was slated to be shipped back to the minors for yet another season after the spring of 1929 when the eagle-eyed commissioner spotted a problem.

Mancuso did well in 1929 and would get another look in spring training of 1930. When the Cardinals decided to send poor Gus down one more time, the commissioner intervened. Landis stated that the Cardinals had kept Mancuso in the minors too long and gave them the choice of either trading him to another team or keeping him up with St. Louis. If the Cardinals couldn't do one or the other, Landis was prepared to set the catcher free. The Cardinals decided to hang onto Mancuso, and as 1930 began they would be happy that they did keep him.

Besides the Mancuso affair, the Cardinals also had to name a new pilot. Bill McKechnie was less than pleased at the shoddy way he had been treated by Breadon. First he won a pennant in his first year as manager, then gets demoted to the minors. After that, McKechnie was returned from exile when his replacement failed. McKechnie decided to leave, and Breadon let him go. With McKechnie gone the Cardinals then turned to Gabby Street, who had gone 2–0 as interim manager in 1929, to be the skipper for 1930.

To aid Street in his quest to get the Cardinals back to the top, Rickey bought third baseman Sparky Adams from the Pirates and picked up outfielder George Fischer for practically nothing. George Watkins, another farm product, was also brought up to bolster the outfield. Other than these players, Rickey stuck by his usual plan to keep the nucleus of the previous season's roster intact. When a nucleus contains Jim Bottomley, Chick Hafey, Frankie Frisch, and Taylor Douthit, it's wise to be complacent. On the hill, Grover Alexander was sent to his original team for two players of little note. The Phillies would now have to deal with Alex's bouts with the bottle. Also added from the minors were Bill Hallahan, who would join Haines, Syl Johnson, and Rhem as a key pitcher on the staff.

As 1930 dawned, the Depression was worsening around the country. In St. Louis, the two ball clubs that always had to keep a close watch on all money-related matters were bracing for expected declines in attendance. Both clubs saw shrinking gate receipts in 1929, and with the uncertainty of the Depression looming, another big drop would put both teams in the same bind that they were in during the Federal League war of 1914–15.

Both leagues also worried about the effects of the Depression and decided that a juiced-up ball might bring people to the ballpark to watch an increase in high-scoring games. What baseball did *not* need by 1930 was more hitting. In 1929 the American League had posted a .284 average, led by the Detroit Tigers' .299 mark. Three A.L. clubs had scored 900 runs, and the league ERA was 4.24. Detroit could hit but not pitch, as evidenced by its 4.96 ERA. In the National League, offense had been even more plentiful. Three teams had hit over .300, two had scored 900 runs (one just missed doing that by 3 runs and another by 2), and three had collected 300 doubles. At 4.71, the league had an ERA worse than the American's by nearly half a run. Brooklyn had posted a 4.92 ERA, and that wasn't even the worst. Boston had a 5.12 mark, and the Phillies came through with a disgusting 6.13 ERA! Needless to say, the Phillies led the majors in runs allowed with 1,032, even

77

though that was balanced by league-leading totals in homers (153), average (.309), and slugging percentage (.467).

Despite all of the offense 1929 featured, many teams saw their attendance drop, the Cardinals and Browns being two examples. Still, bosses in both leagues figured that even more hitting would bring in more people. As things would turnout, 1930 would be a zany season for the majors and the St. Louis Cardinals as well.

IV

As pennant races go, the 1930 National League battle was one of the tightest. Just before Opening Day, new St. Louis skipper Gabby Street stated, "I am anxious to make good in my first year as a major league manager, and that is also why I consider myself fortunate. Given an initial assignment and handed a group of players like those on the Cardinals is enough to make anyone feel well fixed." Some people picked the Cardinals to win, but most experts had the Cubs winning their second straight flag. After all, the Chicago club had won the 1929 flag by ten and a half lengths over the Pirates. The Cardinals had few worries about hitting, with their future Hall of Famers still looking good. The pitching was another story, though. "Our pitching seems to be our only big problem," said Street. As things turned out, pitching would be a problem of almost every team in 1930.

The Cardinals got off to a flying flop, dropping into the cellar after the Brooklyn Robins of Wilbert Robinson came to town and swept a 4-game set in early May. As expected, the Cardinal pitching staff was struggling, and all the hitting in the world wasn't making much difference. Batting averages in both leagues were skyrocketing at this early juncture, and both leagues had batters over the *.400* mark in droves. ERAs in the 5.00s were commonplace, as double-digit scoring became the norm. The Cardinals had scored 20 runs in the last 3 games of their series with the Robins, and all they could show for that was 3 losses. It looked like a long summer in St. Louis.

Attendance figures showed that the increase in scoring was having dubious effects. Three National League teams were running ahead of 1929's gate pace, but much of that had to do with the pennant race. Five American League teams were running behind their 1929 paces, including the Philadelphia Athletics, who were running away with their second straight flag, and the St. Louis Browns, who most certainly could not afford a drop at the gate. The poor Browns were en route to disaster, one of epic proportions. The Browns would open the new decade in sixth place and would end it on the verge of extinction.

As for the Cardinals, after the 4-game fiasco against the Robins, the pitching staff began straightening out. St. Louis spent the next three weeks going 15–1 and moving into first place ahead of Brooklyn. The Cubs and Giants were also clawing their ways to the top, making the race a four-team affair. After they downed the hot Cubs and a decent Pirate team a few times, the Cardinals had a streak of 17–1 over the last three and a half weeks. It looked like the Cardinals were going to win a flag for 1930.

Wrong. An injury wave saw second baseman Frankie Frisch (now a fan favorite after a first year of vilification due to the Hornsby trade), shortstop Charlie Gelbert, outfielder Chick Hafey, and first baseman Jim Bottomley come down with various ailments. As a result, the Cardinals plunged to below the .500 mark again and they found themselves in fourth place, with the Robins occupying the top spot.

June saw the Cardinals struggling in virtually every facet of the game. Catcher Jimmie Wilson went down with an injury, but luckily the commissioner forced the Cardinals to keep rookie Gus Mancuso. Mancuso ended up hitting .366 and doing well in handling a shaky pitching staff. In games on the field, the Cardinals had as much trouble catching the ball as they did throwing it. On June 15 the Cardinals allowed 3 quick Brooklyn runs on an outfield error and it looked like another Cardinal loss was coming. Luckily, the Robins were really generous and made 5 miscues themselves as the Cardinals rallied against Brooklyn ace Dazzy Vance to win 9–4. The Cardinals went on to make 183 errors in 1930, a total surpassed by only the Pirates and last-place Phillies.

On June 16 the Cardinals made a key trade with the Boston Braves, shipping young pitcher Fred Frankhouse and fading pitcher Bill Sherdel for veteran Burleigh Grimes, one of the last of the legal spitballers. Grimes was struggling at 3–5 with the dismal Braves, but he turned out to be a godsend for St. Louis. Still, in June the Cardinals were putting together a 10–15 record for the month as they slowly began to fade behind front-running Brooklyn. It looked like only the Cubs and Giants would have a shot at the Robins.

In early July the Cubs moved into the lead as their outfield featured three .300 hitters, one of whom was Hack Wilson, who was busy hacking a league-record 56 homers and a major-league-record 190 RBIs. The Robins weren't cream puffs either, as Babe Herman was hitting well over .400 at this point in the season en route to a 100-RBI season himself. Herman was joined by shortstop Glenn Wright and first baseman Del Bissonette in topping 100 RBIs. The Giants had their own trio of 100-RBI men in Bill Terry, Mel Ott, and Fred Lindstrom, all future Hall of Famers. Terry was to become the league's last .400 hitter that year, ending up at .401.

It seemed that every team had a lineup filled out top to bottom with .300 hitters and in the National League every team had at least one man en route to 100 RBIs except the Reds. The Phillies pounded out a .315 team average, but it didn't help them escape the basement. A 6.71 ERA might have something to do with that. Overall, the league hit .303 and had a 4.97 ERA. It was truly a pitcher's nightmare in 1930.

Despite his team's bumbling, Gabby Street still was confident that the Cardinals would right themselves and get back into the race. "We are keeping our noses to the wheel," said the skipper. These nice words did little for the team as it went 8–13 on a long road trip in July. The Cardinals then concluded the month with a weak 15–17 mark. As August dawned, the Cardinals seemed dead for the 1930 season.

Gabby Street was still determined to stay in the race and decided to go from an easygoing guy to one who would impose a curfew and a ban on card playing. The increase in discipline seemed to do wonders for the team. Despite an amazing 53 RBIs in the month by Hack Wilson for the Cubs, they could not shake off the Cardinals, even though they had dislodged the Robins from first place. Not even a 16–4 drubbing of the Cardinals could spark the Cubs into a runaway or kill the Cardinals' chances for the flag.

As August closed, St. Louis posted a 17–6 record and stood just 4½ games out of first as Hack Wilson carried the Cubs to the lead.

On September 4 the Cardinals moved past the hard-hitting Giants into second place with a 13–2 beating of the Reds. The Giants were suddenly struggling against the lousy Braves, as they lost 3 in a row in Boston. Three days later the Cardinals swept the Reds in a twin bill and were now 2½ games behind the Cubs as the Cardinals were moving on to New York. The first-place Cubs also had a series against a tough team, the team from Brooklyn. All four contenders were playing in the Big Apple at the same time, a baseball fan's wildest dream come true.

New York writers had ridiculed the Cardinals just a few months earlier over their efforts to attract fans to the park as the team struggled. Indeed, Sam Breadon's club at the time was having trouble drawing as many as 4,000 people at some games, leading him to try the then unconventional idea of Sunday doubleheaders, and there were rumors that he would also try playing night baseball (five years before it was tried by the Reds). "Baseball virtually is dead in St. Louis," wrote New York scribe Joe Vila in July. At that point, Vila was basically right.

Now, though, things had changed. The Cardinals were certainly not dead coming into New York. St. Louis was second to Chicago, and the Cardinals were rolling. On September 8, the Giants sent former Cardinal Clarence Mitchell to the mound and in a rare (by 1930 standards) well-played game he shaded St. Louis 2–1. The Robins helped the Cardinals (and themselves) by downing the Cubs 3–0. The race tightened. The next day the Cardinals put up 4 runs in the eighth to beat the Giants while the Cubs lost again in Brooklyn. On the tenth, the Cardinals rallied late again as they downed the Giants 5–4 while the Cubs spent the afternoon getting shaded 2–1 by the Robins. The Cardinals then wound up the season series in New York by winning 5–2 with another late rally. The Big Apple was half-happy as the Robins returned to the thick of things and half-sad as the Giants seemingly fell out of the race. The Cardinals then moved on to Boston, where they won 2 of 3, while the Robins extended their winning streak to eleven. The *big* series of the Big Apple was now ready to take place.

On August 10, the Cardinals were fourth, 11 games behind the

Robins. Brooklyn led second-place Chicago by 3 and New York by 4½ on that day, as Robin fans had thought of their first pennant in ten years. A month later, the Robins led the Cardinals by half a game and the Cubs by 1. The fading Giants still had a shot, at 5 games out. On September 16, the Cardinals arrived in Brooklyn for a 3-game set. The Robins were already printing tickets for the World Series, as everyone expected the hot locals to beat back the St. Louis club. Unfortunately for the locals, Rube Bressler and Johnny Frederick, two hard-hitting outfielders, were out of action for the series. On the Cardinals, pitcher Flint Rhem was missing as the series was set to begin.

Rhem was slated to start the second game, but he was not seen for some time. Finally, Rhem showed up at the Cardinal hotel on the seventeenth, looking sick as a dog. Rhem explained to Branch Rickey (so the press reported) that he was out walking around town when some thugs pushed him into a car and brought him to New Jersey, where he was forced to consume enough booze to render him useless for the Brooklyn series. After getting him smashed, the thugs had brought him back to his hotel and warned him that he would be a dead man if he pitched against the Robins. Years later Rhem denied this bizarre story (bizarre because Rhem was a noted boozer and it wouldn't take much to force him to imbibe), saying that he was indeed sick, but he was in his hotel room during his disappearance suffering from what he figured was food poisoning. Gabby Street didn't know what to make of this story, but he did not fine Rhem.

Meanwhile, there was some baseball played in Brooklyn. The first game saw Bill Hallahan retire the first twenty Robins until he fumbled a ball by Babe Herman's batting prowess. Hallahan lost his no-hit bid when Harvey Hendrick singled to left with one out in the eighth. Neither team could score when the Robins blew a chance to win it in the ninth with some patented bumbling Brooklyn baserunning on the part of the Daffiness Boys. With two men on, Eddie Moore tried to bunt but popped it up instead, and Gus Mancuso grabbed it on the fly and fired to second, getting a rally-killing double play. In the tenth Andy High, an ex-Robin, doubled, then scored on a single by Taylor Douthit. Brooklyn loaded the bases in the bottom of the frame, and it looked like a

Robin victory was coming when Al Lopez hit a sizzling grounder to Sparky Adams, who converted it into a game-ending double play. The Robins' winning streak was dead.

The second game was just as good. Syl Johnson faced Dolf Luque, and a 2-run Robin lead was overcome by a 2-run homer by Chick Hafey. Going into the eighth, Luque had the lead after Ike Boone homered, but the Cardinals tied it again on a walk, a double, and a sacrifice fly that scored Adams. In the ninth, St. Louis got an infield hit from Charley Gelbert and then a pinch double from Robin reject Andy High that scored Gelbert and Gus Mancuso (who had walked ahead of Gelbert). High noted after the game that "Robinson never thought it necessary to change the signs" when asked how he managed to hit his game-winning double. By this point, the Robins fans were demoralized, as the pennant was slipping away. The next day another former Robin, Burleigh Grimes, went out and downed his old team 4–3. While the Cardinals were disposing of the Robins, the Giants took 2 of 3 from the Cubs, so the Cardinals were now on top by 2 games.

Next the Cardinals visited the dismal Phillies and a run-scoring feast ensued as St. Louis took 3 of 4 by 7–3, 15–7, and 19–16 scores. The last game was really something, as Hallahan was given an 11–0 lead going into the fifth, when the high-octane Phillie lineup began to bang out hits all over tiny Baker Bowl (a stadium so old and decrepit that it made the Cardinals' *old* park look like a work of modern technology by comparison). Hallahan failed to pitch through the fifth but got a cheap win under the scoring rules of the time.

The Cardinals returned home to close out the 1930 season and had to face a tough Pirate team that had given the Cardinals trouble all year. Although the Robins could throw out their World Series tickets by now, the Giants and Cubs still had a shot at the flag. For a change the Cardinals were able to handle the Pirates, by beating them 9–0 on September 25. The next day, Pop Haines downed the Pirates 10–5 to clinch the Cardinals' third pennant in five years. Two days later, in a meaningless game, the Cardinals sent out a rookie by the name of Jay Hanna Dean to the mound and saw him win 3–1. More on "Dizzy" later.

At the end of the regular season the Cardinals had piled up

impressive offensive totals that have managed to still stand after six decades. The Cardinals scored 1,004 runs, a league record that still stands. The Cardinals of 1930 also set long-lasting club records for most hits (1,732), most total bases (2,595), most extra-base hits (566), most RBIs (942), highest batting average (.314), highest slugging percentage (.471), most .300 hitters (11), and these are the ones that have lasted to the present. The pitching set a few club records in the other direction, but it's best not to discuss those on a pennant-winning team. After all, it was the hitting that got the Cardinals to the 1930 flag.

Individually, the Cardinals had a lineup that stacked up favorably against any other in the majors that year. Jim Bottomley hit only .304, as he was starting to decline (not bad for a decline), but still drove in 97 runs. Frankie Frisch hit .346 and knocked in 114 runs. Charley Gelbert hit .304 in his second big league season. Sparky Adams hit .314. Taylor Douthit drove in 93 runs on his .303 average. Chick Hafey slammed 26 homers to lead the club, with 107 RBIs and a .336 average. Behind the plate Jimmie Wilson hit .318 while platooning with Gus Mancuso and his .366 mark. Right field was shared by George Watkins (.373) and George Fisher (.374). Watkins certainly did well as a rookie and hung around a few more years, but Fisher was sent back down after the season and later appeared in a few games for the Browns. His exile is still a mystery.

On the hill Bill Hallahan was the big winner at 15–9. Syl Johnson went 12–10, Pop Haines was 13–8, Flint Rhem went 12–8, and Burleigh Grimes was 13–6 with a club-low ERA, 3.01. It's highly unlikely that the Cardinals would have won the pennant without the crafty Grimes. Overall, the pitching staff was good for 1930 standards, as it posted a 4.40 ERA, second only to the Robins' 4.03.

The Cardinals would have their work cut out for them going into the 1930 World Series. The Philadelphia Athletics won their second straight flag by 8 games and had such an easy time of it that they scouted the Cardinals (and the other three contenders) for all of September. The Athletics had a lineup packed with .300 hitters and had two home run threats in Jimmy Foxx and Al Simmons. Pitchingwise, Connie Mack could brag that he had two 20-game winners in Lefty Grove and George Earnshaw. Grove was baseball's top hurler in 1930, as he posted a measly 2.54 ERA and won 28 while losing just 5 games. He also saved 9 other games. Few people liked the Cardinals' chances.

Game 1 opened in Philadelphia on October 1 and pitted Grove against Grimes. Despite falling behind 1–0 in the second, the Cardinals rallied for 2 in the third as they went on to pile up 9 hits in the game. Grimes was masterful in allowing just 5 hits. Unfortunately, the 5 hits were all extra-base hits, including 2 homers, as the Athletics went on to win 5–2. Game 2 saw another game with few hits and another Philadelphia win. Rhem, Johnson, and Jim Lindsey allowed only 7 hits, but the Athletics put them to good use, as 5 were for extra bases. Earnshaw scattered 6 hits in a complete game 6–1 win over the Cardinals.

After a day off for travel, the series shifted to St. Louis on October 4. Hallahan allowed just seven hits to the Athletics while his teammates supported him with 5 runs, handing Rube Walberg a 5–0 defeat. The next day the Cardinals tied the game at 1–1 with a run in the third, then scored twice in the fourth against Grove as Haines outlasted the Philly ace 3–1. The series was now even, and there was talk that the Cardinals were going to pull off a surprise on the Athletics like they did against the Robins a month earlier.

Such a surprise would have to take place under very difficult conditions after Jimmy Foxx socked a 2-run homer off of Grimes, giving Grove a 2–0 win in relief of Earnshaw. With just one day of rest, Earnshaw went out and started the sixth game, in Philadelphia. Earnshaw went the distance this time while scattering five hits en route to a 7–1 win and a 4-games-to-2 series win for the Athletics over the Cardinals. Both clubs ended the hard-hitting 1930 season by posting sickly averages in the Series. Philadelphia hit just .197 while St. Louis was better by just three points. It was one of the strangest series ever when one compares it to what went on in the regular season. The 1930 series was also one of the lightest-hitting in terms of team average in the entire history of the fall classic.

Despite playing Sunday doubleheaders and talk of night games to improve attendance, the Cardinals still managed to turn a profit. Over 508,000 people went to see the Cardinals battle for the flag, and most of those people came not to see ridiculous high-scoring games but to see a great pennant fight. Big league bosses must have figured as much, and they decided to bring back a ball with less rabbit for the 1931 season. Pitchers were mighty pleased about that kind of news.

The Depression was getting worse and many teams were feeling the pinch, but the Cardinals were in better shape than most. The farm system was still producing high-quality prospects, so any cash the Cardinals made went right back into their organization. Some teams, like the Cubs, were experimenting with allowing radio broadcasts of their games, but Branch Rickey was initially opposed to this idea, fearing people would stay home and listen to the game instead of coming out to the ballpark, especially when the weather seemed bad. The radio decision was one of the few mistakes Rickey would make in baseball, but when he later allowed Cardinal games to be broadcast it turned many people out of St. Louis into Cardinal fans. The Cardinals were certainly far better off than their landlords, the dismal Browns, who by 1930's end were making money more by collecting rent than by putting bodies in the seats. While over half a million people went to see the Cardinals in 1930, a paltry 152,000 went to see the Browns. It was the third worst gate the Browns had ever drawn to that point, and the two worst draws had come during World War I and the Federal League war. Prospects for the Browns were to become even worse, however, much to the benefit of the Cardinals.

For 1931 the Cardinals made the usual few moves. One involved the recall of pitcher Paul Derringer, who would improve a staff that many people thought would be one of the best now that the rabbit ball was shelved. Another was the decision to let that kid named Jay Hanna Dean spend another year in the minors to get a little more seasoning. As things turned out in 1931, the future Hall of Fame pitcher would not be needed.

The Cardinals were picked by many to win, and they did not disappoint. The Cardinals got off to a fast start, leaving expected challengers New York, Chicago, Pittsburgh, and Brooklyn in the dust. At various times the Cardinals had leads of between 10 and 20 games, as the pitching did come through brilliantly. Hallahan led the league with 19 wins, Grimes won 17, and rookie Paul Derringer posted an 18–8, 3.36 record as the aces of the staff. Pop

Haines had a nifty 12–3 season, and Flint Rhem went 11–10. Offensively, Chick Hafey won the league batting title at .349, Frankie Frisch hit .311, and Jim Bottomley hit .348 despite injury, as they were the big guns. The Cardinals were doing so well that Rickey decided to call up some minor leaguers ahead of schedule to see what they could do in the big time. First baseman Ripper Collins hit .301 with 59 RBIs in under 300 at bats, which probably worried Bottomley. Pepper Martin, the "Wild Hoss of the Osage," looked so good to Rickey in spring training that he sold Taylor Douthit to the Reds to make room for him. Martin played center field brilliantly and hit .300 with 75 RBIs as a rookie. Already Rickey was living up to his saying of "better to get rid of a guy a year too early than a year too late'" in his sale of Douthit.

In the middle of September the Cardinals wrapped up the pennant, the first time they did not have to strain to grab it. The Cardinals, like every other team, saw their batting totals drop without the rabbit ball, but the pitching offset things well enough. The Cardinal staff tossed a league-tying 17 shutouts and the hitters collected a league-high 353 doubles and a league-high 114 stolen bases as the home run became less important in the St. Louis arsenal of run-scoring weapons. Despite winning the flag by 13 games, the Cardinals managed to hike their gate up by another 100,000.

The Cardinals' opponent for the 1931 World Series was Philadelphia. The Athletics won their third flag in a breeze and had a pitching staff that this time featured two 20-game winners and a 30-game winner. Rube Walberg and George Earnshaw were the two hurlers who fit in the former category, and Lefty Grove was the latter pitcher. Because of this staff and the strong lineup supporting it (Al Simmons hit .390 *without* the rabbit ball and Mickey Cochrane hit .349, among other great hitters), St. Louis again went into the series as the underdog.

The first game opened in St. Louis on October 1. Gabby Street decided to open with his fine rookie in Derringer, and the Cardinals staked him to a 2–0 lead when 4 Athletic runs came home in the third inning. Philly put 2 more runs across in the seventh, and Grove went on to get a 6–2 complete game victory despite allowing 12 hits, 3 by the rookie Pepper Martin. Game 2 saw Bill Hallahan allow just 3 hits while Martin and Charley Gelbert each drove in a run against Earnshaw in the 2–0 St. Louis victory.

Grove got the ball for the third game on October 5 in Philadelphia and opposed Burleigh Grimes. The Cardinals got 2 runs in the second and 2 more in the fourth, and that was really all that Grimes needed, as he gave up just 2 hits, one being a 2-run homer by Simmons in the ninth. By that time Grimes had a 5-run lead, and he went on to win 5–2. Game 4 saw a reversal of fortunes as George Earnshaw allowed only 2 hits (both by Martin) in blanking Derringer, Jim Lindsey, and Syl Johnson. The final score was 3–0.

The Cardinals took the lead in the series when Hallahan was backed by a 12-hit attack and the Cardinals scored 3 runs off of former Yankee star Waite Hoyt. The Cardinals went on to post an easy 5–1 victory. As the Cardinals returned home for the final 2 games, Branch Rickey must have thought he had uncovered the next great hitter of the age in Pepper Martin. Martin by this time had collected 12 hits off the American League's best pitching staff and had stolen 4 bases on catcher Mickey Cochrane, considered the top backstop in the game. Thus far, Martin figured greatly in every Cardinal rally in the series.

On October 9 Grove finally stopped Martin by making him go 0 for 3. That must have done the trick, as Grove was able to tie up the series again with an easy 8–1 win at the expense of Derringer. Martin was silenced again the next day, but the Cardinals got by anyhow despite getting just 5 hits. The Cardinals scored twice in the first against Earnshaw and then got the key blow in the third with a 2-run homer from George Watkins. The Athletics scored twice in the ninth against Grimes, but Hallahan shut the door in relief and the Cardinals hung on to win 4–2. The Cardinals had captured their second world championship.

Martin was the toast of the town. In the series he hit .500 (a record for a 7-game Series), stole 5 bases, scored 5 runs, and had 4 doubles and a homer among his 12 hits. Everyone praised Rickey for this new find of his, and Rickey must have smiled when he saw what else was growing down on the farm. With people like Martin and Ripper Collins, and Derringer coming up and making good, it looked like the Cardinals would have a dynasty that would win pennant after pennant for years to come.

The Cardinals would be an important factor in the race for some time to come, Rickey figured, but unless he started a rebuilding campaign the Cardinals would simply grow old and sputter. Rickey looked at the roster and saw that Chick Hafey's sinus trouble, which had cost him much playing time over the years, was something that was not going to go away. Jim Bottomley was hurt throughout the year, and it looked like his bat was slowing. Frankie Frisch was no spring chicken himself, as he headed for his mid-thirties, an age for death in the majors in those days. Flint Rhem was a good pitcher, but his drinking could get out of hand. Pop Haines was close to forty. Simply put, alterations had to be considered.

As 1932 began, such alterations were a dangerous idea. The Depression was still worsening, and its possible effect on the gate in the future was still unknown. Many teams had lost money over the last two seasons, and Rickey was aware that a massive rebuilding program would probably kill pennant chances. The Cardinals had to stay in a tight race, at the very least, if they were going to make any money. The pinch of the Depression would hurt the minors more than the majors, so Rickey had to keep an eye on developments there. To make matters even worse, Sportsman's Park wasn't exactly in the best of shape, nearing the age of fifty. The park had not been built to last this long, and some improvement would need to be made or it would come close to being as bad as Philadelphia's Baker Bowl (home of the Phillies). Unfortunately, the Cardinals had a team like the Browns for a landlord and that club was barely breathing at this point. Phil Ball had spent years and plenty of money to improve the Browns but had nothing to show for it except increasing debts. Out of all the teams that existed in 1932, only the Browns had failed to win at least one pennant. Making matters worse was the fact that Phil Ball was now dead and his team seemed about ready to join him. Ball's heirs had never taken much of an interest in the team while Ball lived, and now that he was dead they weren't about to put out any cash to improve the team or its park. It would fall to the Cardinals to improve the park.

The Cardinals were favored to win their third straight flag in 1932, but it was not to be. They got off to a bad start, as the veterans showed signs of age and took longer to recover from injury. Chick Hafey's big bat was gone, as he had been sent to the Reds for two marginal players. Jim Bottomley was plagued by injury, and his once big bat was slowing down. Frisch was less than stellar, as he was no longer hitting .300. Pop Haines had been hit with age and injury and was virtually useless. One of Rickey's biggest mistakes was in trading Burleigh Grimes. Grimes was as old as Haines, and Rickey figured he was through or close to it. Rickey swapped him to the Cubs for Hack Wilson. At that point, the trade looked good, since the pitcher was indeed at the end of the line. But Rickey then swapped Wilson to the Dodgers (formerly called the Robins) for $45,000 and a minor league outfielder who never made it to the majors. In essence, Grimes was traded for nobody and Rickey got rid of a slugger who still had a good year in him. Wilson drove in over 100 runs for the Dodgers in 1932, while nobody on the Cardinals did that. People came and went all year, but most of the players coming through St. Louis did little. As it turned out, Ripper Collins proved he could play at first base and drove in 91 runs and Jay Hanna Dean, now known as Dizzy, posted an 18–15 record as a rookie. The Cardinals concluded the season tied with their usual New York foes for seventh place with a poor 72–82 record.

Now the Cardinals were really in big trouble. The gate slipped alarmingly from over 608,000 to under 280,000. The team lost money. A major housecleaning was in order, and nobody knew what to expect next. The Depression hit even the long-running money-makers like the Yankees hard. The Browns, continuing to do even worse than the Cardinals, did not have any money or desire to fix up the park, which was becoming more and more run-down. The Cardinal farm system was in the red as the parent team called up top minor league players. The minor league teams, stripped of their big gate attractions, saw their gate receipts fall off. Sam Breadon was hinting about moving his team out of St. Louis, but the National League told him to forget it. After all, the Browns were in worse shape, and if any team should move it would be them, was the league's argument. Good as that argument was, it did little to soothe Breadon, who wanted more than logic to put in his coffers.

Probably because of the reconstruction plan that Rickey was trying to implement, he decided to retain Street as skipper despite the team's poor showing in 1932. Street was now going to get some more help in restoring the team to contention. Joe "Ducky" Medwick was deemed ready for full-time play after hitting nearly .350 in a late season trial the previous year. Outfielder Ethan Allen was picked up in one of Rickey's biggest trades to date. Allen came from the Giants to St. Louis along with Bill Walker, Jim Mooney, and Bob O'Farrell. This deal cost Gus Mancuso and Ray Starr. Also acquired was Pat Crawford, an infielder who last played in the big time in 1930, and one Rogers Hornsby, who was cut loose by the Cubs after the 1932 season.

For the second straight year the Cardinals stumbled out of the gate, and this time it cost Street his job. On July 24, with the club playing 46–45 ball, Rickey fired the pilot and named Frankie Frisch as the manager. The move didn't do much good, as Frisch guided the team to a 36–26 finish. Overall, the Cardinals were competitive but not a contender. Rickey's moves did not pan out all too well in 1933, except for the Giants. Mancuso did well handling a rebounding pitching staff, as the Giants won the World Series that year. Hornsby's return to the Cardinals was well received by the fans, but not by the manager or many of the players. Hornsby became a disruptive influence on the team and was cut. The publicity-starved Browns picked him up almost immediately, much to their detriment. Pat Crawford at least became a noted pinch hitter, and some of the deals made after Opening Day turned out well. On May 7 Rickey sent struggling Paul Derringer along with Sparky Adams and Allyn Stout to the Reds for Dutch Henry, Jack Ogden, and Leo Durocher. Durocher improved the infield and added some life to a team that certainly needed some. The Cardinals now had a more youthful team on the field with Durocher, Collins, Medwick, and Martin in the everyday lineup and Dizzy Dean and Tex Carleton in the rotation.

Despite all of the moves since the end of the 1932 season, the Cardinals still were not in contention and still were losing money. The 1933 squad finished at 82–71 and in fifth place, and they were never a factor in the race. Attendance again fell, this time to under 257,000. The ballpark still needed a renovation, but the Browns were still in a coma, as they drew the incredibly tiny total of 88,000 diehards in their games at home. Despite looking at this terrible attendance figure of the Browns, Sam Breadon was still making noise about leaving town. Breadon looked at Detroit as the promised land, but attendance there wasn't much better. The American League was approached by Breadon, but they told him to forget it. Besides, the National League had told him before that they would not allow the Cardinals to go anywhere, especially with the way the Browns were. At this time both leagues tried to upstage one another (especially in the five cities that held teams in each circuit) and neither league wanted to abandon a town, especially a town served by both leagues.

V

As 1934 opened it was obvious that neither league was going to let the Cardinals do anything but stay in St. Louis. Branch Rickey now had to hope that some of the five teams that were considered as good as or better than the Cardinals would be hit by a slump while his own team could avoid one and move into a good race. In his moves for 1934, Rickey took up another player who seemed to be through in Jack Rothrock. Rothrock had last played in the majors in 1932 and hit a less than sizzling .196. In 1933 Rothrock played minor league ball and caught Rickey's eye in his never-ending search for useful players.

After the 1933 season Rickey was approached by the Phillies, who asked if they could talk to catcher Jimmie Wilson about their manager job. Rickey told them they could have him if he could have Spud Davis. Davis was a catcher Rickey's farm developed in the 1920s and he was sent to the Phillies in 1928 for none other than Jimmie Wilson! Now five years later the two teams reswapped their catchers. The Phillies then named Wilson as their new pilot.

These two deals and the call-up of utilityman Burgess Whitehead from the farm (this was now an annual ritual) were the big moves made by Branch Rickey to get the team going. The experts picked the Cardinals for another middle-of-the-pack finish, while the Giants were expected to win their second straight flag.

The Cubs and Pirates were expected to provide the competition for New York.

The so-called experts, namely the sportswriters, held a little meeting with Giant manager Bill Terry in early 1934 to chat about the upcoming season. Terry fielded various questions about his chances to repeat, and then the writer covering the Brooklyn Dodgers asked about that team's chances for the pennant. "Brooklyn? Are they still in the league?" was Terry's reply. When the New York papers printed this statement new Dodger manager Casey Stengel was less than his usual clowning self. Stengel stated as he signed his contract for 1934, "The first thing I want to say is that the Dodgers are still in the National League. Tell that to Bill Terry." The famous rivalry between the New York Giants and Brooklyn Dodgers would now have another chapter added to it, and the St. Louis Cardinals would end up benefiting from it.

The Cardinals opened up the 1934 season at home against the Pirates. Dizzy Dean, by now considered to be the ace of the staff, went out and defeated Pittsburgh 7–1. That same day the Giants opened their season and beat the longtime league patsies, the Phillies, by a 6–1 score. The Dodgers, too, were playing at home, but they lost to the Braves early on before pulling out an 8–7 victory. The big loss that the Dodgers suffered early in the game was Hack Wilson, who hurt his ankle running out a homer. In Brooklyn at that time such happenings were normal.

After Opening Day, the Cardinals went on to lose their next five games while the Giants started out 5–0. After getting the bats going in a 10–1 beating of the Pirates in Pittsburgh, St. Louis dropped 2 more games and owned a 2–7 record, bad enough for a last-place tie with the Phillies. The Cardinals were playing far worse than expected at this point, and people stayed away from the park wherever they played. Suddenly, though, the Cardinals took off, winning seven straight and getting into the first division. The Giants were still the team to beat, as they and the Cubs traded first place for the first few weeks.

Suddenly, Pittsburgh got hot and on May 28 the Pirates were on top, with the Cardinals half a game behind and the Cubs and Giants right behind them. On Memorial Day the Giants visited Brooklyn and were received by more than the usual boos. Fans brought signs reminding the Giants of what their manager had said about the local team and hoped for revenge. No such luck, as the Giants swept a twin bill 5–2 and 8–6. The Cardinals kept pace by taking 2 in Cincinnati by 9–6 and 9–2 scores. Still, the Giants moved into first place a week later, but the Cardinals and Cubs made sure that the Giants wouldn't have it easy.

The antics of the Cardinals delighted the St. Louis fans. Every now and then the Cardinals would enter a restaurant, then would be led by Pepper Martin to their table with a nifty slide right into it. The Cardinals liked to party hard and often and were masters of pulling off plenty of practical jokes. Dizzy Dean was certainly called Dizzy for a reason. Once he stopped by the Giant clubhouse just before game time to chat with skipper Bill Terry, just as the Giants were discussing how to handle the Cardinals. Terry asked him to leave. "That's all right. I know all their weaknesses," was Dizzy's reply. Later in the year brother Paul tossed a no-hitter against the Dodgers in the second game of a twin bill. After the game Dizzy said, "If I knew he was gonna throw a no-hitter in the second game, I would have thrown one myself." Dizzy had pitched "only" a shutout in the first game. Dizzy also predicted that he'd win 30 games in 1934 before the season began. As it turned out, he was right about that. Such was life with the Gashouse Gang.

Throughout the summer the Cardinals played consistent ball but had to settle for a race for second with the Cubs. The Giants seemed to win and lose only when the Cardinals did the same, and as a result the Giants hung onto first place. Slowly, though, the Cardinals started to fade. On August 7 they were 6 ½ games behind the Giants. A few days later the team went to Detroit for an exhibition game, but both Dean brothers decided to skip the game and stayed in St. Louis. Rickey then issued fines, $100 for Dizzy and $50 for Paul.

On August 14 the Cardinals were scheduled to play the Phillies at home. Manager Frankie Frisch found that his top two pitchers, the Deans, were not in uniform. When Frisch ordered them to dress for the game, the Deans refused, and a shouting match ensued. The Deans informed the manager that they were quitting. Frisch suspended them. Evidently, both pitchers were upset at their fines stemming from the missed exhibition game and both balked at paying the hefty (for those days) fines. A few days later Paul (also called Daffy) paid his fine and was restored to the roster. Dizzy still was in a tizzy.

The commissioner of baseball went to St. Louis to try to settle the mess. Landis and Dean the elder finally chatted about the affair, and Dean gave in. Dean paid his fine and apologized for his walkout. Some of the other players, like Leo Durocher, were less than thrilled at the mess, but amazingly, it did not effect the Cardinals very much. In fact, the Cardinals were 6–1 during Dizzy's one-man strike.

Dizzy returned to action on August 24 and picked up a 5–0 victory against the Giants, who were visiting town and still in first place. Dizzy looked as good as new, but then the next day Dean came out of the bullpen to stop a Giant rally but instead failed and picked up a 7–6 loss. The defeat gave the Cardinals a 7-game deficit to ponder. At this point it seemed highly unlikely that the Cards would be able to grab the pennant. The race that most fans now were waiting to see won was the race for second.

A 4-game winning streak closed the gap a little, but then the Pirates inflicted two defeats on the Dean boys in a twin bill on September 3, bringing more despair to St. Louis. A St. Louis paper noted after the double loss: "The two defeats virtually eliminated St. Louis from the 1934 pennant scramble." On September 4 the Cardinals were tied with the Cubs for second place, 7 games behind the Giants. A 6–1 streak pushed the Cardinals to within 4½ games of the Giants, but it still looked hopeless. The sense of hopelessness was magnified on September 12 when the lowly Phillies downed the Cardinals 3–1, with the only St. Louis run coming on pitcher Dazzy Vance's homer. On that same day Carl Hubbel picked up his twentieth win by shading the Pirates 3–2. The end was in sight.

On September 13 the Cardinals went to New York to open up a 4-game series with the first-place Giants. At this point the Cardinals entered this series hoping to play for pride rather than pennant. The Cardinals lost 2 of 3 to the Giants the last time they faced the Giants in St. Louis, so a split in this series was the best they could look for. In the first game Paul Dean faced Fat Freddie Fitzsimmons and they hooked up in a twelve-inning thriller. Ducky

Medwick got on base in the twelfth and then scored on a fly out by Bill DeLancey. Leo Durocher then came through with an RBI single. The Cardinals won 2–0. The next day Hal Schumacher beat Bill Walker 4–1 to keep the Cardinals 5½ games back. After a rainout on the fifteenth, both teams ended the series with a twin bill on the sixteenth. The Polo Grounds were jammed with a record crowd exceeding over 60,000, as the fans were ready to buy tickets for the World Series after the day's action was over. In the opener Dizzy Dean outpitched Schumacher 5–3, and in the second game Paul Dean and Carl Hubbell entered the eleventh with the score tied 1–1. Pepper Martin then led off the eleventh with a homer, and Medwick came through with an RBI single. The Cardinals won that game 3–1.

Despite cutting the deficit to 3½ games, the Cardinals were still given little chance to win the flag. Still, the Cardinals had a favorable schedule that had them facing the weak Dodgers, the fading Pirates, the mediocre Braves, and the dismal Reds. The Giants disposed of the Reds while the Braves were beaten twice by the Cardinals, so the situation was unchanged. On September 21 the Cardinals swept two from the Dodgers (which featured the Paul Dean no-hitter) while the Giants downed the Braves. The deficit was reduced half a game when the Braves nipped the Giants in extra innings, while the Cardinals were rained out on the twenty-second. The next day both teams split twin bills.

In the season's final week, the Cardinals downed the Cubs once while splitting two with the Pirates. During this time, the lousy Phillies took 2 from the Giants, cutting the Giant lead to 1 game. The Giants had 2 straight off days to worry about a choke as the Cardinals hosted the Reds for the first 2 games of a season-ending 4-game set. On September 27 the Cardinals downed the Reds 8–5, Bill Walker beating ex-Cardinal Paul Derringer. The next day Dizzy Dean picked up his twenty-ninth win by shutting out the Reds 4–0. The Cardinals had done the near impossible. They had tied the New York Giants for first place.

September 29, 1934, will go down as a great day in the history of both the St. Louis Cardinals and the Brooklyn Dodgers, and as a dark one in the history of the New York Giants. On that day, the Cardinals faced the Reds while the Giants hosted the Dodgers with the pennant on the line. The Giants had held first place since June 6 and were now in danger of going down in history as one of the big chokers in baseball. Worse, the Giants had to face the team that Bill Terry had mocked earlier in the year. The Dodgers were long since eliminated, but Casey Stengel wanted to show that Brooklyn was still in the league.

Thousands of Dodger rooters packed the subways and headed to the Polo Grounds to see their team give the Giants hell. These two teams already had a tense rivalry, but this brought out the very best of it. People carried posters and banners proclaiming that Brooklyn still was in the league. The Dodgers proved it as well as Van Mungo faced Roy Parmalee and the Dodgers supported Mungo with a ten-hit attack. The Dodgers won the game 5–1. The Cardinals did their part by downing the Reds 6–1. The Cardinals now had sole possession of first place, 1 game ahead of the Giants.

On September 30 the Giants knew what had to be done. They had to beat Ray Benge while Dizzy Dean had to lose to former Cardinal Syl Johnson. Easier said than done. Dean had 29 wins while Johnson had 21 losses for the last-place Reds. Still, the Giants hoped. The Giants were glad to knock Benge out before he completed an inning. After an inning the Giants held a 4–0 lead. Dutch Leonard was summoned from the bullpen by Stengel, and he managed to stop the Giants for the next six-plus innings. The Dodgers began chipping away, and Freddie Fitzsimmons was sent to the showers in favor of Hal Schumacher. At that point, the Giants had a 5–4 lead. Later "Prince Hal" threw a wild pitch that tied the game at 5–5. While this was going on, the scoreboard showed the Cardinals were leading. The mostly Dodger crowd cheered. In the tenth the game was still 5–5 when the Dodgers put two men on. Bill Terry called on Hubbell to put out the fire. Instead of putting out the fire, he poured gas on it by walking a man to load the bases, then proceeding to give up 2 runs on a fumbled grounder. By the time the inning was over, the Dodgers held an 8–5 lead. The chances for a first ever pennant playoff looked dead. Rookie pitcher Johnny Babich retired the side easily in the tenth, and the Giants had blown the pennant. At St. Louis, Dizzy Dean fulfilled his preseason prediction by tossing a 9–0 shutout for his thirtieth win. St. Louis was crazed with joy. It took a 20–5 streak to get the

Cardinals into the World Series, but they had done it. New York would have to burn those series tickets that they had printed earlier in the month, just like Brooklyn had to four years earlier.

Dizzy Dean was sensational throughout the season, as he posted a 30–7 record and a 2.66 ERA. Brother Paul was no slouch at 19–11. Tex Carlton had an ERA over 4.00, but he still went 16–11. Offensively, the Cardinals got a league-leading 35 homers from Ripper Collins (as well as a .333 average and 128 RBIs), a .319 average from Medwick as well as 106 RBIs, and a .305 average from second baseman and manager Frisch. Jack Rothrock, Rickey's reclamation project, hit .284 with 72 RBIs and a league-leading 647 at bats and provided great defense in right field. In short, the rather miraculous season was a total team effort. The gate responded by improving to over 120,000, decent but not enough to make much profit. The World Series would come in handy for making some extra money.

As fate would have it, the Cardinals faced Detroit in the series, the same Detroit that Sam Breadon had wanted to move his team to not too long ago. The Cardinals knew the manager and catcher of the Tigers, Mickey Cochrane, from two previous series with the Philadelphia Athletics. The Tigers got a good fight from the Yankees in the regular season, but with a 101–53 record they beat out the New Yorkers by seven lengths.

Game 1 took place in Detroit on October 3. Over 42,000 people packed the ballpark to see the Tigers play in their first series since 1909. Dizzy Dean got the ball and faced General Crowder, a late-season pickup from Washington who went 5–1 down the stretch. Before game time Dizzy, who was asked about the Cardinals' chances in the series, said that although he couldn't win 4 straight, he "could win 4 out of 5." In the game the Cardinals put together a thirteen-hit attack and bombed Crowder 8–3. In the second game Hallahan faced Schoolboy Rowe and they hooked up in a duel that went twelve innings. As usual, the Cardinals needled their opponents, being led by pinch hitter Pat Crawford. Still, the Tigers went out and evened the series with a 3–2 win.

The third game moved to St. Louis on October 5. Paul Dean outpitched Tommy Bridges and beat him 4–1. The next day Detroit collected 13 hits of their own and handed Bill Walker a 10–4 beating. This game scared the daylights out of the Cardinal fans when Frisch made the strange move of inserting Dizzy Dean as a pinch runner for Spud Davis. Pepper Martin hit a grounder to second, and as Dean ran to second to break up the double play attempt he went in standing up. Billy Rogell's throw hit Dizzy right in the head, nearly knocking him out. Dizzy left the game via stretcher, and X rays of his head "showed nothing," as it was reported. Dean didn't seem to mind that he got hit on the noggin, since he told Frisch he wanted to pitch the next day. The 1934 Cardinals, being what they were, did send Dizzy out to pitch against Bridges the next day. Dean pitched a good game but lost 3–1. Dizzy seemed fine after his "beaning."

As the series shifted to Detroit for the last 2 games, the air was tense. Both teams were less than happy with the umpiring, and the two teams had played some hardball. In game 2 Medwick crashed hard into Cochrane, angering Tiger fans. The Cardinals got on the catcher good after that, and he was so miffed that he wanted to beat up Pat Crawford, his chief tormentor. Game 6 was a battle between Paul Dean and Rowe, and it was hard fought. Jo Jo White went hard into second, knocking Frisch down when he tried to steal second. Cochrane was spiked when one of four Cardinal runs scored. Despite all of this rough play, there was a ball game played and it showed the Cardinals to be the better team, as they won 4–3.

The final game, on October 9, pitted Dizzy against Eldon Auker. The Cardinals scored seven times in the third, and the game was practically over when a near riot ensued. In the sixth Medwick slid hard into third and tangled with Marv Owen. Owen stepped on Ducky and Medwick followed with a kick. The umpires broke it up and Medwick tried to patch things up, but Owen waved him away. In the bottom of the inning Medwick was in the center of a garbage storm when fans threw whatever they could find at him. The umpires feared that a riot would break out. The baseball commissioner was at the game and ordered Frisch to take Medwick out of the game. Frisch wasn't happy, but he did as he was told. The Cardinals then completed their 11–0 win without further incident. St. Louis was the world champ again.

The exciting series did well enough to put the Cardinals in the black for 1934. Breadon was pleased that the Cardinals had won a rather surprising pennant. Even though the Browns increased their gate with Rogers Hornsby as the manager, they still drew poorly, and Breadon was now sure he could outlast the Browns if it came down to having one team or another move.

Branch Rickey did his usual thing for the 1935 season, which was make few moves. Terry Moore was the phenom for the new year, and he would be put in center field. The Cards were expected to battle with the Giants and Cubs for the flag, and most people picked the Cardinals to win the race.

The Cubs entered 1935 with a new owner, chewing gum king Phil Wrigley. Wrigley issued orders for the Cubs to win the flag in his first year as owner. Manger Charlie Grimm, a St. Louis native, certainly did not join in the chorus of people who sang another Cardinal pennant song. "The best I can see for them is a second-place finish with the Cubs first," said Grimm. Grimm's team finished a strong third in 1934 and had handled both the Giants and Cardinals well. The Cubs also picked up Tex Carleton from the Cardinals for two unimportant pitchers.

The Giants got off to another good start and took the initial lead. St. Louis also started well and was a close second, with the Cubs close behind them. As was often the case in those days, the New York press proclaimed another World Series with the front-running Giants seemingly a shoe-in. "The runaway which the Giants are making has the National League by the ears," wrote one local scribe. The Giants were probably taking orders for series tickets by the time that line was being written.

In the second half the Cubs' use of a five-man rotation started to turn them around. Frisch noticed that, and he also put together a five-man rotation, featuring the Dean brothers, Bill Walker, Bill Hallahan, and Pop Haines (who was still effective at age forty-two). The Giants' lead shrank as the Cubbies and Cardinals were winning briskly with their five-man rotations. In head-to-head play the Cubs were tormented all year by the Cardinals, who had beaten them ten out of fourteen in the seasons series by July. The Cardinals took 2 more out of 3 in early August as the Cubs started to sputter. Meanwhile the Cardinals were closing in on first place as the Giants did the fade. The Cubs did their part to help move the Cardinals into first by taking three out of four from the Giants in New York in late August.

After a Labor Day sweep of the Pirates in a twin bill, the Cardinals held a two-and-a-half-game lead on the Cubs and a 2-game lead on the Giants. The Cardinals went on to post a 6-game winning streak while the Giants finally dropped out of the race. The Cubs then moved into second place at his time, as they began launching one of the greatest assaults in the late stages of any pennant race ever. The Cubs were winning daily, but the Cardinals kept pace and held onto first place.

On September 13 (a Friday) the Cardinals still held first and were trailing 10–6 when Dizzy Dean came into the game. The Cardinals rallied to tie it, but Dean gave up three runs in the tenth and the Cardinals lost. That same day the Cubs downed the Dodgers 4–1 in their tenth straight win. The Cardinals and Cubs were virtually tied for first. Frisch worried that the Cardinals would look like the '34 Giants and decided to rely mostly on the Deans for the rest of the season. This move was to do little good for the Cardinals (and especially Paul), as the Cubs kept on winning. The Cardinals were busy losing three of four to the Giants and finally fell out of first on the fourteenth.

St. Louis was running out of gas as Frisch panicked. The pitching staff was losing confidence, as only the Deans got the call practically every day. Despite the Chicago onslaught, many still thought that the Cardinals could pull out the flag, but the pitching staff had little left to offer. The Dean boys were doing a commendable job, but it would take more than just two pitchers to get this Cardinal team (or any other, for that matter) to win its second straight pennant.

The Cubs, meanwhile, kept winning. Chicago swept 4 from New York by scores of 8–3, 5–3, 15–3, and 6–1. On the twenty-fifth the Cubs shaded Paul Dean 1–0. Two days later the Cubs took 2 from the Cardinals by 6–2 and 5–3, completing a twenty-one-game winning streak and giving the Cubs the pennant by 4 games over St. Louis. "Boys, there ain't gonna be any Gashouse Gang in the World Series," said Cub manager Grimm, whose team was dubbed "the Grimm Reapers." The Cub streak was more impressive than even the one of the '34 Cardinals.

The Cardinals might not have won a pennant in 1935, but at least they gained a good rival in the Cubs. Much has been made about the Cardinal-Cub rivalry over the years, but truth be told, there isn't much basis for it. Baseball has had far stronger rivalries in its history. During the 1890s the Boston Beaneaters and Baltimore Orioles waged savage battles against each other as they fought for the National League flag year after year. The Brooklyn Dodgers–New York Giant rivalry was probably the most fierce over a prolonged period of time. Both teams played just about as close to each other as geography would allow. When the Dodgers first joined the National League in 1890 (by leaving the American Association), Brooklyn was an independent city that was looked down on by New York. Even after Brooklyn became part of greater New York in 1898, Brooklyn and New York (Manhattan, that is) looked at each other with scorn. A Giant-Dodger game always had the potential for much bloodletting.

It seems that proximity is the key to the Cardinal-Cub rivalry, but even this doesn't make for an automatic feud. The Yankees and Red Sox are near each other, and in 1904 these two teams were in a wire-to-wire race. However, the rivalry between these two teams did not flourish early on, because when one team contended the other did not. Only after the Yankees provided Boston with a good reason to hate them (buying up the best Red Sox did the trick) did the Yankee-Red Sox rivalry begin to take off. Proximity helps in a rivalry, but if that was the only basis for a feud, then the Pirates and Phillies should draw huge crowds any time they face each other. If anything, the Cardinals had a stronger rivalry with the New York Giants than with the Cubs in those years. The Giants were hated throughout the league for having been rich and successful for years, and just about every time the Cardinals were involved in the pennant chase (through 1935) the Giants were right there to play a role in that race. Later the Cardinals would have a strong feud with the Brooklyn Dodgers and a pretty good one with the New York Mets. The New York Yankees also would provide the Cardinals with a pretty good rival in future series. The Cardinal-Cub rivalry does draw well even today, since fans from each city can travel to the enemy city, but after 1945 the Cubs and Cardinals have rarely been involved in a wire-to-wire race at the same time and the feud has been somewhat cooled.

VI

The Cardinals saw their attendance improve to over 500,000 in 1935, and the good pennant race put them in the black. The Depression still gripped the nation, and other teams were still in the red. The Browns were a total disaster when they drew just over 80,000 people for the year. Crowds of under 100 were regularly seen at Sportsman's Park when the Browns were at home. The Cardinals could draw many people in a week, and to put that measly gate in perspective, compare that total to the total gate that a 1954 twin bill between the Yankees and Indians drew in Cleveland (over *86,000*). Sam Breadon now didn't mind assuming the landlord's responsibility of maintaining the park.

As 1936 opened, Branch Rickey set out to improve the ball club. The Cardinals shipped farm product Burgess Whitehead to the Giants in exchange for Roy Parmalee, Phil Weintraub, and cash. Second baseman Stu Martin and first baseman Johnny Mize were deemed part of the future and brought up for the season. The Cardinals were expected to contend, and many picked them to win. The Cardinals got off to a good start and stayed with the Giants, Cubs, and Pirates in the pennant race, but there were problems. Pilot Frankie Frisch was nearing the end of the line and gave way to Stu Martin, who went on to hit .298. Ripper Collins was slowing down and Mize got more playing time, and he ended up driving in 93 runs, with a .329 average. Paul Dean, showing the effects of too much pitching with not enough rest in late 1935, went 5–5 with a 4.60 ERA and never was effective again. The pitching in general was taxed as it became mediocre. Only Dizzy Dean was reliable, and he was pitching in 51 games, hurling 315 innings, and getting worn down as the season was ending. Rumor had it that Frisch was through as manager, with players plotting behind his back. Leo Durocher looked like the next Cardinal pilot.

Nineteen-thirty-six was a disaster in Rickey's view. The team faded in the second half and had to scramble at the end to get into third place ahead of the Pirates. The Giants won the flag and were 5 games ahead of St. Louis (and Chicago, who tied with the Cardinals). Gate receipts fell as the team did its fade. A housecleaning was in order. Rickey cut veterans and made some deals. In one with the Dodgers he picked up infielder Frenchy Bordagaray and pitcher Dutch Leonard. In another with the Cubs he shipped Ripper Collins to Chicago with Roy Parmalee in exchange for Lon Warneke. More rookies were recalled in Mickey Owen, Don Gutteridge, Don Padgett, and Jimmy Brown.

If 1936 looked bad to Rickey, 1937 was even worse. The rookies came through, Mize became a top slugger in the league, and Ducky Medwick won the Triple Crown with 31 homers, 154 RBIs, and a .374 average. Warneke won 18 games as the big winner and Bob Weiland won 15 after Rickey rescued him off the junk heap. Despite these performances, the Cardinals started slowly, as the Giants and Cubs made the pennant race their own private party. In July, Dizzy Dean started the All-Star game and took a line drive off of his foot. The Cardinal ace had a broken toe but tried to pitch through it, changing his delivery and hurting his arm in the process. Despite winning 13 games in 1937, Dizzy Dean would never be the same again. The Cardinals needed a late-season spurt to get to fourth place, 1 game ahead of the usually dismal Boston team. Continuing dissension on the team did not help matters.

After the 1937 season ended, the Cardinal bosses were looking at a team going backward. The farm system continued to supply stars to the parent team, but the Cardinals were not making progress. Attendance continued to slip. The Frisch situation was still messy, since he was still considered a fine skipper and firing him would turn away the fans. With Dizzy having arm trouble the pitching staff lacked someone who would inspire confidence. Rickey made some more trades and recalled yet another rookie from the farm in Enos Slaughter. The Cardinals hoped for the best for 1938, but instead it turned out to be a dismal year.

Just before Opening Day the Cardinals traded Dizzy Dean to the Cubs for three players and some cash. The fans booed. The fans got plenty of exercise in booing all year long, as the team got off to its worst start since 1932, quickly sinking to the second division and avoiding the cellar only because the Phillies were even worse. The pitching stank, and the hitting, aside from Mize and Medwick, was poor. The Cardinals found themselves fighting the Dodgers and Boston to avoid seventh place. The press had speculated for some time that Leo Durocher would replace Frisch when the time came, but when that time actually arrived Durocher was in Brooklyn. Fans or no fans, Rickey had decided to fire the manager, and on September 10 the ax fell. Coach Mike Gonzales took the helm and posted a 9–8 finish. Overall, the Cardinals ended up in sixth place with a less than great 71–80 record.

Rickey probably thought he had made too many trades after 1937 was over and that was why the 1938 Cardinals did so poorly. In any event, Rickey decided to stand pat when it came to the roster. Mort Cooper was the Cardinal "Rookie for the Year" of 1939, as he was recalled from the farm. He joined a team full of farm products. Mize, Medwick, Stu and Pepper Martin, Gutteridge, Brown, Moore, Slaughter, Padgett, Owen, Bob Bowman (another newcomer for '39), Cooper, and Bill McGee were the most important members of the Cardinals, and all came from Rickey's farm. Ray Blades, a former Cardinal player, was selected to lead the 1939 squad.

The Cardinals started strong and took hold of first place quickly. The hitting recovered and the pitching did an amazing turnaround. Curt Davis, the only key Cardinal not from the farm, posted 12 wins, while 5 other hurlers won at least 10 games. Cooper went 12–6 with a 3.25 ERA as a rookie, and Bowman went 13–5, 2.60, in his first year. The Cardinals stumbled a little near the end as the Reds, led by Bill McKechnie, stormed into first place late in the season. The Cardinals ended up going 92–61, and they finished 5 games behind the Reds.

The Cardinals had righted themselves, and by this time they were gaining new fans by broadcasting their games over the radio. Rickey saw that the attendance of other teams that broadcast their games was not cut and that those teams had attracted new fans from areas that had no big league ball. In time the Cardinals would broadcast their games throughout the South and West (since St. Louis was at the time the southernmost and westernmost big league city), drawing fans from outside of town. The Browns, on the other hand, were a hopeless case, and they never did broad-cast their games as heavily as the Cardinals.

The Depression was winding down, and the economy was recovering in both the nation and baseball. Rickey came out of the Depression well. It was estimated that he made about $50,000 a year in salary, got a cut in the club's profits, and owned a little stock in the team. The Cardinals were clearly *the* team in town, despite the fluctuating attendance, and it had turned a bad Browns team sour on the town. Rumor had it that the Browns would be sold and moved, but few people were interested in a team that drew poorly and had few good players, no gate appeal, and a tradition of failure. While the Cardinals had made a nice profit since the mid-1920s, the Browns had lost more and more money. The Cardinals were on the high road and the Browns were on the low road, and prospects for the Browns did not look good.

Rickey again made few moves for 1940, as the hard-to-figure Cardinals were picked to contend. The Reds and the Dodgers, now led by Leo Durocher, were also expected to go for the flag. In the past, the Cardinals would usually do poorly when picked to con-tend, and this year proved no different. The Cardinals fell off to a 15–24 start before Blades was sacked. Mike Gonzalez then came out of the coaching box to post an 0–5 record before the Cardinals dipped into the minors for a pilot. Billy Southworth, who was deemed not ready after a stint as skipper of the team in 1929, was brought back for the second time. This time Southworth got the Cardinals going, with a 69–40 finish. St. Louis claimed third place in 1940, 16 games in arrears of the Reds.

Before the 1940 season was over, the Cardinals made a trade with the Dodgers, sending the fading Curt Davis and the not fading Ducky Medwick to Brooklyn for four young players and $125,000. Branch Rickey needed to clear a spot for another farm product named Johnny Hopp, who would hold the spot open for a guy named Stan Musial. Besides, the money looked too good for Rickey to pass up, so away went the popular Medwick. This trade would be a big one for Brooklyn in the upcoming season.

After the 1940 season, Rickey saw that his farm system had plenty of prospects left to keep the Cardinals going, so as usual, he passed on the trading block. Hopp was slated to replace Medwick, and Earl White would bolster the pitching. Max Lanier had looked good as a rookie in 1940, so the pitching would not be a problem. At short, Marty Marion covered a lot of ground, and he was a pesky hitter. The hitting was certainly good, as the Cardinals' total of 119 homers led the league in 1940 and their .276 average was second.

At about this time Rickey and Breadon were beginning to disagree on which direction the Cardinals were heading. The trade of Medwick was not popular among the fans, but since the Dodgers added cash to the deal (one probably made at the request of their pilot, Durocher) Rickey could scarcely refuse. Despite the Cardinals' being the top team in town and all of the profits rolling in, the Cardinals still were in a small market and were sharing it with the Browns. From Rickey's view a couple of rash moves one way or another could easily push the team back into the bad shape it was in when he first arrived. Any time a team offered cash to Rickey in a trade he would certainly go for it. Breadon probably figured that since the Cardinals were tops in town they could do as they pleased. The Browns had not been a factor in the Cardinals' financial picture for some time, and Breadon's point of view could be understood. Still, there was always the chance that the Browns would indeed be sold to someone who would try to turn that disaster in the right direction. Rickey had that in mind, and any time Rickey saw reports of the Browns being for sale he worried.

Rickey's other problem was player salaries. Since guys like Mize and Medwick were top players, they wanted top dollars. At least when the Cardinals stank salaries could be kept low, but not now. Rickey was notorious in his dealings with players over salaries. "We didn't win with you, and we can not win without you" was the type of line Rickey used on players when the teams he ran didn't win the flag. Breadon thought that the salary squabbles were silly and costing him players in money-related trades, but the owner himself was known to be tight with money. There's little doubt that the Medwick trade came about due to some salary fighting. Still, despite all of this, Rickey would stay with Breadon for a little while longer, just in time to see the Cardinals start their golden age.

VII

The Ducky Medwick deal was a big one that caused ripples in both St. Louis and Brooklyn. Besides doing it for monetary reasons, the Cardinals sent Medwick to the Dodgers because of his loss of gate appeal. When Medwick first came up he was a fan favorite, but by the time the 1940 season began the relationship between player and fans had crumbled. Medwick was being booed regularly at Sportsman's Park for perceived indifferent play, and he grew surly as a result. When the Dodgers offered the hefty sum of $125,000, the Cardinals could not believe their eyes and gladly took the money by sending Ducky east.

Baseball observers were amazed at that sum of over $100,000. Brooklyn was now being run by Larry MacPhail, a man who had done well running minor league teams and had taken the Reds from being a disaster and turned them into an eventual world champion (in 1940). MacPhail also brought night games to the majors while running the Reds, and he also put the Dodgers under lights soon after his arrival at Ebbets Field. MacPhail's work with the Dodgers by the time 1941 came had been truly amazing, and in a way he did for the Dodgers what Branch Rickey had done for the Cardinals back in the 1920s.

When MacPhail went to the Dodgers he went to a club that had done almost nothing except lose games and money over the previous few years. When Dodger owner Charlie Ebbets (the man who built the club's park and named it after himself) died in 1925 his two partners took over the club. A week after Ebbets was buried, one of the partners died (after catching pneumonia at Ebbets's funeral, no less) and the surviving partner found himself at odds with that partner's heirs, who happened to be his own nephews and nieces. At the center of the problem was the status of pilot Wilbert Robinson, who had run the team for some ten years at the time. One side wanted to keep the popular skipper, while the other side wanted to dump him. Robinson had won two flags at Brooklyn, but by 1925 the Dodgers (named Robins in his honor) were starting to fade. The two sides kept battling over the status of Robby, and somehow Robby managed to keep his job for some time. Unfortunately for the pilot, his team rarely was in the hunt and losses began to pile up on the ledgers as the Dodgers played in a three-team market where the Giants and Yankees kept winning year after year.

In 1930 it looked like the Dodgers would finally win a pennant, as they went into September holding the lead over three other teams. As we have already seen, Brooklyn did not win the flag but faded to fourth. After one more season at the helm, Robby was finally removed. His record reflects just how mediocre the Dodgers were under his leadership: 1,397 wins, 1,395 losses. Max Carey then took the helm and did little better.

By the time Casey Stengel arrived to run the team, the Dodgers were feeling the pinch of the Depression more than other teams. Money was being lost in large sums as the Dodgers continued to fail on the field. Stengel did provide comic relief, but that is not why managers are hired. The anti-Robinson faction died out, causing instability in the front office. The Dodgers plunged into the second division, and it looked like it would be decades before a contender would emerge in Brooklyn. The Dodgers were in exactly the same sorry shape as the Cardinals of the 1910s had been. If anything, the Dodgers were in *worse* shape, since they had to battle *two* successful teams in town and were in the possession of a bank by the time MacPhail arrived in 1937.

MacPhail took a look at the bankrupt team, and he did not like what he saw. Trades were made and veterans were cut left and right. Some semblance of a minor league system was established (although it would be years before the Dodgers' minor league system would compete with the Cardinals'). MacPhail began paying off debts that had piled up since the 1920s while rebuilding the team and getting the bank out of the picture. In 1939 he named Leo Durocher, a man who knew how to win from his days with the Yankees and Cardinals, as manager of the Dodgers. The Brooklyn faithful were happy, as the colorful Durocher was regarded as a possible genius. In his first year Leo took the Dodgers from seventh to third and brought the style of the Gashouse Gang to Brooklyn. Durocher and coach Chuck Dressen were master bench jockeys and gave the opposition hell in every game. Durocher also was no shrinking violet when it came to hard play. Hard slides and "sticking it in their ears" was the type of play that turned the Dodgers from laughingstocks into a team that was respected and despised. When the Dodgers finished second in 1940, the money began to roll in. MacPhail was not one to save, and when Medwick became available MacPhail sent plenty of dough west. People were amazed that a team like the Dodgers would part with such cash after being so poor just a few years earlier. It seemed suicidal, since nobody knew for sure if the Dodgers were really ready to go for a pennant. If the Cardinals were an example of financial restraint in building a team, then the Dodgers were the reverse. They spent heavily as the team built itself by adding veterans from other teams. The Dodgers now looked like the old Giants in their spending spree. In 1940 the price the Dodgers paid for Medwick was extremely high, especially coming at the end of the Depression.

The Medwick trade was popular in Brooklyn. The Dodgers were proving to their fans that they were serious in going for the pennant. Medwick, vilified in his last years in St. Louis, became instantly popular in Brooklyn. An incident just after the deal cemented the fans with Medwick when Ducky was beaned by the Cardinals in a tight game between the two teams. The Brooklyn fans were angered by the beaning, feeling that it was intentional. The Dodgers were still battling Cincinnati at that time, and the loss of Medwick was costly. Durocher, who certainly had no love for his old team, would now try harder than ever to torment St. Louis. Bad blood had been spilled by the Medwick incident, and the hatred between the Cardinals and Dodgers would not subside until over ten years later. A most lively feud was about to begin.

Entering 1941 the Dodgers were favored to win the flag. The Reds, winners of two straight pennants and the 1940 series, were expected to not win three straight flags but were not expected to fold either. The Cardinals, with that home-grown roster of theirs, were also expected to be tough. The Cardinals decided to pick up more Brooklyn money when they traded catcher Mickey Owen east for Gus Mancuso and cash, adding more interest to the upcoming Cardinal-Dodger rivalry.

The Reds got off to a so-so start and went on to struggle for much of the season. The Dodgers and Cardinals started well, making the pennant race a two-team affair for most of the season. Both teams battled in and out of first all year long, with the specter

110

of the military draft looming large. The year 1941 saw war clouds heading toward the nation, and the military was starting to reach into baseball for manpower. Detroit Tiger slugger Hank Greenberg had already gone into the service early in the season, and Hugh Mulcahy of the Phillies was drafted even before the season started, when the Cardinals and Dodgers went at it in their first meetings of the season. Durocher was at his needling best (or worst, depending on the viewpoint) when the Cardinals were the enemy. The Medwick beaning of the previous year made the Brooklyn fans yell louder and longer any time St. Louis came to town, and it didn't help matters that visiting ball players had to walk through a gauntlet of screaming fans just to get to the clubhouse in Ebbets Field. Hard slides, high and tight pitches, and flashing spikes were the norm when the Dodgers and Cardinals hooked up throughout 1941. Both teams would see overflow crowds in their parks when they got together. Branch Rickey must have been mighty pleased in finding such a great rival.

The Cardinals finally fell out of first for good in September 1941, but they kept up the heat on the Dodgers, waiting for them to falter so that they could sneak back into the top slot. September also saw the call-up of one Stanley Frank Musial, "the Man," who would go on to become the greatest of all Cardinal hitters. The arrival of Musial came at a good time, since the Cardinals were suffering a rash of injuries, which might have cost them the 1941 pennant. With Enos Slaughter and Terry Moore hobbled by injury, another outfielder was welcome relief for skipper Billy Southworth. Musial got into 12 games that month, hitting a brisk .426 in 47 at bats with a homer and 7 RBIs. The spurt from Musial helped, but it was not enough. The Dodgers kept winning and in the end the injury wave on the Cardinals was too much to overcome. The Cardinals ended up second with a 97–56 record, 2 ½ games behind Brooklyn. Cardinal fans were probably chuckling when the hated Dodgers went on to lose the series after dropping the key fourth game. That was the game where former Cardinal catcher Mickey Owen mishandled a spitball into a passed ball, triggering a 4-run, game-winning rally in the ninth by the Yankees. Maybe Rickey saw the headlines in a crystal ball when he sent the promising Owen to Brooklyn. At this point, everybody was raving at the way the

Mahatma (as Rickey was now also being called) was coming up with great players from the farm. That Musial kid had really looked good in the heat of a tough race for the pennant, and great things were expected of him. He certainly did not disappoint.

Stan Musial was born in Donora, Pennsylvania, on November 21, 1920, the same year that the Cardinals were finally turning their miserable selves around. As a kid, Musial liked to pitch, although he also played other positions and he eventually turned into a pretty good hitter. Still, it was as a pitcher that the Cardinals signed the eighteen-year-old Musial in 1938, assigning him to Williamson in the Mountain States League.

Musial the pitcher did not remind anyone of another Lefty Grove. Wid Matthews was sent to Williamson in 1938 to see what was wrong with Musial, who was en route to a 6–6 season with a less than stellar 4.66 ERA. Matthews reported back to St. Louis: "Arm good. Good fastball, good curve. Poise. Good hitter. A real prospect." Rickey always had patience with prospects, knowing that some players took longer than others to develop. The Musial kid was in his first minor league season, so there was still time to get him straightened out.

Musial the hitter was also not anything big at that time, but the Cardinals decided to convert him as his pitching improved, but his control did not. A scouting report stated that Musial was too wild to be a pitcher, so it as now time to work on his hitting. In 1939 Musial hit .352 as he began to pinch-hit when not throwing. A year later, the Man was sent to Daytona Beach, where he made the transition to the outfield while still pitching from time to time. Stan hit just 1 homer in 1940, but his nice swing produced a .311 average. It looked like the Cardinals had a singles hitter on their hands.

The Cardinals next sent their outfield prospect to Springfield in the West Virginia League. Musial was done with pitching, and he now concentrated on power hitting. The Man smacked 26 homers and drove in 94 runs in only 87 games while swatting .379. Evidently Burt Shotton, a big league manager in the past (and in the future), put plenty of confidence in Musial in the spring of 1941 when he told him, "I think you *can* make it as a hitter." Shotton then recommended that Musial be turned into a full-time outfielder. The

Man didn't finish 1941 at Springfield, but his 26 homers still led the league. Next was a trip to AAA ball at Rochester, where Musial hit the top minor league hurlers for a .326 mark. On September 17, St. Louis called and the man named Musial came to the big leagues for keeps. Jim Tobin of the Bees (the Boston Braves' name at that time) was the first victim of a Musial hit that day, and on the Pirates, Rip Sewell was the first victim of a Musial homer. The Man had arrived.

After finishing close to the top in 1941, the Cardinals went to work on getting up that high in 1942. The war was in full swing for less than a week when, on December 11, the Cardinals sent Johnny Mize to the Giants for Johnny McCarthy, Ken O'Dea, Bill Lohrman, and $50,000. This trade shocked Cardinal fans, since Mize was the only true, proven power hitter on the team. This deal was needed, since room had to be made for Musial, and it was in line with Rickey's saying of "better to get rid of a guy a year too early than a year too late." Mize proved to have several fine years left, but in the long run the trade worked out great for the Cardinals.

Entering 1942, the Cardinals were still untouched by the draft and they had the makings of a dynasty. Musial would play left field and help form one of the great outfields in baseball history. Enos Slaughter, the original "Charlie Hustle," was in right, and Terry Moore caught everything but a cold in center. This trio could also pound the old horsehide. The infield was rebuilt, with slick-fielding Whitey Kurowski taking over third base and Johnny Hopp shifting from the outfield to replace Mize at first. Marty Marion already was regarded as the top shortstop in the league, and he would be paired with Creepy Crespi at second. The backstop was Walker Cooper, who was turning into a fine defensive receiver and a tough hitter.

Walker's brother Mort was one of the many excellent pitchers that the farm was now turning out. Johnny Beazley, Max Lanier (regarded by many as the league's toughest pitcher in his time), Howie Pollet, Murry Dickson, and Ernie White joined Cooper in rounding out a home-grown pitching staff that would be murder on any lineup. Howie Krist (another farm product) couldn't even break into the 1942 starting rotation despite a 10–0 record the previous year. Only Lon Warneke and Harry Gumbert among the main pitchers of the 1942 Cardinals came from other teams. In fact, all of the regulars, pitchers and hitters, on the '42 squad, came from the farm, except for the two aforementioned hurlers.

Entering Opening Day, the Cardinals and Dodgers were both favored to win the pennant. The Cardinals started well, but the Dodgers took off on an amazing streak, one that made the Dodgers look like they were going to break the 1906 Cubs record for most wins in a season (116). The Cardinals were busy whipping everyone else in the league as well, but they were not threatening the win record and had to settle for second place in the early going. The Dodgers were whipping the daylights out of every team in head-to-head play as Durocher and his crew reminded one and all who the big shots in the league were. One team that didn't think the Dodgers were going to run off with the flag was the Cardinals, who swept a 4-game set in St. Louis against the Brooklyn brutes in early May. Manager Southworth kept calm, as he expected the Dodgers to slow down after their hot start. "They haven't had their slump yet," said the St. Louis skipper. People around the league replied, "Yeah, sure, a team like that will slump."

One look at the 1942 Dodgers roster shows why nobody took Southworth's remark seriously. Six pitchers were to win at least 10 games for Brooklyn that year, established guys who came from other teams, like Johnny Allen (10–6), Larry French (15–4, 1.83 ERA), and Cardinal reject Curt Davis (15–6), who got special attention from the fans in St. Louis as a former hero now with the hated Dodgers. This trio of pitchers wasn't even the front of the Brooklyn pitching machine. Kirby Higbe went 16–11 for the year, and Whit Wyatt was the ace at 19–7. Hugh Casey (he of the spitball that got away in the 1941 series) was the bullpen ace with thirteen saves (then a big total).

The lineup also looked strong. Dolf Camilli, Billy Herman, Pee Wee Reese, and Arky Vaughan formed the infield, and all but Reese had been around for some time with other teams. Pete Reiser (who Branch Rickey called the greatest outfielder he ever saw when *he* joined the enemy), Dixie Walker, and Ducky Medwick comprised the outfield, and all could hit. Mickey Owen wasn't a great hitter, but he was great behind the plate. Augie Galan was no cream puff coming off the bench, and had to stay there, because the outfield had no room for him. This team could dominate, and for the first half of 1942 it did.

In late May, the Cardinals and Dodgers played 5 in Brooklyn. The Dodgers took 4 of the games in a heated atmosphere featuring a fight between Marion and Medwick. Creepy Crespi jumped in and had a few licks with Ducky, and Jimmy Brown (who shuttled between second and third that year for St. Louis) did battle with Walker. After this melee concluded, the Cardinals were looking at a 7½ game deficit. The spirits of St. Louis were flagging, but Southworth still felt the Cardinals would cash in when that Dodger slump finally came. Thus far, such a slump seemed nowhere in sight.

By the All-Star break the Cardinals were on a pace to win 94 games, a good total that can win a pennant in many years. But at that point the Dodgers were heading for a possible 102 wins, which is even better for bagging the flag. Lon Warneke was sold to the Cubs before the game, and many people were mad about that, claiming that the front office was quitting. The Dodgers looked like a dynasty in the making as they tried to win their second straight pennant. Larry MacPhail, though, felt it was a good idea that the team be reminded that the season was only half over and that the slump that Southworth had predicted had to be avoided. MacPhail attacked the team for getting too confident (but not too arrogant) and emphasized that they had better hustle and run up an even bigger lead before expecting a World Series check. It was time to "stop playing mister nice guy and kick some butt" was the message MacPhail was trying to get across to a team with an 8-game lead.

It sure seems strange that the boss of a team leading by 8 in midseason would virtually bawl his team out for not being even further ahead, but that's the way it was with the '42 Dodgers. The Cardinals were not about to fold, and they would give MacPhail fits. In July, the two contenders met in another series, this time in St. Louis, and it was highlighted by a fight between Musial and pitcher Les Webber after the hurler hit the Man on Durocher's orders. The Cardinals swept a twin bill the day of the fight, the second game going 14 innings before Terry Moore knocked in Marty Marion with the winning run. Pete Reiser probably wrecked his career earlier in the game when he smashed into the concrete

115

wall trying to catch what turned into an inside the park homer by Enos Slaughter. Reiser hit .310 for the year, but after taking the batting crown in '41, it was obvious that Reiser would never be the same.

Despite the double defeat, the Dodgers still held first place and kept on winning, albeit at a less frequent pace. The Cardinals certainly were picked up by the 2 wins, and they continued to stay right behind the Dodgers. Then the Dodgers finally began to hit their slump. On August 8, Whit Wyatt was beaten by the dismal Bees 2–0. Durocher was in fine form, as the needling got heavy and head-hunting got out of control. The Dodgers looked like they were starting to panic by trying to shave the Bees. At this point, the Dodgers were becoming the team most likely to be invited to a lynching—its own, thanks to their bloodletting style of play. The National League issued orders to the Dodgers to cut back on the beanballs, but it did little good. Other teams, like the Cubs, brawled with the Dodgers and tried to beat them at their own game, but all it did was incite possible riots.

The Cardinals, playing more sedate ball, refused to give up. An 8-game winning streak just ended when the Brooklyn beasts arrived for the last time in St. Louis. The usual acrimony went on, but for a change, there was no wrestling to go with the game. Max Lanier downed the Dodgers 7–1 in the opener; then the Cardinals went out and tied the game the next day in the thirteenth before winning an inning later. Game 3 was one that duplicated the previous game in the score, 2–1, again in favor of the home team, and it took 10 innings to play. The Dodgers escaped town with a conventional 4–1 win in the last game, still in first by 5½ games. "We'll keep after them," said the pilot of St. Louis. Indeed they did.

On September 10 the top two teams in the league were in the Big Apple, the Cardinals visiting the Giants while the Dodgers hosted the Cubs. Lon Warneke, who had been sold by the Cardinals earlier in the year to the Cubs, started for Chicago and downed Brooklyn 10–2. Meanwhile, lefty Howie Pollet knocked off the Giants 5–1. The Dodgers now saw their lead cut down to just 2 games. The Dodgers were 94–44 after that day's action and were now 10–9 in their last 19 games. The Cardinals, at 92–46, were 27–5 in their last 32 contests. Now the two teams were to meet with the pennant on the line in a 2-game set in Brooklyn.

Mort Cooper did not have a regular number on his uniform that year, and for a strange reason. Every time Cooper went for a win, he would get into the uniform of the man whose number matched Cooper's win total if he was victorious on that day. On the eleventh, Cooper was wearing Coaker Triplett's uniform, number 20, as he went for win number twenty. No Dodger got to second base that day as Cooper tossed a three-hit shutout, winning 3–0. On the twelfth, Max Lanier got the call and he pitched a gem. Whitey Kurowski belted a 2-run homer in the second, which was enough to give Lanier a 2–1 win. Durocher had a fit when the umpire called Mickey Owen out on a close play in the seventh, but it did no good. The Dodgers and Cardinals were now tied for first.

The next day, the Cardinals lost to the last-place Phillies 2–1 in the ninth at Philadelphia. The Dodgers had a shot to keep first place for themselves, but instead they dropped a twin bill to the Reds. The Cardinals now led by half a game. The Dodgers were so incensed over the 2 losses that they sent the Reds a telegram accusing them of sending out the best pitchers they had against the Dodgers. The Reds replied with an X-rated telegram of their own. The Dodgers, who had looked like world beaters such a short time before, now were in their desperate hours.

Both teams won at a brisk pace for the rest of the season, but the Cardinals now were in the driver's seat. The Dodgers entered September 27 still hoping that they could regain the lead. But time had run out, because the Dodgers, although beating the Phillies 4–3 on that day, saw that the Cardinals were beating the Cubs. Ernie White killed off the Dodgers by nailing the Cubs 9–2 in the first game of a twin bill that day, clinching the pennant for the Cardinals. After winning the second game, the Cardinals posted a club-record 106–48 mark, giving the Dodgers a second-place finish despite their 104–50 record. The Brooklyn team was 2 games out when the season ended. The "St. Louis Swifties," as New York sports cartoonist Willard Mullin called them, had done the amazing, going 43–9 down the stretch. The Cardinals led the league in practically every important team category, topping the league in runs scored (755), fewest runs allowed (482), doubles (282), triples

(69), average (.268), slugging (.379), strikeouts by pitchers (651), shutouts (18), and ERA (2.55). Stan Musial, in his first full year in the bigs, hit .315. Mort Cooper led the league with a 1.78 ERA and 22 wins. It was a true team effort.

The 1942 World Series pitted the Cardinals against the Yankees for the third time in the history of the classic. Both teams had split the first two series played between them, and the odds-makers favored New York to take the championship for the second straight year. The Yankees had won their pennant rather easily and had a club that was as well rounded as the Cardinals.

The series opened on September 30 in Sportsman's Park, and it was Cooper facing Red Ruffing. Both pitchers breezed along for 3 innings until the Yankees scored one in the fourth and another in the fifth. Ruffing was gunning for a record 7 series wins and he held the locals hitless until Terry Moore singled with one out in the eighth. Unfortunately, the Cardinals were seemingly dead by that point, since the Yankees scored 3 more runs in the top of the frame to increase their lead to 5–0. It looked like a whitewash was coming after 2 more runs were scored by the visitors in the ninth, but the Cardinals launched an attack in the end. With one out left in the game, the Cardinals raked Ruffing for several hits and walks before Spud Chandler put out the fire with the tying runs on base. Four errors by the Cardinals helped the Yankees hang on to win 7–4.

The next day it was the Yankees' turn to play catch-up. The Cardinals scored 2 quick runs in the first off of starter Ernie Bonham. After the Cardinals tacked on another run in the seventh, Johnny Beazley looked like an easy winner. Instead, Charlie Keller cracked a 3-run homer in the eighth off of the 21-game winner, tying the game. In their eighth, though, the Cardinals came right back when Musial doubled home Slaughter to give St. Louis the final lead. In the ninth, the Yankees tried to rally again when Tuck Stainback tried for third on a hit, but Slaughter threw into third and Whitey Kurowski put the tag on Stainback, killing the rally.

In game 3 at New York, Ernie White and Spud Chandler pitched a great game. In the third, Kurowski scored on a hit by Jimmy Brown, a run that was aided when Marty Marion had a "do-over." The Yankees protested that Marion hit the ball twice with his bat when trying to bunt, so he had to bat again. Marion then got an infield hit on the "second" at bat. The Cardinals added another run in the ninth when Slaughter singled home Brown. White got the win in the 2–0 victory. In the fourth game, Cooper and Hank Borowy faced each other, but neither lasted to the finish. Entering the fourth, the Cardinals were behind 1–0 when Borowy was savaged in a 6-run attack. The Yankees countered with 5 runs of their own in the sixth, tying the game up and sending the Cardinals ace to the shower. St. Louis tacked on 2 runs in the seventh and 1 more in the ninth, and those runs made reliever Max Lanier a 9–6 winner. Atley Donald took the loss in relief for New York.

In the fifth game, the Cardinals had another four-error game, but this time the Cardinals overcame. St. Louis fell behind 1–0 in the first, tied it in the fourth, was down by 1 after that frame ended, then tied it in the sixth as Beazley pitched well. In the ninth, Kurowski belted a 2-run homer off of Ruffing, breaking the veteran's try for an eighth series win. The Yankees tried to rally in the ninth, but a pickoff and a blown bunt gave the Cardinals a 4–2 win and 4 straight series wins as they captured their first world championship since 1934 and their fourth in six series appearances.

Thus the Cardinals had overcome incredible odds to post another world championship. The Dodgers had gotten off to a record-setting pace but still failed, as the Cardinals caught and finally passed them, winning fans in many cities tired of the vicious tactics of the Brooklyn team. The Cardinals then slayed the mighty Yankees, taking 4 straight after dropping the opener. No team had beaten the Yankees in 4 straight series games since the Giants did it in 1922. Now the Cardinals were the kings of baseball, the St. Louis Swifties that hustled their way from also-rans to the top of the heap. Stan Musial proved to be a helluva player, even if he did hit only .222 in the series. The home-grown Cardinals were a family, a team that got along better than others, a team that had major league players coming to St. Louis with experience of playing with one another down on the farm. At this time, other teams had farm systems, but no team was able to put out so many great players, and this made the Cardinals the only big league team that was composed mainly of men coming from within their own organization. The farm system was the wave of the future, and teams that did not realize it were going to be in the second division. It's no coincidence that the top two teams of 1942 got to the series thanks to a great farm system. The Yankees had found the way in the other league, and that's why they were on top over there.

Keeping the Cardinals at the top via the farm system was going to be tough for the next few years. World War II was claiming more and more players at both the major and minor league levels, and baseball wondered if it should keep going. President Roosevelt told the commissioner that as long as it was possible, baseball should continue operations, since people working at night for the war effort would then have some diversion to escape to. Night games would be curtailed, especially in the East. Baseball had a good race in 1942, so the prospects for attendance were good. The minors contained a lot of draft-age players, so the Cardinals were worried about a possible loss of many prospects. It would not be the first time if it did happen. A few years earlier, in 1938, the Cardinals lost about 100 minor leaguers when Commissioner Landis let them become free agents, due to "irregularities" in the way the Cardinals were running their farm system. One player who got away in this decision was Pete Reiser, who went on to have some fine years with the Dodgers. Branch Rickey seethed over that decision but he made sure that it would not occur again.

As 1943 opened, the Cardinals were shocked to find that they would be without the services of Branch Rickey. The Mahatma had decided that the challenge of running the Cardinals had passed, and there were also rumors that he and Sam Breadon no longer could get along. Evidently, *philosophical differences* were the cause of the rift between Rickey and Breadon and Rickey decided to leave. What made the decision so shocking was the fact that Rickey not only was leaving St. Louis, but he was going to the hated Brooklyn Dodgers. Larry McPhail had gone into the military after the 1942 season was over, and the Dodgers pursued Rickey with the lure of more money and more power, lures that Rickey found too good to pass up. The Mahatma would go on to build a great farm system for the Dodgers (who were still relying mostly on trades to build the team) and bring about the integration of the majors, a move that was to become just as important as the creation of the farm system.

Things looked even tougher for the Cardinals on the field. First, Sam Breadon decided to take over the general manager job himself, which scared the players, because he was thought to be even tighter with money than Rickey. Stan Musial was holding out for a bigger raise, and Breadon was playing hardball with him. Eventually, both sides settled their differences and Musial signed. Second, the war now took away Slaughter, Moore, Beazley, and Crespi before the season opened and Pollet was due to leave soon. Two-thirds of the best outfield in the league were gone, and Musial, who was only in his second year, would now have to be the big gun in the lineup and a leader in the clubhouse. The war's pinch was being felt all over baseball as more stars were being taken, so at least the Cardinals were not alone in losing key men.

Harry Walker, brother of Brooklyn's Dixie Walker, took over in center field while Debs Garms (acquired by Breadon in a *trade!*) would platoon with Johnny Hopp in left in the early going while Ray Sanders and Lou Klein formed a new right side of the infield. Harry Brecheen would replace Beazley in the rotation. All of the replacements did the trick, as St. Louis got off to a good start. As expected, the Dodgers were right in the race, and it looked like the two teams might reverse the roles that they had played the year before. In July, the two bitter enemies were again at each other's throats after Les Webber, by now becoming Public Enemy Number One in St. Louis, tried to stick a few into the ear of Musial. Walker Cooper then followed with a ground out and stepped on Augie Galan, the Dodger first baseman. Mickey Owen then jumped Cooper, and the usual fight broke out. The fight put plenty of kick into the Cardinals, who took 4 straight from the Dodgers en route to 11 straight wins. Once the streak was over, the Cardinals had a nice lead as the Dodgers faded away.

The war had, at this time, another effect on baseball. Besides taking players, the military took rubber, so the baseball had a new center. Nineteen-forty-three was the year of "balata ball," the name given to the cheapened substitute for rubber in the center of the baseball. Balata was heavier, and the use of the "balata ball" caused plenty of low-scoring games. Run scoring was down compared to the same point in 1942, and attendance dipped as well as the kind of baseball played before 1920 was making a comeback. Teams that still had old baseballs were allowed to use them, and in games that used the old ball hitting did improve. Once the difference between the old and new baseballs was proven, the balata ball was altered to be livelier.

No matter what ball was used, the Cardinals had little trouble hitting or throwing it. Musial won the batting title that 1943 season with a nifty .357. (Maybe he would have hit .400 if the balata ball wasn't used at all.) Every regular hit at least .280 that year, except Danny Litwhiler, who, after coming in another Breadon deal, took over in left field and hit "only" .279. Despite going into the service, Howie Pollet won the ERA title at 1.75 (until 1950, a pitcher could win the ERA crown by pitching 10 complete games, rather than pitching as many innings as his team's games played) and Max Lanier had a 1.90 mark while Mort Cooper checked in with a 2.30 ERA, so the Cardinals had the three lowest ERA pitchers. Overall, the Cardinals dominated the league. They finished the year with a 105–49 record, 18 games ahead of the Reds and 23 ½ games ahead of the slumping third-place Dodgers. The Cardinals were tops in team batting, slugging, ERA, shutouts, complete games, strikeouts, and fewest runs allowed. Breadon had shown himself to be good at doing something Branch Rickey was always reluctant to do— making trades.

The Yankees also dominated their league in 1943, taking the flag by 13½ over the surprising Washington Senators. (The war years seemed to transform longtime losers in the American League into surprising contenders, as 1944 would prove.) The Yankees topped their league in runs scored, triples, homers, slugging, ERA, complete games, and fewest runs allowed. Most people considered the series a toss-up as to who would win. The Cardinals surprised the Yankees in 1942, so another St. Louis win would not shock this time. The Yankees, being the Yankees, would not shock anyone in any given series if they won.

Because of wartime travel restrictions, the first 3 games were slated for New York, and this would seem to give the Yankees the edge. The series opened on October 5 and pitted Lanier against Spud Chandler. An error and wild pitch by Lanier proved costly to the Cardinals, as the Yankees took advantage and picked up a 4–2 win. The next day the Cardinals evened the series as Cooper gave up just six hits and was staked to a 4–1 lead going into the ninth. The Yankees rallied for 2 runs in the ninth, but Cooper hung on to pitch a 4–3 complete-game victory. In the third game the Cardinals took a 2–1 lead into the eighth when the Yankees got a bases-loaded triple by Billy Johnson off of Al Brazle, part of a 5-run rally that caused the Cardinals to lose 6–2.

Back in St. Louis on October 10 to resume the series, the Cardinals turned to Lanier to even the series. Lanier gave up only four hits in seven innings and left trailing 1–0. Ray Sanders scored on an error to tie it in the seventh, but reliever Harry Brecheen allowed an eighth-inning run that beat him 2–1. The next day Chandler scattered 10 hits en route to a 2–0 shutout win against Cooper. The Yankees had regained the world championship.

Despite the series loss, the Cardinals were still a strong team that looked to dominate as the 1944 season arrived. The Cardinals lost some more players to the war, such as Lou Klein, but that farm system continued to churn out excellent replacements. Emil Verban took Klein's place at second, and he would prove to be a fine replacement. (No, Cubs fans, Verban did *not* play for your team in 1945; he was still a Cardinal then.) Overall, the Cardinals were lucky to retain the nucleus of their 1943 lineup, including Musial. The pitching staff, though, was hit hard, but replacements like Ted Wilks, Fred Schmidt, and George Munger came in and did the trick.

The Cardinals jumped off to a great start, and the race was over before it even started. The Pirates of Frankie Frisch provided a little competition, but it was indeed little. The Dodgers were no fun at all in 1944, as they plunged right into seventh place, shocking everybody. Sam Breadon was pleased as his team went out and beat every other team's brains out day in and day out. The year was certainly sweet for Breadon, as the team of his former employee, Branch Rickey, was struggling while his own was now the best in baseball. However, there was one thing that worried Breadon greatly, and it was something he had not worried about for a long time.

The St. Louis Browns were finally rising from the dead. This longtime disaster had made some steady progress under the leadership of Luke Sewell but still had not attracted much attention. Then, in 1944, the Browns found themselves in a pennant race, something they had known little about since the mid-1920s. Breadon looked with horror as his landlord battled the Yankees in some games that actually had some importance. The Browns began bringing in nice-sized crowds as they battled the Yankees and Tigers for the flag. The boss of the Cardinals feared that the longtime losers were going to recapture St. Louis from him after all the years of hard work and much money had been poured into his club to make it tops in town.

As 1944 progressed, the Cardinals saw their gate receipts fall off, thanks to the lack of a contender in the National League. It was certain that the Browns rose to contention not because they were a great team, but because their regulars (all 4-Fs) were not drafted into the war. The other teams in the American League had lost players like Bob Feller, Ted Williams, Joe DiMaggio, and Hank Greenberg, and here were the Browns with George McQuinn, Mark Christman, and Mike Kreevich staying with their team and getting the job done. The Browns had not caught up with the league; the league had finally caught up with the Browns by sinking to their level. It was still hard to believe, though, that a team that was just three years earlier due to be packed off to Los Angeles (but was saved by Pearl Harbor) was now in the hunt. Needless to say, Browns attendance more than doubled. Breadon bristled.

In late September the Cardinals had already wrapped up the pennant in convincing fashion, but the Browns were still in the race. In the last weekend, the Browns took two from the Yankees while the Tigers lost, giving the Browns their first pennant in their forty-two-year history. Fans went berserk with joy, as the series would be an all St. Louis affair. Nineteen-forty-four was the year of St. Louis.

In town, many people wanted to see the Browns win the series just for the sake of sentimentality. The Browns were one of only two teams that, entering 1944, never claimed a world championship. (The other team was the Brooklyn club, but at least they won three pennants to this point.) The odds certainly did not favor the Browns, who led the American League only in most strikeouts in posting a rather weak 89–65 record to claim the pennant. The

Cardinals, on the other hand, had gone 105–49 and led the National League in runs, doubles, homers, batting, slugging, strikeouts, shutouts, ERA, fewest runs allowed, fewest errors, most double plays turned, and fielding. For a change, the Cardinals were in the role of the heavily favored villain while the Browns were in the role of beloved underdog.

Not since 1922 had a World Series been played only in one park. (That year, the Giants and Yankees both called the Polo Grounds home.) The Cardinals had the home field advantage in the first 2 games, and in the first game Mort Cooper faced Denny Galehouse. Cooper was great, allowing just 2 hits in 7 innings. Unfortunately, both came in the fourth. Gene Moore singled and then George McQuinn homered, giving the Browns a 2–0 lead. A sacrifice fly by Ken O'Dea scored Marty Marion in the ninth, but the Browns hung on to win 2–1. Bedlam ensued, as the mighty Cardinals were down by a game already.

The second game was a hard-fought battle pitting Max Lanier against Nelson Potter. The Cardinals scored 1 in the third and 1 in the fourth to take the first lead, but the Browns then tied it in the seventh with 2 runs off the tough Lanier. The score remained tied at 2 when the Cardinals squeezed across a run in the eleventh. Ray Sanders singled, went to second on a sacrifice, then scored on pinch hitter O'Dea's single. Blix Donnelly won the game in relief, while Bob Muncrief lost it.

In the third game the Browns were the home team, and after it was over Sam Breadon probably was scared to death about losing St. Louis to the Browns. After the Cardinals got a run in the first, the Browns put up a four-spot in the third and sent starter Ted Wilks to the shower before it was over. The Cardinals picked up another run in the seventh, but the Browns got 2 insurance runs in the bottom of the frame to wrap up a 6–2 win. The A.L. champs now had a 2–1 lead in the series, and thoughts of a world championship danced in the heads of Browns fans.

Harry Brecheen got the ball for the fourth game and was opposed by Sig Jakucki. Musial cracked a 2-run homer in the first, getting the Cardinals rolling. The Cardinals scored 2 more in the third and 1 more in the sixth en route to a 5–1 win over the Browns. The fifth game was another pitching duel, as Cooper and

Galehouse faced each other. Galehouse allowed only 6 hits, but 2 of them were solo homers by Sanders and Danny Litwhiler. Cooper scattered 7 hits and picked up the 2–0 win. The Cardinals were now in the driver's seat, where most people had thought they would be. On October 9 the series wound up with Lanier downing Potter 3–1 after the Cardinals erased a 1–0 deficit by scoring 3 in the fourth. The Cardinals were world champs for the second time in three years, and Sam Breadon was relieved. Had the Browns won the series, St. Louis might have turned into a Browns town or at least given the Cardinals a tough time financially, like in the early days of Phil Ball. But it was not to be.

The Cardinals saved St. Louis for themselves, and they did it with some fine players. Musial won the Most Valuable Player award in 1943, and one year later Marty Marion got the honor. (He hit .267 and fielded brilliantly.) The draft, though, was to reach into St. Louis again, this time taking, among others, Stan Musial. Still, the Cardinals had a tough team to beat, and more replacements were brought in. For 1945 the Cardinals put Johnny Hopp (who had seen his playing time cut in recent years despite having solid years) in right field and called up a guy named Red Schoendienst to play left field, although he was basically an infielder. The pitching staff lost some more men, but Ken Burkhart was recalled from the minors and he would do well. The Cardinals were the heavy favorites to win their fourth straight flag despite their losses, and they would become the first team since the 1936–39 Yankees to do that if they would make it. The last (and only) National League team to do that was the 1921–24 Giants.

The Cardinals started well, but so did the Cubs, who had finished 30 games behind in 1944. Charlie Grimm was back in Chicago as the skipper, and he was getting good years out of people like Andy Pafko and Phil Cavarretta. Sam Breadon, who was making more trades in three years as the general manager than Branch Rickey seemed to make in his over twenty years in the job, picked up Buster Adams from the Phillies and bought pitcher Red Barrett from the Braves. Both players played key roles in the Cardinals' 1945 pennant chase. Adams drove in 101 runs with 20 homers and a .292 average while Barrett posted a sensational 21–9 record for St. Louis after going 2–3 for the Braves. It seemed that Breadon was one helluva trader.

Still, the two big moves were not enough to get the Cardinals that fourth straight flag. The infield of 1944 was left intact and the newcomers were great, but the Cubs were just a little better. The Yankees sold Hank Borowy to the Cubs (which killed the Yankees' chances for their league's pennant), and his 11–2 record with a league-leading 2.13 ERA was enough to get the Cubs into the series. The MVP award and batting title both went to Cavarretta. The Cardinals, though, were plenty tough. Whitey Kurowski became a fine hitter, batting .323 with 21 homers and 102 RBIs. The other three infielders hit between .276 and .278. Hopp hit .289. Schoendienst hit .278 and played well in left. On the hill, Barrett was joined by Burkhart (19–8, 2.90) as half of a potent one-two punch. The Cardinals did not lead the league in any team categories, but they finished just 3 games out at 95–59.

Breadon still kept an eye on the Browns, who were again in a pennant race. The Browns were joined by the Yankees and Tigers again, and also by another longtime disgrace in the Senators. As the season wore on, the Browns looked like they would win the flag while the Cardinals would not, which worried Breadon, but the Tigers ended up winning the flag when Hank Greenberg came back from the war late in the season and hit some key homers down the stretch. The Browns ended up in third place, 6½ games out. Breadon was pleased in that respect, as the Cubs faced the Tigers in a series that one scribe said "neither team [was] good enough to win."

Nineteen-forty-six would prove to be a big year, as hundreds of major and minor league players were released from the military and returned to play ball. All of the Cardinals' top stars were back in town, and they joined the guys who had done a good job filling in for them. The Cardinals had to make adjustments on the club to field their best possible team. Buster Adams would sit on the bench despite his fine 1945 season. Red Barrett would virtually disappear for 1946 after his brilliant year. It seemed like many of the World War II replacement players were unfairly discarded or ignored after the war was over, but there was only so much room on the roster. People like Barrett and Adams, Nick Etten (1945 RBI champ in the A.L.), and Tony Cuccinello (second in the A.L. with a .308 average in '45), and scores of others who played well and led their leagues in something ended up fading away on the field after the war and in the minds of their fans. It seemed like a cruel joke that the stars of World War II baseball were at the top one day and were gone almost overnight.

The Cardinals got their old stars back and got a new manger to lead them in Eddie Dyer. Billy Southworth, who had served the Cardinals well as a player in the 1920s, a minor league manager in the 1930s, and big league skipper in the 1940s, decided to leave the team for more money and a chance to build the perennially inept Boston Braves. Dyer was another longtime Cardinal employee who had done well in the minors and was brought up as another low-key manager, just like Southworth. Dyer was deemed the man to restore the Cardinals back to their now familiar perch atop the league.

Dyer decided to make some changes on the field. Stan Musial was shifted to first base, replacing Ray Sanders. At second, Red Schoendienst would take over for Emil Verban. The left side of the infield would remain in place with Marty Marion at short and Whitey Kurowski at third. Enos Slaughter would man right field again while Dyer decided to experiment in the other two outfield spots. Behind the plate, a rookie named Joe Garagiola would get some playing time. The pitching staff looked fearsome with Johnny Beazley, Max Lanier, Howie Pollet, Harry Brecheen, Al Brazle, Murry Dickson, and Ken Burkhart slated for much work.

One thing that greatly disturbed Sam Breadon, and his fellow owners for that matter, was a new organization called the Mexican League (not to be confused with the current minor league of the same name). The Pasquel brothers of Mexico decided to start a new major league by luring the top players of the National and American leagues with huge cash offers. Many players went after the big bucks in Mexico, even though baseball commissioner Happy Chandler (who replaced Kenesaw Landis in the job after his death in 1944) warned that any player jumping to the Mexican League would be suspended for five years. Despite the warnings of Chandler and the owners, many went to Mexico hoping to find paradise. Instead, most players who went to the new league found disaster.

The Cardinals opened the 1946 season as a favorite even though the Cubs were the defending champs. The Cardinals lost their first game 6–4 to the Pirates, but they did start off well. Unfortunately, the Dodgers of Leo Durocher also played well and moved into first place. The Dodgers were now bona fide contenders again, and their attitude was the same as it was in 1942, the last time the Dodgers had been in a race wire to wire. More hard sliding, more flashing spikes, more "stick it in his ear" came from the Brooklyn team as they regained their title of "Most Hated Team" in the National League. New players had done little to calm the Dodgers of Durocher down.

The Cardinals carried on, winning at a good pace. In May, the Cardinals went to Brooklyn to play the Dodgers for the first time in 1946. As usual, there was a good series. As usual, there was trouble. Max Lanier picked up an 11-inning victory to open the series, but as usual the game took a backseat to wrestling. This time, Enos Slaughter was the man being shaved by the Cardinals' favorite pitcher, Les Webber (what was it about Webber? This man went only 23–19 with a 4.19 ERA in six big league seasons, but he always seemed to be at the right place at the right time when it came to the Cardinals—in his ear; in his ear!) when the usual fight broke out. Slaughter bunted and Webber was run over as he went to field it. As most baseball fights went, this one was over quickly and no one got hurt. The Cardinals did well in the series, and then they left, still in the hunt. On this eastern trip, the Cardinals did lose big when it came to the roster. Three players—Max Lanier, Lou Klein, and Freddie Martin—decided the money offered for jumping to the Mexican League was too good to pass, so the trio headed south. The result was a suspension by Happy Chandler. When the three players got to Mexico, they discovered what other players had learned before them: that the Mexican League was falling apart and that the wealthy Pasquel brothers were losing their wealth. Not enough players jumped to Mexico to make the new league viable, and it was heading toward oblivion, taking with it the careers of many good players. Some players would get back to the "real" majors and do well (like Sal Maglie), but others, like

Max Lanier, would have only marginal success when they returned, their best years lost during the suspension (although most players were allowed to return before the five years passed). The Cardinals lost a key man who was 6–0 at the time. Breadon was furious, but there was nothing he could do. Stan Musial was also contacted by the Mexican League right after Lanier left, but lucky for both Musial and the Cardinals, Musial decided to stay put.

The Lanier defection was disastrous. The Cardinals went into a tailspin while the Dodgers kept winning with consistent ease. The Cubs and Billy Southworth's Braves were now gaining ground on the Cardinals from the other direction, and the Cardinals were heading for fourth place. On July 2 the Dodgers were 7½ games ahead of the Cardinals and it looked like the Brooklyn team was going to win the pennant. Then the Cardinals turned it around, closing the gap between themselves and Brooklyn while leaving the Cubs and Braves in the dust. On July 14, the Cardinals returned home to face the Dodgers in a 4-game set and were 4½ games out. The Cardinals swept a twin bill to open the series, winning 5–3 in the first game and taking the second 2–1 on a Kurowski sac fly in the twelfth. The Dodger lead was cut to 2½ games. The next day, the Cardinals pounded out a 10–4 win, cutting their deficit to 1½ games. The Cardinals then delivered the big blow when they got a pinch 3-run homer from Erv Dusak in the bottom of the ninth with the Dodgers ahead 4–2. The Dodgers lead shrank to a measly half game. The Cardinals moved into first two days later when they downed the Phillies while the Dodgers lost. But the Cardinals would not stay at the top for long.

At this point in the season, Howie Pollet was Atlas, holding up the Cardinals' pitching staff by pitching with practically no rest. When Lanier jumped to the Mexican League, Pollet had told Eddie Dyer that he would be available to pitch in relief if he got one day off after every start. It was not that the Cardinals were getting poor pitching from the rest of the staff, but Pollet figured that a good lefty would be best used if he was often used in key games. Besides, it would free up some time for the others, since Pollet had what's known as a "rubber arm," one that doesn't need much rest to stay effective. Pollet would turn out to be the league's best pitcher in 1946.

The Dodgers moved back into first place on July 24, even though the Cardinals beat them 2 out of 3 in Brooklyn soon after regaining first. Still, the Cardinals did not let up, staying close to the Dodgers for a month, looking for an opening. In late August the Dodgers returned to St. Louis for another pivotal 4-game set. On the first day, the Dodgers opened a twin bill by shading Pollet 3–2. In the second game, the Cardinals outslugged the Dodgers by a 14–8 score. In game 3, St. Louis moved into first with Murry Dickson's 2–1 win. The next day saw Kirby Higbe put Brooklyn back in a tie by winning 7–3. The day after that, the Cardinals jumped back into first alone by beating the Giants while the Dodgers were being beaten by the Cubs in Chicago. St. Louis soon held a 2½ game edge over Brooklyn.

In early September the Dodgers hosted the Cardinals in the last meeting of the two teams for the year. Brooklyn had won 9 of 10 entering this series and trailed by 1½ games. On the twelfth, Pollet knocked off the locals with a 10–2 win, leading from beginning to end. The Dodgers came through with a 4–3 win the next day at the expense of George Munger, who had returned from the military just a few months earlier. In the series finale, Durocher decided to be a wiseguy (in keeping with his reputation around the league) by sending a struggling youngster named Ralph Branca to start. Dyer packed his lineup with lefties, and after pitching to one batter, Branca was removed, and lefty Vic Lombardi was brought in. Or was *supposed* to. Instead, Branca was left in and wiseguy Durocher found that Branca was pretty good, as he allowed only 3 hits in winning 5–0. The Dodgers were just a half a game out.

The season continued as the Cardinals and Dodgers kept winning. The Cardinals still held first, but the Dodgers would not die. On September 27, the Dodgers tied the Cardinals for first with two days left in the season. The next day, the Dodgers knocked out the Braves 7–4 in Brooklyn while the Cardinals downed the Cubs in a night game at home. On the twenty-ninth, the Cubs shut out the Cardinals' hope for a flag by beating them 8–3. But the Dodgers also failed to come through with a win when former Cardinal Mort

Cooper blanked them for the Braves 4–0. The first tie for first in major league history was achieved. Brooklyn and St. Louis both held 96–58 records.

In New York, National League president Ford Frick flipped a coin and the Dodgers won the toss. The best of 3 playoff opened in St. Louis with an ailing Howie Pollet facing Ralph Branca (oh boy, *two* playoffs in one lifetime!), as Durocher hoped for lightning to strike twice. The only lightning coming in this game came from Cardinal bats, as they got 3 hits in the first inning, good for a run. The Dodgers tied it in the third, but then the Cardinals put the game away (and Branca, too) by getting 2 runs in the bottom of the third. In the seventh the Dodgers made it 3–2, but the key insurance run came when Musial tripled and scored on a single by Joe Garagiola. Pollet went on to kill a Dodger threat in the eighth and picked up his twenty-first win by a 4–2 score.

On October 3, after a travel day, the playoff resumed in Brooklyn. Murry Dickson faced Joe Hatten, and in the first an Ed Stevens RBI single scored Augie Galan, giving the locals a 1–0 lead. Ecstasy turned to agony in a hurry for Brooklyn when the Cardinals launched a 13-hit attack on Hatten and five unlucky relievers. In the second, St. Louis scored twice on a Marty Marion sac fly and an RBI single by Clyde Kluttz. In the fifth, 3 more runs came in when Enos Slaughter tripled home 2 runs and then scored on an Erv Dusak single. By the time the ninth inning finally rolled around, the Cardinals were ahead 8–1. The Dodgers rallied for three in the bottom of the frame, but it was too little, too late. The Cardinals clinched the pennant with a 98–58 mark and a win in the first pennant playoff ever.

The stats showed that the Cardinals won the 1946 pennant in their usual fashion. St. Louis was tops in runs scored, fewest runs allowed, doubles, average, slugging, complete games, shutouts, ERA, fewest errors, and fielding. Howie Pollet, despite an ailing arm that came from not warming up properly in a late-season game, went 21–10 with a 2.10 ERA. Pollet led the league in wins, ERA, and innings pitched as he became the league's top pitcher. Enos Slaughter was the RBI champ with 130, and Stan Musial picked up the batting title at .365. The Cardinals got fine years from almost everybody on the team, as everybody contributed in some way to the pennant-winning effort.

The 1946 World Series pitted the Cardinals against the hard-hitting Boston Red Sox. The Red Sox, under owner Tom Yawkey, were making their first visit to a series since 1918, when they beat the Chicago Cubs. The Red Sox had a tough lineup led by Ted Williams and had four topnotch starting pitchers; two of them, Tex Hughson and Boo Ferriss, won 20 games. Boston had won their pennant in a breeze, 12 games ahead of Detroit.

The series began on October 6 in St. Louis, and the Red Sox sent Hughson against Pollet. Both hurlers pitched well, with the Cardinals leading 2–1 in the ninth when Pinky Higgins hit a weird grounder that got through for an RBI to tie up the game. In the tenth, Rudy York cracked a homer to give Boston a 3–2 win. In the second game, Mickey Harris opposed Harry Brecheen and the latter was brilliant, allowing just four singles as the Cardinals scored 3 runs for him. St. Louis won the second game easily, 3–0.

After a travel day the series went to Boston. Boo Ferriss gave up only six hits as the locals got 3 first-inning runs and went on to beat Murry Dickson 4–0. In the fourth contest, the Cardinals did some hard hitting of their own for George Munger, pounding six pitchers for a 12–3 rout. Boston took a 3–2 series lead when Joe Dobson downed Pollet 6–3. Back in St. Louis for the sixth game, Brecheen scattered seven hits as he defeated Mickey Harris 4–1. The series was now tied at 3 games apiece.

The exciting seventh game took place at Sportsman's Park on October 15, and it had Dickson against Ferriss. Into the eighth inning Boston faced a 3–1 deficit, when they fought back. Glen Russell got a pinch single, then went to third on a pinch double by George Metkovich. Eddie Dyer brought in Brecheen, and he was escaping the danger until Dom DiMaggio doubled home the tying runs. In the bottom of the eighth, Slaughter singled against Bob Klinger. With two out and Slaughter still at first, Harry Walker hit a shot into left-center field. Slaughter took off at full speed and was rounding third when Johnny Pesky made what's now known in Boston as "the Hesitation" when he held onto the ball just a second too long when he was surprised to see Slaughter trying to score. Pesky fired it home, but Slaughter safely slid in, giving the Cardinals a 4–3 lead. Boston put a man on in the ninth, but Brecheen retired the Red Sox easily and the Cardinals were world champs for the third time in five seasons.

The Cardinals were clearly the top team in baseball again. They had beaten a hard-hitting team with solid pitching in the series after surviving another tight pennant race with a fine Dodger team. The Cardinals drew over a million people for the first time in their history in 1946, an amazing feat for a team in a small market that had to share it with another team. True, the increase in the gate was due to the end of the war, but a team that plays poorly will not draw well under any circumstances. After all, the Cardinals outdrew four teams in the league and some more in the other.

Looking back at the 1942–46 Cardinals, it is hard to believe this team is not considered among the all-time greats. The Cardinals won four pennants and three world titles in those years, and in the one year they didn't win the pennant they were a very close second. From 1942 to 1944 the Cardinals won either 105 or 106 games, quite a feat at any time in baseball history. The Cardinals had excellent hitting, tight defense, and stingy pitching, and in the years they won the pennant the team topped the league often in most categories. The Cardinals averaged 102 wins a year from 1942 to 1946, and few teams can match such an average over a five-year period. Still, this club is slighted when talk of the all-time greats starts.

It is unfortunate that the World War II years of baseball have always been downplayed. True, the quality of the major leagues was down at that time, but many players did well in those years and are now forgotten. Yes, some longtime losers like the St. Louis Browns and Washington Senators rose to challenge a team like the New York Yankees (whose teams of the war years seem to get more credit for their play than the Cardinals, even though the Yankees won only two flags in those years) a couple of times, but that should not detract from the overall fine play seen in the big leagues at that time. The St. Louis Cardinals should not be penalized for doing well from 1942 to 1946 simply because of the war. Those Cardinals teams may not have been *the* greatest of teams in baseball history, but they certainly should merit consideration as one of the best. After all, when will another team come along and win about 102 games per year for five years while being built almost entirely from its farm system? And win four pennants and three world championships to boot?

VIII

The Cardinals entered 1947 as the most recent dynasty in the game. As usual, they were picked to either win it or at least stay close to the top. The Dodgers were also favored to win the flag. Jim Hearn was added to the pitching staff from the minors for the 1947 campaign, adding another good arm to a strong pitching staff. It looked like St. Louis was ready for another flag.

The Cardinals got off to a flying flop, dropping 9 in a row early on as the Dodgers took off. Stan Musial had appendicitis. The team was slumping at the plate. Rumor had it that in Brooklyn the Cardinals would forfeit rather than play a team that had a black on it, one named Jackie Robinson. Obviously, that Rickey was at it again. The forfeit talk passed as the Cardinals did play in Brooklyn and were whipped by the locals, now under leadership of the more sedate Burt Shotton. (Leo Durocher was suspended for hanging around with gamblers.) In June, the Cardinals found themselves in an unfamiliar and uncomfortable place: last place. Another rumor now stated that Sam Breadon was ready to sell the team, one that looked like it was going from dynasty to disaster in just one year.

Then the Cardinals rose from the dead. Breadon picked up Ron Northey in a deal, and he did well. Ducky Medwick returned as a pinch hitter and did well. The rest of the hitting came around as Musial recovered from his illness. The Cardinals swept 4 from the front-running Dodgers, a sorely needed tonic for St. Louis. By August, the Cardinals were back in where they belonged and won 8 straight as they began pressuring Brooklyn.

As September opened, the Cardinals were making the Dodgers sweat yet again. St. Louis had closed to within 5 games of Brooklyn when injuries hit. Red Schoendienst went down. Then Whitey Kurowski. For a change, the Dodgers handled the Cardinals easily in the last month, going 7–3 against them in ten head-to-head meetings. The Cardinals got close, but this time they could not pull it off. The Dodgers picked up a 94–60 record, finishing 5 games ahead of the Cardinals. Still, the Cardinals battled back from the cellar and got back into the race, so the year wasn't a total loss.

As things turned out, those rumors about Breadon selling the club were true. Breadon was seventy years old and spent 1947 looking for a buyer who would keep the Cardinals in town while continuing to run them right. Breadon was worried that if he died while owning the team his wife would run the team into the ground, like former owner Mrs. Schuyler Britton did. Or even worse, the Cardinals might end up like the Dodgers of the 1920s and 1930s, falling into the hands of feuding heirs who would run the team into the ground so badly that a bank would have to take over the team. Once a bank took over the club, who knew what would happen? The bank might simply sell the team to outside interests, who might get permission to move the team to one of many cities that were now clamoring for big league ball.

In November 1947 Breadon sold the team to Robert Hannegan and Fred Saigh. The new owners pledged to keep the Cardinals in St. Louis while running the team as prudently as possible. The new owners expressed interest in building a new stadium for the Cardinals but decided to remain the tenants of the Browns for the time being. Everyone agreed that Hannegan and Saigh had bought themselves one of the top teams in baseball. Sam Breadon, the man who had bought into one of the worst teams baseball ever had, one that knew nothing but failure on the field for decades and was heading for bankruptcy, had allowed Branch Rickey to turn a total disaster around, and now he was able to turn over a team that other teams were emulating. Sam Breadon proved that a team in a small market could not only survive, but flourish. The Breadon way was tough for many players and even fans to swallow, but it worked brilliantly. The way Sam Breadon (and Branch Rickey) turned the Cardinals around is a lesson that the struggling ball clubs of today should follow in building up themselves, rather than crying about being in small markets and saying they can't compete with the bigger and richer teams.

The Cardinals made a few more moves for 1948 and hoped to get back to the top for their new bosses. Instead, the team was hit hard by injuries to several key players and staggered at the start. Stan Musial, though, was a rock. The Man rang up his best numbers ever in 1948 while winning his third MVP award. (The others came in 1943 and 1946.) Musial led the league in runs (135), hits (230), doubles (46), triples (18), RBIs (131), average (.376), and slugging (.702) as well as in total bases. Musial had to carry the team, as the hitting was in a slump in the first half. In the second half, the Cardinals finally came through as they made a move. The Cardinals had little trouble with the Dodgers in their head-to-head meetings in the early part of the season, but now it was the usually bad Boston Braves that were the team to be dealt with. Billy Southworth had done an amazing job taking that poor brother of the Red Sox and turning it into a contender. The Dodgers had been in last place, but they finally got their act together to join the Cardinals, the Braves, and the also surprising Pirates in the four-team race. The Dodgers began beating the Cardinals regularly in the second half, and that helped to keep the Cardinals out of first place. Late in the season the Cardinals went to Boston in an attempt to stave off elimination. St. Louis knocked out Brave ace Warren Spahn, and it looked like the Cardinals were on their way, as they won. But the Braves took care of business, and they eventually went on to outlast the Cardinals by 6½ games.

After the 1948 season, it was becoming obvious that the Cardinals were starting to have some problems. The two new owners were at odds over who would have the greater influence in the day-to-day affairs of the team and also how much money should be spent in running the team. An even worse problem was that the Cardinal farm system was no longer churning out great players. Other teams had finally sent out scouts in greater numbers to sign young players to their farm systems. It did not help matters that the Cardinals were ignoring black talent at this time while other teams did not. In the long run, this big error would damage the Cardinals severely.

Still, St. Louis was a club not to be taken lightly in 1949. A few changes were made (like the selling of Murry Dickson to the Pirates for $125,000), and the St. Louis squad was expected to contend, if not win. Eddie Dyer was still considered a fine pilot despite two straight second-place finishes, and many thought the Cardinals would get the job done in 1949. Things weren't helped by the sale of Dickson, at the behest of Bob Hannegan. Not long after the deal, partner Fred Saigh bought Hannegan out. Fred Saigh was now the chief of a team many thought would win the pennant.

The Cardinals started well, as they were in good health for the first time in three years. As usual, the Dodgers were right there in the race, holding first place. It looked like another Cardinal-Dodger battle, as the rest of the league was not up to the task this year. Both teams went back and forth, trading first and second place. At the All-Star break, the Dodgers led by just half a game. The Cardinals also got a boost at this time when the three jumpers to the Mexican League—Lou Klein, Freddie Martin, and Max Lanier— were allowed to return from their exile under commissioner Happy Chandler.

After the break the Cardinals invaded Brooklyn for a series of 4 games at Stan Musial's favorite enemy park. George Munger outpitched Preacher Roe as a Musial homer helped St. Louis to a 3–1 win. The next day saw the Cardinals scratch their way back from behind in the ninth as they shaded the Dodgers 5–4. In game 3, the Man put on a hitting clinic by going four for four in hitting a single, a double, a triple, and a homer (hitting for the cycle) as he led the Cardinals to another win and first place. The last game ended in a tie, so the Cardinals left Brooklyn in first place.

As August came, the Cardinals and Dodgers were still duking it out. In a tough pennant race like the one in 1949, every game is closely scrutinized, every play is considered pivotal, for it could lead to the loss of 1 game, and 1 game could spell the difference between finishing first and finishing second. Years later, Musial still recalled a game against the Giants in August that might have made the difference in the 1949 race. In the game that the Man recalled, the Cardinals got a 2-run homer from Nippy Jones in the first that seemed to give them a 2–0 lead. Wrong. The third base umpire had called a balk on the pitcher, and the homer was disallowed. The Giants then went on to win the game 3–1. Under the rules of the time, the team getting the homer in such a situation did not have the option to take the homer or the balk (who would have taken the balk?), so the Cardinals ended up losing the game.

As Musial stated in his autobiography: "In a race that close, every quirk of fate seems to sneer and jeer." How true.

In September, the two contenders were slumping when the Cardinals went to Brooklyn for the latest in a long series of pivotal games at Ebbets Field. In the first game of a twin bill that made up for the July tie, the Cardinals got a 5–3 win. Musial was doing his usual thing in Ebbets Field, that is, making the locals cry in their beers with more hits. A homer in the second game gave Howie Pollet a 2–0 lead. Unfortunately, Pollet was facing one of the toughest clutch pitchers ever in Preacher Roe. Roe was a tough cookie to swallow at any time of the year, but in the big games he was something special. After the homer, Roe settled down and the Dodgers fought back to win 4–3. Don Newcombe, a man who's been accused of not being like Roe for ages (unfairly), then pitched a neat shutout in the series finale. Then the Cardinals visited the Polo Grounds to take on the Giants, now managed by Leo Durocher. Leo was in fine form (stick it in his ear; stick it in his ear), but the Cardinals took 3 of 4.

The Dodgers next paid a visit to St. Louis for a big series (again) to determine who would go to the World Series. The Cardinals were up by 1½ games, and the Dodgers were ready, sending Newcombe in to open the series. Max Lanier, who had struggled after his return, battled with Newcombe in a great game. In the ninth, the game was scoreless when the Cardinals loaded the bases. Joe Garagiola, who seems to poke fun at his career nowadays despite being a darned good catcher and clutch hitter, then came through with a single, giving Lanier a 1–0 win. Roe then came up with another gem as he shut out St. Louis 5–0. In the series finale, Joe Hatten easily downed the locals with a 19–6 massacre. The Dodgers were still in second, but only by half a game.

The season continued with a trip to Pittsburgh, where Murry Dickson, late of the Cardinals and now of the Pirates, was waiting for revenge for the trade that had sent him to such a weak team. The Pirates were not happy with a slide that Enos Slaughter made into the plate when the two teams met at Sportsman's Park. Now the Pirates were stating that they'd rather see the Dodgers win the flag than the Cardinals. It seemed that the two contenders had now reversed roles in the eyes of the rest of the league. Under Leo

Durocher everyone hated the Dodgers while the Cardinals were better liked. Now the Pirates called the Cardinals beasts and wanted revenge.

The Cardinals entered Pittsburgh exhausted but still on top. The Pirates were out of the race and wanted badly to get St. Louis. In the first game, the Cardinals lost a tough game 6–4 when a guy named Tom Saffell hit his second homer of the year (and of his life, one of just six in his four years in the bigs), a grand slammer that killed George Munger. Two days later, Murry Dickson went out and knocked off Gerry Staley 7–2 while the Dodgers swept 2 from the Braves. The Cardinals were out of first. The St. Louis nightmare continued in Chicago, when the Cardinals blew a lead to the last-place Cubs and lost 6–5. The next day, the Dodgers were beaten by the Phillies, so the Cardinals still had hope to sneak into first. Instead, Harry Brecheen gave up three runs early and the Cardinals were on their way to a 3–1 loss to the Cubs. Despite the two losses to Chicago, the Cardinals *still* had a shot. St. Louis finally downed the Cubs 13–5 as Pollet won his twentieth game. All that was needed now was a Phillies win against the Dodgers, but it didn't happen. The Dodgers took ten innings, but they shaded the Phillies by 2 runs to win the pennant.

And so the 1940s ended for the Cardinals. The St. Louis Cardinals had taken the baseball world by storm in the 1940s, winning four pennants and three world championships. St. Louis also had an all-city series in 1944. The Cardinals finished second five times and third once. In every single season the Cardinals posted a winning record. Except for 1940, the Cardinals were in the race from start to finish every year of the decade. Besides winning four flags, the Cardinals showed their mettle by finishing second by only 1 game (1949), 2½ games (1941), 3 games (1945), 5 games (1947), and 6½ games (1948). In the 1940s, the Cardinals won 960 games and lost 580, the best mark in baseball during the decade. (The Yankees were second with a 929–609 mark.) The Cardinals had a .623 winning percentage in the 1940s, meaning they averaged a 96–58 record for each season of the decade. With three 100-win seasons the Cardinals were the only team in the National League to get over that mark more than once. (The 1942 Dodgers, you'll remember, won 104 games but finished second.) Only the Yankees had more than one 100-win season besides the Cardinals (1941 and 1942), so the St. Louis Cardinals can be considered *the* team of the 1940s.

Despite all of the impressive things that the Cardinals had accomplished in the 1940s, change was inevitable. The Cardinals entered the decade possessing perhaps the finest mind the game ever had in Branch Rickey. Rickey set the trends that other teams followed, but only after the Cardinals had reached the heights of champs. With Sam Breadon as the supreme boss, the Cardinals not only won often, but they won with class, and they earned the respect that they were entitled to as a dominating team. The Cardinals had gotten to the top in a way that could be termed the Cardinal way, which meant spending money wisely, teaching players in the minors the fundamentals until they become automatic, building the big league club's nucleus from within the organization, and making a few prudent trades. While other teams built themselves mostly with trades, getting old and costly players in the process, the Cardinals had built up their team cheaply and through young players who would be around for a long time. This was the way of Breadon and Rickey. But by 1950, they were no longer around.

Part IV

The House of Cards in a Breeze (1950–59)

I

Yes, Sam Breadon and Branch Rickey were no longer around as a new decade opened. For the first time since the dismal 1910s opened, the Cardinals would open a decade without the two titans of St. Louis baseball. Still, the Cardinals were not hurting, at least on the surface. Fred Saigh seemed to provide sound leadership after buying out his partner. The Cardinals certainly held title to the best hitter in the National League in Stan Musial, a man who had done much already, and he wasn't even thirty yet.

But there were problems, big problems. Since other teams had by now caught onto the idea of a successful farm system, the Cardinals had trouble signing new prospects. The Yankees were sending scouts all over the place as they tried to maintain their dominance in the American League. Worse, Branch Rickey was over in Brooklyn as 1950 began and he sat atop a formidable minor league empire of his own. Prior to Rickey's arrival in 1943 the Dodgers had had only a small minor league system while the big league club, building itself by trades, let many youngsters languish in the minors. Rickey changed things by expanding the Dodger farm system as he went all over to look for any prospects that might make good in the majors someday. Branch Rickey also realized that sooner or later it would be time to integrate the major leagues, and in this respect he was again ahead of his peers. Building the minor league farm system and signing Jackie Robinson have to go down as two of the biggest developments in baseball in this century. For decades the Negro leagues were bypassed as a talent pool for the majors to explore, even though players in the Negro leagues were some of the finest around. Between other teams catching up to the Cardinals with minor league systems and integration, the Cardinals would suffer a great deal in the 1950s.

As 1950 opened, the Cardinals were certainly looking around

145

and seeing that Rickey's experiment in integration was working. Rickey was taking a big chance when he signed Robinson, because most owners here happy with keeping the majors all white. Robinson was certainly talented, so Rickey had no worries about him being a poor player. The reaction of other teams when playing against Robinson was what worried Rickey most. Before recalling him to the Dodgers for 1947, Rickey asked Robinson to pledge that for his first three years in the majors he would not fight if he was insulted. Rickey feared that if Robinson got into a fight it not only would trigger a riot, but it could also end the integration process. Robinson agreed not to fight.

As was expected, the Dodgers themselves had qualms about having a black on their team. One faction, led by Dixie Walker (who was highly popular in Brooklyn and dubbed "the People's Cherce" by the fans), wanted no part of the Rickey experiment. Rickey responded by offering to trade any Dodger player who had problems playing with a black man. Most of the malcontents were silent, while a few like Dixie Walker were traded, although Walker stayed until after the 1947 season ended. Commissioner Happy Chandler warned that any team thinking about not playing the Dodgers because of Robinson's presence would be dealt with harshly. Chandler was not to be taken lightly, since Mexican League jumpers were still banned at that point, so Chandler had proved that he would be tough if necessary.

Bench jockeying was a common thing in those days, and it could get nasty even when it was white against white. Some managers, like Leo Durocher, were masters at this art, an art used to rattle the opposition. Rookies were most likely to be needled, and many would indeed get flustered from it. With Jackie Robinson being a *black* rookie at a time when racism was far more acceptable than it is now, it was a given that Robinson was going to have a tough time. Some players would certainly try to also hurt the rookie physically if it was possible.

Robinson endured all kinds of abuse in 1947, but he played through it all and did well. The reaction of the St. Louis crowd was expected to be the most hostile, since that city was the southernmost in baseball back then. Big crowds came out to see the Dodgers and their "experiment" and the crowd did get on

Robinson, but it wasn't any worse than in other cities. It was certainly natural to curse Robinson as being a member of an enemy battling the locals for first place, but it was also difficult for some, reprehensible as it was, not to hurl racial slurs at baseball's first black player.

Considering what he went through, Robinson had a fine rookie year, as he hit almost .300 and led the league in stolen bases while doing a good job at a new position (first base; Robinson was really a second baseman but was moved to first because Eddie Stanky was highly regarded as a leadoff man and fielder). Also, Robinson was named as the first ever Rookie of the Year for 1947. Rickey's experiment worked, and the Dodgers led other teams in signing black players. Before 1947 was even over, the Cleveland Indians also saw the light and called up Larry Doby from the minors, making him the first black to play in the American League. Cleveland was owned by Bill Veeck, another progressive thinker who would have done something to top even Branch Rickey had he kept quiet about it. In 1943 the Phillies were up for sale and Veeck wanted to buy the team, then a perennial cellar dweller. Before buying the club, Veeck told commissioner Kenesaw Landis (not a progressive thinker) that when he bought the Phillies he was going to stack it with black players. Horrified, Landis arranged for a new buyer, and the plan was dead. Had Veeck managed to implement his plan by placing the best Negro league players on the dismal Phillies, he might have owned the first team to go from worst to first in a season.

It was no accident that the Dodgers were becoming a power-house with black players playing key roles on the club. Roy Campanella became the league's best catcher, and Don Newcombe was a topnotch pitcher (and one of the best-hitting ones as well). The Giants also went after black players, and they helped a team that was recently a doormat become a contender. Even the St. Louis Browns, a team that needed help in the worst way, tried to get themselves off the floor by signing a black player in Hank Thompson. Thompson would have certainly helped the Browns draw some sorely needed black fans to their games had they kept him, but instead they let him get away to the Giants, where he had some good years in New York. Despite seeing the other teams doing well with blacks on their rosters, the Cardinals dragged their feet on the integration issue until it was too late.

Overall, the Cardinals' financial picture looked good. Fred Saigh made his money in real estate, and the market was booming in the aftermath of World War II. The "Baby Boom" was under way, and people were making more money to buy houses with. Not only did people have enough money to buy houses, but they also had money to go to the ballpark. Attendance figures around baseball were increasing each year for most teams (unless your team was the St. Louis Browns), and more teams were making nice profits. The Cardinals were now so wealthy that they were making all of the needed improvements at the park and more or less made it their own, even though they were still just tenants. Soon the Cardinals would have a park of their own, but not in the way that they thought.

That new invention called television was becoming very popular in America at the start of the 1950s, but ball clubs worried about it. People might want to stay home and watch Milton Berle rather than go to a baseball game, and this kind of thinking scared owners. Like radio a generation earlier, this new technology had the potential to kill attendance, but the owners were intrigued at the possible good uses that television could be put to. The three teams in New York had already tried the new medium by putting some of their games on the tube, and attendance was not harmed. (Most teams used TV at first to show a few road games before expanding the use of the medium to show almost all games.) The Cardinals took the plunge into TV with a few games, hoping that it would attract new fans, but they did not plunge too deep. Radio was still king for baseball, and the Cardinals had thousands of fans in the South and West as a result of an extensive radio network. Being in contention certainly helped the club attract new fans via radio. The Cardinals were hoping that they would keep on getting new fans as the 1950 season opened, but there was a wind swirling around the Cards that would not be very beneficial for them.

II

On the field the 1950 Cardinals got off to a good start, bunching together with the Dodgers, Phillies, and Braves in the early going. When the Cardinals went to Brooklyn for the first time that year, the usual good crowds turned out to see the usual tough battles between the locals and St. Louis. The Dodgers, though, went out and took the first two games, then stormed back in the last game, one that would be the microcosm of the Cardinals' 1950 season and their play for the whole decade as well. St. Louis jumped out to an 8–0 lead when Brooklyn mounted a late rally. In the ninth, third baseman Tommy Glaviano made three errors, helping the home team score 5 runs and giving the Cardinals an embarrassing 9–8 loss. Disaster was now in the cards. Injuries began to pile up all over as the Cardinals slowly slipped out of contention. In July the Cardinals were on top, but then the Giants made a move and the Cardinals began to slide toward the second division. The hitting was inconsistent, and pitchers like Al Brazle, Harry Brecheen, and Gerry Staley were losing it. Howie Pollet and Max Lanier were still good, but they hardly were given adequate offensive support. First base was becoming an unproductive spot, and the outfield was also having its problems. Stan Musial shifted from first to the outfield and back as the Cardinals tried to find a potent lineup at a time that the league was getting "home run fever." Only the Reds failed to hit 100 homers in 1950, and they missed by just one. The Cardinals were next to last in homers with 102 and were dead last with 23 stolen bases and sixth with a .259 average. The Cardinals were still getting decent pitching, but it wasn't enough. St. Louis concluded the 1950 season with a fifth-place finish on a 78–75 record. It was their worst season since 1938. Eddie Dyer, one of the few pilots to lead his team to a world championship in his first year, was forced out.

Popular shortstop Marty Marion took over as manager for 1951. Marion decided to stay off the roster as a player, so Solly Hemus, a farm product, was given the job at short. Nineteen-fifty-one began on a bad note when the Cardinals caught the flu on a trip east, making them feel miserable. They began to resemble a vaudeville team with some of their performances. Once the Cardinals scored just one run in a game despite putting eighteen men on base by various means. Frequently the club lost games in the enemy's last at bat. This new version of the Cardinals was certainly turning off the fans as attendance began to slip. The front office resorted to trades to shore up the team, with dubious results. On June 15, the Cardinals shipped Howie Pollet, Ted Wilks, Joe Garagiola, Bill Howerton, and Dick Cole to the Pirates for Wally Westlake and Cliff Chambers. Only Chambers for the Cardinals and Howerton for the Pirates did well, as the trade did little good for either team.

The Cardinals plodded along despite players coming and going with amazing speed. The once hot Cardinals-Dodger feud was now cooled somewhat as the Dodgers began to feast on the now mediocre Cardinal pitching. Brooklyn was now clearly the top team in the circuit, and in 1951 it looked like they would claim an easy pennant. The Giants played well and were catching the Dodgers that year, but the Cardinals gave them fits. Still, it was becoming a two-team race as the season was winding down, and one of the two teams was not St. Louis. In September the Cardinals played a weird twin bill when they beat the Giants in the first game and lost to the Braves in the second, but by this time nobody cared. Stan Musial won his second straight batting title and the Cardinals finished third with an 81–73 record, but finishing 15½ games out made 1951 a failure.

Marion did a decent job as a rookie manager, but Fred Saigh was impatient. Marion was allowed to go to the Browns and he returned as an active player, but his days were numbered. The Cardinals next made a sensational trade, sending Max Lanier and Chuck Diering to the Giants for Eddie Stanky. For years Stanky was regarded highly as a possible manager while playing hard-nosed ball for the Giants, Dodgers, and other teams in his almost ten years in the majors. Stanky was a fine leadoff man who drew over 100 walks frequently, and he was cut right out of the mold of Leo Durocher, a man he played for on two teams. Indicative of Stanky's nature was his nickname of "the Brat." Many figured that the Brat would be able to turn the Cardinals into a contender in his first year as pilot, and it seemed like the team was in a time warp. Some forty years earlier the Cardinals had pinned their hopes on a deal with the Giants that brought them Roger Bresnahan as a highly regarded manager. Like Yogi Berra was to say, "It was déjà vu all over again."

Stanky promised to stir things up in St. Louis after the Cardinals were led for years by sedate skippers. In spring training the Brat verbally lashed many of his players that he thought were not hustling, setting a serious tone for the 1952 season. The Cardinals had picked up Dick Sisler (a man they gave up on in the past) to provide some sock at first base and they had former Yankee Billy Johnson at third for a whole year, so the Cardinals were expected to battle Brooklyn and New York for a title in 1952. Unfortunately, as the season began Fred Saigh was under fire for tax trouble and the Cardinals again faced the prospect of being sold, possibly to out-of-town interests. But Saigh's problems would not be a big deal for the team until a little while later.

The Eddie Stanky Cardinals got off to an expected start when the Brat engaged in a hot discussion with an umpire, one that nearly erupted into a full-scale fistfight. Both parties were fined, and the umpire decided to quit. Chalk one up for the new skipper. Next Stanky told some writers to "go to hell" when they questioned one of his decisions. The Brat's temper was seemingly out of control when the Cardinals began playing like their old selves. In a June twin bill at New York, the Cardinals were being humbled by the Brat's old mentor, Leo Durocher, with an 11–0 score when the Cardinals erupted. By the eighth inning the Giant lead was cut to 11–10 and it was time for Durocher to seethe. One inning later, the game was over, and the Giants emerged as 14–12 losers. St. Louis then took the second game, and the Cardinals were in the race.

St. Louis played hard-nosed baseball, and it paid off in a 10-game winning streak. The hitting was timely and the pitching was solid as young Eddie Yuhas became an ace reliever. In August the Cardinals won eight in a row and seemed poised to move into first place after bumping the Giants to third. The Dodgers, though, were too tough to handle, and when Brooklyn beat St. Louis in September, the Cardinals began to slip back. The Cardinals went 88–66 and finished third, just ahead of the Phillies and close to the second-place Giants. Stan Musial won his third consecutive batting title, and Stanky got a two-year deal to manage. It seemed like the Cardinals were back.

III

Nineteen-fifty-three turned out to be a most important year for the St. Louis Cardinals, perhaps *the* most important. Eddie Stanky's arrival had been expected to aid the attendance figures in 1952, but it didn't. The Cardinals drew 913,000 fans that year, and it was the third straight year that gate receipts fell off. The 1952 total was also the first under a million since 1945. This decline was worrisome.

Fred Saigh's problems were now the problems of the Cardinals and St. Louis as well. In January, Saigh was convicted of tax evasion, and he would have to go to jail, which led to the possibility of front office chaos. The Cardinals certainly did not need the publicity and headaches that Saigh's trouble was bringing, not when they were having attendance problems, farm problems, and a tough road ahead on the big league field. The Cardinals were now in big trouble.

The farm system was no longer turning out great players. Solly Hemus and Eddie Yuhas and others coming from the farm system were good players, but not great ones. In the past, the Cardinals were able to come up with future Hall of Famers like Bottomley, Hafey, Dean, Medwick, Musial, Mize, and Slaughter, but none of the current players were going to get to the Hall unless they bought a ticket. The lack of blacks in the Cardinal organization at all levels was certainly hurting, especially when other teams had superstar blacks in the majors like Jackie Robinson, Roy Campanella, Don Newcombe, Willie Mays, and Larry Doby, among other fine black players. The Cardinals had nothing like the Negro leagues to draw black players from anymore, because those leagues were dying due to the increasing recruitment of their players by the majors. Nobody in the Cardinal system looked like a Mays or even a solid but not great player like Hank Thompson, and this was a major problem. The Cardinal minor league system was drying up.

While the Cardinals were suffering from problems from within, they were also being pushed hard by external forces. The Browns had fallen on hard times after winning the 1944 pennant. In 1945 the team was in the hunt, but in the next season they returned to their usual home in the second division. The Browns continued to lose money and began selling off their top players, mostly to the Red Sox. People began joking that the Browns were little more than a Red Sox farm team, but that was basically the truth. There always were rumors that the Browns would be sold and then moved, but nothing ever came about. Nobody wanted to own a team that had a long tradition of losing, was in poor financial straits, and was second banana to another team in their own park. Besides, the American League was not yet ready to lose a town to the National League (since both leagues always were trying to outdo each other), even if visiting teams were leaving St. Louis with almost nothing in gate receipts.

In 1951, a possible savior for the Browns came in the person of Bill Veeck. Veeck was a maverick who loved all kinds of promotions to lure fans to the park. The man knew what he was doing when he arrived in St. Louis. The Browns were a disaster in every sense of the word, but Veeck loved a challenge. After working for the Cubs for a few years, Veeck bought the Milwaukee team in the minor league American Association and turned that team around. In 1946 he had purchased the Indians, a team that had been doing nothing for some time. A year later the Tribe was going in the right direction as Veeck brought in the American League's first black players. In 1948 Cleveland went to its first World Series in twenty-eight years and they won it in six over the Boston Braves. After the 1949 season, Veeck decided to sell out after feuding with several of his fellow owners.

When the American League allowed Veeck to buy the Browns, it did so reluctantly. Veeck always had to scrape and scratch for money to buy his teams, but he always came through and the league had been taking one last shot at saving its St. Louis team. Veeck set out to steal the town for his team and came up with zany promotions featuring a midget hitter (who later popped out of cakes on the club's behalf) and the hiring of former Cardinal greats, like Rogers Hornsby (the Browns had few greats in their history, but the one man that they did have in George Sisler was busy as a

Dodger employee) and then Marty Marion, to run things, but Cardinal success did not rub off on the Browns. Once Veeck allowed the fans to manage the team by flashing cards to a coach in a rocking chair atop the dugout, and the fans seemed to know what to do, as the Browns pulled off a rare win. Veeck, strangely, didn't try this again, probably fearing he'd have to pay 2,000 people to manage the team while profits were nowhere to be seen.

Veeck promised not to sell his top players when he first arrived, but when crowds of 2,000 or less became the norm he had no choice if he wanted to continue operations. The Browns could not cut good radio or TV deals, since stations did not want to pay good money to broadcast games that nobody even cared about. Other teams were less than thrilled to still go to St. Louis and barely be able to pay for their expenses with their portion of the measly gate. The owners tried hard to get Veeck out when it was clear he could not save the team. Veeck himself realized that things seemed hopeless as 1953 opened and wanted to move the team. The league was beginning to change its mind about moving the team but said that as long as Veeck was in charge the team would stay put. The league was willing to have the Browns suffer more losses before having Bill Veeck still among its ranks.

While the Browns were still stuck in St. Louis despite Veeck's efforts to move them, Fred Saigh had a talk with some people in Milwaukee about buying his team and moving the Cardinals there. Now St. Louis was facing the real possibility of losing *both* its teams. Milwaukee was a fine baseball town and it was clamoring for big league ball, even though it was the top minor league city of the Boston Braves. Before Saigh got too heavily involved with the men from Milwaukee and went to the commissioner to get approval to sell, St. Louis came up with a viable alternative in Anheuser-Busch, the large brewery. Saigh indicated that if the brewery made a good offer he would accept it, even if it was less than the offer from Milwaukee, in order to keep the Cardinals in St. Louis. When Busch offered $3.75 million to Saigh, a deal was made, and on February 20, 1953, the Cardinals were acquired by Anheuser-Busch. August A. Busch, Jr., or Gus, as the press called him, would become the new head of the club. Gus pledged to get the Cardinals going on the road back to the top, but it would be some time before it was to happen.

Once the Cardinals announced that they were staying put, a whole new age in baseball began. A month after the Cardinals were sold, the Boston Braves decided to pack their bags and head west. The National League for years had been watching the situation in Boston with disgust as the Red Sox became the preferred team in town. At one time, the league had considered Boston a holy city of sorts and would fight tooth and nail any attempt by another league to put a team there. When Ban Johnson put a team in Boston in 1901 it triggered a vicious feud between the American and National circuits. Soon the Red Sox became the darlings of Boston while the Braves spent most of the time in the second division. The National League realized that it was finally beaten in Boston, and in March 1953 the Braves became officially known as the Milwaukee Braves. It was the first time a team was moved in the big leagues since the American League's Baltimore Orioles became the New York Highlanders (later Yankees) in 1903. The age of franchise moving had begun, and before it would end twenty years later it would finally claim the Cardinals' chief tormentors of long standing among its victims.

IV

After all of the preseason drama was settled, the Cardinals were ready to go for a pennant in year one of the Busch ownership. Ironically, the Cardinals were the first team to play the Milwaukee Braves at home, and the game in Milwaukee was a good one—for the locals, that is—when the Braves downed the Cardinals 3–2 in 10 innings. The Brat was more restrained in 1953, as the Cardinals were playing well, despite a slow start by Stan Musial. At the All-Star break the Cardinals were still in the hunt. Suddenly the Dodgers took off on a streak that left the rest of the league in the dust. Despite Stanky getting on Jackie Robinson's case all year (like the previous year), nothing could shake the Dodger star or his team. St. Louis got some great hitting out of Red Schoendienst (.342) and Musial (.337), but neither could get the batting title. In a year of extra-hard hitting (Brooklyn hit 208 homers, scored 955 runs, and batted .285), the Cardinals had the same problems as every other team in the pitching department. Harvey Haddix won 20 to become the ace, but Gerry Staley's 18 wins were overshadowed by a high 4.00 ERA. Young Stu Miller pitched frequently for the 1953 Cardinals, but he showed little of his future greatness by going only 7–8 with a 5.56 ERA. Overall, the Cardinals ended up fourth with an 83–71 record in their first year under the Busch administration.

Nineteen-fifty-three might have been unsuccessful on the field for the Cardinals, but their season was far better than that put out by the Browns. Again the American League pressured Bill Veeck to sell after the Browns ended up in last place with a 54–100 record under Marty Marion. Again Veeck refused to sell, asking instead that he be allowed to move the Browns to Baltimore. The league again refused. The league, however, was fighting within itself when it came to the Browns. One faction wanted the Browns to move to Baltimore while another favored Los Angeles. The side favoring the latter was defeated on the grounds that having only one team on the west coast would be too costly in terms of having teams going that far for just one series. The Baltimore faction had its own trouble, since putting the Browns there would put them in a congested section that contained the always bad Washington Senators, the equally bad Philadelphia Athletics, and the Philadelphia Phillies. The situation involving the Senators was especially touchy, since the Baltimore team would play right next to them. The American League had enough trouble pitting the Browns against a team in the other league, so how could they allow that bad team to compete against another poor team from the same league? The weird part about this situation was that the Senators were one of the teams that favored Baltimore over Los Angeles, probably thinking that a rivalry might develop between the two bad teams. On October 1, 1953, Bill Veeck sold the Browns to Baltimore interests. The new owners were approved by the American League, and they announced that the team would be moved to the eastern city for 1954. Ban Johnson's attempt to run the Cardinals out of St. Louis had failed. The miserable St. Louis

Browns were no more, and as the Baltimore Orioles they became an American League powerhouse.

Now, for the first time since 1919, the Cardinals had a stadium all to themselves, and Sportsman's Park would have its name changed to Busch Stadium in the future. For the first time since 1901 the Cardinals had St. Louis all to themselves. They were now the holders of their own future and no longer had to worry about what their erstwhile landlords were up to. With Gussie Busch running the team, the Cardinals no longer had to worry about leaving town or who would sponsor their radio and TV games. At this point, the Cardinals looked like they finally had put their economic worries behind them for good. St. Louis was truly a Cardinals town now.

Nineteen-fifty-four looked like a nice year with the Browns finally out of the picture. The Cardinals decided that Enos Slaughter was washed up and sent him to the Yankees in exchange for Mel Wright, Bill Virdon, and a minor leaguer just before Opening Day. The old guard was passing. Stan Musial was the only regular from the Cardinals' glory days still playing regularly and doing well. Al Brazle, the other man who played in a series with the Cardinals, was at the end of his fine career and Gerry Staley was winding down, as this trio could swap stories about big games in Brooklyn and how September used to mean important games were coming rather than meaning that the season was ending. Vic Raschi, once a fireballing pitcher on the great Yankees pitching staff of the late 1940s and early 1950s, could understand what they were talking about when he was picked up for $85,000, but most of the other Cardinals had not known what a pivotal September series was.

The Cardinals had a good lineup with Musial, Schoendienst, Ray Jablonski, and Rip Repulski coming off fine 1953 years, and the pitching looked pretty good on paper, as Raschi joined Staley, Brazle, and Harvey Haddix in forming a seemingly tough pitching staff. The Cardinals also finally came up with a black player when Brooks Lawrence joined the mound corps. Eddie Stanky was still the boss of this crew and most people expected the Cardinals to compete, but few picked them to win, as the Brooklyn Dodgers

157

were a virtual dynasty by this time. (They had won 105 games the year before.)

Those with weak stomachs probably got very sick in 1954, as the team plunged to the lower echelons of the league. Wally Moon did a great job replacing Slaughter (who was busy proving he was not washed up in the other league), but an indication of things to come came on Opening Day when the Cubs, who had finished seventh in 1953, bombed the Cardinals 13–4. Later in April, the Cubs destroyed the Cardinals again, this time in Chicago and by a 23–13 score. Hitting was falling off around the majors compared to 1953, but the Cardinals and Cubs certainly did not seem to know it. St. Louis could hit the old horsehide, but throwing it was a probably unbearable torture. Too many times the Cardinals were involved in 8–7 type games, and more often than not the Cardinals were on the losing end of such scores. Things weren't helped by an injury to top starter Harvey Haddix in midseason, although Brooks Lawrence came through with solid pitching performances.

Eddie Stanky was frantic looking for ways to win a game. The Brat was at war all year against the umpires, needled enemy teams endlessly, and tongue-lashed his own players when he felt they needed it. Stanky stopped at nothing to get a win. In the second game of a doubleheader in St. Louis, the Cardinals lost to the Phillies when the umpires thought Stanky was going out of his way to try to get the game cut short with the Phillies in the lead. A fight broke out to stall things nicely; then the game plodded along at a slow pace as Cot Deal took his time throwing the ball all over the place. Stanky's tactic failed when the umpires forfeited the game to the Phillies. The Brat ranted and raved at that game and did again when he was fined and suspended, but the forfeit stood. To date, this was the last time a National League game was won by forfeit.

The forfeited game might have seemed endless, but the season was even slower in coming to an end. But end it did, and the results were not good. The 1954 Cardinals plunged into sixth place with a dismal 72–82 record, the team's first losing mark since 1938. Among the highlights of the dismal year were the 18 wins by Haddix, a 15–6 rookie year by Lawrence, and 35 homers, 126 RBIs, and a .330 average out of Musial. Other hitting notes included

Jablonski's .296 year with 104 RBIs, Schoendienst's .315 mark, and Moon's .304 rookie season. Despite all of the poor play in the season, the Cardinals improved their gate to over a million. The departure of the Browns certainly helped.

Eddie Stanky was retained for the 1955 season even though the Cardinals were going downhill. St. Louis brought up Ken Boyer and Larry Jackson from the minors in an attempt to turn the team around. Musial was sent back to first base, and Jablonski was sent to the Reds with Staley for Frank Smith. Nobody gave the Cardinals a chance to win in 1955, and the Cardinals did not prove anybody wrong. St. Louis stumbled out of the gate at a 17–19 clip, when Stanky was fired and replaced by former Cardinal star Harry Walker. The Cardinals rushed prospects up too fast, and most of them couldn't hack it. Many old-timers failed to do the job as well, and the team found itself fighting with the Pirates to avoid the cellar. The Cards were now indeed like a house of cards trying to stay up in a breeze, only now the breeze had turned into a hurricane.

Harry Walker could do little as he watched his once awesome team end up in seventh place with a terrible 68–86 record. Musial had his usual good year and got help from rookie Boyer (.264 with 18 homers and 62 RBIs), Bill Virdon (.281, 17 homers, 68 RBIs), Moon (.295, 19 homers, 76 RBIs) and Repulski (.270, 23 homers, 73 RBIs). Haddix went 12–16 with an ERA over 4.00. Lawrence was even worse, with a 6.56 ERA to go with a 3–8 record after getting the Opening Day start. Jackson went 9–14 with an ERA over 4.00. In short, the pitching stank.

By now, the Cardinals were playing a game called musical managers. Since Eddie Dyer left after the 1950 season the Cardinals had had Eddie Stanky, Marty Marion, and Harry Walker run them, and none of these guys had turned the Cardinals around. For 1956, the man chosen to restore St. Louis to respectability was former pitcher Fred Hutchinson. Hutch had been a good pitcher in his days with the Tigers, and he was quite familiar with adversity. After all, he had pitched for the 1952 Tigers, the worst of all the dismal Tigers teams of that time, as well as managing them, so Hutch had guts. (In 1952 the Tigers lost a club-record 104 games.)

Minor call-ups and trades had given the Cardinals a new look for 1956. Don Blasingame was the new second baseman, and Alvin Dark was the new shortstop. The pitching staff was rebuilt, and most of the changes came after the season began. On June 14, the Cardinals made a big trade with the Giants. The Cardinals shipped Red Schoendienst, Jackie Brandt, Bill Sarni, Dick Littlefield, and Bobby Stephenson east in exchange for Dark, Ray Katt, Whitey Lockman, and Don Liddle. This trade came a month after the Cardinals shipped Bill Virdon to the Pirates for Bobby Del Greco and Littlefield. The Cardinals meant business and these deals proved to fans that the team was committed to building a winner. Dark became a regular and Del Greco got plenty of time in center field, but on the whole the trade to get all of the players from the Giants (or all of the players acquired from the Pirates, for that matter) did not pan out.

The man who engineered all of the deals during the season and the one that sent Brooks Lawrence to the Reds, in one of his first deals, was Frank Lane. Lane was called Trader for a reason— he masterminded the trades of literally over a hundred players in his long career as general manager for several teams. Lane figured that it certainly could not hurt a losing team like the Cardinals to swap some bodies in the hope of improving the team. At least the new faces would keep fan interest in the club high. Many of Lane's trades were of dubious value when looked at today, but some did work. Overall, it has been said that Lane traded so much just for the sake of making a deal. (In 1960 Lane would end up trading his manager of the Tigers to the Indians for their manager in mid-season.) At the time Lane made his Cardinal deals, though, there was no doubt that they made St. Louis a better club. Still, the Cardinals got off to a good start prior to the May and June swaps, and in time the deals began to not pan out.

Amazingly, Lane was also working on another deal that would have sent Stan Musial to the Phillies. Just before the June 15 trading deadline, Musial was to go to the Phillies for Robin Roberts. Musial's business manager (sort of an agent, in the days before agents were all over the place) and Gussie Busch killed that deal before it went through, so the two future Hall of Famers stayed in the cities where they began their careers.

As the season went on, the Cardinals began to fade. The

Dodgers, Reds, and Braves began to pull away, leaving the Cardinals behind. The trade of Brooks Lawrence certainly hurt the Cardinals and helped the Reds, since Lawrence won 19 games for his new team, turning them into a contender while his old team began to struggle. The Cardinals were no longer in the hunt in September, but they had fun playing spoiler. St. Louis swept 3 from Cincinnati, then tortured Milwaukee to death in the final series of the year by beating the Braves while the Dodgers wrapped up the flag in the process. The Braves' season-ending 2–1 loss in St. Louis left them one game behind Brooklyn.

The 1956 Cardinals were nothing to jump for joy over, but they did improve to fourth place with a 76–78 mark under Fred Hutchinson's leadership. The Cardinals still hit the ball, led by Musial (.310, 27 homers, and a league-high 109 RBIs), and the pitching improved as Murry Dickson returned (13–8, 3.07 ERA) and joined Herm Wehmeier (12–9) and Vinegar Bend Mizell (14–14) as the top three winners on the Cardinal pitching staff. Still, there was room for improvement, and Trader Lane figured that a little more dealing might just do the trick.

St. Louis went into 1957 needing changes, and Trader Lane made them. Lane picked up Del Ennis from the Phillies for Rip Repulski and Bobby Morgan; then he made a big deal with the Cubs, getting Sam Jones, Eddie Miksis, Hobie Landrith, and Jim Davis in exchange for Jackie Collum, Tom Poholsky, Ray Katt, and a minor leaguer. The Cardinals also dipped into the minors and made some more moves, as the Cardinals were expected by Gussie Busch to do some wire-to-wire contending for a change.

The Cardinals opened in Cincinnati and won. The Reds were expected to contend, along with the Braves and the Dodgers, but the Cardinals got off to a good start. On the suggestion of Busch, third baseman Ken Boyer was moved to center, and he did a good job while Eddie Kasko took over at third and did the job. Then the usual pitching problem popped up again and the Cardinals were back to the task of getting over the .500 level.

Then St. Louis put together eight straight wins and got back into the race. Rookie Von McDaniel came up and gave the Cardinals some great pitching to get the team going (his brother Lindy was also with the team in 1957), and he led a turnaround on the staff.

For a change from the norm of the last few years, the Cardinals kicked the Dodgers around, as their dynasty was at an end. Next the Cardinals disposed of the Reds and moved into the top spot as the All-Star Game was coming; this year the game was in St. Louis.

At this point, the Cardinals looked like the team to beat in the National League. Lane's 1957 deals worked out well and were not of dubious value, as his 1956 moves were. Sam Jones was having a good year, and Del Ennis was having a great year. Ennis joined with Wally Moon and Stan Musial (who was gunning for another batting title) in forming a tough middle of the lineup. Entering August, St. Louis was leading a five-club race and the prospects for a flag looked good as a long homestand was coming up. Then disaster struck. The Cardinals dropped nine in a row and began slipping out of the race. The Braves, who had picked up former Cardinal Red Schoendienst from the Giants earlier, began making their move, as Red was hitting better than ever.

The Cardinals, though, were not dead yet. St. Louis took three of four in Milwaukee and got back into the race. Despite an injury to Musial, the Cardinals kept hanging in there, even though the Braves were now in first. In the final weeks the Cardinals battled hard, but tough losses in games to the Reds and Braves finally ended the St. Louis quest for a title. The Braves won the flag by eight games over the second-place Cardinals. At least Musial won the batting title with a .351 mark.

St. Louis posted its best season since 1949, and manager Fred Hutchinson was hailed as the best Cardinal skipper since Eddie Dyer, after having the team in a season-long pennant race. Frank Lane's moves were also praised, but Lane had left not long after the 1957 season ended due to conflicts with Busch over trades. Busch had questioned Lane's 1956 moves (like just about everyone else), and Lane was less than pleased at that. Plus there was the fact that Busch killed some of Lane's proposed trades (like Musial for Robin Roberts), so Lane felt that his authority was being undermined. Once 1957 ended Lane went to the Cleveland Indians and was replaced by Bing Devine.

After the trading frenzy of Frank Lane and the good year the Cardinals were coming off of, St. Louis decided to stand pat going into 1958. Bad move. The Cardinals might have had a good year in 1957, but they still ended up 8 games back, so some moves were needed. Despite doing next to nothing, the Cardinals were favored by some to win the 1958 flag and most people expected that at least the team would stay in the hunt. Wrong. The Cardinals got off to a slow start, and many of the young players who made 1957 so good made 1958 so bad. Injuries had hampered Wally Moon all year, and he dropped to a .238 season. Von McDaniel proved to be one of the biggest flashes in the pan and was sent back to the minors, never to return. Brother Lindy joined him down on the farm and he turned in a bad year, but he would bounce back and have a long, fine career as a reliever. Larry Jackson split twenty-six decisions. Eddie Kasko hit .220. Del Ennis went from 24 homers and 105 RBIs to just 3 homers and 47 RBIs as he was hit by injury. Stan Musial got off to a bad start (probably because of the Dodgers and Giants leaving for California; Musial was unstoppable in the Polo Grounds and especially in Ebbets Field) and he ended up hitting just 17 homers while driving in a paltry 62 runs, easily his most punchless season since becoming a regular in 1942 (although he did hit .337). Fred Hutchinson, genius of 1957, became the dope of 1958 (at least in the eyes of his critics) and was sacked with less than two weeks left in the season. Stan Hack took over, but in the end the Cardinals ended up sixth with a 72–82 record for 1958. If nothing else, the Cardinals came up with a pretty good center fielder that year. The kid was Curt Flood, and he hit .261 as a rookie. Oh, yeah, Musial also got his three thousandth career hit, on May 13 in Chicago against Moe Drabowsky. This event was easily the highlight of 1958 for St. Louis.

Nineteen-fifty-eight may have been a long nightmare, but 1959 would be even worse. Solly Hemus was tabbed to run the Cardinals, and the former Cardinal infielder had his work cut out for him. St. Louis made a few moves in the off-season, like shipping Wally Moon to the Dodgers for Gino Cimoli, but nothing would work out. One move did pan out, though, when Sam Jones was dealt to the Giants for Bill White. Still, this one trade did little for 1959. Hemus stated that Musial would be rested more frequently in 1959 in order to conserve his strength, which meant enemy pitchers would see less of the still most dangerous man in the St.

Louis lineup, even if he was thirty-nine. The Cardinals lost to the Giants on Opening Day, and the disaster of 1958 became the disaster of 1959. Compared to the previous season, the Cardinals seemed to avoid the crippling injuries and got better hitting, but the pitching was getting worse. So was Stan Musial, who was off to the worst start of his career.

The Cardinals were again in the second division, and now there was talk that Musial was through as a hitter. At the middle of the season the team was going nowhere, as the pitching stank. Lindy McDaniel was back and he was a busy man cleaning up a lot of messes as a reliever. McDaniel posted a 13–8 record with 15 saves in 1959 as he became the top hurler on the Cardinals. Larry Jackson and Vinegar Bend Mizell gave St. Louis a chance at victory, but they were not enough. Musial tailed off in the second half of the season, and his final numbers were a .255 average with 14 homers and 44 RBIs, as he got more rest than expected. The Cardinals ended the season with a 71–83 record, bad enough for seventh place. Not since the early days of Rickey and Breadon had the Cardinals finished so poorly.

The Cardinals saw their gate shrink as their win total shrank. The Cardinals had entered the 1950s as a premier team and left the decade as a loser. St. Louis went 776–763 for the decade, easily their worst mark for a decade since the 1910s. As the 1960s opened, some changes would have to occur to right the Cardinals again.

Part V

The Cardinals Fly High Again (1960–68)

I

As the 1960s dawned, one thing was certain—the Dodgers and Giants were the top teams in the National League because they had been the first two teams in the circuit to tap into the large pool of black and Latin players while other teams simply watched and did little else. It was also certain that the Cardinals were in such a mess as they were because they went from trendsetters to trend followers when it came to black and Latin ballplayers. The Cardinals were certainly not *the* last team to go after blacks and Latins (that distinction falls on the Red Sox, who finally added a black player in 1959, twelve years after the Dodgers brought up Jackie Robinson), but because they were not one of the first, the Cardinals paid the price. Throughout the 1950s the Dodgers, Giants, and Braves dominated the league while the Cardinals were, at best, a mediocre team during the same decade. It was no coincidence that the teams that had players like Mays, Aaron, and Campanella were at the top, while the team that had players like Del Greco, Grammas, and Landrith were not.

Fortunately, the Cardinals eventually saw the light and began to go after black and Latin players and now, in 1960, the St. Louis farm was packed with these players and they would soon restore the Cardinals back to the top of the heap. At the big league level the Cardinals had already tried Curt Flood in center field, and he was doing fine. They also gave a cup of coffee to Bob Gibson late in 1959, but he was not quite ready yet. Bill White was picked up from the Giants, and he was already producing at first base and the outfield. More players were to come.

Overall, 1960 was a restless year for baseball. Three National League and two American League teams had moved to new cities, and more teams had plans to move as well. Cities still lacking major league baseball were still clamoring for teams. It certainly was idiotic that the National League had no team in New York after having two sound teams there for decades. New York was the biggest city in the country, and it was a money-maker for baseball in both leagues for years. The importance of New York was such that Ban Johnson risked full-scale war with the National League when he placed a team in New York for his American League. The angered city tried to lure the Pirates, Phillies, and Reds to town, but these teams were not interested in moving. Next, New York big shots tried to form a new league, called the Continental League, to give cities lacking major league ball a team to call their own. New York was to be included in this new league, and Branch Rickey was called in to help found the new circuit. Both established leagues were worried about another war similar to the 1914–15 Federal League war and decided to come to an agreement with the new outfit. Both leagues then announced plans to expand by two teams within the next few years, so New York would get a new National League team.

As for the Cardinals, a rebuilding was in order for 1960. The Cardinals shipped second baseman Don Blasingame to the San Francisco Giants in exchange for shortstop Darryl Spencer and young Leon Wagner. The St. Louis team also picked up pitcher Ron Kline from the Pirates for Gino Cimoli and Tom Cheney. The Cardinals' infield for 1960 would contain Bill White at first, Julian Javier at second, Spencer at short, and Ken Boyer at third. Stan Musial would join Curt Flood and Joe Cunningham in the outfield. A platoon behind the plate would have Hal Smith doing most of the catching. The pitching staff would have second-year man Ernie Broglio joined by Kline, Lindy McDaniel, Larry Jackson, and Ray Sadecki in doing most of the flinging. The big question for 1960 was: can Musial still hit?

Musial wasn't going for a batting title in 1960, but he still could swing the bat well while doing a decent job in left field. St. Louis started off slowly, though, and people thought that another bad year was in store. The last time the Cardinals posted three straight losing years was in 1918–20, so it was forty years since Cardinal fans had tasted losing in large bites. Solly Hemus (retained as skipper despite the poor 1959 season) was frantic as he tried all kinds of players out to get the right combination of youth and experience to turn the club around. The aforementioned 1960 lineup was tried only after much experimentation on the part of Hemus, and once it began to click Hemus stuck with it. Musial was having a decent year, but there was talk that he would be going to the Pirates, who were at the top at the middle of the year. Musial stayed put, and even though he wasn't playing on an everyday basis in 1960, he had good numbers for the year.

Meanwhile, the Cardinals found themselves in a pennant race for the first time since 1957. The Pirates were at the top, followed closely by the Braves and Cardinals. In August, the Pirates began to falter and the Cardinals made their move, beating Pittsburgh at Busch Stadium a few times before going to visit the league leaders while holding onto second place. The Cardinals went into Pittsburgh down by 5 games of a 4-game set, the first game going 12 frames. The Pirates had to battle to win a series-ending twin bill by going extra innings to get the nightcap, but they did it and the Cardinals began to slowly slip back. The Cardinals ended up third in 1960, just 9 games behind the Pirates and 2 games behind the second-place Braves. Nineteen-sixty was a most pleasant surprise indeed, as Ernie Broglio led the league with twenty-one wins in his second big league season.

Solly Hemus did well with a team expected by most to do nothing in 1960, so he was brought back for 1961. Entering 1961 the Cardinals were expected to battle for the flag and a few people thought they were good enough to take it. As seemingly is the case when the Cardinals are expected to do well, they got off to a weak start. Hemus, who had experimented in 1960 until he found the right combination that produced a good team, experimented again in 1961. This time, Hemus could not come up with the right combination and the result was inevitable. After starting off 33–41 and nowhere near the pennant, Hemus was fired and replaced by Johnny Keane. Keane was perhaps the most religious and quiet man the Cardinals had ever employed, aside from Branch Rickey. Keane oozed patience and was always an optimist, always figuring that if things were going bad they would soon change. Keane's calm leadership seemed to do the trick. St. Louis posted an 80–74 mark at the end of the year, going 47–33 under Keane.

Although the 1961 Cardinals were a disappointment, the making of a fine team was already evident. First baseman Bill White was developing into a slick fielder and a top clutch hitter after failing to cut it as an outfielder in his first Cardinal year. At second, Julian Javier was an acrobat, scooping up ground balls and making great plays so fast he was dubbed "the Phantom." Ken Boyer was by this time one of baseball's top third basemen. Not only was Boyer a top fielder, but he was a big gun in the Cardinal lineup, as his 24 homers, 95 RBIs, and .329 average in 1961 showed. Curt Flood was also hailed as one of the top center fielders in the game, and as a hitter he was a tough cookie. An injury bothered Flood in 1961, but he still hit .322 that year in over 300 at bats. On the hill, Ray Sadecki had a good second year in 1961, going 14–10. Bob Gibson, who had no problem throwing inside even at this point in his career, was 13–12 with a 3.24 ERA. Gibson was coming on as a power pitcher, as he fanned 7.07 batters per 9 innings, a rate topped only by Sandy Koufax and Stan Williams of the Los Angeles Dodgers. Curt Simmons was only 9–10 in 1961, but the veteran pitched in tough luck, as his 3.13 ERA showed. A few spots needed shoring up, like shortstop and catcher, but in time those holes would be filled in. Those holes and a little more depth in the pitching were needs that would hold the Cardinals back for a little while longer.

Nineteen-sixty-two brought about a change in the National League when it increased in size from eight to ten teams. The last time the league's size changed was sixty-two years earlier, when the twelve-team National League dropped four of its teams. The last time the National League brought in new teams was seventy years earlier, when the league brought in St. Louis as one of four cities absorbed from the American Association. The American League had expanded in 1961, coming up with the Los Angeles Angels and the new (but certainly not improved) Washington Senators (which replaced the old and equally bad team of the same name that became the Minnesota Twins after the 1960 season ended), and neither team looked like world beaters. For 1962 the National League came up with the New York Mets and the Houston Colt .45s as its two new teams. The two new N.L. clubs would make the two A.L. clubs look good by comparison, especially the Mets.

Like all of the other teams, the Cardinals kept their top players out of the expansion draft used to stock the two new teams. With the league now containing ten teams, the Cardinals were picked for a middle-of-the-pack finish, which now meant ending up fourth, fifth, or sixth. Julio Gotay was recalled from the minors to fill in the troublesome hole at short, while Gene Oliver and Carl Sawatski were elated to split the catching chores. Ray Washburn was called up to add depth on the pitching staff, but otherwise the Cardinals entered 1962 with a roster that had ended the 1961 season in fifth place. With the schedule lengthened by eight games to 162 games due to expansion, the Cardinals hoped to improve their win total over 1961.

The Cardinals performed another historic first in 1962 when they opened the season in Busch Stadium. Nine years earlier the Cardinals were the opposition in the first home game the Milwaukee Braves ever played. Now the Cardinals would be the first team the New York Mets *ever* faced. On April 11, 1962, the Mets began their life (and one of the worst seasons ever by a team) by balking home a run in the first inning en route to an 11–5 loss to the Cardinals. The Cardinals didn't know what to make of this win, since they gave up 5 runs to a team of rejected ballplayers, but they did score 11 runs in the game. Such confusion was understandable when one played the 1962 Mets.

The Cardinals played well in the early going, but they were nothing to jump for joy about. Minnie Minoso, picked up in the off-season, was expected to provide some pop and dazzle in the lineup, but instead he suffered all kinds of injuries and was virtually useless for the entire year. Soon four teams pulled away from the pack and battled it out for the pennant, and the Cardinals were not one of those four teams. Instead, the Cardinals found themselves in a battle for fifth place with the now fading Braves and the suddenly good Phillies. The Cardinals got good hitting all year long, especially from Stan Musial, who was in a fight for the batting title at age forty-two. The Man was playing every day again, as Johnny Keane told him he could still get the job done. Musial was no Gold Glove in left field, but he certainly did not make a fool of himself at that position. In the middle of the year Musial got his 3,431st hit, breaking Honus Wagner's National League record for most hits in a career. Evidently, the two new teams helped Musial in his quest for a batting title, since he battered the weak staffs of

Houston and New York (using Musial's old haunts in the Polo Grounds as a home) with plenty of hits.

The Cardinals might have been out of the pennant race by September, but they made sure they had a finger in the pie when it came to giving other teams trying to grab the flag a rough time. On September 23 the Cardinals throttled the Dodgers 12–2 as they bombed Los Angeles ace Don Drysdale. While the Dodgers lost, the Giants won. On the twenty-seventh, the Cardinals downed the Giants 7–4 to keep the Dodgers in the race. The next day St. Louis shaded the Dodgers 3–2 to keep San Francisco alive. On the twenty-ninth the Cardinals shut out the Dodgers 2–0 while the Giants won again. In what was supposed to be the official end of the regular season, the Cardinals forced a 3-game playoff between the Giants and Dodgers when they beat the Dodgers 1–0 on September 30. If the Cardinals couldn't get into the series, then at least they made things interesting for the two teams trying to get there.

On paper the 1962 Cardinals had a good year. Bill White hit .324 with 20 homers and 102 RBIs. Julian Javier hit .263. Ken Boyer hit .291 with 24 homers and 98 RBIs. Curt Flood stayed healthy and batted .296. Stan Musial ended up third in the batting race with a .330 mark. The pitching staff got a 16–11 year from Larry Jackson, a 15–13 year from Bob Gibson, 12–9 years out of both Ernie Broglio and Ray Washburn, and a 10–10 year from Curt Simmons. All of these personal stats were nice, but somehow the Cardinals posted only an 84–78 record and finished sixth, 17 ½ games out of first. In a year when pitching was down and hitting was up due to expansion, the Cardinals posted a league-high seventeen shutouts.

After the 1962 season it was obvious that the Cardinals were a competitive team, but they were not contender material. General manager Bing Devine looked around and saw that shortstop was still a problem and that as long as the Cardinals did not have a full-time catcher to aid the development of young pitchers like Gibson and Ray Sadecki, St. Louis would be good enough to stay above .500, but that would be all. No pennant could be expected until these long-standing problems were finally solved.

Devine looked around the majors and did not find a catcher that would come cheap or would be able to handle the young pitchers, so he turned to the minors. Tim McCarver had been given a couple of cups of coffee by St. Louis and was sent back down to get more seasoning. McCarver was a good handler of pitchers and a pesky hitter, so Devine decided to bring him up for more than just a sip. Next Devine had to find a shortstop who could both hit and field. Julio Gotay hit surprisingly well in 1962 (.255) but was found wanting with the glove on an everyday basis. The Pirates decided to part with Dick Groat, a slick-fielding, fine-hitting shortstop who had won the league's MVP award in 1960. Devine jumped at the chance to get Groat, and he swapped Gotay and pitcher Don Cardwell (who was picked up from the Cubs a month earlier) to get him and pitcher Diomedes Olivo.

Devine also decided to shore up the outfield, and before the Groat deal he swapped Larry Jackson, Lindy McDaniel, and Jimmie Schaffer to the Cubs for Don Cardwell, George Altman, and Moe Thacker. Altman had pop in his bat, and he was the key to this deal as far as the Cardinals were concerned. Devine was now satisfied that he had filled in two holes that had plagued the Cardinals for years and he had also picked up a hard-hitting outfielder in case Stan Musial could no longer hack it at age forty-three.

St. Louis started 1963 well, staying in the race with Los Angeles, San Francisco, the amazing Philadelphia Phillies of Gene Mauch, and Cincinnati. Entering June, the Cardinals were leading the race when they visited Houston. The Colt .45s played in a former minor league park in those days and it was the bane not only of the visitors, but of the home team as well. Terrible heat and humidity and huge flies coming from a nearby swamp like an air force squadron made for little fun at this ballpark. All of these accouterments, plus poor lights ("If they're gonna play night games here they should at least get lights," said Mets outfielder Richie Ashburn in 1962) caused the Cardinals to lose 2 games to the Colt .45s, triggering a slump by the St. Louis hitters that caused an 8-game losing streak. The Cardinals visited California, where the always pitching-packed Dodgers put St. Louis bats to bed in a hurry; then it was on to see the Giants, who were also rude hosts, with their big bats and some good pitching from Juan Marichal. By the All-Star break the Cardinals were in fourth place and the normally potent Cardinal bats were silent.

In the second half, the Cardinals finally got their bats back in order as the pitching staff was also becoming one of the best in the league. By this time, Bob Gibson was proving to be a top pitcher in the league, as he started to appear among league leaders in many categories. Ernie Broglio also looked like a pitcher with plenty of good years ahead of him (both he and Gibson were twenty-eight in 1963), and veteran Curt Simmons was providing leadership among the starters. Ray Sadecki was still finding himself, but he would indeed find himself soon.

After the break, Stan Musial announced that 1963 was his last year with the team. The Man had collected all kinds of records and awards in his career and felt that it was time to hang up the spikes at age forty-three. Musial was feeling the effects of playing in the most games in National League history up to that time. On the Cardinals' last trip through the league, every city feted the Man as he was winding down his great career with 12 homers and 58 RBIs in only 337 at bats.

While St. Louis was busy giving Stan Musial a grand send-off, the Cardinals were still in the race. Bing Devine had made the right moves as Dick Groat tightened the defense and provided a solid bat. Tim McCarver took charge behind the plate and coaxed fine performances from the pitching staff while hitting .289 as a rookie. George Altman provided timely hits as he took over in right field. Devine was being hailed as a genius as the players he acquired were doing better than many people expected.

In late August the Cardinals were fading when they battled back by sweeping the Phillies, triggering a 9-game winning streak. The bats were hot now, and enemy pitchers were getting burned. The Cubs sent 20-game winner Dick Ellsworth out, and he was bombed. Warren Spahn was having another 20-win season himself (his last), and the Cardinals disposed of him as well. In the middle of September the Cardinals swept a twin bill from the Braves that concluded a 10-game winning streak. At that point, St. Louis had won 19 of 20 and were 1 game behind the Dodgers when they visited the Cardinals for a key series. The Dodgers entered this series 1 game ahead of the Cardinals, so first place was on the line.

In the opener, Johnny Podres faced Broglio and both pitchers were doing well when Tommy Davis drove in a run with a cheap single. One inning later, in the seventh, Stan Musial belted his last homer ever, tying the score at 1–1, but the Dodgers won the game with 2 runs in the ninth off of reliever Bobby Shantz. The next day Sandy Koufax came up with a 4–0 shutout against Curt Simmons. The series then ended with St. Louis leading 5–1 in the eighth when a Dodger rally tied up the game. Los Angeles went on to win the game and extend their lead after downing St. Louis 6–5 in thirteen innings. The Dodgers left town with a 4-game lead, and the Cardinals got no closer. A few days later the Dodgers clinched the pennant and it was all over.

Despite not winning the flag, the Cardinals proved they were finally bona fide contenders in 1963. St. Louis won 93 games, the highest total that they had reached since 1949. All of Devine's moves worked brilliantly. Dick Groat hit .319 while driving in 73 runs. Tim McCarver hit .289 as a rookie. George Altman hit .274. This trio was joined by Bill White (.304, 27 home runs, 109 RBIs), Ken Boyer (.285, 24, 111), Curt Flood (.302), and Julian Javier (.263) in forming a potent lineup and an excellent defensive unit. The pitching staff also excelled. Bob Gibson went 18–9, 3.39. Ernie Broglio went 18–8, 2.99. Curt Simmons posted a 15–9, 2.48 year. Ron Taylor became a fine reliever with a 9–7 mark and 11 saves. Veteran Bobby Shantz also saved 11 games while going 6–4 with a 2.61 ERA. The Cardinals were now a proven team that everyone had to take seriously.

As 1963 concluded, St. Louis gave a nice good-bye to Stan Musial. People now wondered what the Cardinals would do without their clubhouse leader, a man who had played with the team for almost twenty-two years. For the first time in memory the Cardinals were lacking a hitter that was of superstar potential and did not come from anywhere else, but from the minors. Ken Boyer was certainly a fine hitter and he did come up from the minors, but not many people figured that he would be a Hall of Famer. Besides, Boyer was with the team for less than ten years, so *if* he kept on playing like he had thus far for another ten years, then maybe he'd get to the Hall of Fame. Bill White had already posted some big years for the Cardinals, but he was with the team even less long and he came from another team on top of that. The pitching staff certainly had some good candidates for heroes in

Bob Gibson, Ernie Broglio, and maybe Ray Sadecki, but pitchers don't play on an everyday basis. It was time for an adjustment in the thinking of Cardinal fans. There were no Musials, Medwicks, Mizes, Slaughters, Bottomleys, or Hafeys coming any time soon. The fans would most certainly adjust.

II

Entering the 1964 season, it was hard to believe that the St. Louis Cardinals had not finished in first place since 18 years earlier. The thing that irked most Cardinal fans was the fact that in those 18 years the Cardinals were rarely in a wire-to-wire race. Since 1950 the Cardinals had been in a wire-to-wire race just three times (1957, 1960, 1963), and in all three of them the Cardinals were no closer than 6 games out at the end. Gussie Busch, boss of the club, was a fan first and a boss second when it came to the Cardinals, and he was well aware of how badly the Cardinals had played in the last 18 years after several years of sustained excellence. It was time to bring the flag back to St. Louis.

Bing Devine was now under intense pressure to put out a pennant winner. Devine's moves for 1963 panned out very well, but they still did not make the Cardinals a champ. More depth was needed for the pitching staff, so the Cardinals sent George Altman and Bill Wakefield to the Mets for their top starter in Roger Craig. Craig had labored for two long and hard years as a Met, posting 10–24 and 5–22 records as that team's ace while leading the league in losses in 1962 and 1963. Craig, however, had good stuff and had played on winners with the Dodgers, so the veteran was expected to pitch far better for a team loaded with good offense. Devine also saw that the Cardinals were lacking a good leadoff man. After the 1963 season there weren't many good leadoff men around, but Devine would solve that problem later on.

As 1964 opened, the Cardinals were clearly a team picked by some to win the flag. But there were other teams that also merited consideration as well. The defending world champion Dodgers were certain to be a factor. Sandy Koufax and Don Drysdale were, by this time, the most potent one-two pitching punch in the game.

Besides having the two ace pitchers, the Dodgers also had some fine hitters in Tommy Davis (the batting champ of 1962 and 1963), Willie Davis, Frank Howard, Ron Fairly, and the game's best leadoff man, Maury Wills. Wills had set a record in 1962 by stealing 104 bases and entered 1964 as the league's top thief for the last four years. Johnny Podres was a tough number-three starter, and Ron Perranoski was one of the top relievers in baseball.

The Giants also were a tough team. In 1963 the Giants finished third, after winning the flag the year before. San Francisco boasted a powerful lineup featuring 1963 homer king Willie McCovey, Willie Mays, Orlando Cepeda, Felipe Alou, and former batting champ Harvey Kuenn. The Giants also had a solid pitching staff led by Juan Marichal, who was the league's top winner in 1963 (tied with Koufax) and also containing Jack Sanford, Billy O'Dell, and Bob Bolin. A young guy by the name of Gaylord Perry was trying to get into this rotation, but he couldn't quite make it in 1963. Still, Perry looked good and he would make it in 1964.

The Reds also were a team to look out for. Cincinnati most certainly had a potent lineup of its own, which centered around Frank Robinson. Robby had an off year (for him) in 1963 when he hit .259 with "only" 21 homers and 91 RBIs. Still, the Reds were murder in 1963 as Vada Pinson took up the slack by hitting 22 homers, driving in 106, and batting .313 for the year. Robinson and Pinson were joined by young Pete Rose (a .273 hitter as a rookie) and Gordy Coleman and Leo Cardenas, the latter two usually fine hitters but two who had struggled in 1963. Cincinnati also had fine pitching with 23-game winner Jim Maloney (who threw almost as hard as Koufax) heading a rotation that also had Jim O'Toole, Joe Nuxhall, and John Tsitouris doing well in 1963.

Milwaukee had been in decline ever since just missing out for its third straight pennant in 1959 (the Dodgers beat them in a playoff), but the Braves still had a tough lineup. Hank Aaron was the 1963 leader in RBIs and homers (tied with McCovey), and he was one of the league's top stars for years. Eddie Mathews was still knocking balls out on a regular basis, and these two sluggers were joined by veteran Lee Maye and youngsters Denis Menke and Joe Torre, two players that everyone agreed would go on to do some heavy damage to pitchers before they were through playing. The

177

Braves also had a hard-hitting kid in the minors by the name of Rico Carty, and he was considered to be the top jewel in Milwaukee's system in 1963. In 1964 Carty would have a great rookie year, joining a most potent lineup. The Braves figured to be in the race as long as they got pitching that was better than the pitching they got in 1963. Warren Spahn was 42 in 1963, but he still had enough to win 23 games that year, and in one of the greatest pitching duels of the post–World War II era, Spahn and Juan Marichal pitched 16 scoreless innings against each other until the Giants won it 1–0 on a Willie Mays homer. Spahn might have been a superman in 1963, but unless other pitchers did their share, 1964 would not see a pennant flying over Milwaukee.

The final team to watch in 1964, according to the experts, was the Phillies. The story of the Phillies in 1963 was quite amazing when one saw what the Phillies were like in the years before that one. After winning the flag in 1950 in surprising fashion against the Dodgers, the Phillies began a gradual decline. By the late 1950s the Phillies had become a second division club despite having players like Robin Roberts and Richie Ashburn on the roster. Eddie Sawyer, who managed the 1950 "Whiz Kids" (called that because the 1950 Phillies had so many young players) was sent packing in 1952 after getting off to a bad start, but by 1958 he was back at the helm, leading the Phillies to the depths of the second division. After managing the Phillies to a loss in the 1960 season's first game, Sawyer resigned, saying, "I'm 49 and I want a chance to be 50."

The Phillies next turned to their minor league system and saw a 35-year-old manager doing well named Gene Mauch. Mauch had been around in the majors with several teams, but as a player he did little, hitting .239 in nine years. One thing Mauch liked to do when sitting on the bench (which was often, thanks to his weak stick) was question his manager on strategy during games. Mauch must have done well in asking questions, because he had his minor league teams always in contention when the Phillies offered him the job of leading a lousy big league club. Mauch said he would take the job, and he was on his way to Philadelphia.

It's likely that Mauch required plenty of antacids when he saw the mess that was the Phillies in 1960. Mauch spent the year mostly observing, while the Phillies spent another year losing all over the place. The team made some moves for 1961, but evidently they weren't the right ones, as the Phillies endured one of their worst seasons ever. Mauch wanted to get rid of many players (who could blame him?), including a fading Robin Roberts. The Phillies dragged their feet on this issue of Roberts, and then they came up with a record that nobody will want to break—a losing streak of 23 games. When the Phillies returned home after almost a month of nonstop losing, the team was welcomed by a crowd of crazed fans celebrating the win. The 1961 Phillies would have gone down in the book as the absolute worst team of the 1960s (they were 47–107) had expansion not created the 1962 Mets. Mauch, who was highly praised in the minors, was now being thought of as just another lousy manager who would quickly fade away to the place that most fired pilots end up going to.

Then came "the miracle" of 1962. First, it was considered miraculous that Mauch was back in 1962 as the Phillies' manager. Then it was miraculous that the Phillies had a decent spring. Finally, it was really miraculous that Mauch had his team trying to play .500 ball in the season. Suddenly a sow's ear was turning into a silk purse in Philadelphia. People like Clay Dalrymple were hitting .270. The Phillies were beating real teams (the Mets and Colt .45s were considered almost minor league teams at the time) on a somewhat regular basis. The club finally was getting some production from the lineup as Don Demeter, Johnny Callison, and Roy Sievers were driving in runs at good paces. Art Mahaffey became an ace. Jack Baldschun was putting out fires in the late innings. Philadelphia fans were amazed at the way their team was now turned around. In 1962 the Phillies became only the fourth team in the twentieth century to go from 100 or more losses in one year to a .500 or better record the next. Not since the 1946–47 Philadelphia Athletics had a team turned around so radically in so short a time. To put this accomplishment in some perspective, the feat of turning 100-game losers into a .500 team in a year's time has happened just eight times in this century, so it was no wonder the fans in Philadelphia were in ecstasy.

Gene Mauch was now hailed as a genius. Certainly it was no small feat to manage a team that put out so well only a year after being stomped on daily, but to hail Mauch as a genius was a bit much. Nonetheless, Mauch was indeed an outstanding skipper and he deserved praise for what his team did in 1962. The players themselves certainly deserved praise for the feat, but as is often the case in such an amazing turnaround, the manager gets too much credit while the players don't get enough. Philadelphia now praised Gene Mauch to the high heavens.

In 1963 the Phillies got off to a great start and were in an actual pennant race. The Phillies were tormenting teams that nobody thought they could even compete with, teams like the Dodgers and Giants. The Phillies were streaking after the All-Star break in 1963 and were very close to the top in August when they began to drop back, thanks to a sweep by the Cardinals. At the end of 1963, they were 87–75 and in fourth place, the best season the team had since winning the pennant in 1950.

Now Gene Mauch was being hailed in Philadelphia as possibly the greatest manager who lived. First Mauch took the team from the depths and brought it to .500. Now Mauch had taken a team expected to do nothing in 1963 and had it in the race almost wire to wire. Philadelphia was under the grip of pennant fever in 1963, when the Phillies were closing in on the top spot, and now the town was in sight of water after fourteen years of being in a desert. Gene Mauch was becoming a victim of his team's success as the Philadelphia fans, known to be some of the toughest, raised their expectations for 1964. Phillies fans not only expected their team to contend, but they were now expecting a pennant. "Genius Gene Mauch had better deliver the flag in 1964, or else" was now the attitude in the city that hadn't had a winner in a long time. Philadelphia was impatient. The acquisition of Jim Bunning from Detroit was expected to do the trick. The Phillies certainly had flaws, like any other team, but Philadelphia expected those flaws to be overcome, and easily, too.

Outsiders picked the Phillies to do well, and a few picked them to win, but being more objective, the outsiders noted that the Phillies had flaws and that unless the team played extremely well, the Phillies would not win the flag. When the season began the Phillies did start well, going 10–2 and claiming the top spot. The Cardinals began on a sluggish foot and found themselves in the middle of the pack with teams like the Pirates and Cubs, who nobody picked to do anything, battling with St. Louis to stay out of eighth place.

Bing Devine was worried over the start of the Cardinals. Like Philadelphia, St. Louis was expecting a flag in 1964, but unlike the Phillies, the Cardinals were struggling in the second division. At least the Cardinals weren't the only expected contender having a poor year. The Dodgers relied too heavily on Koufax and Drysdale when Podres was out, and when the hitting just wasn't there Los Angeles found itself with St. Louis, Chicago, and Pittsburgh in trying to avoid getting too close to the still awful Houston and New York squads. The Phillies were in and out of first place, trading the spot with the Giants, Reds, and Braves (who were not getting good pitching from the now washed up Spahn, but that lineup overcame much).

The Cardinals' bad start began all kinds of rumors. Stan Musial's retirement was the reason, some said, that the Cardinals were struggling. Maybe if the Man came back it would help? Then there was the rumor that pilot Johnny Keane would be fired. Another rumor indicated that Bing Devine didn't do enough in the off-season to improve the team, so he was history. The Cardinals still lacked a leadoff man like Maury Wills that could get on base a lot and score plenty of runs while Bill White and Ken Boyer knocked him in. Curt Simmons, Ray Sadecki, and Ernie Broglio certainly were not breezing along for a Cy Young Award. Trades were proposed but never pulled off, for one reason or another. Going into June the Cardinals were still serving as a punching bag while four teams were still bunched at the top, trying to take permanent hold of first place.

On June 15, 1964, the Cardinals perpetrated highway robbery on the Cubs, although at the time few people who followed both teams took notice. Bing Devine sent Ernie Broglio (3–5), Bobby Shantz (1–3), and Doug Clemens (.205) to the Cubs in exchange for Paul Toth (0–2), Jack Spring (0–0), and Lou Brock (.251). As the stats (at the time of the trade) show, nobody was doing backflips in either St. Louis or Chicago when the deal was made. On the Cardinals' side, Brock was the key. Lou Brock was highly regarded by the Cubs when they first brought him up in 1962 and thought he would be more of a power hitter than he had shown at the time of his trade to St. Louis. Brock gave some hint of being a power hitter when he homered into the center field stands against the Mets in the Polo Grounds. Brock put a ball where even Babe Ruth could not put one, even when the Polo Grounds was Ruth's home park from 1920 to 1922. The Cardinals were more interested in Brock being their leadoff man rather than being another Ducky Medwick or Johnny Mize. Some people actually thought in Chicago that Lou Brock would be another Willie Mays, a kind of player who could break open a game with either speed or the long ball. Unfortunately for the Cubs, by 1964 Brock had proven he was not going to be another Mays. Instead, he would prove to the Cardinals that he was one of the all-time great leadoff men.

Left field was a mess when Brock arrived, so Johnny Keane put Brock and his .251 average there. At the time of the deal Brock's .251 mark fit in nicely, as the team was not hitting as well as it had done in 1963. Brock's arrival did little good for St. Louis initially, as the whole team was trying to get its act together. The Phillies were still leading a "Gang of Four" as the Reds, Giants, and Braves stood close to Philadelphia, waiting for a Phillies slump to unseat Gene Mauch's crew from the top.

At this time the Phillies were getting fine pitching from newcomer Jim Bunning, who tossed a perfect game against the Mets on Father's Day in New York. Holdover Chris Short was also doing a fine job, and Art Mahaffey and Dennis Bennett were also capable behind Bunning and Short. The Phillies made a deal of their own, sending fading first baseman Roy Sievers to the Washington Senators for reliever Ed Roebuck. Roebuck joined Jack Baldschun in doing a fine job putting out fires in the late innings. Johnny Callison was having an MVP-type season, and everybody was raving about rookie third baseman Dick Allen, who was tearing up the league himself. Wes Covington and Tony Gonzalez were also hitting well, despite nagging injuries, and this quartet was giving the Phillies some good hitting. Although the middle infield was a mess and first base had a revolving door situation while the catchers were not hitting, few people were worried about the Phillies not hanging onto first place. Not yet, anyway.

In July, the Cardinals finally started to make a move. St. Louis began to pass the still disappointing Dodgers, the still bad Cubs, and the still struggling Pirates as they climbed into the first division, even if it meant St. Louis was only in fifth place, still seemingly light-years away from the Big Four. Curt Simmons and Ray Sadecki began to find themselves and began winning with some consistency. Lou Brock was hitting far better than he ever did for the Cubs, and he became the leadoff man that the Cardinals had long lacked. Brock was now challenging Maury Wills for the top spot in steals. Bill White and Ken Boyer were happy to see Brock get on base and steal bases, for it meant more RBI chances. Mike Shannon was recalled from the minors to play right field (another problem spot after George Altman was sent to the Mets), and he did a fine job with the bat and glove. The Cardinals were jelling and were certainly better than the five teams behind them in the standings, but they were not quite ready to make a move on the four teams ahead of them.

Bing Devine was blasted for sending veteran Bobby Shantz to the Cubs in the Brock deal back in June. Shantz had done a fine job in the St. Louis bullpen since he was picked up, but when he started weakly in 1964 he became expendable. Ron Taylor was also having his problems in the bullpen, and young Mike Cuellar (a future perennial 20-game winner with the Baltimore Orioles) was not the answer either. Late in July Devine recalled ancient 37-year-old Barney Schultz from the minors to bolster the bullpen. Schultz was so-so in a couple of earlier stints with the Cardinals, but Devine needed somebody to get the job done. Schultz came up and took charge of the Cardinal bullpen, which ended the bullpen crisis for 1964.

In August, the Cardinals were still feeling their way around when many people began losing hope that the team would bring home a flag in 1964. St. Louis had expected a pennant this year, and even though the team started badly, the fans still believed that the team would turn it around. In early August, the Phillies picked up slugger Frank Thomas from the Mets to fill in their first base hole. It now appeared less likely than ever that the Cardinals would win in 1964, since the Phillies now added another big bat to a pretty good lineup, even if they were having injury problems. In the middle of the month, Gussie Busch also figured that the Cardinals were not going to make it, so he fired general manager Bing Devine.

The sacking of Bing Devine surprised many people. Devine was highly regarded around the majors as a good trader who helped build the Cardinals from a doormat in 1958 to a contender five years later. True, the Cardinals in mid-August 1964 were not setting the baseball world on its ear, but they were still a good team getting better. The effect of the firing on the team was stunning. The Cardinals began to pick up the pace and began winning more consistently. There was a rumor that Busch wanted to fire manager Johnny Keane at the same time he let Devine go but decided to hold back on that move. Keane was popular with the team, and his ouster at that point in the season would probably have sent the team right back into the second division after they had gotten to the threshold of making a serious run at the flag. Keane was retained, but rumors had it that nothing short of a flag would keep Keane in his job after the season.

In early September the Cardinals began to pick up a head of steam, pushing their way past the Braves, whose pitching shortage was now too much for their great lineup to overcome. Next the Cardinals squeezed by both the Giants and Reds, and by mid-September the Cardinals were in second place. The Phillies, though, were now increasing the distance between themselves and the other contenders. On the twentieth, the Phillies were leading both the Cardinals and Reds (who were now tied for second) by 6½ games. The Phillies were still dogged by injuries, and this time they had sustained a big one when first baseman Frank Thomas broke his thumb a few weeks back. Still, the Phillies held the lead, despite that one of the Phillies' biggest problems, a lack of depth on the bench, was now being exposed when people like Ruben Amaro and John Herrnstein were playing first base. People in Philadelphia were now getting anxious to buy tickets for the World Series against whoever would win a tight three-team race in the American League between the New York Yankees, the Chicago White Sox, and the Baltimore Orioles.

September 20 began a stretch that has now been called "the Great Phillie Fold." At this point, Milwaukee was dropping out of the race due to pitching problems. The Giants were also having problems, even though they had a fine team all around. The 1964 Giants had many Latin players on the team, and many of them liked to speak Spanish. Manager Alvin Dark decided to ban the speaking of Spanish in the clubhouse, which did not sit well with the Latin players. Many of the Latin players felt that Dark did not like them. Some of the black players also felt the same way about Dark. Soon, there was dissension on the Giants. Many outsiders felt Dark was a decent manager, but he did not get the job done with a roster full of stars and now there was another season seemingly slipping away without a pennant in San Francisco. Sure, Dark ran the 1962 team that won the flag, but it took a tough playoff against the Dodgers to do it, then the Giants lost the series to the Yankees in 7 games. Dark was a born-again Christian whom many people felt was a bit of a hypocrite. When Dark admitted he had an extramarital affair it led to his firing, but by the time the ax fell the season was over and the Giants won nothing for 1964.

That left the Cardinals and Reds as the only two teams left to possibly pressure the Phillies. Cincinnati was hitting the ball even better than the year before, and their pitching was also tough. The Cardinals now had their act together, so they felt confident of victory. Many people, though, felt that the only race left in the National League was the one for second between the Cardinals and the Reds.

The Phillies were home on September 20 to open a 7-game homestand. Meanwhile, the Cardinals were on the road to face the still miserable Mets. On the twentieth, the Cardinals lost while the Phillies and Reds both won. This was the day the Phillies' lead was at 6½ games over both clubs. The next day, the Reds visited the Phillies while the Mets waited for the Cardinals. On the Cardinals' travel day the Reds beat the Phillies, so the Reds were now 5½ games out while the Cardinals were alone in third place, 6 games out. By this time, Gene Mauch had decided to do something that the Cardinals themselves had tried but had failed to do in a pennant race.

In 1935 the Cardinals were in a tough race with the Cubs when manager Frankie Frisch decided to rely mostly on the Dean brothers to win a second straight flag. The result was a failure, as the Cubs launched a 21-game winning streak and captured the flag ahead of the Cardinals. Both Deans were tired from the overwork, and Paul Dean developed a sore arm from overuse, ruining his career. Now, almost thirty years later, Gene Mauch decided to rely mostly on Jim Bunning and Chris Short to win a pennant for Philadelphia. Entering September 22 Mauch's plan had already been implemented and the results were mixed. Still, Mauch decided to stay with the plan.

On the twenty-second the Reds downed the Phillies again while the Cardinals beat the Mets. The Phillies now held a 4½ game lead on the Reds, with the Cardinals 5 out. The Cardinals remained 5 out the next day when they lost to the Mets while the Reds put the sweep on the Phillies by beating them yet again. Cincinnati was now 3½ out. People in Philadelphia were starting to get nervous, as the Reds were now within striking distance of the Phillies while the Cardinals lurked not too far behind.

September 24 found the Cardinals sweeping a doubleheader while the Phillies lost to the hard-hitting Braves. The twin-bill sweep began an 8-game winning streak for the Cardinals, which certainly came at the right time. The Reds were off that day, so the Phillies ended the day leading the Reds by 3 and the Cardinals by 3½. On the twenty-fifth, more bad news struck the Phillies. The Braves beat them again while the Cardinals won and the Reds swept a twin-bill. The Phillie lead was cut to just 1½ games over the Reds with St. Louis only 2½ out. The twenty-fifth was really galling for the Phillies because Chris Short was having a good game (on short rest) and had the Braves under control when they fell behind in the eighth. Johnny Callison hit a homer in that frame to tie it; then the Phillies tied it again in the tenth on a Dick Allen homer. The Braves then scored twice in the twelfth, and the Phillies were dead.

As September 26 began, the Phillies were in the middle of a 10-game losing streak. During that day's game, the Phillies lost it in the ninth when Bobby Shantz (yeah, the former Cardinal of earlier in 1964 was now a Phillie after the Cubs thought he was through) gave up a triple to the less than speedy (even then) Rico Carty. The Cardinals kept pace by winning that day, as did the Reds. Art Mahaffey started that day for the Phillies, and when he struggled it made Gene Mauch more determined than ever to now stick to his Bunning-Short pitching rotation. The Reds were now only half a game out, the Cardinals just 1½ behind.

The Philadelphia nightmare continued when they faced the Braves yet again on the twenty-seventh. By now, the Braves were just about back into the race with their beatings of the Phillies. Jim Bunning went out with short rest and was given a 3-homer barrage by Johnny Callison for aid. Instead of winning, Bunning and the bullpen were savaged by a 22-hit attack by Milwaukee as the Braves won a slugfest 14–8. The Cardinals won again to keep pace, and now the Giants were just 4½ games out as they tried to put their problems behind them. The big news, though, was a doubleheader sweep of the Mets by the Reds, which moved Cincinnati into first place, a game ahead of the Phillies. St. Louis was now just half a game out.

The next three days pitted the Phillies in head-to-head games with the Cardinals. Bob Gibson, now proving to be a tough clutch pitcher, downed the tiring Chris Short in the first game 5–1 in St. Louis. In the second game Ray Sadecki posted a 4–2 win over Dennis Bennett as the Phillies lost their ninth in a row while the Cardinals won their seventh straight. In the series finale, Curt Simmons disposed of his old team by downing Jim Bunning 8–5. While this 3-game series was going on the Reds lost 2 games, so the Cardinals entered an off day on October 1 in first place for the first time all year. The Reds dropped to second, 1 game out, while the Phillies were in third place, 2½ games out. The Giants and Braves were no longer in the hunt. While the Cardinals and Phillies were off on October 1, the Reds won, so they were now just a half game out of first. All three teams had a shot at the flag with 3 games left in the season. Now St. Louis was in the driver's seat, since they ended the year at home against the last-place Mets while the Reds hosted the Phillies.

On October 2, the Phillies put an end to their 10-game losing streak by shading the Reds 4–3. Meanwhile, the Cardinals were expecting to easily down the Mets, who owned a dismal 51–108 record coming into the game. Instead, Al Jackson tossed a 1–0 shutout against Bob Gibson. The shock was unreal. How could a miserable team like the Mets beat a team like the Cardinals, and in their own park? The next day, the Phillies and Reds were both off due to a quirk of the schedule while the Cardinals and Mets went at it again. This time, the Mets allowed 5 runs, but with the 5

187

homers of their own the Mets defeated the Cardinals 15–5. A few days earlier everyone laughed at the Phillies for blowing their lead. Now the Cardinals were the ones being laughed at as they were in danger of losing the lead themselves, at home, against the Mets.

October 4, 1964, the Phillies sent Jim Bunning to face the Reds while the Reds sent John Tsitouris to face the Phillies. Bunning had some rest for a change, and he was sharp. All three teams had a shot at a three-way tie for first at this point, so this game was a must for the Reds. Instead, Bunning handcuffed the hard-hitting crew from Cincinnati 10–0, knocking them out of the race. The Cardinals needed a win to clinch the flag, and Curt Simmons faced Galen Cisco. The Mets knocked out Simmons and took a 3–2 lead, but in the bottom of the fifth the Cardinals got 3 runs to take the lead. Bob Gibson came on in relief, and the Mets closed the gap a bit, trailing 5–4 when the Cardinals scored thrice in the sixth and thrice in the eighth. The Cardinals clinched the pennant with an 11–5 win in one of the greatest pennant races of all time, if not *the* greatest pennant race.

When the dust cleared, the standings showed the Cardinals owning a 93–69 record, with the Phillies and Reds tied for second at 92–70 and 1 game out. The Giants finished third with a 90–72 mark, 3 games out, and the Braves were fourth with an 88–74 record, just 5 games out. Did the Philadelphia Phillies really choke, as everyone maintained steadfastly after the season ended? Yes and no. The Phillies did lose 10 straight at a bad time in the schedule, and that streak most certainly hurt. Gene Mauch did show signs of either panic or overconfidence by relying so heavily on Bunning and Short, panic by thinking that no other starter was good enough to win games down the stretch, and overconfidence in thinking that Bunning and Short were so good that these two pitchers alone would be able to slay the rest of the league in the stretch, while holding a nice lead in the standings. If one looks at the streak and the way Mauch used his starting rotation in these lights, one can say that the Phillies did indeed choke in 1964. After all, had the Phillies won just one game in that losing streak the race would have been altered and the Phillies might have won after all. But on the other hand, perhaps the Phillies were simply overrated going into the season. In Philadelphia expectations were high, while outsiders at first thought the Phillies would contend but not win. Once the Phillies got off to their 6½ game lead, even the objective outsiders got caught up in "Phillie Fever," and when the Phillies lost the flag these outsiders joined the Philadelphia crowd in screaming, "Choke!" despite the fact that most outsiders didn't think the Phillies were pennant winners in the first place. As a result, the "Phillie Fold" has come down to us today as something of a legend in baseball history, something that should have never happened at all, says the legend.

When one sees what kind of team Gene Mauch had in 1964, one can see the job he did was almost as amazing as the one he had done in 1962. Injuries dogged the Phillies all year, and Mauch had a weak bench to work with even before the season began, so when people like Frank Thomas went down, Mauch had to improvise a bench, playing a middle infielder like Ruben Amaro at first, for example. True, a good team is supposed to overcome injuries, but when a team lacks depth, it will usually fall out of the race quickly (if it was supposed to contend when healthy). The pitching staff also was hit by a lack of depth. Art Mahaffey was the Phillie ace in 1962, but in 1963 and 1964 Mahaffey was bothered by injury and wasn't close to the 19-game winner that he was in 1962. Few starters outside of Bunning, Short, and Dennis Bennett did well for the Phillies in 1964, so starting pitching was a glaring weakness as well.

Finally, a look at the 1964 Phillies lineup shows why the Phillies did not win. At first base John Herrnstein (.234, 6 home runs, 25 RBIs) got plenty of time at the Phillies' revolving door position. The Cardinals got a .303, 21, 102 year out of Bill White that year. Deron Johnson went .273, 21, 79 for the Reds. Orlando Cepeda went .304, 31, 97 for the Giants. Even Walt Bond of the light-hitting Colt .45s produced a .254, 20, 85 season for Houston. At second base, Tony Taylor hit .251, but at least he gave the Phillies a solid glove. Shortstop was a mess with Bobby Wine (.212), Cookie Rojas (.291), and Ruben Amaro (.264) all taking turns at the position. Every other team in the league had stability at the key infield position at short, but the Phillies did not. Virtually every team in the league had stability behind the plate as well, while the Phillies went with Clay Dalrymple (.238) and Gus Triandos (.250) there. The Phillies had no speed, as they stole just 30 bases. Overall, the Phillies lineup compared unfavorably with the lineups of the other first division teams, as well as with the lineups of Pittsburgh and Chicago. Overall, the Phillies' pitching (aside from the bullpen) was little better than the Braves, Dodgers, Cubs, or even Mets. When one looks at the material Gene Mauch had to work with in 1964, one is amazed how he kept the Phillies in the race wire to wire in 1964. Instead of being condemned as the man who blew the pennant, Gene Mauch should be commended for leading a mediocre club in a tough pennant race, despite lacking an All-Star lineup, pitching depth, and a good bench. If anything, Mauch's 1965 Phillies were better than his 1964 Phillies, even though they finished sixth, 11½ games out.

No matter what one thinks about the 1964 Phillies, the fact remains that the Cardinals were the top team in the National League that year. After overcoming a poor start, St. Louis played excellent ball in the second half of the year, and especially after Bing Devine's firing. Old Barney Schultz was a godsend for the bullpen, picking up 14 saves while posting a 1.64 ERA in less than half a season's work. Bob Gibson became the big man in the starting rotation when he posted a 19–12 record while fanning 245 batters (second in the league). Ray Sadecki finally found himself and went 21–11. Veteran Curt Simmons went 18–9. Offensively, the Cardinals also picked up after the All-Star break. Bill White posted another fine year, going along with a slick glove at first. Ken Boyer was named the MVP of the league with a .295 average with 24 homers and a league-high 119 RBIs. Tim McCarver hit .288. Dick Groat got 70 RBIs despite hitting just one homer. But the biggest contributor to the Cardinals' 1964 pennant was Lou Brock. Brock hit .348 after coming from Chicago, and he finished second to Maury Wills in steals with 43. Brock gave St. Louis the leadoff man it lacked for so long, and he was outstanding. Brock also formed a part of a fine outfield with Mike Shannon in right and the man many hailed as the best center fielder of his time in Curt Flood (.311 in '64) between the two newcomers. The Cardinals survived turmoil, a bad start, and a grueling pennant race and were now going to their first World Series in eighteen years.

The Cardinals survived a tough pennant race to get to the

1964 series, and so did the Yankees. Nineteen-sixty-four was one of the most hectic years the Yankees went through in the pre-Steinbrenner years. Former Yankee catcher Yogi Berra retired in 1963 and was named the team's skipper for 1964. Many had questioned this move, believing that the players would take advantage of their jovial former teammate. The Yankees then started 1964 slowly, as the White Sox and Orioles took turns sharing the top spot. Many people thought the Yankees were getting out of control under Berra and wanted him fired. Privately, the team's owners thought they indeed had made a mistake in naming Berra as pilot, but they decided to do nothing until the end of the year. In the later stages of the season, the turmoil with the Yankees exploded into "the Harmonica Incident." Utilityman Phil Linz was playing a harmonica on the bus after a tough Yankee loss when Berra told him to stop. Linz thought the manager was kidding and kept on playing. Berra then slapped the harmonica out of the hands of Linz, and a fight was narrowly averted. The owners filed away this incident for future reference, and then the Yankees took off, playing like past Yankee teams. In the end, the Yankees won their fifth straight flag by 1 game over the White Sox and 2 over the Orioles as Berra became one of the few skippers to win a flag in his first year on the job.

The 1964 World Series began on October 7 in St. Louis. The Yankees were slightly favored to win it due to their experience of playing in many previous series. Whitey Ford started against Ray Sadecki, and neither man lasted a full 9 innings. In the sixth, the Yankees led 4–2 when the Cardinals exploded for 4 runs when Mike Shannon hit a 2-run homer, pinch hitter Carl Warwick hit an RBI single, and Curt Flood hit a run-scoring triple. Ford failed to finish the frame when he hurt his arm, and he would not appear in the rest of the series. The Yankees scored once in the eighth, but St. Louis countered with three runs in the frame as Barney Schultz shut the door. The Cardinals won the game 9–5.

Bob Gibson's importance to St. Louis was evident in the second game. After eight innings the Yankees were ahead by only a 4–2 score when Johnny Keane sent Charlie James to hit for Gibson. James doubled but did not score. In the ninth the Cardinal ace was replaced by Schultz. This time the top bullpenner didn't have it, and the Yankees quickly disposed of him and two other pitchers, scoring four times in the ninth. New York starter Mel Stottlemyre went the distance as the Yankees won 8–3.

Two days later the series resumed in New York, and it was a fine day for both Curt Simmons and Jim Bouton. Both pitchers were hurling beautifully in the game as the Yankees got an RBI double from Clete Boyer (Ken's brother) in the second. In the fifth Simmons helped himself with an RBI single to tie the game. The game remained tied at 1 when Simmons was lifted for a pinch hitter after allowing just 4 hits. In the bottom of the ninth, Barney Schultz again came into the game, but he didn't work for long. Mickey Mantle slammed the first pitch Schultz threw for a game-winning homer. Bouton, who allowed only 6 hits in his complete game, took the 2–1 win. The Yankees now led in the series 2 games to 1.

The Cardinals tied up the series the next day with a quick game. Sadecki was given the ball against Al Downing, but he failed to escape the first inning. A double by Bobby Richardson and singles by Mantle and Elston Howard produced a quick 3–0 Yankee lead against Sadecki. Roger Craig came out of the bullpen, and he then proceeded to throttle the locals the rest of the way. In the fifth inning, the Cardinals took the lead when Ken Boyer came through with a grand slam homer, and that blow made Craig a 4–3 winner. The game was over in under two hours and twenty minutes.

On the twelfth, Bob Gibson was given the ball against rookie Mel Stottlemyre and both hurlers were effective. The Cardinals took a 2–0 lead into the ninth, when the Yankees broke through to tie it up. Mantle was safe on an error when Joe Pepitone ripped a line drive off of Gibson's side. Gibson quickly grabbed the ball and threw Pepitone out by only seconds. Tom Tresh then homered to tie the game, so the play on Pepitone was pivotal. In the tenth, Bill White walked against Pete Mikkelson, then went to second on Ken Boyer's bunt single. After a force out, Tim McCarver delivered a 3-run homer to bag a 5–2 win for Gibson, who went the distance.

Back in St. Louis on the fourteenth to conclude the series, the Yankees tried to stave off a series loss by sending Bouton against Simmons. The Cardinals took a 1–0 lead in the first, but the Yankees fought back with 1 run in the fifth and 2 in the sixth. In the eighth,

Pepitone ripped a grand slammer, highlighting a 5-run outburst that sent Simmons to the showers. The Cardinals scored solo runs in the eighth and ninth, but it wasn't enough, as the Yankees won 8–3.

Bob Gibson got the call for the seventh and final game of the series, and he again faced Stottlemyre. Both men pitched 3 scoreless innings when St. Louis scored 3 in the fourth and 3 more in the fifth to give Gibson a 6–0 cushion. Mickey Mantle cut the lead in half when he belted a 3-run homer in the sixth, but in the seventh Ken Boyer hit a solo homer to make the score 7–3 in favor of the locals. In the ninth the Yankees threatened when they got homers from Clete Boyer and light-hitting Phil Linz. Johnny Keane stuck with Gibson despite the late New York rally. Gibby ended the game by getting Bobby Richardson to pop out to second, giving St. Louis a 7–5 win and its first world championship since 1946. Gussie Busch and the city of St. Louis expected a championship in 1964, and the Cardinals came through splendidly. St. Louis erupted in euphoria.

Thus the Cardinals were world champs, but one more story was left for 1964. The day after the series ended, on October 16, the Yankees made a stunning announcement—manager Yogi Berra was fired. This news rocked baseball for only a little while when even more bizarre news came from St. Louis that same day— Johnny Keane had quit as manger of the Cardinals. Evidently, Keane was upset at the way Bing Devine had been treated in August and he had made up his mind to quit no matter what the Cardinals did in 1964. The demise of both World Series managers only a day after the series was unprecedented and shocked all. Less than a week later the Yankees delivered another shock when they hired Johnny Keane to manage them in 1965. Yogi Berra moved on to the Mets as a coach a year after taking the Yankees to a series as a rookie pilot, and Johnny Keane took over the team that his old club beat in that same series. Keane's move to the Yankees proved disastrous. In 1965 the Yankees showed their age and their lack of a good farm system to new owner CBS by plunging into sixth place with a 77–85 record, their first losing record in forty years. Johnny Keane could not get along with his new players, a hard-partying lot featuring Mickey Mantle and Whitey Ford. The next year, 1966, the Yankees got off to a dismal 4–16 start under Keane when he was fired. It was obvious that the great New York Yankees dynasty was over and Keane had lost control of the team. Johnny Keane left the game after his firing and died on January 6, 1967, at age 55.

III

The St. Louis Cardinals were world champs for 1964, and they now found themselves without a manager. A little while after Keane quit, the Cardinals named Red Schoendienst as the new pilot. Schoendienst was highly popular when he played for the Cardinals from 1945 into 1956. Red broke into the majors as an outfielder even though he was middle infielder in the minors, but he was capable in the new position. In 1946, Schoendienst was moved to second base, where he excelled for the rest of his career. In 1956, Trader Lane sent his second baseman to the Giants in a deal that most Cardinal fans were outraged about. Red knew about winners, playing on the 1946 world-champion Cardinals and two more pennant winners at Milwaukee in 1957 and 1958, the former team winning the series. In 1961 the Cardinals brought back Schoendienst as a pinch hitter, and he led the league in pinch at bats and pinch hits in 1962. After getting into six games in 1963, Schoendienst retired and became a coach. Now Red Schoendienst the manager had the task of trying to win a second straight world championship going into 1965.

The Cardinals entered 1965 with some new faces. Roger Craig and Charlie James were shipped to the Reds for Bob Purkey. Purkey posted an 11–9 record with a 3.04 ERA for Cincinnati in 1964 while being nagged by injury. At one time Purkey was the Reds ace, but injury kept him back. St. Louis also picked up pitcher Tracy Stallard and infielder Elio Chacon from the Mets for Johnny Lewis and Gordon Richardson. Stallard was one of the top Mets hurlers of 1964, even though he led the league with 20 losses while winning 10. Stallard's 3.79 ERA was outstanding on a Mets team that posted a league-high 4.25 ERA. Chacon would bolster the bench. The Cardinals also bought Tito Francona from the Indians for pinch-hitting duty and to fill in in the outfield. Overall, the Cardinals did very little to their roster, since teams are hardly anxious to strengthen the defending world champion.

The Cardinals were expected to contend in 1965, maybe even win. The Phillies, Reds, Giants, and Braves were all expected to provide the competition for St. Louis, just like they did the year before. The Cardinals started weakly again while the aforementioned teams were joined by the rejuvenated Dodgers and the Pirates in a tough six-team battle for the flag. Many people were worried that the Cardinals would not get back into the race, while others figured that the Cardinals would simply repeat their 1964 performance. St. Louis had trouble holding leads in the late innings as the bullpen repeated the 1964 season all over again before Barney Schultz arrived. This time, Barney Schultz was hit hard and often and Ron Taylor was struggling so badly that he was sent to the Astros (the new name of the Colt .45s) with Mike Cuellar for Chuck Taylor and Hal Woodeschick on June 15. The deal for Woodeschick was a great one for St. Louis as well as Houston. Cuellar would have some good years for the Astros as a starter while Woodeschick would solve the bullpen problem for the Cardinals for the next two years.

Still, the Cardinals struggled. The hitting fell off as Ken Boyer and Bill White were not driving in runs like they did the year before. Lou Brock was hitting well and stealing bases, but he was not the .348 hitter that he had been in 1964. Dick Groat struggled to hit .250. The Purkey deal failed, as he was bombed almost every time he pitched. Curt Simmons was showing signs of age as he had an ERA over 4.00. Ray Sadecki was hammered over and over again as his ERA went over 5.00. Injuries reduced Julian Javier and Mike Shannon to poor hitters. St. Louis ended up getting good years out of only Brock (.288 with 63 steals), Tim McCarver (.276), and Curt Flood (.310 with a club-high 83 RBIs). Bob Gibson broke the 20-win barrier for the first time as he went 20–12 in 300 innings with a 3.07 ERA and 270 strikeouts (third in the league). Ray Washburn had a decent year at 9–11, 3.62, and Nellie Briles showed promise with a 3–3, 3.50 record as a spot starter/long reliever. Tracy Stallard went 11–8 with a 3.38 ERA, and Woodeschick posted fifteen saves with a 1.81 ERA after coming from Houston.

Overall, 1965 was a disaster for the Cardinals. Like their

opponent in the 1964 Series, the Cardinals ended the year sixth, with a poor 80–81 record. Major changes would be in order to get the Cardinals back on track. A few weeks after the season ended, the Cardinals made a big trade with the Mets, sending former MVP and ten-year man Ken Boyer to New York in exchange for Al Jackson and Charley Smith. Then, in an even bigger deal, the Cardinals sent their other slugger, Bill White, along with Dick Groat and Bob Uecker, to the Phillies in exchange for Art Mahaffey, Alex Johnson, and Pat Corrales. These were the major moves that the Cardinals made (in addition to some lesser ones) to improve themselves for 1966. The Cardinals would rely more heavily on farm players to do the job as regulars. Smith was elated to be the third baseman while Dal Maxvill was elevated to regular status (he was a utilityman for the last few years) at short. Mike Shannon was given the right field job full time. Tim McCarver was the catcher, and Curt Flood and Lou Brock completed the outfield. First base would be a revolving door until someone proved that he could play the position well on a daily basis. The pitching, led by Bob Gibson, was expected to be solid, as the failures of 1965 were swept out. Ray Sadecki, who was dismal in 1965, was expected to right himself and pitch more like he did in 1964, so the load on Gibson would not be too heavy. Although the Cardinals made many changes, they were not expected to win the flag, but were expected to move into the first division, however.

The Cardinals started 1966 the same way they started the previous two seasons—poorly. St. Louis was getting good pitching, but the hitting was even worse than in 1965. Nellie Briles was losing games by 1–0 and 2–1 scores frequently as the offense contributed virtually nothing. St. Louis was again mired in the second division when on May 12 the Cardinals played their first game in their new home—the new Busch Stadium. Busch Stadium featured all of the modern accouterments that the old Busch Stadium (formerly Sportsman's Park) lacked, and it was bigger than the old ballpark. The old Busch Stadium, originally the home of the St. Louis Maroons of the Union Association and then the home of the American League's St. Louis Browns, was finally abandoned after eighty-two years. Part of the old stadium still stands today.

Despite having a new home, the Cardinals continued to be

mediocre. Bob Gibson was pitching better than ever, and he had to with the way the hitting was in order to win. Besides Nellie Briles, Al Jackson was also finding it hard to win, even though he was throwing well. Jackson probably thought he was still with the weak-hitting Mets, as he lost plenty of low-scoring games for his new team. Charley Smith was hitting better than expected, but he was not the answer at third, so a parade of players came and went as they were found lacking in one area or another. Julian Javier and Dal Maxvill were a great double play combination, but they could not hit a lick. Mike Shannon provided some surprising pop and Curt Flood was becoming the top RBI man when St. Louis made a key trade.

Four days before the Cardinals played in their new home for the first time, they sent struggling Ray Sadecki to the San Francisco Giants for Orlando Cepeda. Cepeda was a good-fielding first baseman who had been one of the league's top sluggers for years. Since first reaching the majors in 1958 Cepeda had driven in 96, 105, 96, 142, 114, 97, and 97 runs in his first seven seasons while hitting between 24 and 46 homers in each of those years. Cepeda also hit .300 six times, and in 1961 he out-homered the likes of Mays and McCovey, Robinson and Aaron, while leading the league in RBIs. Most people thought that Orlando Cepeda was heading for the Hall of Fame as he put up some eye-popping numbers.

But there was something wrong. Cepeda developed a reputation of not giving his all, of being too conceited, and of being a clubhouse lawyer. Many people figured that he was the biggest enemy of Al Dark when he managed the Giants and that he was leading a movement to get Dark fired, a movement that was killing the Giants' chances at a pennant every year that Dark was in San Francisco. Such dissension in 1964 probably was the key reason why the Giants just missed the flag themselves. In 1965, Dark was gone and Herman Franks was at the helm. Franks was no shrinking violet, and people wondered how he would get along with the slugger. Cepeda missed 1965 due to injury, but when he returned in 1966 it didn't look like he and Franks were going to be good pals. At the time of his trade, Cepeda was hitting .286, so the Giants probably felt that they would never win a pennant with Cepeda on the team and got rid of him.

Cepeda's arrival in St. Louis brought an end to the mess at first base. The Cardinals finally had a bona fide home run threat in their lineup and began to play better. Cepeda got along well with everybody in his new city, and while he wasn't hitting like he did before 1965, he was still better than anyone the Cardinals had tried at first up to the trade.

The Cepeda trade made little impact on the Cardinals overall in 1966. The team continued to languish in the second division for most of the year, moving ahead of the Braves (spending their first year in Atlanta) and Phillies every now and then. Briles and Jackson continued to lose tough games as the Dodgers, Giants, and Pirates were making it a three-team race. Ray Washburn continued to develop, and Joe Hoerner was turning into an ace reliever. Overall, 1966 was simply a year for personal achievement rather than collective greatness. Larry Jaster tied for the league lead in shutouts with five, and all of his blankings were against league champ Los Angeles. Tim McCarver hit thirteen triples for the year, becoming the first catcher to lead a league in that category. Nellie Briles had a 3.21 ERA to go with his hard-luck 4–15 mark. Al Jackson fared little better with a 13–15 mark to go with his fine 2.51 ERA. Bob Gibson went 21–12 with a 2.44 ERA and 225 strikeouts as he finished third in wins, fourth in strikeouts, and fifth in ERA. Joe Hoerner had 13 saves with a 1.54 ERA in 57 games. Cepeda hit .303 with a club-high 17 homers. Curt Flood's 78 RBIs led the team (the lowest total to lead the team in that category since the shortened season of 1919, when Rogers Hornsby led with 71 RBIs), and Lou Brock was the league champ in steals with 74.

Teamwise, the Cardinals were mediocre. The team hit just .251, a mark that was better than only the ones of the Giants and Mets. St. Louis hit only 108 homers, which was better than only the Mets' total. The Cardinals did lead the league with 144 steals, as they had to rely on steals and speed in general to generate runs. The Cardinals' ERA of 3.11 was topped only by the Dodgers' 2.62, and St. Louis threw nineteen shutouts, one less than the Dodgers. The biggest deal, though, was in the standings. St. Louis finished sixth again, this time with an 83–79 record. Despite finishing 12 games out, the Cardinals drew a team-record 1,712,980 fans, an increase in attendance of about 500,000 from 1965. Most of those people came to see the new ballpark, not the mediocre team playing in it. More changes were needed to transform the Cardinals into a contender.

St. Louis went to work on building for 1967 right away. The Cardinals were gambling that Orlando Cepeda would hit like he had prior to his injury, so they kept him at first base. More power was needed to supplement Cepeda, so the Cardinals sent Charley Smith to the Yankees for Roger Maris. Maris had hit 61 homers in 1961 and had been a big power hitter in New York for some time, but injuries had reduced him to a struggling hitter who was being booed in New York. Maris was less than happy playing for a now dismal Yankee team and getting booed for his trouble, so he was thrilled to go to St. Louis. With Maris coming to the Cardinals, Mike Shannon would be bumped out of position, so Red Schoendienst decided to move him to third base, replacing the now departed Charley Smith. Maris was in decline, but he could still do the job in right field.

Next the Cardinals looked around their minor league system for help and decided that two pitchers, Dick Hughes and Steve Carlton were ready. Speedy outfielder Bobby Tolan was also recalled in case Maris underwent a complete breakdown. Fine-looking prospect Alex Johnson was also deemed ready for part-time play, and pitcher Ron Willis was also recalled to bolster the bullpen. St. Louis chose to retain the nucleus of 1966 for 1967 by leaving Julian Javier and Dal Maxvill as the keystone combo, Lou Brock and Curt Flood in their usual outfield slots, Orlando Cepeda at first, and Tim McCarver as the catcher. Most trades that the Cardinals made simply shored up their bench strength.

When the 1967 season was due to open, the Cardinals went into it with a different building plan than the one they had used in the last few years. Under Branch Rickey, the Cardinals hardly ever made a trade, using their farm system to stock the team with stars and even replacements for utilitymen. Rickey felt that he paid good money to start up an extensive farm system, so he wanted his money's worth. Every now and then Rickey would deal when he felt the player that was needed could not be supplied by the minors. Most of the time when Rickey did deal he would basically send surplus players to other teams in exchange for cash. This sort of deal filled the Cardinal coffers with sorely needed (at that time) cash while cleaning out the minors of players deemed not good enough to be of any use in St. Louis.

Eventually, as other teams began to catch on to Rickey's idea, the Cardinals had to alter their way of improving the team. Under Sam Breadon (after Rickey left) the Cardinals made more deals than ever and they did not always involve cash. (By then, the Cardinals were making plenty of money.) Other teams began to rely on their farm systems to fill in their needs, so they no longer went to the Cardinals to buy surplus players. As is the case with a trade, the Cardinals won some and they lost some over the years. The trading frenzy of Frank Lane in the 1950s began to overshadow the farm system. The Cardinals soon relied too heavily on trades while their minor league system was drying up, and the result was a succession of poor-playing Cardinal teams on the field.

In the early 1960s the Cardinals began to go back to the farm to stock the team. Now that St. Louis was pursuing black and Latin players, the Cardinal system was able to revive after some dry years, and that's how the Cardinals returned to the top in 1963–64. Trades were still important, so the Cardinals found the right mix of trades and recalls from the minors to win the World Series in 1964. After 1964 the Cardinals miscalculated and tried to fill in a few holes with trades that did not pan out, and the result was a mediocre team that did nothing in 1965 and 1966.

Now, as the Cardinals entered 1967, they went back to the Branch Rickey way of thinking. The nucleus of the 1967 Cardinals would be a home-grown one. Bob Gibson, Tim McCarver, Curt Flood, Dal Maxvill, Mike Shannon, Dick Hughes, Ray Washburn, Steve Carlton, Bobby Tolan, Julian Javier, Nellie Briles, Ron Willis, Larry Jaster, Joe Hoerner, and Phil Gagliano were the big names on the 1967 Cardinals who were all products of the Cardinal farm system. Gussie Busch was gambling that by basically standing pat the Cardinals would be able to get back into contention. Other teams were in flux as 1967 was coming. Sandy Koufax retired after the year, so that would have some effect on the Dodgers. The Mets finally escaped last place in 1966, so maybe they would do what the Phillies had done in 1962. The Reds had had a bad year in 1966, so nobody knew which way they were going. Leo Durocher was busy rebuilding the Cubs, so he might be a factor. The Giants and Pirates were tough, but with Willie Mays getting older his age might adversely affect his team. The Braves were trying to improve their pitching, and maybe Phil Niekro was the answer. The Astros had pitching, but the hitting was under suspicion, since youngsters Jimmy Wynn, Rusty Staub, and Joe Morgan might be stars or flops at that point. The Cardinals figured that by being complacent they might be able to push past all nine of the other teams that were in flux. Only time would tell if the Cardinals could pull it off.

IV

As Opening Day 1967 approached, the experts decided that the Dodgers were not good enough to win their third straight flag, since Sandy Koufax retired while Don Drysdale was coming off of a 13–16 season. Los Angeles was expected to drop to the middle of the pack, along with St. Louis, while the Giants and Pirates, the two teams that just missed out in 1966, were expected to battle it out for the top spot in 1967. St. Louis was regarded as having good pitching, but the hitting was still suspect. Now that the Cardinals played in a much bigger park they would have to emphasize speed more than ever before in order to score runs. The Dodgers of the early to mid-1960s proved that a team with good pitching, speed, and defense could indeed win pennants even if they lacked power. In 1965 the Dodgers were world champs even though they hit just 78 homers. The Cardinals would now try to duplicate the Dodgers' success.

When the season opened, the Pirates got off to a shaky start as pitching problems canceled out their fine hitting. The Giants did not falter, and they were joined by the Cardinals, Reds, and Cubs in getting off to a good start. St. Louis was getting better than expected hitting while the pitching was doing its expected thing. The Giants, Reds, and Cubs all had more power hitting, but none of these teams had the pitching depth or the pervasive speed of the Cardinals. As the season progressed the Cardinals began to break away from the pack as Dick Hughes became a top hurler and

Steve Carlton showed that he had fine control to go with a nasty fastball. Bob Gibson, of course, was still the ace, and he looked like he would win another 20 games. Offensively, Lou Brock was hitting around .300, and he was hitting some homers as well (no, he was not trying to prove to the Cubs that he really was another Willie Mays) while leading the league in steals. Curt Flood was going for the batting title. With Brock and Flood getting on base so often, Orlando Cepeda had plenty of RBI chances and most of the time he cashed in big, as he began to hit like he did before his 1965 knee injury. Julian Javier suddenly added some pop to the lineup as well while becoming an all-around threat with the stick. Even Mike Shannon and Tim McCarver began hitting the long ball, despite the large size of their new home.

In the middle of July the Cardinals were cruising along in first place, leading by four games, when a potential disaster hit. On July 15 the Cardinals were playing the Pirates with Bob Gibson on the hill. In the fourth inning Roberto Clemente hit a line drive right off of Gibson's leg for a single. This reminded people of when Gibson was hit by a line drive from Joe Pepitone's bat in the 1964 World Series. In this game, where the legend of Bob Gibson grew, Gibby waved off the trainer and insisted he was fine. Gibson pitched to two more batters before collapsing on the mound. In the club-house came the frightening news—Gibson had a broken leg. Despite having the leg broken by a line drive, Gibson still wanted to keep on going, but after two batters the break worsened. Gibson would miss the next two months at the very least, and all of a sudden the Cardinals looked like they would fold up and go home after losing their ace.

Wrong. Instead of folding, the Cardinals actually played better than ever as the other pitchers chipped in to compensate for the loss of Gibson. The Giants continued to dog St. Louis, but the Reds and Cubs began to fall back. In August the Cardinals began to put on a spurt just as the Giants finally began to waver, moving St. Louis further and further away from the pack. The Cardinals' blend of speed and timely homers was quite a devastating mix for victory, and with all of the pitchers sharing the load the Cardinals were able to build a head of steam and move into a permanent hold of first place. In September Gibson returned, won 3 games while looking like he never was gone, and the race was over. St. Louis finished ten games ahead of the Giants while posting a 101–60 mark.

Compared to 1966, 1967 was most definitely a year for collective greatness. Orlando Cepeda led the league with 111 RBIs while hitting 25 homers on a .325 average. Curt Flood was third in the batting race with a .335 mark. Lou Brock led the league with 52 steals. Julian Javier hit .281 while driving in 64 runs. Mike Shannon had 77 RBIs. Tim McCarver hit .295. Roger Maris brought a winning attitude to St. Louis while batting .261. Five Cardinals hit at least 10 homers. Light-hitting Dal Maxvill got 41 RBIs out of a .227 average. Defensively, Flood was his usual brilliant self in center, McCarver became the best catcher in the league, and Javier and Maxvill looked like two acrobats turning double plays. Maris still played well in right field, Brock and Cepeda looked sharp at their positions, and Shannon made a fine transition from outfielder to third baseman. Overall, St. Louis hit 115 homers, good enough for fourth in the league while being the only team to steal 100 bases, so the offense made an amazing about face from the dismal performance of 1966.

Pitching, though, was what made the Cardinals tough. At 3.05, St. Louis finished tied for second in team ERA. The individual performances were great. Dick Hughes became the big winner with Gibson missing two months. The rookie went 16–6 with a 2.67 ERA. Nellie Briles moved from long relief to starting and compiled an amazing 14–5 mark with 6 saves and a 2.43 ERA. Steve Carlton went 14–9 with a 2.98 ERA. Ray Washburn was the worst starter with a 10–7, 3.53 year. (Yeah, he should have been shot for such a bad year.) Bob Gibson didn't show any aftereffects of his broken leg as he ended up 13–7 with a 2.98 ERA. In the bullpen Ron Willis won 6 and saved 10 as a rookie while posting a 2.67 ERA. Joe Hoerner won 4 and saved 15 with a 2.59 ERA. Larry Jaster, Al Jackson, and Jack Lamabe all pitched well as starter/relievers.

The Cardinals had breezed to a pennant despite losing their top pitcher and inspiration in Bob Gibson. St. Louis was now favored to win the World Series against Boston. The Red Sox had won their flag in astounding fashion. Since the mid-1950s the Red Sox had been at best a mediocre team that never was in the race.

In 1966 the Red Sox–Yankees rivalry took on a horrible new twist when both teams fought to finish ninth. Boston won that battle by half a game, thanks to some rained out games that were not made up. Boston hired Dick Williams to manage the 1967 Red Sox, a team that everyone agreed was going to have another battle for the basement. Williams, though, had other ideas. He ranted and raved, straightening out attitudes and destroying egos along the way to Opening Day, saying that the Red Sox were going to be in the hunt for first place, not last place. A few months later the Red Sox were involved in possibly the most grueling race in American League history. The Red Sox, White Sox, Tigers, Twins, and for a time Angels were all at each other's throats. Like the 1964 National League race, the 1967 American League race saw teams moved into and out of the top slot seemingly every minute. Every day teams checked the scores to see if the other contenders had lost. Entering the final week four teams still had a shot and a four-way tie was possible, just like 1964 in the N.L. On the final day the Red Sox completed the "Impossible Dream" by beating the Twins, while the Tigers lost to the Angels. Boston had a fine roster of players led by Cy Young winner Jim Lonborg and MVP and Triple Crown winner Carl Yastrzemski, and it was hoped by some that the "miracle" Red Sox would beat the favored Cardinals to complete one of the great turnarounds in baseball history.

The 1967 World Series began on October 4 in Boston. Due to pitching frequently in the last two weeks, Jim Lonborg was passed up by the Red Sox to open the series, and in his place stepped Jose Santiago. Santiago had had a fine year as a starter and reliever, and he was opposed by Bob Gibson. Gibson, who liked to work fast (please bring him out of retirement!), did his usual stellar job in a big game. In the third the Cardinals supplied him with a 1–0 lead when Lou Brock singled, went to third on a Curt Flood double, then scored on a Roger Maris ground out. Santiago then did the best thing possible for a pitcher—he homered for himself. The game remained tied at 1 when Brock singled, stole second, then came home on two ground outs. Gibson then went on to complete the game, winning 2–1. Gibby allowed just six hits and a walk.

The next day Jim Lonborg was available to pitch, and pitch he did. Lonborg was devastating, allowing just one man to reach base—Julian Javier on a double in the seventh—in pitching one of the greatest games in series history. Lonborg was backed by a pair of Carl Yastrzemski homers—a solo shot in the fourth and a 3-run shot in the seventh that paved the way for an easy 5–0 win against Dick Hughes.

The series moved to St. Louis on the seventh for the third game. Nellie Briles got the ball against Gary Bell, and the Cardinals scored quickly. Brock tripled and scored on a Flood single in the first, and two more runs came in the second when Tim McCarver singled and scored on a Mike Shannon homer. Bell failed to last the second frame and was replaced by Gary Waslewski. In the sixth Boston got a run when Jose Tartabull singled home Mike Andrews (he of series infamy in 1973, when A's owner Charlie Finley fired him for making errors), but the Cardinals countered with an RBI single from Maris in the bottom of the same frame. Reggie Smith homered in the seventh, and Orlando Cepeda doubled home a run to complete the scoring in the game. Final score: Cardinals 5, Red Sox 2.

Bob Gibson faced Jose Santiago again in the fourth game. Again the Cardinals scored early when Maris hit a 2-run double and RBI singles by McCarver and Dal Maxvill all produced 4 runs in the first, knocking out Santiago in the process. St. Louis got 2 more runs in the third when McCarver drove in a run with a sac fly and Javier doubled home another run. It took Gibson 2 hours and 22 minutes to dispose of Boston in the opener, but in this game he took just over two hours to win 6–0.

The Red Sox were facing elimination when they sent Lonborg against Steve Carlton in the fifth game. The Boston ace was superb, allowing just three hits as the Red Sox supported him with just six hits, but they came at the right times. Ken Harrelson drove in Joe Foy in the third with a single, and the score stood at 1–0 with Boston entering the ninth. The Red Sox then scored 2 insurance runs when Elston Howard singled with the bases loaded, scoring one run, while another run scored on a bad throw from Maris. The 2 runs were big, because Maris homered in the bottom of the ninth, cutting the Boston lead to 3–1. Lonborg completed the game and won by the 3–1 mark.

Back in Boston on the eleventh Dick Hughes faced Waslewski,

and neither pitcher had it. Boston scored a run in the second on a Rico Petrocelli homer. St. Louis bounced back with 2 in the third on RBI singles by Brock and Flood. In the fourth, Boston retook the lead when Yaz homered, Smith homered, and Petrocelli homered, knocking Hughes out and giving the Red Sox a 4–2 lead. Still St. Louis did not die, tying the game in the seventh when Brock popped a homer himself. The Red Sox then put an end to the game when they plated 4 runs in the bottom of the seventh as the Cardinals sent three relievers to save Jack Lamabe from defeat. Hal Woodeschick's arrival an inning later gave the Cardinals a record for most pitchers used in series game—eight. John Wyatt won the game in relief 8–4 over Lamabe.

That brought the series to a seventh game, pitting the two aces against each other. Jim Lonborg was coming back on short rest while Gibson had his usual rest, and once again St. Louis took the lead first. In the third, 2 runs scored when Maxvill tripled and scored on Flood's single. Flood then came home himself when Lonborg threw a wild pitch. In the fifth Gibson homered and then another run came in when Brock singled, stole two bases, then scored on Maris's sac fly. By this point it was obvious that Lonborg had nothing and Gibson was just too much to take. St. Louis picked up three more tallies in the sixth to finally send Lonborg to the showers. Boston scored single runs in the fifth and eighth, but it was too late. Gibby scattered 3 hits en route to a 7–2 complete-game win, giving the Cardinals their eighth world championship in the last 41 years. Since 1926 the Cardinals had accounted for nearly 20 percent of all World Series wins (through 1967), and the 1967 title, like many of their others, came as a surprise to the so-called experts. The Cardinals were picked for a middle of the pack finish, and instead they won all the marbles in rather easy fashion. An incredible total of 2,090,145 people flocked to Busch Stadium in 1967 to see an exciting Cardinals team overcome the odds. The Cardinals, who once drew more flies than people to see them play, were the only team in the majors in 1967 to draw 2 million fans, and it was easily a club record.

The Cardinals were riding high after the 1967 World Series. St. Louis was ecstatic over the Cardinal win and their new style of play. The Cardinals had reached the top of the mountain with tight defense, blazing speed, and home runs at the right times. But the biggest thing that got the Cardinals glory was pitching. Pitching, that often overlooked aspect of the game that Hall of Fame manager Connie Mack said was "90 percent of the game." Many agreed that Mack was right with his statement. Pitching, pitching, pitching. In 1967 the pitching seemed better than ever. The Chicago White Sox were in the race from beginning to end, and it wasn't because of their hitting. The 1967 White Sox hit just .225, a mark more suited for the pre-1920 dead ball era than for the post-1961 expansion era. The Yankees, once the hardest of the hard-hitting teams, hit only hard times in 1967. With their dynasty over, the Yankees equaled the White Sox in batting futility at .225. Only the Washington Senators were a worse-hitting team at .223. The American League hit just .236 in 1967. Five years earlier the A.L. hit .255. The National League also had some weak-hitting teams in 1967. The Braves, playing in tiny Fulton County Stadium and having a lineup of Hank Aaron, Felipe Alou, Joe Torre, Mack Jones, Rico Carty, and Denis Menke, batted just .240 for the year. The Phillies of Dick Allen, Johnny Callison, and Bill White hit .242. The Dodgers, one year after winning their second straight flag, batted just .236 with Willie Davis, Ron Hunt, and Ron Fairly in their lineup. The Mets and Astros were hardly expected to hit well even though they were six years old in 1967, but at .238 and .249, respectively, these teams were actually *regressing*. The 1967 Mets actually hit four points lower than their horrid 1962 predecessors. The Astros saw their average shrink six points from their 1966 mark. Something was clearly wrong here.

Why was hitting in such decline going into 1968? The American League got some heavy hitting in 1961 when the Angels and Senators were brought into the league. The next year the National League saw hitting soar when the Mets and Astros joined the circuit. The bosses of the major leagues were shocked at the effect expansion was having on pitching. People were upset that the quality of baseball in general had suffered when the two leagues expanded and the pitching had really taken its lumps. Still, it seems that when the major leagues expanded (the A.L. in 1961, 1969, and 1977 and the N.L. in 1962 and 1969), not only were there more .300 hitters and 100-RBI men created, but there seemed to be an *increase* in the number of 20-game winners on the pitching side. In 1960, the American League had no pitchers winning more than 18 games. A year later, with expansion, two pitchers won 20. Two pitchers won 20 games in 1961 in the National League. A year later, with expansion, four pitchers won 20. In 1968, the "Year of the Pitcher," three N.L. pitchers and four A.L. chuckers won 20. A year later, with expansion, nine N.L. hurlers and six A.L. mounds-men won 20. Only in 1977 did the number of 20-game winners stay unchanged (3 in 1976 and 1977), so it might be said that expansion has elevated baseball to new highs, both on the hitting and pitching sides.

But 1967 was not an expansion year, and even though 20-game-winning pitchers did not explode across the land, batting averages were clearly sinking. Teams were scoring less runs than even in pre-expansion years, as hitting in general was returning to the days of the dead ball. The owners, worried that there was too much hitting coming from expansion, decided to adjust the strike zone in 1963 to give fans a break from a flurry of 8–7 games. The new strike zone ran from the batter's shoulders to the bottom of his knees, so the enlargement of the strike zone was having a definite effect by 1967. Could the hitting actually get *worse* in 1968? People wondered as another year was fast approaching. They would soon see that, yes indeed, the hitting could really get worse.

Nineteen-sixty-eight stands out in American history as one of the most strife-torn, divisive years ever experienced. The Black Power movement was growing. Vietnam was becoming a national nightmare, with no end in sight. Riots were breaking out all over the country. Sex, drugs, and rock and roll were widening the generation gap. Anyone following the authorities was deemed "square." The upcoming election for president promised to be a bitter affair. It seemed like the United States was going to hell in a handbasket in 1968. The entire world was undergoing upheaval. In France students demonstrated against the government. In Czecho-slovakia the communist government tried to "liberalize'" itself, much to the dismay of the Soviet Union. China was still undergoing the "Cultural Revolution." Every day the headlines screamed bad news from one place or another. And all of this was just in the first three months of 1968. Worse was yet to come.

The St. Louis Cardinals were ready to defend their world championship as 1968 dawned. The Cardinals made no major changes to their roster for the new season and simply improved their bench, primarily by adding catcher Johnny Edwards to give Tim McCarver a rest. Bob Gibson was pronounced fit as a fiddle after his leg healed well (as if his 1967 World Series performance didn't confirm that). The Cardinals were favored to win again, since they had a rather easy time in winning the flag in 1967. The Giants, Reds, and Cubs were deemed as the only teams with a shot at dethroning the Cardinals.

The 1968 baseball season began on a bad note. On April 4, Martin Luther King, Jr., was assassinated, triggering riots in many major league cities. Several teams voted not to play on Opening Day in memory of King. Commissioner Spike Eckert decided to go along with teams not wanting to play, since a ballpark full of people at a time like this could be a disaster waiting to happen. Some teams wouldn't have been able to play even if they wanted to. The Cubs were slated to open in Cincinnati, but they were confined to their hotel when Cincinnati imposed a nighttime curfew. Other teams, like the Dodgers, were reluctant to postpone their openers but went along when their opponents voted not to play. Nineteen-sixty-eight could have also been called the "Year of Postponements" as a result of the King murder and other terrible events.

A few days later the Cardinals began their season with a loss to the Cubs. Bob Gibson took the loss, and he would struggle for two months to get his record over .500 despite pitching the best games of his life. (That includes his outstanding postseason games as well.) The Cardinals were not hitting the ball. Nineteen-sixty-six's bad hitting was back two years later. Orlando Cepeda, the big RBI man in 1967, was driving in few runs. Lou Brock and Curt Flood were not getting on base enough. Julian Javier was having a tough time at the plate, as was Tim McCarver. Dal Maxvill, regarded as the Cardinals' worst hitter, was now the team's most consistent hitter. Gibson had to throw a no-hitter to even come close to a win. Nellie Briles looked like he would duplicate his hard-luck 1966 season. Steve Carlton, Ray Washburn, and Larry Jaster were all pitching well, and still they were around the .500 level. What was going on?

What was going on was simple—baseball had been caught in a time warp and sent back to 1908, a time when most homers were of the inside the park variety, when stealing a base was the main offensive weapon, when a bunt meant plenty. All over the majors, hitters were having a terrible year in early 1968. Triple Crown winner Carl Yastrzemski was struggling to hit .270. Frank Robinson, a Triple Crown man himself in 1966, looked like just another mediocre hitter. The Yankees were sinking to depths even worse than the ones they reached in 1967—as a team, they were hitting barely over .200. The Cubs, featuring Ernie Banks, Billy Williams, and Ron Santo, were shut out in 4 straight games, covering 48 innings where the Cubs failed to score. The White Sox went 39 straight innings without a run themselves, but at least they were not expected to hit. A flurry of 1–0 games were being played everywhere. Shutouts in general increased as every team developed an outstanding pitching staff. The Indians had five hard throwers in Sam McDowell, Luis Tiant, Sonny Siebert, Stan Williams, and Steve Hargan, and in 1967 this collection of chuckers pitched Cleveland to eighth place. Now, in 1968, people were hailing the Indians as the greatest pitching team since the dead ball era. Unfortunately for Cleveland, the hitters supporting such a staff were some of the worst, so the Indians had to be content with a battle with the Orioles for second place.

Baseball officials were worried sick over the total lack of hitting around the majors. The low-scoring games were turning off the fans, and big league bosses were desperate to revive hitting (as well as attendance). Some magnates suggested moving the pitching rubber back. Some suggested that three balls be enough for a batter to walk. Other ideas included having only eight batters in a game (pitchers would not have to bat, nor would someone hit for them), a permanent pinch hitter for the pitcher (the function of a designated hitter today), letting pinch hitters bat more than once in a game, and leaving pitchers in for at least 5 innings, regardless of what they were doing at the time that inning came. One idea had a pitcher never leaving a game until the inning was over, but it did not mention what was to be done with a pitcher who was hurt during an inning. Shrinking the strike zone and lowering the mound five to ten inches were also discussed, but nothing was done with these ideas until after the season.

Meanwhile teams had to scratch and claw for runs. The team most successful at that sort of play in 1967 was the Cardinals, and they started to do it well enough again in 1968 that their excellent pitchers were finally winning some games. St. Louis was bunched together with San Francisco, Cincinnati, and Chicago in the early going, but as these slugging teams were still waiting for the big bats of Willie McCovey, Ernie Banks, and Tony Perez to wake up and lead them, the Cardinals were running off with the flag on the feet of Lou Brock. St. Louis reverted to the kind of play that had earned them the name of "St. Louis Swifties" in their 1942 pennant-winning season.

On June 6, Robert Kennedy was assassinated, which upset many people, including ball players. Spike Eckert called for more postponements when Lyndon Johnson declared a day of mourning for the murdered senator. Most teams complied, but others were miffed. The Giants were still in the race at that point when their opponent for Bat Day, the Mets, voted to not play; the Giants were less than pleased. There was a large crowd at Candlestick Park (despite the poor hitting and the presence of a new team across the bay in the Oakland Athletics), and the Giants did not want to lose the gate. The Mets remained steadfast against playing, and the game was postponed.

The Cardinals continued to play bustling ball as Orlando Cepeda continued to struggle, like many other big hitters. Bob Gibson was only 3–4 entering June despite having an ERA under 1.00. The Cardinals finally began to score some runs for Gibby starting in June, and his win total began piling up. By the All-Star break Gibson was on target to break the record for most shutouts in a season (16, set by George Bradley of the first National League team St. Louis had in 1876 and tied by Grover Cleveland Alexander in 1916 with the Phillies) as well as the record for lowest ERA in a season (1.01 by Dutch Leonard of the Red Sox in 1914). It was incredible that dead ball era records were being threatened in the expansion era. Gibson was becoming the talk of the National League even though Juan Marichal was en route to winning 26 games and despite the fact that people were still amazed at the fact that hitting could be so bad.

The All-Star Game itself showed what kind of year 1968 was. The finest hitters of both leagues were gathered in Houston, and they were all put to shame. The Astrodome was certainly no paradise for any hitter under any type of season (the Astros beat the Mets in a game in the Dome earlier in the year 1–0 in 24 innings), but this was really making the midsummer classic a bore. Willie Mays drove home a run with a ground out in the first, and that was it. The only noteworthy event at the game came when Harmon Killebrew of the Twins tore his hamstring, putting him out of order for the rest of the year. Just what the pitchers needed, one less slugger to deal with.

The Cardinals left the break holding a lead, and then they went to work on extending it. Despite the racial climate of 1968 and all of the turmoil other teams had, the Cardinals played well together because they got along well together. Bob Gibson was the big man in the clubhouse, and everybody looked up to him as if the greatest player in history was in their midst. By 1968 it could be said that as Gibson went, so went the Cardinals. Gibby had already proved himself to be the winner of clutch games: the 1964 pennant clincher, two games in the World Series that year, and three more in the 1967 series. When Gibby tried to pitch right after breaking his leg the year before one couldn't help but be in awe.

If Stan Musial was the greatest hitter in the long history of the St. Louis Cardinals (sorry, Rogers Hornsby fans), then Bob Gibson was the greatest pitcher in Cardinals history (sorry, Dizzy Dean fans). For a man who seemed so indestructible on the mound, Bob Gibson had had a rather surprising childhood. Born in Omaha, Nebraska, on November 9, 1935 (seems like November is a great month for the Cardinals, since not only Gibson was born in that month, but so was Stan Musial), Gibson was usually sickly as a child, suffering from rickets, asthma, and other serious ailments. Gibson's family feared for him getting any sicker, but the sickly little kid grew up to be a six foot, one inch tall athlete who did well in basketball and baseball. When Gibson graduated from Creighton University in 1957, he got offers to play basketball with the Harlem Globetrotters and baseball with the St. Louis Cardinals.

Gibson played basketball for a year, then decided to quit and concentrate on baseball. In 1960 Gibby came up to St. Louis for good after posting a 3.33 ERA with 48 strikeouts in 76 innings during a 1959 cup of coffee.

Gibson spent 1960 moving from the bullpen and the rotation and back to the bullpen again as he struggled with a 5.61 ERA that year. A year later, patient Johnny Keane put his highly touted righthander in the rotation and he won 13 games. In 1962 Gibson reduced the number of walks he allowed (a league high of 119 the year before) to 95 while fanning 208 batters and leading the league with 5 shutouts. Bob Gibson had arrived.

As the Cardinals improved, so did Bob Gibson. In 1963 the Cardinals rose to contention and Gibson began to pitch in big games. If Gibson didn't win the big games, he at least kept his team in them. Pressure didn't faze him. Gibby began to throw inside more to make sure batters weren't getting any edge on him. While Gibson seemed surly toward the media and fans, he was a far more amenable person than Rogers Hornsby was most of the time. Gibson's teammates held the pitcher in high esteem, and he got along just fine with everyone in the clubhouse, joking around and playing pranks on guys. On the mound, though, Gibson was in his own world. "Get off my mound" was the ace pitcher's phrase for catchers trying to talk strategy. Gibson did not need to discuss strategy—he simply disposed of the enemy with his own plan. Indeed, the opposition was the enemy to Gibson, and he never talked to the enemy during a game, not even his teammates at All-Star games, unless they were fellow Cardinals.

In 1964 Gibson won 19 games, including the pennant clincher. A year later he won 20 for the first time. In 1966 Gibson won 21. Gibson fanned over 200 men each year from 1962 through 1966 and led the league in blankings with five in 1966. It seems strange that with all those strikeouts Gibson never led the league. It's easy to see why when one notices that the National League had hard throwers at the time, guys like Sandy Koufax, Jim Maloney, Don Drysdale, Juan Marichal, Bob Veale, Chris Short, and many others.

Entering 1967 it seemed like Bob Gibson would continue to increase his win total for the seventh straight year when Clemente's line drive hit him. Still, Gibson came right back to win

3 games in September and posted another 3 wins in the World Series, all complete games, no less. If Gibson avoided arm trouble, the experts said, he would probably go to the Hall of Fame with a pile of records and awards. As things turned out, the experts were very much right. As 1968 dawned, many people considered Bob Gibson to be the top pitcher in the game and he was yet to deliver his greatest season.

In August, hitting around the majors continued to be laughable. Bob Gibson was putting the final touches on a personal streak of 16 straight wins. Other pitchers were also doing very well. Don Drysdale pitched 58 straight scoreless innings, breaking a dead ball record set by Walter Johnson. (It would have been great to match Johnson in his prime against Gibson in 1968—both would probably pitch their greatest games ever.) Denny McLain of the Detroit Tigers was en route to the first 30-win season since Dizzy Dean did it for the Cardinals in 1934. In the American League five pitchers had an ERA under 2.00. The Mets were on their way to a team strikeout record for batters. Bob Gibson himself still had an ERA just under *1.00* while he threatened to break the Drysdale record himself right after it was set.

As Gibson became the best of all pitchers in 1968 the Cardinals were playing nearly 60 games in 55 days. Many felt the Cardinals would falter during this stretch, allowing other teams to get back into the race. Wrong. St. Louis kicked butt during the tight stretch, and when it was over, so was the race. Bob Gibson finally was hammered (if that's what it can be called) when the Pirates got four runs off of him, putting his ERA over 1.00 for the rest of the year. Still, the Cardinals were stealing, bunting, and clutch hitting their way to another flag. In September came something that could only have happened in 1968 or the dead ball era. On the seventeenth in San Francisco, Gaylord Perry tossed a 1–0 no-hitter against the Cardinals. The next day Ray Washburn got even by no-hitting the Giants 2–0. A few days later the Cardinals clinched their second straight flag for the first time since 1944 and the champagne flowed yet again. Nineteen-sixty-eight was the twelfth year that the Cardinals were league champs.

St. Louis posted an amazing season, and Bob Gibson was the key. Gibby made thirty-four starts and completed twenty-eight of them. The Cardinal ace won 22 while losing 9, struck out a league-high 268 batters, and had a league high of 13 shutouts. In 305 innings he allowed just 198 hits and 62 walks, and Gibson also set a record by posting a 1.12 ERA, the lowest mark in this century for a pitcher throwing 300 innings or more. (It should be noted that earned runs were not compiled before 1913 and research has shown that some pitchers prior to 1913 had lower ERAs, but they are not recognized as the ERA champs. Also, there was some dispute as to whether Gibson did indeed set a record for the lowest official ERA for a pitcher with 300 innings. In 1913 Walter Johnson was declared the ERA champ with a 1.09 mark in 346 innings. However, it seemed that his final appearance in that year was ignored in the stats of the year because he was clowning around and decided to give up a few extra hits to his friends on the opposing team. Some runs scored and they were earned. When this last appearance was included in the final stats for Johnson years later, his 1913 ERA jumped up to 1.14. *The Sporting News* says Johnson had a 1.14 ERA in its *Complete Baseball Record Book*, while *The Baseball Encyclopedia* lists Johnson's 1913 ERA as 1.09. It is up to the reader to decide if Gibson did or did not set the record in 1968. This author says he did.) Gibson was simply awesome in 1968, and he was easily the greatest hurler of the season. Bob Gibson's 1968 performance must go down in history as one of the greatest years a pitcher ever had in any era and probably *the* best since 1920.

Despite doing a feeble job early in the year, the Cardinal lineup ended up with some good numbers. Julian Javier hit .260. Dal Maxvill hit .253. Mike Shannon hit .266 with 79 RBIs to lead the team. Curt Flood hit .301 (good enough to lead the American League, but it would have been only fifth in the National League); Lou Brock hit .279 while winning another stolen base crown. Overall, the Cardinals led the league with 48 triples and were second in steals with 110. (The team that led in this category, amazingly, was the hard-hitting Pirates, but then they had Maury Wills that year.) The offensive totals looked weak compared to other teams', but the Cardinal lineup did enough to win 97 games, tops in the circuit, and that's all that counts in the end.

There was no doubt as to the prowess of the Cardinals pitching staff. Besides Gibson, St. Louis got fine years from Nellie Briles (19–11, 2.81), Steve Carlton (13–11, 2.99), and Ray Washburn (14–8, 2.26) as all of the starters tossed at least 215 innings. (Try finding a staff with 4 hurlers tossing 200 innings today.) Larry Jaster was only 9–13 as his ERA soared (for 1968 standards) to 3.54. The bullpen was anchored by Joe Hoerner and his 8–2, 1.47, 17-save year. The Cardinals had slain all of the hard-hitting clubs in the National League in 1968 with this staff. Now it was time to slay a hard-hitting team from the American League in the World Series— the Detroit Tigers.

The Tigers had missed out on winning the flag in 1967 by just 1 game, and they were determined to bring it home for the first time since 1945 in 1968. Denny McLain set the American League on its ear with a 31–6 record to go with a 1.96 ERA (fourth in the league) as he became the first pitcher to win 30 games in 34 years. Dizzy Dean, the last man to do it, was in Oakland as an announcer when McLain got number 30.

McLain wasn't the only star on the 1968 Tigers. Al Kaline had been with the team since 1953, and he finally got to a series despite being injured much of the year. Mickey Lolich won 17 games and was obscured by McLain in the regular season. (He was to fix that soon.) Norm Cash, Dick McAuliffe, Jim Northrup, Willie Horton, Bill Freehan, and Mickey Stanley all had pop in their bats as eight Tigers hit at least 10 homers, 36 coming from Horton. (St. Louis had only two batters with 10 homers in Orlando Cepeda and Mike Shannon.) Detroit also had strong pitching and tight defense as they breezed to their title by 12 games over the Baltimore Orioles by winning 103 games. The Cardinals would have their hands full with such a solid team as an opponent.

The 1968 World Series began on October 2 in St Louis, and it was filled with many ties to the past. In 1934 it had taken the Tigers 25 years to get to a series. In 1968 it had taken them 23 years. The last time a pitcher won 30 games was 1934, and he was on a pennant winner. Now, in 1968, the first 30-game winner in 34 years was on a pennant winner. In 1934 the Tigers and Cardinals opened the series on Wednesday, October 3, and 34 years later they opened the 1968 series on Wednesday, October 2. And like 1934, the 1968 series was to go 7 games.

216

Denny McLain faced Bob Gibson in one of the most highly anticipated matchups in series history. Expectations for a 1–0 game were high, but it was no contest. Gibson easily fanned leadoff man Dick McAuliffe to start the game, and it was a scoreless affair until the fourth, when McLain walked Roger Maris and Tim McCarver. Mike Shannon singled to drive in Maris, and when Willie Horton's throw got away McCarver and Shannon moved up an extra base. Julian Javier then singled in both men and the Cardinals had a 3–0 lead. In the seventh Lou Brock hit a solo homer, making it 4–0 St. Louis. McLain, who failed to go six innings, took the loss as Gibson was pitching one of the greatest series games ever. After pitching out of trouble in the sixth, Gibson simply dominated the Tigers with one strikeout after another. In the ninth, the ace fanned Al Kaline to give him 15 strikeouts, tying a record set by Sandy Koufax in 1963. Gibson said he wasn't aware of the record at the time, which is likely, since Gibson always was in his own world on the hill, but he did notice the crowd cheering loudly. Victim number sixteen was Norm Cash, and it set a new mark. Gibby then concluded his pitching clinic by fanning Willie Horton for his seventeenth "K," giving him yet another complete-game victory in the series record book. Gibson allowed just 5 hits in his masterpiece.

In the second game Mickey Lolich faced Nellie Briles in a battle of the number-two pitchers. Lolich was supplied with a 2–0 lead going into the sixth when Horton homered in the second and Lolich popped a homer himself in the third. In the sixth Detroit got another homer, this time from Cash, and two more runs on a bases-loaded single form McAuliffe. St. Louis scored once in the bottom of the frame when Orlando Cepeda singled home Lou Brock. The Tigers, though kept going, scoring 1 more run in the seventh and 2 more in the ninth. Lolich was in control all the way as he scattered six hits en route to an 8–1 win over Briles.

On October 5 the series moved to Detroit as Ray Washburn was pitted against Earl Wilson. The locals scored first when Kaline hit a two-run homer in the third, but the lead did not hold up long. In the fifth Brock singled and stole second, then scored on a Curt Flood double. Roger Maris then walked, and Wilson left with hamstring trouble. Pat Dobson replaced Wilson and got an out

217

when McCarver hit a 3-run homer, giving St. Louis a 4–2 lead. McAuliffe cut the lead to one run when he homered in the bottom of the frame, and the score remained 4–3 St. Louis until the seventh. Orlando Cepeda ripped a 3-run homer to provide some insurance in the seventh, and that was all for the game. Washburn got the win, Wilson the loss, and Joe Hoerner the save.

The next day was a rematch of the first game. Denny McLain was far less effective than ever as he gave up 2 runs in the first, one on a Brock leadoff homer and another on Shannon's RBI single. Two innings later McLain was gone after McCarver tripled home and Shannon doubled home 2 more runs. Detroit used five relievers in the contest in an attempt to stop the bleeding, but they failed. In the fourth Gibson popped a homer and Maris got an RBI out of a ground out. St. Louis then came up with 4 more in the eighth, but by then it was all over. Gibson allowed a solo homer to Jim Northrup in the fourth that ruined a shutout, but despite that and trouble with rain Gibby allowed just 5 hits in going the distance for a 10–1 win.

At this point the Cardinals had a 3 games to 1 lead in the series and it looked like they were going to win the flag and the series two straight years. Fewer than 5 teams had won a series after getting behind 3 games to 1, and the final two games were slated for St. Louis if the Tigers won the fifth game at home. The two Gibson-McLain matchups were very disappointing for baseball fans in general and Detroit fans in particular; Gibson had easily outpitched the Tiger ace both times, and McLain looked like a completely different pitcher from what he was in the regular season. An ailing arm had something to do with that, but McLain had pitched through it in the past. Tiger manager Mayo Smith seemed to win on his gamble of shifting center fielder Mickey Stanley to shortstop so he could put Al Kaline in the lineup, so maybe another gamble was needed. One was soon coming.

On the seventh Smith sent Lolich to face Briles again and disaster seemed certain when Cepeda cracked a 3-run homer in the first inning. Detroit battled back by getting 2 in the fourth on a Cash sac fly and a Northrup single. In the seventh Briles left after giving up a single to Lolich. Hoerner came in and quickly the Tigers loaded the bases. Kaline singled home 2 runs, and then another run came in when Cash got a single. Lolich hung around to go the distance in a 5–3 win.

Back in St. Louis, Mayo Smith decided to gamble and sent McLain against someone other than Gibson. Ray Washburn got the ball, and he got into trouble quickly. In the second inning Detroit scored twice for a 2–0 lead. Then came an eruption of historic proportions that was especially shocking since it came in the "Year of the Pitcher." In the third frame McAuliffe walked to open the door on a 10-run attack unseen since the Philadelphia Athletics scored ten in an inning that wiped out an 8–0 deficit against the Chicago Cubs in the 1929 Series. (At least 1929 was a hard-hitting year, so the Athletics' performance could be understood.) Northrup highlighted the inning with a grand slam homer, the first in a series since Joe Pepitone did it against the Cardinals in 1964. Needless to say, the Cardinals went down to defeat, this time by a 13–1 score.

After the shocking debacle of the day before, the series was tied at 3 games apiece. Detroit sent Lolich to face Gibson, and both pitchers went the distance. In the seventh, Gibson got two quick outs when the Tigers got singles from Cash and Horton. Northrup hit a shot to center field that Curt Flood misjudged; first he ran in, then shifted into reverse, but he just missed making a brilliant catch. Northrup got a 2-run triple out of the blow, and then he scored on a Bill Freehan double, giving the Tigers a 3–0 lead. In the ninth, Don Wert singled home another run for a 4–0 Detroit lead. Mike Shannon hit a solo homer in the bottom of the ninth, but it was too little too late. Lolich got the 4–1 win, and the Detroit Tigers were world champs for the first time since 1945. Bob Gibson was finally beaten in a big game.

V

So the St. Louis Cardinals had to settle for simply being the National League champs for 1968. On paper, the Cardinals had a great year nonetheless. The team looked like a possible dynasty waiting to happen, since many of the players were still rather young and seemed to have good baseball left in them for several years to come. Tim McCarver was recognized as the top catcher in the league (Johnny Bench of the Reds was just a rookie in 1968), and he had done a great job handling a fine pitching staff while providing timely hits and showing some power and speed. (He ran well for a catcher, as his thirteen triples in 1966 showed!) Mike Shannon looked like an up-and-coming slugger and was improving every year. Lou Brock was now regarded as the best leadoff man in the game. Curt Flood was a tough hitter who caught anything hit in center. Julian Javier and Dal Maxvill looked like a long-lasting double play combination, with the former a proven clutch hitter and the latter improving greatly at the plate in 1968. Orlando Cepeda was a question mark, since he slumped badly in the regular season and some thought it was a combination of age and that bad knee from 1965 that caused the bad year. Cepeda did hit well in the series, so simply throwing him away would be foolish. The pitching staff was outstanding, led by Bob Gibson and having guys like Nellie Briles and Steve Carlton (who was fooling around with a slider at this time but he didn't have it mastered—yet). Joe Hoerner had a rough series, but he was a fine-looking reliever who seemed to be ready to burst onto the scene as one of the first great relievers. (To show how important relief pitching was becoming at this time, it was decided to make saves an officially kept statistic starting in 1969.) It seemed like the Cardinals would win many pennants for years to come. But it was not to be.

During the 1968 season the owners looked around at the craziness going on in baseball. Pitching was making the .300 hitter an endangered species. Attendance was falling not only because of the lack of offense, but because of expansion. When both leagues expanded to ten teams, it created the same type of problems that had existed in the National League back in the 1890s. Every year the pennant race seemed to be a two- or three-team race, and it was usually the same teams in the hunt (Baltimore and Boston) year after year. On the other end of the scale the same teams were at or near the bottom year after year (the St. Louis Browns, you will recall from earlier, were a perennial disaster at that time, battling with Louisville and Washington to stay out of the National League basement in the 1890s), usually the teams taken in from the defunct American Association. In effect, when the National League absorbed four of the association's teams, it was almost the same as when the majors expanded in the 1960s. Three out of four of the old association teams (now "expansion" teams) were losers in all facets of the term. Attendance in the 1890s declined as the lack of tight pennant races involving a single, long twelve-team league left most teams out in the cold. After years of financial hardship, the National League owners finally cut the league down to eight teams. Things were still rough for longtime losers like St. Louis, but overall the National League did better with eight teams than with twelve.

In the 1960s the same sort of problems existed. While the California Angels surprised people every now and then by posting a winning season (in 1962, 1964, and 1967), they were still basically losers. The Washington Senators were even worse, posting losing records in every year of their existence (through 1968, that is) and ending up in the second division all of the time. The Houston Astros were little better than the Senators (at least they never lost 100 games like the Senators did in their first 4 years), never winning more than 72 games in their 7-year history. The Mets, of course, were a legendary loser by this time. In 1968 the Mets avoided the cellar for only the second time in their history and they were jumping for joy when they posted a "fine" record of 73–89, their best ever. Even though these four expansion teams seemed light-years away from just being respectable (never mind winning a pennant), the majors announced that there would be four new teams coming in 1969. The American League would put teams in Kansas City and Seattle while the National League would field clubs in San Diego and Montreal. At least both leagues decided to split into two divisions, so fans could have four pennant races instead of two to look at. Naturally, there were (and still are) problems with this setup. The champs of each division would face each other in a "championship series" to see who would go to the World Series. The problem was that one division might produce an exceptional team (that would ruin any chance of a race in that division) while the other division might produce a mediocre champ. The mediocre champ might then get hot enough to beat the exceptional champ and get into the World Series, supposedly as the "best" team of its league, cheapening the series in the

221

proccss. Over the years this has happened, with blatant examples being the 1973 Mets (82–79) beating the Reds (99–63) and the 1987 Twins (85–77) beating the Tigers (98–64). In both instances (and a few others) fans were cheated by seeing a clearly inferior team going to the World Series (and sometimes actually winning *that* as well) while the far better teams that they had beaten in the championship series (commonly called the playoffs) sat at home and winced. When the 1984 Cubs lost to the Padres in the playoffs after holding a 2–0 lead in the series, the owners finally woke up and made the playoffs a best of 7 affair. Not only did that *not* solve the problem of weak teams getting to the World Series, but now the playoffs have the potential to overshadow the 7-game World Series (like in the 1986 playoffs in both leagues). That the best of 7 playoff idea (and the whole idea of having playoffs at any length, for that matter) was generating more money for the owners than they were making in the past had nothing to do with the idea(s) being implemented; so said the magnates. Sure.

People thought that expansion for 1969 would automatically improve hitting, as it had in 1961 and 1962, but the magnates were not so sure, so they came up with a few rules changes. First, the strike zone was shrunk down, and second, pitching mounds would be lowered from fifteen inches to ten inches in height. During 1968 this idea was being advocated by many people (especially hitters!) and some pitchers said that not all mounds were created equal. Some pitchers said the mounds in New York's Shea Stadium (home of the Mets and fireballers Tom Seaver and Jerry Koosman) and Dodger Stadium in Los Angeles were higher than other mounds, probably to give even more of an edge to power pitchers (as if they needed help) in those two cities. The teams denied that their mounds were illegally high in 1968, and for 1969 the umpires would be given devices to measure mound heights. Even to this day some people maintain that the hill in Dodger Stadium is illegally high, but it has yet to be proven. Many pitchers were upset when they heard about the new rule on mound height, and Bob Gibson stated that he couldn't throw any more shutouts with the new rule. As it turned out, Gibson tossed 19 more shutouts after 1968, won 20 games twice, 19 once, and threw a no-hitter, so Gibson lost little to the rule change.

The magnates of baseball hoped the changes for 1969 would work out. Hitting in the National League was bad, but Pete Rose hit a fine .335 to win the batting title and four men hit thirty homers. In the American League, things were far worse. Five pitchers had ERAs under 2.00. Three batters hit thirty homers. Carl Yastrzemski won the batting title with a .301 mark, the worst ever to win a title, and Yaz had to finish fast to get that far up. Every team hit below .240 in the A.L. in 1968; only Oakland hit "well" by hitting a league-high .240. The Yankees continued to go from sluggers to cream puffs as they posted a sickening .214 team average, the worst mark posted by a team since the White Sox hit just .211 in 1910. Overall, the entire A.L. hit .230, the worst mark for a league since 1908. In 1930 everybody complained there was too much offensive fireworks going on and the dead ball put in use in 1931 cut the hitting down well enough to satisfy most people (come to think of it, isn't it ironic that the Cardinals lost the World Series in the "Year of the Hitter" *and* the "Year of the Pitcher"?), so the moves for 1969 were hoped to pan out.

Part VI

The Redbirds Become Deadbirds (1969–79)

I

As 1969 opened, the Cardinals found themselves in a weird geographic position. The National League announced that its Eastern Division would contain the New York Mets, the Philadelphia Phillies, the Chicago Cubs, the Pittsburgh Pirates, and the new Montreal Expos, and the St. Louis Cardinals. The Western Division would contain the San Francisco Giants, the Los Angeles Dodgers, the Houston Astros, the Cincinnati Reds, the Atlanta Braves, and the new San Diego Padres. One look at a map of the United States shows that Atlanta and Cincinnati are closer to the Atlantic Ocean, and both cities are in the Eastern time zone, while St. Louis and Chicago are farther from the Atlantic and in the Central time zone, yet here were the Reds and Braves in the West while the Cardinals and Cubs were in the East. League bosses said the two teams in the Midwest were placed in the Eastern Division so the Cardinal-Cub rivalry could remain strong. Huh? Why wouldn't the Cardinal-Cub rivalry be strong if they were in the other division? Geographically, it would have made sense to put the Cardinals and Cubs in the West (where they could continue old rivalries with the Dodgers and Giants) while putting the Reds and especially the Braves in the East. Baseball's illogic was even more visible when the American League placed the Chicago White Sox in the Western Division of its circuit. The American League at least looked at a map before setting up its divisions, so Chicago was given two different geographic identities; in the National League it was an Eastern city while in the American League it was a Western city. Go figure.

Besides having been placed in the East, St. Louis had a more important issue to deal with. Right fielder Roger Maris decided to retire after the 1968 season, and talks to bring him back for another year failed. Maris hit with little power in his two years with the Cardinals as a bad wrist plagued him. Still, Maris was a big favorite

227

in St. Louis and brought leadership, class, and experience to the club while still doing well in right field. Gussie Busch was fond of Maris and tried personally to coax another year out of him, but the former home run king decided to retire and that was that. Right field was now up for grabs and Red Schoendienst could have shifted third baseman Mike Shannon back to his old position, but that would have created a hole at third and besides, Shannon did a grand job at the new position. A trade for a right fielder was in order.

On October 11, 1968, right after the World Series was over, the Cardinals sent promising outfielder Bobby Tolan and promising pitcher Wayne Granger to the Reds for veteran outfielder Vada Pinson. Pinson was one of the most underrated hitters of the 1960s as a member of the Reds. Twice he led the league in at bats. Twice he led the league in hits. Twice he led the league in doubles. Twice he led the league in triples. Once he led the league in runs scored. Pinson had four years where he collected 200 hits, four years he scored 100 runs, two years he drove in 100 runs, and four times he hit .300. Six times Pinson hit 20 homers, but despite all of this Vada Pinson rarely got any attention outside of Cincinnati because a man named Frank Robinson was his teammate and he was hacking his way to the Hall of Fame. This trade seemed to be a good one for both teams, since Tolan and Granger were highly regarded youngsters who were dealt away because there was no place for them on a team of veterans, and Pinson was the veteran that the Cardinals wanted to fill in the right field hole with. Trades made after the 1968 year of pitching prowess were really risky, though, because there were many questions about hitters and pitchers. Was that slugger over the hill or was it just because of the freaky year that he hit poorly? Was that pitcher really *that* good or was it because of the freaky year? Pinson hit .271 in 1968, which was good, but his 5 homers and 48 RBIs were not so good and they were the worst totals of Pinson's career at that point. Was he over the hill or was it the freaky year?

The Cardinals were clearly lacking the thump that they got in 1967, especially from the bat of Orlando Cepeda. After winning the league's MVP award in 1967, Cepeda's numbers slipped badly in 1968 as he hit 16 homers, drove in 73 runs, and had a .248 average.

Again the "freaky year" question came up. Cepeda swung the bat well against the Tigers in the series, so the Cardinals were really in a quandary. Finally, St. Louis decided to swap him. Bing Devine had returned to town after he left the Mets, and on March 17, 1969, the Cardinals pulled off a big trade when they sent Cepeda to the Braves for Joe Torre. The Mets, lacking thump even more than the Cardinals, tried hard to get Torre from Atlanta, but the Braves insisted on getting too many youngsters in return for Torre, and one of those youngsters was a wild pitcher named Nolan Ryan. The Mets then made the smart decision to keep Ryan and passed on Torre (although the Mets made an even worse decision than the one they would have made when they sent Ryan *and three other players* to the Angels to get washed-up Jim Fregosi), so Torre was still available and the Cardinals picked him up. Joe Torre had served as the catcher for the Braves since their days in Milwaukee, and he was coming off a year that the "freaky year" question had to be applied to. Torre hit .271 with 10 homers and 55 RBIs in 1968. A year earlier he hit 20 homers with 68 RBIs. And before 1967 Joe Torre was a bona fide masher who could pop 30 homers, knock in 100 runs, and hit .300 while doing a decent job behind the plate. Was it age or the freaky year that reduced his numbers?

With Tim McCarver behind the plate Joe Torre would have to be moved to a new position. First base was open after Cepeda left, so Torre worked out at the position and did well enough to get the job. Aside from Torre and Pinson coming to the Cardinals, the team decided to stand pat. Julian Javier and Dal Maxvill would still be the men around second. Mike Shannon was still the third baseman. Pinson joined Lou Brock and Curt Flood in forming a solid outfield. McCarver would again have the pleasure of handling one of baseball's top pitching staffs.

People speculated what effects would be stemming from the new divisional setups. Both leagues decided that a team would play its five divisional rivals eighteen times each (nine home and nine road games) while playing each of the six teams in the other branch twelve times each (six at home and six away). Previously, a team would face each of its nine rivals eighteen times a year (before expansion in 1961–62 it was twenty-two times against seven rivals), so teams had thirty-six games against the two expansion patsies in each league. From 1962 through 1968 everyone loved to play the Mets and Astros, since they could get into the race by whipping these two sorry teams on a regular basis. In the Eastern Division of the National League, the Cardinals were placed in a seemingly weak field. In 1968 Leo Durocher's Cubs finished third for the second straight year, and many thought that this was the team to beat. When Durocher took over the Cubs in 1966 he said, "This is not a ninth-place club," and he was right, as his 1966 Cubs crashed into the cellar, evicting the Mets out of their usual tenth-place home. Durocher then made several moves, and the next year was a dramatic success. Everyone thought the Cubs were ready for a breakthrough in 1969.

Aside from the Cubs, the Cardinals looked at a weak field. The Pirates were a hard-hitting team, but in 1968 their bats, too, went a bit cold, while they lacked depth in the pitching department. The result was a mediocre 80–82 record for Pittsburgh. The Pirates would need more pitching if they were going to be a factor, was the thinking. The Phillies were clearly in decline. After the debacle of 1964 the Phillies spent the next two years competing decently, but it seemed like the Phillies had their spirit broken in 1964. Gene Mauch presided over a team that finished 82–80 and in fifth place in 1967 and a team that was under .500 in 1968 when he was fired. The Phillies lacked hitting and were close to the cellar by the end of 1968. Mauch, though, wasn't unemployed for long. The Montreal Expos hired him to be their pilot for 1969, and nobody expected the new team to do anything in the new year. The Expos had some fine players in Rusty Staub and Maury Wills as the year opened, but expansion teams never do anything in their first year. Finally, there were the Mets. People expected the Mets to finish ahead of the Expos and that was it. Maybe the Mets would edge past the Phillies, but even that might be too much for a team that had had seven straight losing records since being born in 1962. St. Louis was in a good position by being in the East, since the Giants, Reds, and Braves, three of the league's better teams in 1968, were over in the West. Nineteen-sixty-nine was to be a year when the Cardinal-Cub rivalry was to flourish more than ever before, said the experts. It did not turn out that way, though.

Once the 1969 season began, the Chicago Cubs broke out to

an early lead while the Cardinals and Pirates battled for second place. The Mets, Expos, and Phillies all met the expectations of the fans and formed the second division. The changes in the rules concerning the shrinking strike zone and lowered mound seemed to work out well, as offense was getting back to the levels of about five years earlier. The Cardinals' offense improved a great deal as Julian Javier's batting average rose to its 1967 level and Joe Torre began to hit with his old power. Five Cardinals were en route to at least 10 homers for 1969, up by 8 from the previous year. Vada Pinson provided the pop that St. Louis sought in right field, but his average fell and he seemed to be in decline all around. Still, the pitching, led by Bob Gibson, was effective.

Despite the improved lineup and the continued good pitching, the Cardinals were quickly falling out of the race, as the experts seemed right about the Cubs. Chicago had one fine club in 1969; the infield had Ernie Banks, Glenn Beckert, Don Kessinger, and Ron Santo from first to third, Randy Hundley was the catcher, and the outfield contained Billy Williams and usually Jim Hickman. The pitching staff was led by Fergie Jenkins and also had Billy Hands, Ken Holtzman, and Dick Selma in the rotation, with Phil Regan and Ted Abernathy in the bullpen. The only weak spot seemed to be center field, as the 1969 Cubs had three Hall of Famers on their roster (Banks, Williams, Jenkins). After getting off to a fine start, the Cubs seemed destined to win. Leo Durocher lost none of his fire as his Chicago team played as hard and earned as many detractors as his old Dodger and Giant teams did in New York in the 1940s and 1950s.

The Cardinals also had to contend with a tough club in the Pittsburgh Pirates. The Pirates were a hard-hitting crew featuring names like Roberto Clemente, Willie Stargell, Al Oliver, Matty Alou, Bill Mazeroski, Richie Hebner, and Manny Sanguillen in their powerful lineup. Oliver, Hebner, and Sanguillen were all rookies in 1969, and this trio looked like it had a fine future ahead of it. The other boppers were around for some years, and Clemente and Stargell were both on their way to Cooperstown. Even the Pirates' pitching was coming along in 1969. Bob Veale (a forgotten man when people discuss the flamethrowers of the 1960s) could still bring it, even though he often pitched in tough luck. Dock Ellis and

Bob Moose both showed promise, and Steve Blass was improving. Jim Bunning also was a member of the Pirates in 1969, but it looked like he was running out of gas by then. The bullpen was a bit spotty, but still the Pirates were becoming a tough team to beat.

By the time June arrived, the Cardinals were in trouble. St. Louis was struggling to play .500 ball and suddenly the pitching staff had its problems. Ray Washburn was having trouble winning. Nellie Briles was trying to break even as he was being hit hard. The bullpen was having big trouble holding leads. Joe Hoerner was still effective, but he was having problems with a bum arm. On the hitting side, Vada Pinson was struggling. Dal Maxvill began to revert to a light hitter again. Tim McCarver still was not hitting with the power that he had before 1968, and his average was also down. Mike Shannon also began to stop hitting with authority. Suddenly the Pinson deal looked like a steal for the Reds. While Vada Pinson was struggling in St. Louis, Bobby Tolan began to blossom as a power hitter who could also hit for average and steal bases, and Wayne Granger became one of baseball's top relievers. As things turned out, the Vada Pinson deal was the first in a long line of many deals that backfired on the Cardinals in the next few years, a result of which was the ruining of a fine ball club.

Road trips to the West were becoming a nightmare. In 1969 the league's top-hitting teams (except the Pirates) were in the West as Cincinnati featured six batters with at least 82 RBIs, four men with 20 homers, and three .300 hitters; San Francisco featured the league's top slugger of 1969 in Willie McCovey (45 intentional walks tell plenty) as well as Willie Mays, Bobby Bonds, and Ron Hunt; Atlanta featured a revived Orlando Cepeda to go with Hank Aaron, Felipe Alou, Rico Carty, and Tony Gonzales; even the usually weak-hitting Houston team had Jimmy Wynn, Joe Morgan, Denis Menke, and Doug Rader. These teams were murder on every team's pitching staff, and the Cardinals had their hands full with these teams. Los Angeles had their usually tough pitching staff, which had seventeen-game winner Don Sutton dwarfed by twenty-game winners Claude Osteen and Bill Singer in 1969, and this club tormented St. Louis hitters. It looked like a long year was in store for the Cardinals.

A month later, by July 1, the Cardinals were still out of the hunt. The Cubs were still soaring, and these now amazing Mets seemed to be for real, as they had a firm grip on second place. Mets mania began sweeping the nation as fans began to pull for that longtime loser to move into first place, even though the long-suffering Cubs hadn't been to the top in twenty-four years themselves. At this point, the Cubs were starting to irritate teams all over the place as Ron Santo began clicking his heels in joy after every Cubs victory. Leo Durocher was still promoting his theory of intimidation with his "stick it in his ear" philosophy. Fergie Jenkins and Dick Selma had great fastballs at that time, and getting hit by one of them was no fun. Teams tried to beat the Cubs at their own game, but by this time Chicago was ahead by plenty, so it seemed futile.

Finally, in July the Cardinals began to right themselves, after spending most of the first three months under .500. St. Louis took three out of four at home from the Cubs early in the month, which delighted the local fans. St. Louis also began to fatten up on such patsies as the Phillies and Padres while moving past the Pirates into third place. Bob Gibson continued to be the ace, as his earlier claims of being unable to pitch well with a lower mound proved groundless. After his brilliant 1968 season, Gibson probably could have won pitching from a hole, much less a mound. Steve Carlton continued to show improvement, and they looked like a one-two, righty-lefty punch as potent as the Koufax-Drysdale combination was for the Dodgers just a few years earlier.

As August proceeded, the Pirates got hot and moved back into third. St. Louis did decently against the West this time around, so they remained over the .500 mark. A month later, the Cardinals suddenly had a shot at second place. The Cubs were fading as the Mets charged into first place, and now the Cubs had to worry about both the Cardinals and Pirates catching them from behind. Chicago was self-destructing rapidly, but they continued to upset their enemies with their hard style of play. It was now becoming obvious that St. Louis would not finish first, so Bob Gibson expressed the sentiments of most baseball fans when he said, "I hope the Mets win it." The Cardinals did their part to help the Mets to their division title by beating the Cubs five out of seven in two tough series in September, then lost to the Mets themselves in New

233

York when Joe Torre hit into a double play on the twenty-fourth, which gave the Mets the title. A few days earlier the Cardinals' 1969 season was exemplified when Steve Carlton struck out a then record 19 Mets on the nineteenth, but he lost the game 4–3 when Ron Swoboda hit a pair of 2-run homers. It was that kind of year for the Cardinals, and the Mets, too. St. Louis ended 1969 in fourth place, a game behind the Pirates, five behind the Cubs, and thirteen behind the Mets. So much for a possible St. Louis Cardinals dynasty.

II

Gussie Busch was a very wealthy man. He headed one of America's largest companies in Anheuser-Busch, which was one of the world's biggest breweries. Busch knew beer well, but his big passion was baseball. When the brewery bought the Cardinals in 1953, Busch put himself in charge of the Cardinals, a team he loved. Gussie Busch was not only the boss of the Cardinals, but he was also the biggest fan of the team. Unfortunately, there seems to be a problem when the man running a baseball team also is a fan of the team he runs, especially if the man does not know much about the day-to-day operation of a ball club. Even owners who knew the game inside out over the years have tended to cause the team trouble with well-intended moves. At the end of 1969, it seemed that Gussie Busch, owner and top fan of the Cardinals, was using a hands-on approach in running the club. True, the Cardinals had people in the role of general manager over the years that Busch presided over the club, but it seemed that the general manager was directly responsible to the owner when it came to trades and salaries, unlike the setup of other teams, where the general manager usually deals with the owner through intermediaries on an infrequent basis. Most teams had owners that were distant from the club, content to let experienced baseball men run their teams, but Busch was not of that ilk. Busch was no dope when it came to baseball, but the boss began to suffer from the same affliction that strikes all other "hands-on" owners—the need to make changes on spur-of-the-moment fan emotionalism, changes that can have bad consequences.

The Cardinals franchise had already undergone such changes by the time Gussie Busch arrived. In the 1890s Chris Von Der Ahe (who also made his fortune in beer; isn't that ironic?) was most certainly a hands-on owner. Von Der Ahe was sort of a Bill Veeck type of guy—one who would hang around the fans and pick up some ideas about what he should do with his team. Von Der Ahe the fan made moves based on emotionalism, and the moves proved to be a disaster. Even when the Cardinals were in the American Association and called the Browns, Von Der Ahe would trade a player who made a key error to lose a game, even if he got little in return for a star player. Chris Von Der Ahe continued this sort of rule when his team joined the National League, and when it came to managers Von Der Ahe put George Steinbrenner (another highly emotional owner-fan who liked the hands-on approach) to shame. We have already seen the effects on the franchise that Von Der Ahe wreaked with his methods as the emotional owner-fan with a hands-on approach. Helene Britton knew far less about baseball then did Von Der Ahe, and although she was far less of a fan and didn't care much for the team, her firing of Roger Bresnahan as manager looks like a move that a Von Der Ahe would have made.

Gussie Busch was far less emotional than Von Der Ahe when it came to the franchise, but Busch did make some seemingly rash moves by the time 1969 was over. Bing Devine's firing in 1964 was more or less a shock, and then bringing him back a few years later (Devine had moved to the Mets after his firing) also raised some eyebrows. Busch also changed managers frequently before Red Schoendienst became the pilot. (Six skippers took the helm between 1953 and 1961.) Busch suggested trades to his general managers, and he blocked the trade of Stan Musial to the Phillies (a great move on the boss's part). Busch was very unhappy at the way the Cardinals performed in 1969, and now he decided to take an even bigger hands-on role in handling trades. The next few years would be rough for the Cardinals as a result.

On October 7, 1969, the Cardinals consummated one of their biggest deals ever, and one that was a disaster for them as well.

St. Louis shipped Tim McCarver, Curt Flood, Joe Hoerner, and Byron Browne to the Phillies for Dick Allen, Cookie Rojas, and Jerry Johnson. Almost immediately there was trouble. Flood, one of the best center fielders ever to play the position, liked playing for the Cardinals, a team that was always competitive. The Phillies were a bad team that lost almost 100 games and avoided the cellar only because of the arrival of the expansion Expos. Flood refused to go to Philadelphia. The Cardinals were upset, fearing the trade would be canceled by Commissioner Bowie Kuhn. The Phillies were anxious to dump Dick Allen, who was getting a reputation for being a troublemaker despite being the team's top player. Both teams wanted the trade to go through. Finally the Cardinals and Phillies sat down and figured out what to do. On April 8, 1970, the Cardinals sent minor leaguer Willie Montanez to the Phillies in place of Curt Flood, and the deal finally went through. Flood, a proud man, refused to be treated like chattel, and if he couldn't play for the Cardinals, he would simply go to court and challenge the reserve clause that had made him (and all other players) merely a piece of property to be bought, sold, or swapped (if not released) at the whim of his team. As things turned out, Flood lost his case, tried to hook on with the Washington Senators in 1971, then left the game after playing poorly for a few games. Curt Flood is currently doing well in business.

After the Curt Flood trade was first made, the Cardinals then made another deal. On November 21, 1969, the Cardinals sent Vada Pinson (who hit only .255, a career low) to the Indians for Jose Cardenal. The Cardinals were not through with their housecleaning with that deal, as they then sent Dave Giusti, along with Dave Ricketts, to the Pirates for Carl Taylor and a minor leaguer. This trade turned out to be another disaster for St. Louis. St. Louis also sent Ray Washburn to the Reds for George Culver. These were the major moves that the Cardinals made in their attempt to get back to the top. People shook their heads and wondered why the Cardinals made so many moves after winning 87 games in 1969, but more head shaking was yet to come.

The Cardinals started 1970 poorly, fighting the slightly improved Phillies and the greatly improved (but still bad) Expos to avoid the cellar. In fairness to the Cardinals, many of their off-season moves were made in an effort to make room for minor leaguers trying to get to the big show. Joe Hague took over at first base (Joe Torre was moved to third) and did a good job. Leron Lee replaced Vada Pinson in right field, and he struggled. The Cardinals got rid of Tim McCarver because they had a kid who would speak his mind while hitting for average and power and also doing a good job behind the plate. The switch-hitting kid catcher was highly touted, and his name was Ted Simmons. Simmons did not look like the greatest catcher that the Cardinals ever had when he first came up, batting just .243 with 3 homers as a part-timer. Jose Cardenal did a good job in center, but he was not Curt Flood. Dick Allen was moved from first to third to right, and despite all of this shifting about and playing in big Busch Stadium, Allen had a great year, hitting .279 with 34 homers and 101 RBIs.

Offense was not much of a problem for the 1970 Cardinals, but pitching was. Steve Carlton chalked up 19 losses, and Nellie Briles was battered all over the lot with a 6.22 ERA. Young Mike Torrez went 8–10 with an ERA over 4.00. Bob Gibson was a rock amidst all of this chaos, tossing almost 300 innings while going 22–7 with a 3.12 ERA. The bullpen was a total disaster. Carl Taylor did well with a 3.12 ERA and a club-high 8 saves, but that was not enough. Great relievers were in St. Louis in Wayne Granger, Dave Giusti, and Joe Hoerner, but only when the Reds, Pirates, and Phillies were in town. Mudcat Grant had a great year for the A's, and all the Cardinals got was nothing but some cash when they sent Grant to Oakland in the off-season. Most of the moves the Cardinals made helped the teams that got St. Louis players more than they helped the Cardinals. The 1970 season was a total disaster. The gate dipped only slightly, but the won-lost total dipped far more as the Cardinals went 76–86 for the year, three games out of the basement.

The Cardinals had to go back to the drawing board after the fiasco of 1970. Trades were made again in an attempt to make St. Louis respectable. After the 1970 season ended, the Cardinals sent Dick Allen (now becoming a nomad) to the Dodgers for Ted Sizemore and Bob Stinson. Sizemore was slated to bump Julian Javier out of his second base job despite his still doing a good job. St. Louis then sent Nellie Briles and Vic Davalillo to the Pirates for

Matty Alou. Most people thought that the Cardinals got the better of that deal, and they were right. The Cardinals also shored up their weak bullpen by sending utilityman Jerry DaVanon to the Orioles for zany reliever Moe Drabowsky. Backup catcher Jerry McNertney was picked up from the Brewers for Carl Taylor in a multiplayer deal.

Going into 1971 the Cardinals were expected to be a middle-of-the-pack team, since their moves improved them, but to expect the Cardinals to be contenders seemed a bit much. The Pirates and Cubs were the favorites, and both teams played well in the early going. The Cardinals got off to a better start than the year before, but they were still taken lightly. Then the Cubs underwent plenty of dissension and began to fade and the Cardinals charged past them into second place. Joe Torre was having an outstanding year, hitting over .350 most of the year and driving in runs in bunches, sparking the club in the process. Joe Hague was a flop in his second year at first, but other players took up the slack. Matty Alou hit over .300 all year and gave the Cardinals production in right field unmatched since Wally Moon played the position in the mid-1950s. Young Jose Cruz had a decent year in center field after Jose Cardenal got off to a bad start and was sent to the Brewers in a July trade. Ted Sizemore did a fine job at second as Julian Javier was sent to the bench. Lou Brock was by now the undisputed base-stealing king, and he was hitting over .300. Ted Simmons became the catcher full-time and also hit over .300.

The Pirates had an outstanding team in 1971, but the Cardinals dogged them to the end. St. Louis's revival came about thanks to a turnaround in the pitching. Bob Gibson slipped to 16–13 for the year, but he did toss a no-hitter at Pittsburgh on August 11, stifling a hard-hitting lineup. Rookie Reggie Cleveland split 24 decisions, young lefty Jerry Reuss split 28 decisions, and Steve Carlton won 20 games for the first time in his career when he went 20–9. The bullpen did a fine job as Moe Drabowsky, Don Shaw, and Frank Linzy (picked up from the Giants in the middle of 1970) won 11 games while saving 16 (a good total in those days). The Cardinals closed to within a couple of games of the Pirates in late September, but Pittsburgh was too good, as Dave Giusti was almost unhittable late in the 1971 season, and the Pirates wrapped up their second straight title by 7 games over the second-place Cardinals. St. Louis improved its win total by 14 in 1971.

After the 1971 season was over came a bad episode that led to another bad trade on the Cardinals' side. Steve Carlton felt he deserved a hefty raise for winning 20 games in the year. At that point, Bob Gibson had been finally overshadowed by another pitcher on the team for the first time since 1964, so in effect Carlton was the ace of the rotation, at least in 1971. Gussie Busch got in on the contract talks this time and was very unhappy over the demands of his top lefty. Carlton was firm and so was Busch, and since Busch had the upper hand, he decided to use it. On February 25, 1972, the Cardinals traded Carlton to the Phillies for their top starter in Rick Wise. Wise was a solid pitcher who won 17 games for a last-place club in 1971, so the Cardinals were not getting a lemon. Still, the trade turned into one of the all-time worsts for St. Louis. Wise had two okay seasons with the Cardinals before he was swapped again, while Carlton pitched the Phillies back to health, won four Cy Young awards, and headed for the Hall of Fame. Without a doubt Gussie Busch was in on this deal, and after it backfired he began to leave his hands off of the team for the most part, asking only to be consulted on possible trades before they were made.

Nineteen-seventy-two began with the Cardinals making few moves, as they figured that the odds of the Pirates winning a third straight division title were too high. The Cubs were fighting among themselves, and Leo Durocher was having his problems trying to keep his talented but underachieving club under control. The Mets had solid pitching but a weak lineup and had had two straight mediocre years. The Phillies and Expos were both building for the future and were not regarded as factors in the pennant race. Many thought the Cardinals would win the flag in 1972 despite doing little to shore up the team. But then the pennant races that were coming took a backseat to some very important news.

During the spring of 1972 the players' union wanted to have a new pension agreement with the owners. The union wanted a larger piece of the TV revenue pie, and the owners balked at such an idea. The union stated that TV revenue was increasing while contributions to the player pension fund did not match the

239

revenue increases. The owners viewed the union as a threat and decided to take a hard line in dealing with the pension issue, even though many of the owners did not get along and had opposing ideas on how to deal with the union. Gussie Busch was one of the leading hard-liners, and he played a key role in this and future issues dealing with the players' union. Busch advocated that the players be allowed to strike so that the union would end up collapsing from financial hardship (sort of the attitude taken by NFL owners in the 1987 football strike) on the players. The other owners agreed. Meanwhile the players on each team took votes on whether or not they should strike.

The impasse continued throughout the spring. The union informed the owners that if nothing was done to settle the pension dispute by March 11, the players would strike. The owners put up a firm front to the union while in private the owners bickered over what to do. Some teams in small markets like the Brewers, Orioles, and Royals feared that a strike would bring catastrophe on their clubs, so the owners of these clubs tended to favor a softer stance. Teams like the Cardinals, who were making more money than some teams in bigger markets, continued the hard-line stance, and the owners decided to join the hard-liners.

On April 1, 1972, the first strike of players in this century took place. When the strike began, many people feared that the entire season was going to be wiped out. All games were canceled until further notice. The owners figured that the players would drop their support of Marvin Miller, the head of the players' union, as soon as they began to feel the pinch in their wallets. Wrong. The players stood firmly behind Miller, and the strike went on. Fans were upset and supported the owners against "greedy players." More moderate owners (usually from the smaller markets) continued to nag at the hard-liners like Busch and Walter O'Malley of the Dodgers to make a settlement with the union. Finally the moderates prevailed and the strike was settled.

Each team lost an average of eight games to the strike (which were not made up) as the season opened late. Just before the season began, the Cardinals made another trade that was destined to fail by sending Jerry Reuss to the Astros for Scipio Spinks and Lance Clemons. Earlier the Cardinals had disposed of Julian Javier by sending him to the Reds for washed-up Tony Cloninger. This last trade left Lou Brock and Dal Maxvill as the only two non-pitchers left from the pennant-winning Cardinal team of only four years before. (Mike Shannon was released in 1970, and Larry Jaster went to the expansion draft after 1968.) Soon even Maxvill would be gone.

The Cardinals opened the 1972 season as a favorite for the flag, and they played before small crowds everywhere they went, residue of the strike. St. Louis started poorly, as Joe Torre (MVP in 1971) got off to a slow start and the hitting in general was sluggish. The Pirates took off like a rocket and were breezing along while the Cardinals tried hard to overtake the Mets and Cubs for second place. Joe Hague got off to another weak start, and he was shipped to the Reds for Bernie Carbo in May. Matty Alou became the first baseman by default, and Carbo spent some time in right field with Luis Melendez. Lou Brock was having another good year, and Ted Simmons was becoming the second-best catcher in the league. (A guy named Johnny Bench held the number-one title in Cincinnati.) As the season wore on, it was obvious that the Cardinals were going nowhere. Alou was sent away in a deal for some minor leaguers as was Dal Maxvill. Several players came and went, but the offense was at its worst point since 1966. Bob Gibson posted 19 wins in his last effective year, while posting a 2.46 ERA. Rick Wise had a 3.11 ERA but was on his way to a 16–16 year as the boo birds got on him (Steve Carlton was leading all pitchers in everything in 1972 for the last-place Phillies), and Reggie Cleveland pitched as well as he could without good hitting support. The bullpen was again weak as the Cardinals sent the relief crew of 1971 out of town.

Overall, the 1972 season was a disaster. The Cardinals saw their attendance drop by over 400,000 while the team posted a dismal 75–81 record, bad enough for fourth place. Cardinals fans were becoming disgusted with the lousy trades that the team had made over the last few years, and few people could blame them. Wayne Granger became a top reliever in baseball after leaving the Cardinals, posting 27 and 35 saves in 1969 and 1970 for the Reds. Dave Giusti became a top bullpenner himself, getting 26, 30, and 22 saves for the Pirates in 1970, 1971, and 1972. Bobby Tolan hit

.305 with 21 homers and 93 RBIs in 1969 for the Reds, then went .316, 16, 80 in 1970 and .283, 8, 83 in 1972. (Tolan missed 1971 with injuries.) Jerry Reuss went only 8–13 for the Astros in 1972, but a good lefty is hard to come by. Nellie Briles went 8–4 with a 3.04 ERA in 1971 for the Pirates, then went 14–11 for them in 1972, so he was not washed up like the Cardinals thought. Most of the guys who replaced these players on the Cardinals never even came close to matching such numbers. Cardinal fans were really howling mad when Steve Carlton won the Cy Young Award in 1972 for leading the league in wins (27), strikeouts (310), ERA (1.97), complete games (30), and innings (346) and finished second in shutouts (8), all for a Phillies team that went 59–97 with a record that was worse than those of either of the two newest teams in the circuit. Heads were shaking in abject disgust.

The Cardinals now were at a point where they would have to rely more on the minors to get better. Any time a trade proposal hit the media, the fans might get worried that some more lemons were coming to St. Louis. The Cardinals were facing a crisis of faith concerning the team's fans. More lousy trades and people would stay away from the ballpark, but moves to improve the club were now imperative. The Cardinals finished the 1972 season 21½ games out of first, their biggest deficit since 1955.

Red Schoendienst decided to rebuild the infield. Joe Torre would move to first base while two rookies would be recalled. Mike Tyson, normally a second baseman, would take over at shortstop while Ken Reitz would become the new third baseman. Jose Cruz would be given a full-time shot in center field while Lou Brock would stay in left and Luis Melendez and Bernie Carbo would share right. Ted Simmons made catcher one position not to be worried about, and Ted Sizemore would stay at second in the new infield for 1973. On the hill Bob Gibson would anchor the staff, and behind him would be Reggie Cleveland, Rick Wise, and a man who would have to be picked out of the crowd in spring training, if not from a trade. A new bullpen had to be built, and veteran Diego Segui would lead it, backed by a young, flaky lefty named Al Hrabosky and a newcomer of sorts in the fading form of Wayne Granger. In some minor trades (besides the one for Granger) the Cardinals shored up the bench, getting another old face in Tim McCarver

242

from the Expos as the key bench move. St. Louis avoided making big trades involving well-known names, and it seemed just fine with the fans. At least the Cardinals weren't going to get burned by another bad deal while sending stars to other teams. Everyone in St. Louis wondered what kind of team the Cardinals would be like in 1973; would they be the losers of 1970 and 1972 or the better teams of 1969 and 1971? Or maybe something in the middle? Only time would tell.

III

As 1973 opened, the whole Eastern Division of the National League seemed in flux. The Pirates had won the divisional title three years running, and they were a tough club. However, the Pirates entered the new year without their spiritual leader and top clutch hitter in Roberto Clemente. Clemente had been delivering relief supplies to earthquake victims in Nicaragua on December 31, 1972, when his plane crashed in the Caribbean Sea. The Pirate great had gotten his three thousandth career hit in his last at bat of the 1972 regular season (postseason hits don't count), and it looked like he would have another good year in 1973. The Pirates announced that they would retire Clemente's number (21) and asked that he be put into the Hall of Fame immediately, rather than wait the mandatory five years. (The Hall did put him in early.) Despite having a good pitching staff and an excellent lineup, the Pirates would certainly be expected to feel the effects of the loss of their leader.

The Cubs were another team that merited consideration for the division title. They had mystified their fans for the last five years by not once ending up on top. The Cubs had plenty of talent in Billy Williams, Don Kessinger, Glenn Beckert, Ron Santo, Jim Hickman, Randy Hundley, Fergie Jenkins, Rick Reuschel, Burt Hooton, Milt Pappas, Jack Aker, and, new for 1973, Rick Monday, yet this collection of fine hitters, fielders, and pitchers had not gotten the job done. Leo Durocher, one of the all-time great managers, just couldn't bring home the flag, and 1969 became an albatross around his neck the same way that 1964 had become

Gene Mauch's albatross. Internal dissension worsened over the years, and finally Durocher was sacked in favor of the more sedate Whitey Lockman. Nineteen-seventy-three was Lockman's first full year as the Cubs' pilot, and some people thought that maybe his calmer leadership would get the job done in Chicago.

The Mets had fine pitching for some time, led by Tom Seaver. Jerry Koosman, Jon Matlack, and newcomer George Stone gave the Mets one of the league's top rotations. Tug McGraw anchored a deep and solid bullpen, and the Mets also had strong defense. Mets watchers figured that the team would go only as far as their hitting would take them, and in the last three years the hitting hadn't taken them too far. Rusty Staub had been an excellent hitter with the Astros and Expos when the Mets got him for four players. Staub got hurt in his first year with the team, and that ruined flag hopes for 1972. A healthy Staub, going with Cleon Jones and John Milner, would make the Mets do more than simply spin their wheels.

Gene Mauch was doing a great job with the Expos as they gradually improved every year. Mauch loved to bunt no matter where he managed (he was always criticized for it, being called predictable by other pilots like Billy Martin and Earl Weaver), even making his power hitters do it when he thought it necessary. Mauch had molded a decent team by having an infield made up of Mike Jorgensen (light hitter, great glove), Ron Hunt (tough as nails and a good hitter), Tim Foli (nicknamed Crazy Horse for his play), and Bob Bailey (underrated power hitter) for 1973. Ron Fairly was a veteran outfielder who could still hit, and the up-and-coming star of the future was outfielder Ken Singleton. Mauch also had a decent pitching staff with Mike Torrez, Steve Renko, hard-throwing Balor Moore, and rookie Steve Rogers in the rotation, backed by one of the most durable pitchers ever in Mike Marshall in the bullpen.

Even the Phillies looked like they might be on the rise. Steve Carlton was miles ahead of the other starters, although Ken Brett and Jim Lonborg were no slouches in the past. Offensively was where the Phillies had more talent. Willie Montanez was a slick fielder and an underrated power hitter, Larry Bowa was a slick-fielding (but still weak-hitting) shortstop, and young Greg Luzinski looked like the next great power hitter of the era. Bob Boone was already doing a fine job behind the plate, and in 1973 the Phillies decided to put another rookie by the name of Mike Schmidt in an everyday job at third to go with Boone and Luzinski (rookies in 1972). The Phillies were the pits in 1972, but with all of the young players coming up and a guy like Carlton leading the pitching staff, the Phillies looked ready to rise in 1973.

Once the 1973 season began, the Cardinals got off to one of their patented slow starts; this time St. Louis managed to dislodge the Phillies from the cellar after starting with a 5–20 record. The Cardinals might have been in last place with their lousy start, but they amazingly were still within striking distance from first place. The other five teams in the division all were sputtering along with rather weak starts themselves as mass mediocrity set in. Bob Gibson's arthritic right arm was having trouble winning ball games, as most of the team's offense slumped. A season worse than 1972 seemed to be in the making.

Soon the scribes began calling the division the National League Least, as all six teams were playing just above or below the .500 mark. The weird thing was that the N.L. East was not the only division playing poorly. The Eastern half of the American League also was mediocre, as teams like the Brewers and Indians took turns sharing first place with teams like the Orioles and Red Sox. At the middle of May, the whole division was under .500, but the A.L. East at least got its act together later on and had a real pennant race that was confined to the real contenders. The N.L. "Least," though, would continue to be a mess right to the end.

At one point the Phillies were on top, and Philadelphia was abuzz with stories of a "miracle" Phillies team that might just go from worst to first in a year. As soon as such talk began to be believed, the Phillies reverted to their usual poor play as that rookie third baseman named Schmidt was awful and Steve Carlton began to get battered often. The Expos were also entertaining notions of a flag even though they were just in their fifth year. No five-year-old expansion team ever won any flag, but when the Expos took first place for a time, it looked quite possible. Montreal, though, lacked depth in the starting rotation, and there was little after Mike Marshall in the bullpen. When the Pirates took over the top spot, things looked normal. Pittsburgh had the best all-around team in the division, and even though they had lost Roberto Clemente, they still had a tough lineup. Willie Stargell was now the unquestioned leader, and he was en route to league highs in homers and RBIs. The big problem with the Pirates was the fact that their top starter in 1972 in Steve Blass (19–8, 2.47) suddenly could not get the ball over the plate. Blass was wild and was getting bombed every time he pitched, and four other fine starters could not compensate (the four were Dock Ellis, Nellie Briles, Jim Rooker, and Bob Moose), even though the lineup had seven men who would go on to hit at least 10 homers that year. The Cubs also held first for a time, but with Fergie Jenkins (who won twenty or more games every year for the Cubs from 1967 through 1972) having an off year, the pitching staff was destabilized and a decent lineup simply could not overcome.

That left two teams that basically did not spend much time in first in the first half of 1973—the Mets and the Cardinals. The Mets were hit hard by all kinds of injuries and soon forced the Cardinals out of the basement. New York was getting great pitching, but with injuries to the lineup the pitchers had a tough time winning ball games. The Cardinals had health, but they were just inconsistent. Rookies Ken Reitz and Mike Tyson were doing well enough with the glove on the left side of the infield, but both were not hitting. Joe Torre continued to slip from his league-leading .363 average and league-high 137 RBIs in his 1971 MVP year. Jose Cruz just couldn't hack it at the plate. On the other hand, Ted Simmons became the big gun in the St. Louis lineup, Lou Brock continued to reign as base-stealing king, and Ted Sizemore was hitting and fielding brilliantly. The Cardinals were even getting great pitching from Rick Wise, Reggie Cleveland, and newcomer Alan Foster, who was picked up for virtually nothing from the Angels. Bob Gibson still was struggling, but as July wore on he was getting back on track.

Suddenly the Cardinals began to make their move for the top. St. Louis began to win with consistency, and they crossed the .500 barrier as August came. The other teams were still in the hunt and one win or one loss could mean a rise or fall of three or four places in the standings. The Phillies began to fade as Steve Carlton followed his greatest season with one that would be his worst. The press in Philadelphia began to attack the idol of 1972, and Carlton began his famed silence that lasted throughout most of the rest of his career. The Pirates, Cubs, Expos, and even Mets still were in the hunt, though, and the Cardinals had to keep winning to stay at the top. St. Louis continued to enjoy good health as August began, but disaster was just around the corner.

Early in August the Cardinals went to New York for a key series (all series within the division were key that year) against the Mets. Bob Gibson was on the hill, and he was returning to form. Early in the game, a ball was hit to Gibby. Gibson scooped it up and ran to first to retire a batter. As things turned out, that was the last time Gibson was ever able to run well on a field again. Later in the game Gibson got on base. He was taking a lead off first when a pickoff throw came. Gibby dived into the sack. Bang! Gibson was on the ground in pain; his knee had given out. The Cardinal ace was taken off the field and examined, and the diagnosis was bad—torn ligaments in the knee. Gibson was through for the year, and now the chances for a flag flying in St. Louis looked bad. The ace of the team was out, and now the Cardinals would have to try to win without their leader.

The Cardinals eventually got to 11 games over .500 in August, and it looked like they would win rather easily. But then other teams began to cut down St. Louis. The Western clubs were tough on the Eastern ones, and St. Louis was no exception. The Mets began to make their move for the top in August after being in the cellar for a long time, and as September came every team but the Phillies had a shot to finish on top. A flag that no team seemed to want to win was up for grabs by almost everyone, and the season was just one month away from ending.

The Mets continued to win in September at a good pace. On the twenty-first the Mets finally got into first place with a weak 77–77 record. The Cardinals were third, just 1 game out with a 76–78 record. The Cubs, in fifth place, were just 2½ games out. Four days later, the Cardinals were 4 out and had a 76–81 mark, so St. Louis could hope for no better than a .500 finish for 1973. Still, the Cardinals had a shot. Even though the Cardinals dropped two games to the Mets in head-to-head play this late in the year, St. Louis could possibly make it by winning the last five games of the year while the Mets went on a five-game losing streak. Of course, the Pirates needed to go 2–4 in the final week, the Cubs had to go no better than 4–2, and the Expos could not play too well against their opponents to help out, but all of this was still possible.

The Cardinals did win their last 5 games to end the year 81–81. The season, however, was still not over. The Pirates had a rainout to make up with the lowly Padres while the Mets and Cubs had a doubleheader in Chicago to play due to rain the previous two days. Entering this final "final" day the Mets owned an 81–79 record while the Pirates were 80–81. The Pirates needed to lose and the Mets had to be swept by the Cubs for the Cardinals to still be alive. A two-way tie would result, forcing a division playoff game. The key was for the Mets to lose their first game in the twin bill; otherwise the Cardinals would be knocked off and the Pirates would be as well. The Pirates lost their game, eliminating them from the race, but the Mets won the first game of the twin bill, giving them an 82–79 record. The second game of the twin bill was rained out, so the Mets' mark was final, and the Cardinals finished 1½ games behind them. A most bizarre pennant race had come to an end.

So the Cardinals just missed out on a flag. There was little doubt in most people's minds that had Bob Gibson not hurt himself in New York, the Cardinals would have won the division. Gibson had been back to his old self at the time of the injury, and it was reasonable to figure that he would have won at least 2 more games in the last 2 months of the season. Two wins sound like nothing, but in the weird 1973 race 2 wins would have meant first place for the Cardinals. Just 1 of those wins coming in the last 2 Cardinal games against the Mets would have made the difference right then and there. Instead of winning a flag for 1973, the Cardinals now worried about Bob Gibson's condition for 1974.

After the 1973 season it was obvious that the Cardinals needed to add some power while getting some outfielders who could get the job done. Jose Cruz was highly touted, but for the most part he was a failure. Luis Melendez was fine as a utilityman, but as an everyday outfielder he was lacking greatly. The Cardinals had an outfielder in their system with speed and a good bat, named Bake McBride, and it was time to give him a shot, so center field would be filled. Right field would have to be filled in by a trade. St. Louis decided to gamble on another deal, and on October 26, 1973, the Cardinals sent Rick Wise and Bernie Carbo to the Red Sox for switch-hitting power hitter Reggie Smith. This trade worked out well for both teams in the long run, and it seemed to signal the end of the Cardinals' era of terrible trades. Smith was a hustling ball player who was nagged by injury in 1973 but still popped 21 homers while hitting .303. Five straight years Smith hit at least 20 homers, three times he hit .300, and twice he had 90 RBIs. On the same day the Cardinals acquired Smith, they also picked up Sonny Siebert from the Rangers to replace Wise in the rotation. Finally, St. Louis made another deal with Boston in December, sending Diego Segui, Reggie Cleveland, and Terry Hughes to Boston for Lynn McGlothen, John Curtis, and Mike Garman. The pitching staff now would have a new look for 1974.

In 1974 every team was considered to be a contender by its fans after what had happened in 1973. The division got off to another weak start, triggering wonder over why a whole division had been playing so badly for such a long time. People figured the second wave of expansion brought more bad things to the game than the first wave did, since now half a league was terrible. This time, though, the division began to play better, as the Mets and Cubs both had genuinely bad years and quickly dropped out of the race. The Phillies and Expos began to fall back after midseason, and the race turned into a conventional one between the Pirates and Cardinals.

The Cardinals' moves off-season were working very well. Lynn McGlothen was a hard-throwing righty who was having an excellent year. John Curtis was also doing well, but it seemed like he never got decent offensive support. Sonny Siebert, once a flamethrower himself, had lost it, but he was still getting by on guile. Young Bob Forsch came up in midseason, and he looked promising. The bullpen of Al Hrabosky, Mike Garman, and Rich Folkers was doing well, closing out rallies that the enemy tried to ignite. All seemed well with Reggie Smith, as he was among the league leaders in batting, homers, and RBIs.

All did not seem well with Bob Gibson. Gibby's knee was not back and it showed, as the Cardinal leader was having a mediocre year. At one time, Gibson's ERA was over 4.00 and the talk was that Gibson had had it and was ready to quit. Still, with the team in the race it would look bad if Gibson just left, so he stayed and endured a painful season.

The other Cardinal who remembered glory days in St. Louis was Lou Brock. Brock was now running at a record pace, and there was much talk that he would break the record set by Maury Wills in 1962 with 104 steals. People thought it incredible that anyone would even approach the Wills record. When Maury Wills broke the old mark for steals (96, set by Ty Cobb in 1915), nobody could believe it. Ty Cobb's record was considered harder to break than even the home run record of 60 that Babe Ruth set in 1927. The thing was that in 1962 the stolen base was still a neglected weapon for scoring and it had been seldom used since the 1920s, as homers were flying out of every park. To show how little stealing was used one should see that in 1949 Bob Dillinger of the Browns led the American League with just 20 thefts.

But Maury Wills was a true pioneer of bringing the steal back to the majors. Ty Cobb's mark had stood for nearly fifty years, and nobody even came close after the 1920s began. Nobody liked the steal anymore, and in his later years John McGraw, longtime manager of the Giants, was heard lamenting the death of "inside baseball," where a stolen base was a big part of run scoring. Maury Wills became the pioneer of all of today's great base stealers by becoming a threat to score every time he got to first while the Dodgers were lacking homer hitters. Wills's 1962 was compared to Maris's 1961, with his 61 homers, and was so impressive that Wills won the MVP award even though the league had great hitting that year. (Wills's teammate Tommy Davis led the league with a .346 average and an amazing 153 RBIs, many coming with Wills scoring like crazy.) If it took fifty years for Wills to break an "unbreakable" record, then Wills's mark should have been safe for at least fifty years as well, if not forever.

Well, twelve years later, Lou Brock was threatening to break the "unbreakable" Wills record. By midseason, the media swarmed where the Cardinals were playing. Brock handled himself well during all of the questions, and he kept hitting above .300, as the Cardinals were in the race. The media circus around Brock took the spotlight off the team as the Cardinals moved into first place as September came, but the Pirates were still hanging tough.

In September, the Cardinals hosted the Phillies and Lou Brock was closing in on the record. Finally Brock took off and beat the throw to Phillies shortstop Larry Bowa for his 105th steal of the season. The unbelievers believed as the record fell to the man who studied base stealing the way a neurosurgeon studies brains. Brock went on to collect 13 more steals for the month and ended with an amazing total of 118 steals for the year.

At the time Lou Brock went into the record book, the Pirates were making their move on the Cardinals. St. Louis was in the lead, but the Pirates began to slug their way closer to the top. In the final week, the two teams still were at each other's throats, but the vast experience of the Pirates was just too much for the Cardinals to overcome. Pittsburgh moved into first place with a rush and ended up beating out the Cardinals by just 1½ games. For the second straight year St. Louis finished a tough pennant race by being less than 2 games out.

Still, the 1974 Cardinals were a solid team. Besides owning the stolen base record, Lou Brock hit .306. Ted Simmons drove in 103 runs. Reggie Smith had 100 RBIs on a .309 average. Bake McBride was Rookie of the Year with a .309 mark. Ken Reitz improved to a .271 mark and was becoming a slick fielder at third. Pitchingwise, Lynn McGlothen went 16–12, 2.70, as the big winner on the staff. The bullpen trio of Hrabosky, Garman, and Folkers went 21–5 with 17 saves. John Curtis, Sonny Siebert, and Alan Foster all did decently without run support. Bob Gibson had a rough year at 11–13, 3.83, even though he led the club with 240 innings pitched. A flag seemed to be soon in sight.

IV

Many people thought that the Cardinals would dethrone the Pirates in 1975 after Pittsburgh had won four titles of the last five. St. Louis made few moves for the year outside of trading Joe Torre to the Mets for former Cardinal Ray Sadecki. The Cardinals hoped that Bob Gibson would come through at age 40 to help them in the quest for the title, and with Torre gone Reggie Smith became the first baseman while another outfield hole was opened. This did not bode well for the new year.

The Cardinals began the season weakly yet again and hovered around the .500 mark for most of the year. The pitching was having trouble, as Lynn McGlothen was now being solved by batters. Ray Sadecki was battered all over the place and sent packing to Atlanta in exchange for Ron Reed. Reed was one of the more effective Cardinal pitchers of 1975, but he suffered from a lack of support. Bob Forsch was developing nicely, and John Denny had a good half season. But Bob Gibson was not helping at all. At age 40 his knee was killing him and so was his arm. Gibson was being pounded every time out and owned a 3–10 record with a 5.04 ERA when he finally called it quits late in the year. Bob Gibson retired with 251 wins, 3,117 strikeouts, 56 shutouts, and a 2.91 ERA in his outstanding 17-year career as the greatest pitcher in St. Louis Cardinals history.

While the pitching struggled, the hitting was also doing less than expected. Reggie Smith had a good year, but it was nothing compared to 1974. Lou Brock dropped to third in steals with fifty-six. Willie Davis arrived from the Rangers in a deal in June, and he brought with him a reputation as bad news. Davis took over in center, and although he hit well, his fielding was off, as he was clearly in decline. Bake McBride moved to right field and did well, but Davis's presence made some uneasy. The Cardinals got through the disappointing season with a weak 82–80 record, good enough for a third-place tie with the Mets.

For 1976 the Cardinals made some moves to shore up the team. St. Louis sent Ted Sizemore to the Dodgers for Willie Crawford. Willie Davis was shipped to the Padres virtually for nothing. Mike Garman went to the Cubs for Don Kessinger. Ken Reitz went to the Giants for Pete Falcone. All of these moves were designed to get the Cardinals back into contention. St. Louis went into 1976 with high hopes, but news more important than the pennant races hit baseball.

Again the players' union and owners were butting heads, this time over the issue of free agency. During 1975, Andy Messersmith and Dave McNally pitched for the Dodgers and Expos, respectively, without new contracts. Under the old reserve clause that bound a player to a team for life (or until a trade, sale, or release did them part), a player was considered a member of the team permanently, because contract language seemed to imply that once a player signed his first deal he was "renewed" by his team each year. In effect, the owners maintained that once they signed a player to a contract, that player was property of the club and after the end of each contract the team could "renew" the deal at its own behest, whether or not the player liked it. The "renewal" of the contract was what the reserve clause was all about, and the clause was in existence for a century. Prior to the creation of the National League in 1876, players from the National Association (its predecessor) tended to jump from one team to another, so the N.L. founders agreed to keep players bound to one team by using a clause that kept them permanently attached to the team with which they signed their first contract. In the past, the reserve clause was challenged, first by the Union Association in 1884, then by the Players League in 1890, but as we've seen, both leagues died after one year. In 1922 the Supreme Court declared baseball a special exception to antitrust laws of the country in the aftermath of the Federal League war, and although Congress looked into the business practices of baseball a few times in the 1950s, nothing was done about the reserve clause. Senators from areas clamoring for big league ball before expansion came always threatened to look into baseball's unique status when it came to the antitrust laws, but the owners always placated the bigwigs by promising to move teams or to expand, and in the 1950s and 1960s they indeed did so.

For decades the owners also maintained that without a reserve clause baseball would be ruined. Free agency would result, and the free agents would all go to the wealthy teams, leaving teams that were poor or in small markets unable to compete; so went the argument. The players also tended to agree with this kind of thinking, and one wonders, if free agency existed in the 1910s and 1920s, would the Cardinals have managed to survive even with Branch Rickey and his farm system? The chances were good back in those days that players like Rogers Hornsby would have gone to the Giants immediately if free agency were around, leaving the

Cardinals without a Frankie Frisch to replace him. It's likely that the owners' argument in those years would have been proven right and many of the oldest teams of today would most likely not be here, including the Cardinals.

But by the 1960s, the players changed their thinking on the reserve clause. They formed a union, and they were tired of being mere chattel. In the past, many players were treated shabbily by owners who were *very* cheap when it came to paying raises. The 1919 Black Sox scandal erupted because White Sox owner Charles Comiskey (yeah, that name is familiar in St. Louis, because he was the same guy you read about earlier when he was with the American Association's Browns) was notoriously cheap, and when gamblers offered big money to throw the series, some of the players jumped at it. In the 1970s, Charlie Finley of the A's was another tightwad who underpaid his great players that had formed baseball's last dynasty (but at least Finley could claim financial duress due to poor attendance in Oakland; Comiskey had no excuse for his cheapness) and lost Catfish Hunter to the Yankees as a free agent when an arbitrator set him free on a technicality.

Now, in 1976, baseball had two pitchers who did not sign a contract that was automatically renewed under the reserve clause. The players contended that since they did not sign a contract, they technically were not under obligation to the teams they were paid by. The clubs maintained that it did not matter that the two men did not sign a contract; they knew years before that they were property of their respective clubs once they signed that very first contract and that the club could renew the pact any time it wanted to, so they were still considered under contract, signature or no signature. Today, it's hard to believe how the owners thought and behaved back then and it looks like a very flimsy argument, but the owners stuck by their guns on this issue. It's even more amazing that a player did not challenge the owners years before 1975 in the way that Messersmith and McNally did, but it was a very risky idea.

Once the 1975 season ended, the players' union filed a grievance on behalf of the two pitchers. Dave McNally decided to retire, but Andy Messersmith's career was now on the line. The union said Messersmith should be a free agent while the owners said no, Messersmith was not free because of the reserve clause. Arbitrator Peter Seitz was agreed to by both sides to decide the matter, and on December 23, 1975, he decided: Messersmith was a free agent, and the union was right; the reserve clause was destroyed. Seitz stated that when a player signed a deal, the player was bound to the team for the duration of the deal and nothing more. The idea of a perpetual renewal clause that bound a player to a team for life was declared dead. The owners were irate and fired Seitz. The magnates then filed an appeal on the decision. On March 9, 1976, the appeal was denied, and now the owners faced the grim specter of a mass of players being set loose and going to rich teams like the Yankees and Dodgers while teams like the A's and Giants faced disaster. The Peter Seitz decision went down in baseball history as one of three moves in this century that changed the face of the game, the others being Branch Rickey's farm system and the arrival of Jackie Robinson on the Dodgers.

As was the case in the 1972 flap between union and owners, Gussie Busch was among those advocating a hard-line. The union was happy that it won free agency, and they could be expected to be tougher than ever to deal with. The Basic Agreement, which governs relations between the union and owners, was running out in 1976, and the owners wanted a new deal that put at least some brakes on free agency. In order to pressure the union, the owners decided to lock the players out of the training camps. People feared that a lockout or strike would cut into the regular season, but the owners finally decided to end the lockout and the season would begin as scheduled. Negotiations on a new Basic Agreement went on into the summer, when both sides agreed to a four-year deal that included some brakes on free agency. Soon the players would embark on a gold rush and the expiration of the new agreement would lead to all kinds of untold grief as sports faced strife on an unprecedented scale.

Whether the lack of a full spring training was the cause or not became a moot point, as the Cardinals got off to a flying flop in 1976. The pitching staff was leaderless with the loss of Bob Gibson, and it was hit hard and often. Offensively, the Cardinals did not exactly thrill anyone either, as only rookie Hector Cruz was on target for a ten-homer campaign. St. Louis was beaten every which way during the year, as only a few players fared well. Ted Simmons went on to the lead the team with just 75 RBIs while the offense got virtually nothing from anyone outside of Simmons, Lou Brock (.301), Willie Crawford (.304), and part-timer Keith Hernandez (.289). John Denny was the ERA champ in 1976 with a 2.52 mark and Pete Falcone had a decent year at 12–16 and 3.23, but the pitching in general was pitiful. The Cardinals plunged into fifth place with a dismal 72–90 record, the first time the Cardinals had lost 90 games in 60 years. Only a worse year by the Expos (who lost 107 games) kept the Cardinals out of the cellar. Red Schoendienst was so disgusted that he quit as pilot, but he stayed with the club in other capacities. Clearly the Cardinals had become a bunch of deadbirds.

The winter of 1976 saw the first ever free agent draft. Longtime stars such as Reggie Jackson, Rollie Fingers, Don Gullett, and Sal Bando were up for grabs as the owners rushed to outspend one another. Gussie Busch, a staunch conservative on all baseball matters, watched in horror as teams like the Yankees, Angels, and even Padres spent millions in their efforts to "buy" a world championship. Busch decided to pass on this madness, even though the Cardinals were not poor and were in big need of some of the free agents. The Cardinal tradition of fiscal prudence would continue to be maintained, even if it was now chic to spend millions to get top players. From now on teams could build themselves a third way besides through trades and the minors, with free agency, but the Cardinals would basically stick with the traditional methods.

The main order of business for the Cardinals was to get a new skipper. The 1976 Cardinals seemed to lack a sense of discipline, and they decided to hire a man who would provide some with Vern Rapp. Rapp's rap was that he was tough and expected his players to obey his orders as if he was a drill sergeant. Players would either run through a wall for him or want to run a sword through him. In any event, Rapp was expected to get the Cardinals over .500 for 1977 and take it from there. St. Louis got Rapp a new third baseman in Ken Reitz from the Giants, as Reitz was now back for his second tour with the Cardinals. Reliever Clay Carroll was also added for 1977, but overall the Cardinals decided to make few moves by getting outside players. Rapp would have to work mostly with the material already on hand.

The Cardinals got off to a better start in 1977 than they had the year before. Unfortunately, the Phillies and Pirates got off to far better starts and the race was between the two Pennsylvania clubs. Vern Rapp's style irked some players, but the team was playing well. Rapp made Keith Hernandez the regular first baseman, and he was hitting well while making outstanding plays around the bag. Garry Templeton was made the regular at short, and he had Hall of Fame written all over him. In mid-1976 Templeton was recalled from the minors and he hit over .320 while making some sensational plays. Templeton, though, was considered a bit lackadaisical, and his defense would confound people; Templeton would make plays that few could make on the one hand, but on the other hand he would botch the simplest of plays. Still Templeton excited fans with his speed and he was as comfortable hitting righty as he was hitting lefty, and he became a top switchhitter. Ted Simmons got his power stroke back, and Ken Reitz was showing some pop as well, as the offense improved in 1977.

The pitching was still in disarray, though, and it was holding the Cardinals back. Bob Forsch was en route to 20 wins, but the other starters were less than stellar. Eric Rasmussen was among the league leaders in losses, and he was the only other pitcher beside Forsch to win in double figures. John Denny was proving to be temperamental and brittle, and he had a poor year in 1977. Pete Falcone also had a bad year, and Tom Underwood's arrival from the Phillies did little to help. The bullpen was spotty, as Clay Carroll and newcomer Butch Metzger (picked up from the Padres) did well while Al Hrabosky, Rawly Eastwick, and others did not. In general the pitching failed and the Cardinals did not improve as much as they could have. Still, the Cardinals ended up winning 13 more games in 1977 than they had the year before and finished third.

After St. Louis progressed to over the .500 mark in 1977 it was expected that they would be a real contender in 1978. The pitching was improved when Pete Vuckovich was picked up from the American League's new team in Toronto, the Blue Jays. Reliever

Mark Littell was acquired from the Royals in exchange for Al Hrabosky, so the bullpen was expected to be effective. The offense was supposed to be productive again, and if the pitching moves worked out, the 1978 Cardinals would be battling the Phillies and Pirates for the flag.

In spring training there was dissension over Vern Rapp's heavy-handedness, and it boded badly for the Cardinals in 1978. The murmuring continued right into Opening Day, and the prospects for a good year in St. Louis were poor. The Cardinals got off to a 5–10 start, and Vern Rapp was fired. Ken Boyer, the popular Cardinal third baseman of the 1950s and 1960s, was named the pilot. Boyer had been considered a leader in his playing days and people thought he would make a good skipper, so his selection was popular. The Cardinals were happy to be relieved of Vern Rapp, but the team continued to falter. John Denny was healthy and doing well, Pete Vuckovich was having a better than expected year, and rookie Silvio Martinez did well. Bob Forsch, though, was not getting help from the offense, and he was the perfect example of what was wrong with the 1978 Cardinals—good pitching but no hitting. Keith Hernandez wasn't even hitting to the level everyone expected, Garry Templeton was not hitting too well, and Ken Reitz was in a year-long batting funk. Newcomer Jerry Morales was a big disappointment, and Lou Brock was having his worst year ever. George Hendrick came over from the Padres, but by the time he arrived it was too late to save the Cardinals. St. Louis plunged into the second division and threatened to unseat the Mets from the basement, but the Cardinals managed to avoid that awful fate by 3 games. But at 69–93, the Cardinals were still bad enough to finish fifth.

The Cardinals were now at a crossroads. St. Louis had not been in a race since 1974, because they kept having trouble with one facet of the game or another. One year the hitting was good and the pitching stank. Another year the pitching was good and the hitting stank. St. Louis needed to get its hitting and pitching in sync if the team was to go anywhere. Cardinal fans were tired of the inconsistency as well; after 1968 the Cardinals failed to draw 2 million, and in 1978 the gate dropped to about 1,200,000, the worst mark since Busch Stadium opened in 1966 (excluding the strike year of 1972). It was time for new blood to be brought in.

Lou Brock was almost 40 and many felt he should quit after hitting just .221 in an injury-plagued 1978, but Brock had other ideas. Brock wanted to leave on a high note and he also wanted to steal the most bases in a career, so he came back for 1979. Ken Boyer decided to get some young players into the lineup and brought up Ken Oberkfell to play for Mike Tyson at second. Highly touted catcher Terry Kennedy was also ready for some playing time, and speedy Tony Scott was given the center field job. A couple of fading relievers were added to back up Mark Littell in Darold Knowles and Will McEnaney, but otherwise the Cardinal roster was left mostly unchanged for 1979.

St. Louis got off to a good start in 1979 and moved into the race for a while as the highly touted Phillies were having a rough year. Brock was hitting the way he used to and was on target for his steals record. Keith Hernandez got off to a hot start and was ahead in the batting race while Garry Templeton was heading for 100 hits from each side of the plate, something no batter had ever done before. The offense was strong and the pitching was weaker than the year before, but it was holding up. Pete Vuckovich and Silvio Martinez became the big winners, and in the second half John Fulgham came up and looked great. Ken Boyer was praised for a fine job of calm leadership as the Cardinals showed great improvement. Ken Oberkfell was hitting over .300 as a rookie and doing a great job at second.

The Cardinals were having a fine year in 1979, but they then began to slip back a bit as the Pirates took charge of the race and the Expos surprised everyone with their best year ever. Montreal had never finished above .500 in a season, but they shot past St. Louis and dogged the Pirates right to the end. As the race became a battle between Montreal and Pittsburgh, Cardinal fans had to be content with watching individual achievements. Garry Templeton had wanted out of St. Louis because he felt he wasn't being appreciated, but in 1979 the fans got behind him and he had a great year when he collected over 200 hits and got 100 from each side of the plate. Keith Hernandez became a fan favorite with his brilliant defense and his .344 average as he won the batting title.

After that year, Hernandez became the first man to share an MVP award when he tied Pittsburgh's Willie Stargell for the honor. Lou Brock swiped his 938th base with a week left in the year to become the all-time steals king. A month earlier Brock also collected his three-thousandth career hit, and he ended the year at .304, when he decided to retire. Overall, the Cardinals were one of the top-hitting teams in the league in 1979 (a league-high .278 average, 279 doubles, and 63 triples), and the pitching held up well. The Cardinals had a shot at 90 wins but dropped 4 straight to the Mets at the end. It had looked like the Cardinals were finally righted, but that was an illusion.

Part VII

Whitey's Redbird Revival (1980–90)

I

After the 1979 campaign the St. Louis Cardinals looked like they were finally in sync. The hitting was fine and the pitching was adequate and visions of a contender danced in the heads of Cardinal fans. Lou Brock, the last man on the team to play for a pennant winner in St. Louis, was gone, so the last link to a glorious past was cut. The Cardinals decided to make moves to make the team a winner in 1980 by shoring up not the pitching, but the lineup instead. St. Louis shipped spare outfielder Jerry Mumphrey and pitcher John Denny to the Indians for Bobby Bonds. At first glance the deal looked good for St. Louis, since Bonds was a top power hitter and base stealer. Unfortunately, Bobby Bonds's fine career was spent as a wanderer in the majors, as the teams he played on failed to win. In 1974, after playing the last of his seven years in San Francisco, Bonds was sent to the Yankees. The Yankees were picked to win in 1975, and Bonds did his part by hitting 32 homers. The thing was, most of the other Yankees did not do their parts and the team failed to win, so Bonds was sent to the Angels. In 1976 Bonds got hurt and missed much of the year, but in 1977 he belted 37 homers with 115 RBIs. But the Angels, who were one of those teams that spent lavishly on free agents in the winter of 1976, failed to win as predicted, and Bonds was off to the White Sox for 1978. Chicago got off to a poor start, disappointing the fans, so rather than wait until after the season to trade Bonds, the White Sox sent him to the Rangers a month into the year. Texas also was expected to win that year, but they didn't either and Bonds found himself with the Indians in 1979. No, the Indians were not expected to win in 1979, and when they didn't, they figured Bobby Bonds was used to traveling, so off to St. Louis he went. Guess who was supposed to contend in the N.L. East in 1980? Bobby Bonds knew the answer, and he probably wondered if he would be the first man to play for every team in the majors before his career was over, as 1980 began.

While the Bonds trade seemed to look good, it had two flaws. One, it strengthened the Cardinals' main strength, the hitting. Two, the deal weakened a Cardinal weakness, the pitching. John Denny was only 8–11 with a 4.85 ERA in 1979, but he did pitch 206 innings and made 31 starts, so at least he could give the Cardinals some innings. Besides, Denny did have good years in 1976 and 1978, so 1980 looked like another good year for Denny if he kept to his two-year cycle. Denny, though, would have to have his good year in Cleveland, if he kept to form.

Ken Boyer saw that the minors were filled with good prospects, and he decided to bring in some more youngsters to improve the club as soon as they were ready. The big problem was that most of the promising youngsters were hitters and not pitchers. The Cardinals had plenty of offense, and what they needed was more pitching. The N.L. East had teams that had good pitching, and they were the teams that were expected to finish ahead of the Cardinals. The Pirates had a tough rotation in 1979 that lacked a man that won as many as fifteen games, yet they won the World Series because five good starters were backed by three top relievers. The Expos were even more frightening, having a great blend of young and veteran starters backed by a bullpen of good veterans who had been on winners elsewhere. The Phillies had a bad year in 1979 because their pitching staff was hit hard by injury, but in 1980 the pitchers were coming back healthy and with Steve Carlton leading the way the Phillies had to be taken seriously. Even the Cubs had a decent four-man rotation and a bullpen led by Bruce Sutter. Only the last-place Mets had a shortage of good pitching, but the one man who did well in 1979 in Craig Swan (14–13, 3.30) was so good-looking to the Cardinals that they actually were rumored to offer MVP and batting champ Keith Hernandez to the Mets for Swan, but the Mets, undergoing a change in ownership, said no. From a pitching standpoint, the Cardinals were clearly heading into 1980 with some trepidation.

Before 1980's races got under way there was more trouble between the players' union and the owners. The Basic Agreement was due to expire, and both sides were haggling over the issue of free agent compensation. The owners wanted teams that lost free agents to get something in return for their lost players, while the union balked at that idea, saying it would harm free agency and make free agency seem more like a trade, where a team gets a new player as compensation for the departing free agent. The battle between both sides raged throughout the spring, and the training time was cut by the players' decision to strike near the end of spring training. The union threatened to extend the strike into the regular season but then delayed the move until May 23 while the players built up a "war chest" in the meantime. Thus the 1980 season began with a threat of a major disruption.

Besides the Bobby Bonds deal the Cardinals did little to alter the roster for 1980 by getting players from the outside. The season began at home against the defending world champion Pirates, and the Cardinals showed that their pitching was just fine as they beat the Pirates 1–0. St. Louis played sluggishly, though, and the pitching began to experience problems. An injury wave began to plague the team, and when it hit the hill there was little in the minors to offer any solution to the pitching problems. Soon the Cardinals began wallowing in the second division as good hitting was canceled by bad pitching. The team was getting out of control and lacking direction. For the third time in five seasons the Cardinals were going through another dismal year, and attendance was way down. Not since the late 1950s had the Cardinals seemed to be so out of order for such a long time. The team was pathetic. A solution was needed, and fast.

II

The solution for the Cardinals was a man who would seize the bull by the horns and put a chaotic situation under control. Such a man would have to be a firm man, one who managed and had success, a man willing to gamble. It would help if the man also knew how to build a team from within, in the old way of Branch Rickey, and he should also know what each player was capable of doing. The man who took over the St. Louis mess would need the guts to make moves that would not sit well with the fans, and the man also had to work well with both veteran players and youngsters. The man was Whitey Herzog.

Whitey Herzog's real first name is Dorrel, but for most of his life he's been called everything but that. Whitey was born on November 9, 1931 (there's that month again, just like Musial and Gibson), in New Athens, Illinois. Herzog was a pretty good ball player, and by 1956 he became acquainted with failure when he made the dismal Washington Senators as an outfielder. The Senators were going through their usual poor year and Herzog fit right in with his .245 average as a rookie, but he learned things about managing by observing skipper Chuck Dressen. Dressen knew success as a pennant-winning manager with the Brooklyn Dodgers just a few years earlier, but he didn't have a chance in Washington. Still, Dressen did the best he could with a roster lacking anyone even remotely resembling Duke Snider or Carl Erskine, and Herzog made mental notes on the strategy Dressen used and also asked questions, just like Gene Mauch was doing at that same time in Boston. Unfortunately, Whitey Herzog was nagged by injury in his playing days, and he did not do very well as a hitter, even though he did hit .291 in 113 games for the Orioles in 1961, a team that also had another great manager of the future in Dick Williams. These two men learned plenty by watching skipper Paul Richards, a man considered one of the best pilots of the late 1950s and early 1960s, in action. Richards did not win a flag in twelve years of managing, but his two 1961 pupils would go on to do quite well.

By 1963, Herzog was through in the majors, hitting .257 for mostly weak teams in his eight years. Whitey had drifted around for a while when he arrived in New York in 1965. The Mets were a disaster at that point, and Casey Stengel was through as manager. A year later, Herzog became a coach under skipper Wes Westrum and saw more failure as the Mets "thrilled" their fans by finishing ninth in 1966. Herzog was getting a reputation for being great with young players, so he was next put into the front office in the player development section, looking for kids who might help a terrible team finally go somewhere higher than next-to-last place. While with the Mets, Herzog saw the team rise to a world championship in 1969 and remain a team packed with pitching that Herzog had a hand in helping develop.

In 1973, Whitey Herzog was regarded highly in baseball and

was given a shot at managing. The Rangers were without a manager when Ted Williams left after the 1972 season, and they decided to give Herzog a shot. Now the Rangers had a pilot, but they were still lacking something important—good players. Herzog tried his best to get a terrible team like Texas going in the right direction, but he found his hands tied. Ownership running the Rangers was losing money and did foolish things to boost attendance, like recalling local phenom David Clyde from the minors too early and against Herzog's wishes. Clyde had some initial success, then hurt his arm, became a big spender and an alcoholic, and finally was out of the bigs in 1980 after the Indians cut him. The team was getting worse on the field, and Herzog was fired with the team in the cellar. After that, Dick Williams asked Herzog if he wanted to be one of his coaches on the Angels. At that point, Williams had already made it big as a skipper, taking the "Impossible Dream" Red Sox of 1967 to the pennant and leading the A's to back-to-back world titles. Herzog agreed to Williams's offer, and he became an Angel coach.

In 1975 Whitey Herzog was contacted by the Royals and asked if he wanted to manage them. Kansas City was close to Herzog's home and the team was far better than the Rangers of 1973, so Herzog said yes. The Royals were one of the few expansion teams that did things right and had some good years by 1975, even though they hadn't won a flag. Owner Ewing Kauffman wanted a winner and figured Herzog was the man to lead the club to the top. In 1975 the Royals finished second after Herzog took over in midseason. A year later the Royals beat out the now fading A's for the division title and Herzog was hailed as a great pilot. Under Whitey's direction, the Royals ran like crazy, played tight defense, and had solid starters, backed by a motley crew of relievers. Other teams built themselves around home run hitters even when they played in a big ballpark and relied on one reliever, but Herzog knew that Royal Stadium was too big for long balls and he did not have a one-man gang in the bullpen, so speed and a deep bullpen were stressed in Kansas City.

The Royals won their division in 1976 and faced the Yankees in the playoffs. They were hard fought and the Royals played tough, but the Yankees prevailed. In 1977 the Royals won 102 games and beat out a couple of fine teams in the Rangers and White Sox easily for the title and again faced the Yankees in the playoffs. The Royals looked like league champs when the Yankees pulled out a late-inning win in Kansas City to win the fifth and final game. Herzog was disappointed and Kauffman was very upset, but both men agreed that 1978 would be the Royals' year. In 1978 the Royals again won the division title and again they faced the Yankees in the playoffs, and despite the Royals' getting three homers from George Brett in the third game the Yankees again won the playoffs, this time in four games instead of five.

By 1979 there was trouble in paradise. Whitey Herzog was no longer getting along with Ewing Kauffman and there were rumors of a firing if the Royals failed to bring home a pennant. Also, Herzog was having trouble with some players who did not like his tell-it-like-it-is style. Later Herzog claimed that drug use by players "cost me a world title in Kansas City," so much of the dissension may have been triggered by drugs. In 1979 the Royals got off to a sluggish start as the pitching faltered. The starters were inconsistent and the bullpen was dismal, but because of hard hitting from George Brett, Hal McRae, Amos Otis, and Darrell Porter, among others, the Royals were in a four-team dogfight with the Angels, Rangers, and Twins. Late in the year the Royals lost a key series to the Angels and Kansas City's quest for a fourth straight title was over. At the end of the year the Royals finished second, just 3 games behind the Angels, but Kauffman was upset that the Royals did not get to the World Series and Herzog was fired. Kansas City was outraged and years later a poll taken in town showed that the worst mistake the Royals ever made was when they fired Whitey Herzog.

As 1980 began, one of baseball's top managers was without a job, and people were surprised. Whitey Herzog decided to relax for the first time in years and did some fishing. Soon Herzog became tired of staying away from the game and wanted to get back in. Meanwhile the Cardinals were staggering around the second division like a headless chicken as St. Louis fought to avoid the cellar. A TV listing in a New York paper noted the team's plight when it stated: "The Mets take on the St. Louis Cardinals in the battle for the basement" just as the Cardinals were set to play the

Mets in New York. The Cardinals were so bad that a magazine did an article on them chronicling the hard-hitting but disappointing team's dismal trip to California. Some players thought the team would snap out of it, and Ted Simmons mentioned the poor start the team had in 1973 when they almost won the flag. Still, the Cardinals were a disaster in 1980.

After that trip to California produced a 1–8 record, the Cardinals were facing a tough trip to their homes. The dismal trip ended just as the May 23 strike deadline came. At the last minute both sides agreed to extend the old Basic Agreement to 1981, and a strike was averted for 1980. The Cardinals were not stranded in California after all, but St. Louis probably wished they were. The team went to Busch Stadium and found small crowds, as people were turned off by 8–7 losses piling up all over the place. In June, some good news finally came.

On June 8 the Cardinals were in Montreal for a twin bill that they would go on to lose. After the first game, Ken Boyer was fired, and interim manager Jack Krol took the helm for the second game. While the Montreal debacle went on, Gussie Busch called a news conference in St. Louis to announce the hiring of Whitey Herzog as manager. Herzog knew what he was getting into when he took the job, and when he met the team he did not like what he saw. The Cardinals were the not proud owners of an 18–34 record, and their play on the field was awful game after game. Herzog saw a team poorly schooled in the fundamentals and a team that many times needed three singles to score one run, as speed was virtually nonexistent. Herzog saw Bobby Bonds having the worst year of his career after having a broken wrist, and he was not hitting homers or for average and he was not stealing bases, not good for a perennial threat to make the 30-30 (homers and steals) club. Herzog saw a team that could not field very well. The pitching staff was abysmal. St. Louis picked up forty-two-year-old Jim Kaat from the Yankees for next to nothing, and this ancient pitcher (he was the last man left to have spent time with the *original* Washington Senators) was actually the top pitcher of the Cardinals. Not only was Kaat used as a long reliever, but he also was used as the closer, and he even hurled a shutout as a starter! Good thing Kaat was in

269

excellent shape or he might have gotten a heart attack from all of the pitching he was doing.

Herzog could not believe that a team with such talent as Bobby Bonds, Keith Hernandez, Ted Simmons, Garry Templeton, Ken Reitz, Bob Forsch, Pete Vuckovich, and George Hendrick could be *that* bad, but it was. Herzog then found out what the problem was as he "was afraid to go into the clubhouse" because "about a dozen players were using drugs heavily," as he recalled years later. Drug use was a big problem in the early 1980s in baseball, as a big trial concerning baseball's drug use would show in Pittsburgh in 1985. Many players admitted using cocaine at that time, and some players threw out names of other drug users. Keith Hernandez admitted he was a cocaine user back in 1980 and it controlled him so much that he referred to the drug as "the devil on this earth." Heavy drug use most certainly is a plausible reason why the 1980 Cardinals were such a terrible team, although injuries also played a big role in that club's downfall.

Despite finding a drug mess that he had not expected, Herzog took the helm and tried to guide the Cardinals to a somewhat respectable finish. Herzog got along great with Gussie Busch, and when Herzog told the owner about what he had found, Busch agreed that a major housecleaning was in order after the season was over. In the meantime the Cardinals began to play somewhat better ball, as Herzog tried to use speed to generate some runs. Herzog also accelerated the use of minor leaguers to bring some enthusiasm to the team. Catcher Terry Kennedy was highly regarded, and he began to play frequently both behind the plate and in the outfield. Tommy Herr was recalled when Ken Oberkfell got hurt, and he did a nice job filling in at second. Leon Durham, another big prospect, was given more playing time in the outfield. The pitching staff was hit hard by injuries, and Herzog called up as many rookies as he could to see who could be useful for 1981. The bullpen remained a major headache even after John Littlefield was recalled. Littlefield did a nice job, but his club-leading 9 saves were just not enough.

The team played much better under Herzog and had compiled a 38–35 record for him when Gussie Busch decided to make another big move. On August 29 Busch fired general manager John

Claiborne and asked Herzog if he wanted the job so he could engineer the upcoming housecleaning. Whitey said yes and took the job. Red Schoendienst came out of the coaching box and took the helm for the rest of the year while Herzog figured out what to do to put the club on the right track. With Schoendienst finishing out the year as pilot, the Cardinals concluded their disastrous 1980 campaign with a poor 74–88 mark, bad enough for a fourth-place finish.

Whitey Herzog now faced the difficult task of breaking up a hard-hitting team that led the league in hitting (.275), slugging (.400), runs scored (738), and doubles (300) while improving the feeble pitching staff (last with a 3.93 ERA and 27 saves) without making the offense too weak. Years ago trades were much easier to make because agents did not exist, few players had multiyear contracts, trade vetoing rights did not exist, and no-trade clauses in contracts were unheard of. Now Herzog would have to deal with all of these factors as well as the free agents that were always around and rules that made it tougher for teams to keep players in the minors too long. Moves had to be made, because the Cardinals as they were after the 1980 season were a bunch of leadfoots that tried to hit homers in a big ballpark. Herzog knew that speed was going to have to replace power in Busch Stadium if the Cardinals were to be a factor in the pennant race. The defense would also have to be beefed up on the artificial turf. Most of all, the Cardinals needed pitching, pitching, and more pitching. The starting rotation needed youth, and the bullpen needed somebody who could go out there and put out fires quickly, rather than pour gasoline on the flames. None of the Cardinals' needs would be filled in cheaply, and Herzog knew this, so he asked Gussie Busch for a blank check to do what he pleased. Busch informed Herzog that as long as he told him what he had in mind ahead of time Herzog would have a mandate to build Busch the winner he desperately wanted. That's all Whitey Herzog needed to hear.

Whitey Herzog began his massive housecleaning of the Cardinals on October 25, 1980, by releasing pitcher Don Hood. At the winter meetings Herzog was ready for some real wheeling and dealing at what became one of the busiest trading sessions ever. On December 7 Herzog signed free agent catcher Darrell Porter.

Porter had been Herzog's catcher on the Royals, and although he was coming off a weak 1980 season, Herzog had always been impressed by his defense. Next came three deals that are now part of Cardinals lore. Jack McKeon, the general manager of the Padres, also had a mandate to clean up his team in order to turn that longtime loser around. McKeon wanted young talent and some pitching, and Whitey Herzog had what he wanted. On December 8 the Cardinals sent catcher Terry Kennedy, pitchers Al Olmstead, John Littlefield, Kim Seaman, and John Urrea, catcher Steve Swisher, and infielder Mike Phillips to the Padres in exchange for pitchers Rollie Fingers and Bob Shirley. Later St. Louis even threw in a minor league catcher in this deal. Next the Cardinals made another big deal on the ninth when they sent outfielder Leon Durham, third baseman Ken Reitz, and a minor leaguer to the Cubs for Bruce Sutter. In 1980 the St. Louis bullpen was a disaster, and now the club had the league's top two relievers. On the twelfth the Cardinals concluded the meetings by sending pitcher Rollie Fingers, catcher Ted Simmons, and pitcher Pete Vuckovich to the Brewers for outfielder Sixto Lezcano, pitchers Larry Sorensen and Dave LaPoint, and outfield prospect David Green. On December 22 the Cardinals completed their housecleaning by releasing outfielder Bobby Bonds. St. Louis was abuzz after all of these moves as the Cardinals underwent their biggest upheaval since the 1899 melding of the Perfectos and Cleveland Spiders took place. Everyone was amazed at the way Whitey Herzog had transformed the team. Herzog threw away his Cards for a new deck of them.

III

As spring training 1981 arrived Whitey Herzog was very pleased at his new team's look. Soon after making all of the moves, Herzog decided to manage the team as well, so he now held two jobs. Herzog predicted that his team would make baserunning the chief weapon of scoring, that defense would be tight, that the pitching would hold up, and that the Cardinals would not only be able to compete but also would win the division. St. Louis would have to battle the defending world champion Phillies and the always tough Expos, who everybody thought were going to win in 1981 after two straight close finishes. The Cardinals were generally expected to battle the Phillies for second place. A tight race in the N.L. East was expected.

St. Louis opened at home against Philadelphia and lost their first game. However, the Cardinals got off to their best start in years with a 9–3 April by beating the teams expected to finish in the division's lower half. St. Louis was getting good pitching and Bruce Sutter was putting out the fires while the Cardinals began using speed to do their thing. Herzog rebuilt his infield. Keith Hernandez remained at first as Tommy Herr became the new second baseman and Ken Oberkfell moved to third. Garry Templeton stayed at short. Darrell Porter was struggling at the plate, but he was calling a good game for the hurlers. The outfield was a bit out of position. George Hendrick, usually a right fielder, was moved to center while Sixto Lezcano, a brilliant right fielder, took over Hendrick's old spot. Dane Iorg, a fine hitter but a bit weak on defense, got most of the playing time in left. Still, the 1981 Cardinals were far better than the 1980 squad in all facets of the game. Fundamentals were stressed in the spring, and the players were executing well. Defense improved and new players did well at new positions. Hendrick did a good job in center, Herr showed great range at second, and Oberkfell made a good transition to third. Lezcano and Hernandez had long been recognized for their defense, and they did their usual fine jobs.

In May the Cardinals were hit by injuries to Porter and pitchers Silvio Martinez and Andy Rincon, but still they were in the race. The Phillies were in the lead, but the Cardinals were right behind them and the Expos were also in the thick of it. St. Louis played through the injuries to stay close, but Herzog was still on the lookout for pitching help. The Astros were loaded with more than enough pitching and Joaquin Andujar was unhappy at having been the low man on the totem pole for some time, so he wanted out of Houston. The Astros needed another outfielder and the Cardinals had one, so on June 7 St. Louis sent Tony Scott to Houston for Andujar. Andujar spent a little time in the Cardinal bullpen, but he was soon to be placed into the rotation. A few days later the Phillies had a 1½ game lead on the Cardinals when bad news came—the players union called a strike.

The mess of 1980 was still not cleaned up as 1981 began, and both the owners and the union were inflexible on the key issue of free agent compensation. The union stated that there would be a strike in 1981 if the issue was not resolved, but instead of negotiating, the owners were busy putting up a strike fund. The hard-liners, led by Gussie Busch, remained firm that they would not be browbeaten by the union. The union, led by Marvin Miller, also remained hardheaded and was putting its own war chest together. The owners decided in January to put a compensation plan into effect without the okay from the union, and the union said it would strike in May if the plan was not scrapped. A judge delayed the strike for a few months while the owners stood by their action. On June 12, 1981, professional sports was hit by its first strike begun after a season began. All games were canceled until further notice.

At first, neither side made genuine efforts to settle the affair, and it looked likely that the whole season would be canceled, just like the 1980 season was in the Mexican League when players there struck. Fans were unhappy, and the media wondered why commissioner Bowie Kuhn was doing nothing to help settle things. Both sides then tried a few talks here and a few talks there, but such talks lasted only briefly and broke up when the atmosphere was nasty. June passed into July and still there was no solution in sight. The fans and media both condemned the two sides for the impasse, and if the season was to resume attendance could be expected to be poor.

Finally, the two sides hammered out an agreement in late July. A player pool to compensate teams losing free agents was set up, free agents were now given a classification so the team losing a player could pick a player from the pool only of a comparable ranking, a convoluted system to determine rankings was devised, and other confusing things dealing with free agents were agreed to by both sides. Both sides also agreed on things pertaining to 1981 and the strike, like players not losing pension time during the strike, that the All-Star game would open the "second half" of the season, and that lost games would not be made up. The owners were also allowed to decide how the 1981 season was to end. Both sides still hated each other and Bowie Kuhn was attacked as being incompetent, but the strike was finally over. More than 700 games were canceled and now the big question was, how would the 1981 season be concluded? The answer would satisfy few.

Fans, players, and owners of teams way out of the race at the start of the strike favored a split-season format, which was last used in 1892 after the National League "expanded" to twelve teams. The teams in first place at strike time (Phillies, Dodgers, Yankees, A's) also favored a split season, since it would assure them of getting into postseason play. The Cardinals and Reds, two teams very close to the top at strike time, were very much against the split-season idea. St. Louis, Cincinnati, and a few other teams wanted to continue the season in the usual fashion, but they were outvoted by the split-season faction.

With the idea passed, the four first-place teams of the first half automatically went into the "miniplayoffs." The team winning the second half would also go to postseason play, but if the first half champ also won in the second half, then that team would face the team with the best overall record in the division. The White Sox stated that they could get to postseason play by throwing games to the A's, making the A's champs in both halves while giving the White Sox the best overall record in the division. Whitey Herzog implied that he might forfeit a game or two if it would help the Cardinals get to the postseason. Bowie Kuhn then came up with the idea of pitting the second half champ against the first half champ if the first half champ did not win both halves. If a team won both halves, then it would face the number two team of the second half. Kuhn the commissioner would take heat for this move as well, and the Cardinals would not forget it.

The second half of 1981 began on August 10, and the Cards now had to start from scratch after being near the top at strike time. Joaquin Andujar was moved to the rotation and he became one of the top starters on the Cardinals as St. Louis continued to contend. Some players, like Darrell Porter and Sixto Lezcano, were having rough years at the plate, but the Cardinals continued to lead in the race. Then came an incident that was destined to change the Cardinals in a positive way. On August 26 at Busch Stadium Garry Templeton was not hustling against the Giants and the fans began to boo him. Templeton, who felt he had always been unappreciated in St. Louis and was very temperamental (when he wasn't voted as a starter in the 1979 All-Star game he said, "If I ain't starting I'm not departing," for the game after he was selected as a backup), began making obscene gestures at the crowd. Whitey Herzog was angered beyond belief, and he yanked Templeton right into the dugout. Templeton was fined and suspended, and he checked into a hospital because of depression. The suspension was lifted and Templeton hit well after returning, but his days in St. Louis were numbered. Garry Templeton was talented and looked like a sure bet to get to the Hall of Fame, but his attitude was souring the Cardinals on him. Herzog even admitted that he would not win a flag in St. Louis as long as Templeton was his shortstop. A trade would have to be made after the season.

Despite the Templeton flap, the Cardinals continued to hold the lead. But then the Expos fired their skipper in Dick Williams and when Jim Fanning took over Montreal began to make a move. In head-to-head play in September the Cards did well against the Expos, but they stumbled against the Mets and Cubs, the two teams at the bottom, and the Expos moved into the lead. St. Louis went only 17–17 in the last month, and the Expos ended up on top in the second half. The Cardinals were very upset that they owned the best overall record in the division at 59–43, yet they did not get to postseason play at all. At 66–42 the Reds had the best mark in the majors, but they also did not get to postseason play. On the other hand, the Royals were 50–53 overall, but they got to postseason play by winning the second half of the season. The Cardinals and Reds blamed Bowie Kuhn for the whole mess and vowed revenge when Kuhn would be considered for another term of office.

Whitey Herzog had a very fine team, but in 1981 he was robbed of the chance to have it in postseason play. The Cardinals had decent pitching, but it had to be improved further if St. Louis was going to advance in 1982. The offense also needed some sparking, since the Cardinals lacked a dynamic hitter near the top of the lineup. Also, there was the Garry Templeton affair, which had left a bad taste in Herzog's mouth. It was time for Herzog to put on his general manager's hat.

On November 20, the Cardinals made a three-team trade with the Phillies and Indians. The Indians sent catcher Bo Diaz to the Phillies for outfielder Lonnie Smith and a player to be named later. The Indians then sent Smith to the Cardinals for Silvio Martinez and Larry Sorensen. Smith was an exciting ball player with great speed and a penchant for slipping on the bases and in the outfield, and he was unhappy about being a part-time player with the Phillies despite being the team's top base stealer and top hitter for average in the last two years. Smith was just what the Cardinals needed—a fast runner who could steal over 50 bases a year. The Cardinals then decided to dispose of Sixto Lezcano, who once was a power hitter for the Brewers but showed little power in 1981 with 5 homers and 28 RBIs. Herzog intended to send Lezcano and Garry Templeton to the Padres for pitcher Steve Mura and shortstop Ozzie Smith, but complications arose.

Previously the Cardinals had tried to trade Templeton for Smith, but the Padres balked. Jack McKeon, better known as Trader Jack, wanted more players, and the deal died. Herzog, however, wanted Smith, and the two teams continued to talk. Ozzie Smith had been one of the best-fielding shortstops since he first came up in 1978, but he was a weak hitter. Smith wanted a multi-year deal to stay in San Diego, with big bucks, but the Padres were wringing their hands over what to do. In 1980 the Padres lost their all-time best player in Dave Winfield to free agency after not giving in to his demands, and now the Padres were facing the prospect of losing their popular shortstop when his pact expired. Trading him would at least bring something of value to the Padres.

The Padres then announced the deal as Smith and Mura going to St. Louis for Templeton and Lezcano. Ozzie Smith was upset over the way contract negotiations were going and he was furious that the Padres simply traded him without even consulting him, so he refused to go. Smith invoked a no-trade clause in his contract, and the deal was stopped. The Padres and Smith bickered over the deal when Smith wanted to know what the Padres intended to do about giving him a new contract or buying out his no-trade clause. The mess continued right into the new year.

Meanwhile, Sixto Lezcano was having second thoughts about going to the Padres and decided to stay in St. Louis. The Cardinals and Padres decided to go ahead with half of the deal, so Lezcano (who had no clause in his contract concerning trades) was sent to San Diego for Steve Mura. The Templeton-Smith portion of the deal was up in the air until the Padres were able to satisfy Ozzie Smith. The Padres now were more determined than ever to get rid of Smith and allowed Whitey Herzog to talk to him. Herzog convinced Smith that St. Louis was heading in the right direction and that he would be well treated if he went to the Cardinals. George Hendrick, a former teammate of Smith's at San Diego, also talked to the shortstop about the Cardinals being a great team to play for, and Smith was ready to go east after the Padres agreed to satisfy him. The Cardinals had other teams coming to them with their own deals for Templeton, but Ozzie Smith was Whitey Herzog's objective and all other teams were put off.

The Padres finally satisfied Ozzie Smith, and the Cardinals also satisfied him with a new salary. Smith was convinced that St. Louis would be a nice place to play and the Cardinals were indeed going in the right direction, so he finally relented. On February 11, 1982, it was made official. Ozzie Smith was now a member of the St. Louis Cardinals. Herzog had his man. Some people thought that the Padres got the better of the deal, since Garry Templeton was a better hitter than Ozzie Smith and at times Templeton could match Smith defensively, but as time proved, it was the Cardinals who got the better end of the deal. The Cardinals now had the best shortstop in their history.

After getting Ozzie Smith, the Cardinals were considered an excellent defensive team. George Hendrick would move back from center to right field. Rookie David Green was highly touted and was given the job in center. Lonnie Smith had never been regarded as a great fielder, but he had more speed than incumbent left fielder Dane Iorg, so he took over the third outfield slot. Ozzie Smith and Tommy Herr would make a nice double play combination. Speed was improved greatly with the arrival of the two Smiths. Pitching continued to be the key question. Because the Cardinals had only added Steve Mura to a decent but not great rotation, many expected the Cardinals not to win, even if they were going to be tough in a wire-to-wire race. Again the Montreal Expos were favored to win it.

On April 6 the Cardinals began the 1982 season in Houston with a 14–3 beating of the Astros. Bob Forsch had little trouble in winning, as the Cardinals ran wild on the Astros. Right off the bat it was obvious that the Cardinals were going to steal plenty of bases and make enemy pitchers and catchers work hard. The Phillies, another expected contender, was off to a slow start, as the Cardinals took off in April. The Expos were hanging close and even the Mets were doing well at that point, but the Cardinals had far better defense than either pretender.

May came and the Cardinals had some problems. Injuries cut down pitchers Andy Rincon and John Martin, two highly touted youngsters. David Green also was injured, and the Cardinals quickly dipped into the minors for help. Dave LaPoint was recalled and was moved into a starter/reliever role. John Stuper was having a good year on the farm, and he also was recalled. Jeff Lahti shored up the bullpen. The biggest move came when Willie McGee was recalled and inserted into center field. McGee provided brilliant defense and a solid bat while also bringing speed. Despite the changes, the Cardinals held onto the top spot. The Expos had terrible defense that caused their fine pitching staff trouble all year. The Mets faded to their usual poor performance, and the Phillies had trouble getting their hitting going. The Cardinals kept on running their way to a flag, and their tight defense made an average pitching staff look and perform abnormally well. Joaquin Andujar finally became a starter full-time, and he was having his best season ever while delighting fans with his antics. Bob Forsch had finally rebounded from a series of mediocre years and was also having a good year. Steve Mura came out of nowhere to have a career year. Dave LaPoint and John Stuper both excelled for stretches, and Doug Bair did a great job at setting up saves for Bruce Sutter.

The offense shined as Lonnie Smith stole bases at a league-leading clip and scored plenty of runs. George Hendrick was the big power hitter, and Keith Hernandez also was busy collecting RBIs. Ozzie Smith was hitting around .250, far better than anyone ever expected, and Willie McGee was hitting around .300, also a surprise. Everybody was busy stealing bases on the Cardinals in 1982 as the team was dead last in homers. The Cardinals game of

August 22 put the whole year on display when third-string catcher Glenn Brummer stole home with two strikes and two outs in the bottom of the twelfth to beat the Giants 5–4.

St. Louis continued to hold the top perch going into September. The Phillies were closing in, but then a big batting slump killed them off. The Expos continued to struggle, and the Pirates lacked pitching to catch them. As the month wore on, the Cardinals easily breezed against the hapless Mets and then the Cardinals went to Montreal for 3 games against the defending division champs. On September 27 the Cardinals beat the Expos for a 4–2 win and clinched their first ever divisional title. It was the first time St. Louis finished first since divisional play began in 1969.

The Cardinals' opponents in the 1982 playoffs were the Atlanta Braves. The Braves had surprised everyone with a record 13–0 start in April and then outlasted the Giants and Dodgers in a tough fight. The playoffs began in St. Louis on October 6, and the Braves got off to a 1–0 lead behind their ace in Phil Niekro, but before five innings were completed rain came and wiped out the game. The next day Bob Forsch faced Pascual Perez and it was no contest. Forsch scattered three hits while St. Louis backed him with a thirteen-hit attack. In the third inning Willie McGee ripped a ball that should have been an inside the park homer, but the rookie stopped at third with a triple. Ozzie Smith then scored him with a sac fly and St. Louis led 1–0. Three innings later the Cardinals sent Perez to the shower with a 5-run outburst by bunching six hits together. The locals added 1 more tally in the eighth, and the Braves lost it 7–0 as Forsch went the distance.

The second game was more exciting, as Niekro came back to start on three days' rest while facing rookie John Stuper. The Cardinals scored once in the first, but Atlanta took the lead in the third on a single and an error that produced two runs. In the fifth the Braves made it 3–1 on a sac fly by Niekro. The Cardinals scratched back in the sixth with a run and it looked like the Braves would take the game when they put two men on in the eighth, but Bruce Sutter came in and got the mess cleaned up. An RBI single by McGee made it a 3–3 tie in the bottom of the eighth. In the ninth both teams had their relief aces in and the St. Louis ace won it when Ken Oberkfell singled home David Green with one out in the frame, giving Sutter a 4–3 win.

On October 10 the Cardinals sent Joaquin Andujar to clinch the pennant in Atlanta against Rick Camp. In the second, St. Louis scored 4 runs when George Hendrick got an RBI single, McGee tripled home two runs, and Ozzie Smith had an RBI single. Camp was history by then, and so was Atlanta. St. Louis scored solo runs in the fifth and ninth, and the Braves were only able to score twice, both runs coming in the seventh. Andujar cruised to an easy 6–2 win, with Sutter getting a save. St. Louis had won its first pennant since 1968.

The Cardinals were favored to easily deal with Atlanta, and they did, but now they would face the tough task of handling the Milwaukee Brewers in the World Series. The Brewers had smashed 216 homers in 1982, making them one of the most powerful teams in baseball history. The Cardinals hit only 67 homers by comparison, the fewest in the league. Milwaukee also had gotten to the series thanks to the efforts of three men Whitey Herzog had sent them—Pete Vuckovich, Rollie Fingers, and Ted Simmons. Vuckovich led the Brewers with 18 wins, Fingers had 30 saves, and Simmons drove in 97 runs. The Brewers were expected to beat the Cardinals, even though they lacked the speed needed to win 4 out of the possible 7 games in big Busch Stadium.

The series began in St. Louis on October 12, and Bob Forsch faced Mike Caldwell. Caldwell was impressive, giving up just three hits, while the Brewers did what they did best—score several runs. In the first inning the visitors scored twice. In the fourth and fifth the Brewers scored solo runs. In the sixth Milwaukee got 2 more runs. In the ninth 4 more Brewer runs came home. The leadoff man got five hits while the number-two man got four in the game. Yeah, Paul Molitor and Robin Yount were murder on St. Louis, as they got nine out of seventeen Brewer hits in the 10–0 win.

The second game looked more like the first when the Brewers held a 3–0 lead after three innings. Charlie Moore doubled home Roy Howell in the second and Milwaukee scored twice in the third when Yount got an RBI on a ground out and Simmons hit a homer in his old home, but this time the locals answered back. Tommy Herr hit a ground rule double and Ken Oberkfell singled in the

281

bottom of the third, and the hits cut the Brewer lead down to 3–2. In the fifth the Brewers added another run on an RBI single by Cecil Cooper, but St. Louis tied it in the sixth on a 2-run double by Darrell Porter. By this time, starters Don Sutton of the Brewers and John Stuper of the Cardinals were gone. In the eighth St. Louis broke through to a win when the Cardinals quickly loaded the bases. Pete Ladd, who had replaced the injured Rollie Fingers as the Brewer relief ace, hit trouble by walking Steve Braun on four pitches. Bruce Sutter then held the visitors in check and saved a 5–4 win for himself by easily disposing of the Brewers in the ninth.

On October 15 the series shifted to Milwaukee for the next 3 games. Joaquin Andujar faced Pete Vuckovich in a battle of the top starters on each side. Both aces were breezing along until the fifth, when St. Louis came through with a rally. With one out Lonnie Smith doubled, Dane Iorg reached first on an error, and Willie McGee slammed a 3-run homer, giving the Cardinals a 3–0 lead. In the seventh the Cardinals erupted again when Lonnie Smith tripled and scored on a bad throw and McGee hit another homer, giving St. Louis a 5–0 advantage. In the bottom of the seventh, the Cardinals were jolted when Simmons lashed a line drive off of the leg of Andujar, forcing the pitcher out of the game. Memories of Bob Gibson's broken leg in 1967 came to mind, but the man who called himself "one tough Dominican" proved to be okay. Milwaukee scored twice on Sutter and in the ninth the Brewers might have pulled off a rally, but McGee robbed Gorman Thomas of a homer with a man on by making a sensational leaping catch. Sutter picked up the save in the Cardinals' 6–2 win.

The next day the Cardinals supplied Dave LaPoint with a quick 4–0 lead, but the rookie could not hold it. In the first Ken Oberkfell doubled, then scored on a single by George Hendrick. An inning later St. Louis picked up 3 more runs and an easy Cardinal win looked likely. But Milwaukee battled back by scoring once in the fifth. LaPoint was at the top of the hill going into the seventh with a 5–1 lead when the Brewers exploded. Jim Gantner hit an RBI double, Robin Yount hit a 2-run single. LaPoint failed to last the inning, as 6 Brewer runs came in and the St. Louis bullpen failed to stop the flood. Jim Slaton picked up a 7–5 win in relief while Doug Bair was charged with a loss.

Bob Forsch faced Mike Caldwell again in the fifth game, and Milwaukee came out on top again. St. Louis tied the game at one when Keith Hernandez doubled home David Green, but the locals retook the lead in the bottom of the third. It was 3–1 Brewers going into the seventh when Hendrick singled home Ozzie Smith. It seemed like the Brewers would counter a Cardinal score by scoring in the bottom of the frame when Milwaukee scored 1 in the bottom of the seventh. In the eighth the Brewers seemingly put the game away when Moore and Gantner each singled in a run to make it 6–2 Brewers, but in the ninth the Cardinals rallied. Hernandez had an RBI double and Hendrick had an RBI single, but Bob McClure relieved Caldwell and got out of trouble with the Cardinals leaving the tying runs on base. Milwaukee won 6–4, taking a 3–2 lead in the series.

The Cardinals returned home on October 19 needing to win the last 2 games. The Brewers home run attack was basically stifled by the allegedly weak Cardinal pitching staff, but the Cardinals were looking at defeat at home.

The sixth game looked like a mismatch as Whitey Herzog gave rookie John Stuper the start against veteran Don Sutton. The weather was as bad as the Cardinals' chances of winning. In the second the Cardinals scored twice when Dane Iorg scored on an error and McGee scored on Tommy Herr's double. Two innings later St. Louis got 3 more runs when Porter hit a 2-run homer and Iorg scored on a squeeze bunt by Herr. In the fifth rain delayed the game for almost half an hour and Sutton left, but before he did he was touched for 2 more runs. In the sixth another rain delay came right in the middle of the 6-run attack by St. Louis. After over two hours, the game resumed, and when the sixth inning was over the Cardinals had a 13–0 lead over the usually hard-hitting Brewers. Despite giving up a meaningless run in the ninth, John Stuper amazingly went the distance as St. Louis evened the series at 3 games each.

One tough Dominican named Andujar lived up to his self-styled billing when he got the ball and faced Vuckovich in the final game. In the fourth the Cardinals took the initial lead when McGee singled and scored on a Lonnie Smith single. Ben Ogilvie popped a homer to tie it in the fifth, and in the next frame the Brewers took the lead when Gantner doubled and scored on a bad throw and Molitor scored on Cooper's sac fly. The 3–1 Milwaukee lead did not last long when Ozzie Smith singled and Lonnie Smith doubled and a walk loaded the bases. Hernandez then singled home the Smiths to tie it up. Hendrick then delivered an RBI single that scored pinch runner Mike Ramsey with the go-ahead run. In the seventh Andujar had a few words with Gantner after the latter man grounded out and a fight was in the making, but the umpires restored order. In the eighth the Cardinals scored 2 insurance runs when Porter and Braun both hit RBI singles. In the ninth Sutter got the side out in order and he got the save as the Cardinals won the game 6–3 and their first world championship since 1967, their ninth overall. Whitey Herzog the manager and the general manager had done a remarkable job of leading a club that was a disaster just two years earlier right to the top. Gussie Busch was overjoyed and so were the fans in St. Louis.

The 1982 season proved that Whitey Herzog was right in just about everything he said and did. Nobody thought that the Cardinals pitching staff would make it through the regular season, much less the postseason, but the much maligned staff did the job. People thought that the Cardinals would suffer from an acute lack of power, but with 200 steals leading the league St. Louis generated plenty of offense. The steals, the bunting, the solid pitching, the tight defense, and the stressing of fundamentals all became the ingredients of a style of play called Whiteyball. The elements were certainly not new in Cardinals history (as the 1934 Gashouse Gang showed), but they had seemed lost in the mists of time. Herzog simply brought the past style of the Cardinals back to the future, and now he was hailed as a genius. The "Cult of Whitey" was now being built by his fans.

Before 1982 was out, the Cardinals were also involved in another big issue, the issue over commissioner Bowie Kuhn. Kuhn's term of office was running out, and his supporters wanted to give him another seven-year term. Busch was less than happy over Kuhn's role in past union-owner disputes, and since the commissioner is hired by the owners, Busch felt he had the right to get rid of an employee who was performing poorly, even if the commissioner was supposed to run *all* of baseball, owners included. Busch also wanted his brewery to increase its sponsorship of baseball games on TV and radio, especially on the national level, and he felt Kuhn was not helpful in that regard. Then there was the flap over the 1981 split-season format that cost the Cardinals a shot at postseason play. Technically, Busch himself was not physically leading the anti-Kuhn front; Busch's representative, attorney Lou Susman, was, but Busch informed Susman in no uncertain terms that he wanted Kuhn out.

All during 1982 Kuhn tried to sway his enemies to his side, and he did succeed in some cases. Busch, though, was still firm on Kuhn not getting another deal. The old Cardinal-Dodger rivalry now was placed on the magnate level when the Dodgers, led by Peter O'Malley, was the team most in favor of Kuhn. The two teams not only had some great pennant races in the 1940s, but once Gussie Busch bought the Cardinals he took an immediate dislike for the Dodgers to heart. Walter O'Malley (Peter's father and boss of the Dodgers from 1950 until his death in 1979) was a shrewd man who worked for the bank that held control of the faltering Brooklyn Dodgers in the late 1930s. O'Malley soon bought more and more stock in the team, until he was able to force Branch Rickey out in 1950. Many owners liked O'Malley because he embraced the idea of making as much money as possible and if that irked fans and the media, then to hell with them. When the Boston Braves wanted to move to Milwaukee, O'Malley voted enthusiastically in favor of it. Once the Braves hit the pot of gold in their new home, O'Malley's eyes grew large. The Dodgers played in a tiny, old ballpark that was located in a crumbling neighborhood and making a profit would be difficult in the future, so O'Malley decided to move his team. His archenemy, the Giants, were in even worse shape, and they were ready to move to Minneapolis when O'Malley asked Giant owner Horace Stoneham if he would like to continue their rivalry in California. Stoneham said yes and both teams plotted moves to the West. New York's politicians fumbled and bumbled badly enough that they made it very easy for both National League teams to leave. O'Malley expected such ineptitude, and he took advantage of it by moving his team.

Busch did not care much for such shady moves. Gussie Busch

liked more to tell it like it is rather than plot secretly in some dark corner. (That's why he got along well with another straight shooter in Whitey Herzog.) As the labor messes of the 1970s broke out, the Dodgers and Cardinals were both on the same side, even if O'Malley and Busch did not like each other. Neither team wanted player strikes, and both took rather hard lines against the union. The Dodgers, though, did favor Bowie Kuhn in most of his actions, and rumor had it that Kuhn was little more than a puppet of O'Malley. Gussie Busch certainly did not like the idea of the commissioner even being thought of being under Dodgers influence, so this potential stooge in Kuhn had to be removed, and Gussie Busch made sure that the Cardinals would try hard to oust him.

Although the Dodgers were worried about Anheuser-Busch sponsoring so many teams (including the Dodgers) locally, they decided to try to turn the Cardinals around on the Bowie Kuhn affair. It was a hopeless task. Gussie Busch remained firm that Kuhn had to leave, and he would not even field calls from Peter O'Malley. Kuhn continued to try swaying enemies, including the very hostile Reds (whose general manager, Dick Wagner, was still fuming over the Reds not making the postseason of 1981 despite having the best record in the majors) and the Yankees of George Steinbrenner (who had several verbal battles with Kuhn over the years and been fined and even suspended by him). The Yankees were expected to be staunchly anti-Kuhn, but a flap between the Yankees and Cardinals over a trade had threatened to move the Yankees to the pro-Kuhn side. After the 1981 season the Yankees sent minor league outfielder Willie McGee to the Cardinals for sore-armed pitcher Bob Sykes. Sykes's arm was so bad that he retired before he even threw one pitch for the Yankees. Willie McGee then went on to have a great 1982 season and drew much attention in the postseason, and this upset George Steinbrenner. Steinbrenner hinted that he might vote in favor of Kuhn unless he received another player from St. Louis. The Cardinals, needing the Yankee vote, decided to placate Steinbrenner and sent him a player. The Yankees remained in the anti-Kuhn camp.

The Kuhn affair continued throughout the summer of 1982. The pro-Kuhn camp wanted the incumbent to stay for another seven years at virtually any cost, while the Cardinals and their supporters were equally determined to oust Kuhn. The pro-Kuhn group tried to keep Anheuser-Busch from expanding their sponsorship of baseball and the Dodgers dropped them completely as a sponsor to force the Cardinals to change their minds, but this only made them angrier. Next the faction for Kuhn tried to have a new setup passed, one where Kuhn would share power with a man who would oversee mostly financial matters in baseball (Kuhn was called incompetent in baseball's financial affairs by some of his enemies, especially when it came to TV deals), but Lou Susman said that was not acceptable. A full-scale war between the two sides of magnates seemed likely and the ramifications of such a war could be disastrous, one that could repeat the near disaster of 1920. Over sixty years earlier, the magnates had fought over the issue of the commissioner and things got so bad that the Yankees, Red Sox, and White Sox were prepared to move into the National League if American League president Ban Johnson would not be restrained by the other five A.L. clubs in his stance concerning the issue. Now a messy situation was unfolding in 1982 and it looked like the Kuhn issue would not be resolved.

On November 1, the pro-Kuhn side decided to call for a vote on the fate of the commissioner. Prior to that time Kuhn and his supporters continued to try to sway votes, and it seemed that some success was being found. The Pro-Kuhns went into the meeting that would feature the vote feeling confident that they would win. The American League was more committed to keeping Kuhn, but the National League was split almost evenly, with the Cardinals, Braves, Mets, Astros, and Reds against him while the other seven clubs favored him. Such a split would force the vote overall to affect Kuhn adversely. Then the vote came. The American League voted 11–3 in favor of Kuhn, and the National League voted 7–5 in favor of Kuhn. Bowie Kuhn had a total of 18 votes out of 26, but it was not enough. Gussie Busch was delighted that the commissioner would not be back for another seven-year term. Until the owners' search committee came up with a suitable candidate, Bowie Kuhn would stay in power, but now he was a lame duck boss. Nineteen-eighty-two turned out to be a banner year for the St. Louis Cardinals: first they won the World Series; then they succeeded in ousting Bowie Kuhn. Gussie Busch was the "King of Baseball" as well as the "King of Beer" in 1982.

IV

On the field the Cardinals now had the difficult task of remaining at the top to carry out. The Phillies moved to add experience in the off-season by adding first baseman Tony Perez and second baseman Joe Morgan to the team. The Pirates had surprised people with an 84–78 record in 1982, so they would be a factor. Once again the Expos were a favorite because of their good starting pitching and tough lineup, and now they seemed to have better defense for 1983. The Cardinals decided to stand pat and hoped that the pitching would come through again in 1983. Whitey Herzog had decided to quit his job as general manager, since he was tired of haggling over salaries and dealing with the players' agents. The Cardinals were expected to contend, but again the Expos were favored to win.

The Cardinals started off well in 1983 and took the lead in a five-team race that involved every team but the Mets. St. Louis was busy stealing bases and was on a pace to exceed their 1982 mark of 200. Lonnie Smith, who almost won the MVP award in 1982, was off to an even better season as he led a strong offense. Still, there were problems on the Cardinals. The pitching was getting more and more spotty. Joaquin Andujar was getting hit hard over and over again, and he was off to a bad start. Bob Forsch was also struggling. Bruce Sutter, who never had a bad year since reaching the majors in 1976 with the Cubs, was having one in 1983, blowing saves all over the place. An even worse problem was being exposed in St. Louis that year. Whitey Herzog was hearing talk of drug use on the team and decided to flush out the users. Herzog announced that if any player who was using drugs came to him, he would be sent to a rehabilitation center and not be punished and any player using drugs who did not confess would be dealt with accordingly. Lonnie Smith came forward and admitted he was a cocaine user. The Cardinals now had to face the fact that one of their top hitters would be gone in a rehab center while the pitching staff was having trouble. Although the 1983 Cardinals had drug users on the team, it was not nearly as bad as 1980, but it was still had enough for Whitey Herzog.

On July 15, 1983, the Cardinals made one of the worst and most unpopular trades in their history when they sent Keith Hernandez to the Mets for pitchers Neil Allen and Rick Ownbey. St. Louis was shocked at this trade. Hernandez had been a Gold Glove winner at first base, a lifetime .300 hitter, an RBI leader, a former MVP, and a clubhouse leader. What most people did not know was that Keith Hernandez had also been a cocaine user. Hernandez stopped using the drug just before the trade, but because he did not come forward when Herzog issued his announcement, the Cardinals decided to trade him. At the time, Herzog staunchly defended the trade by saying he got two sorely needed fine pitchers in the deal and although he hated to lose Hernandez, he felt that the two pitchers would be able to contribute more to a 1983 title than Hernandez would. Still, St. Louis fans were outraged and they would not know of Hernandez's drug use until the 1985 Pittsburgh drug trial.

At the time of the Hernandez trade the Cardinals were beginning a June swoon because the pitching was getting worse. Rick Ownbey was a highly touted pitching prospect in the Mets organization, but the Mets had to include him in the deal to get a premier first baseman like Keith Hernandez. Neil Allen had been one of the league's top relievers since 1980 despite the fact that he pitched for a terrible team throughout his career. The Mets were trying out Allen as a starter and their dismal pitching staff was getting worse when the trade was made, so the Cardinals decided to continue experimenting with him.

June proved to be a tough month for St. Louis as the offense sputtered without Hernandez and Lonnie Smith in the lineup. Ozzie Smith was off to a terrible start, and Tommy Herr was having a great year until his knee blew out. Herr played on with his bad knee until later in the season. The Phillies and Pirates began to make their moves, and the race began to tighten. St. Louis began to struggle in head-to-head play with Eastern teams, including the Mets.

The year plodded on. Andujar continued to be hit hard, and

a trip to the bullpen came. Forsch continued to struggle, and his arm was bothering him. Neil Allen became a top starter for the Cardinals, but the fans booed him any time he appeared in Busch Stadium, the fallout from being acquired for a popular player. Rick Ownbey had control problems and was of little help. Bruce Sutter continued to get shelled. John Stuper and Dave LaPoint were doing a decent job, but they were plagued by arm miseries.

In the second half the Cardinals finally got their offense back together. Lonnie Smith returned and picked up where he left off, going for a batting title in the process. George Hendrick was also going for the title, and he was having another big year. Ozzie Smith began to streak, and his average started to climb. Rookie Andy Van Slyke was having a decent year and was a Herzog favorite as the skipper looked for a position for him. Ken Oberkfell was hitting close to .300. Darrell Porter was rebounding with a good year. Willie McGee showed he was for real with another good year. David Green stayed relatively healthy and was having a good year while moving Hendrick out of right field. (Hendrick moved to first after the Hernandez deal.) Tommy Herr was still hitting well despite his bad knee.

In September the Cardinals still had a shot while the Phillies, Pirates, and Expos were also going for the title. The Cubs had fallen out of the race but were still pesky and the Mets had played their best baseball in years in the second half, so St. Louis faced a tough test. The pitching still was spotty and Tommy Herr was gone by then, but the hitting still was strong. St. Louis had tough battles with the Cubs and Pirates and Mets but managed to beat them enough times to stay in the race. Unfortunately, the Cardinals had trouble with the Expos and especially the Phillies, and they faded back. On the twenty-sixth Forsch no-hit the Expos, but by then it was too late. St. Louis finished 1983 in fourth place with a losing record. Standing pat and not improving the pitching staff in the off-season proved to be fatal mistakes.

The Cardinals realized that standing pat in the winter of 1983 would not do the trick. The division seemed to be in flux. The Phillies were old and even though they were the division's winningest team since 1976, all of those old men were no longer productive and a housecleaning was planned in Philadelphia. The

Pirates had become basically a mediocre team after dominating the division in the 1970s, so they were heading downhill. The Expos were picked year after year to get to the World Series, but in spite of all of their talent Montreal had won nothing but a strike-tainted division flag in 1981 and their won-lost record had been dropping since going 95–65 in 1979. The Cubs had new ownership, and they were determined to field a winner. Even the Mets showed signs of life in the second half of 1983, and their minor league system was ready to send plenty of good players to the big leagues. The Cardinals now had the chance to sink with the fading old guard or rise with the new breed.

Whitey Herzog looked around for help on the outside but saw very little available. Pitching was a priority, since the Cardinal offense had produced a club-record 207 steals, and Herzog had to look at the minors for help. The Cardinals had one outstanding club at the AAA level in Louisville in the American Association. While the Cardinals set a club high with an attendance mark of 2,343,716, the Louisville Redbirds set a minor league record of 1,052,438, drawing more fans than the Indians, Twins, and Mariners at the major league level, and that's because the Redbirds won more games than any other team in the association. It was now time to go back to the minors.

Going into 1984, Whitey Herzog was taking a lot of risks. Herzog was hoping that his starting rotation would improve greatly with what he already had on hand. Bob Forsch and Joaquin Andujar both won 15 games in 1982 and the latter hurler was second in the league with a 2.47 ERA, but both were terrible in 1983. Forsch was only 10–12 with an ERA over 4.00 and Andujar was 6–16, 4.16, as they both had stints in the bullpen and both seemed to have ailing arms. These two past aces would have to rebound if the Cardinals were to contend.

Bruce Sutter was an even bigger worry. In 1982 Sutter pitched in a career-high 70 games while posting a league-leading 36 saves, but in 1983 he was complaining of a bad arm. People began to accuse Herzog of overworking his ace reliever, but everyone concerned said otherwise. Sutter was one of the first pitchers to master the split finger fastball (also called a forkball by some who insist that the split finger is nothing new), a pitch that tends to put much strain on a pitcher's arm, especially on the elbow, so after throwing that pitch for so many years, Sutter's arm was finally feeling the effects in 1983. The effects were bad—a 9–10 record, 21 saves, and a 4.23 ERA in 60 games. Another year of such poor production and the Cardinals would be doomed.

Finally, Whitey Herzog had to hope for continued improvement from his younger players. Andy Van Slyke had one of the best arms in the game, and Herzog looked all over for a place to play him. Van Slyke was considered a power hitter and his bat would be needed in the future, since slugger George Hendrick was getting older and even the speedy Cardinals needed at least one man to drive in all of the speedsters. David Green recovered nicely from his 1982 injuries, and it was expected that he would drive in a goodly sum of runs. Willie McGee knocked in seventy-five runs in 1983, and that was a nice surprise. Tommy Herr was also coming off of knee surgery, and his status was uncertain. When healthy, Herr combined with Ozzie Smith to give St. Louis one of the top double play combinations in the game.

St. Louis would not have an easy start to the 1984 season. Since 1969 the Cardinals had suffered many a disastrous trip to California. In the first years of divisional play the Giants had a tough lineup and the Dodgers always had excellent pitching, and the Cardinals would take their lumps. In the mid-1970s the Giants declined, but they were still tough for the Cardinals to beat, while the Dodgers were busy trying to beat out the powerful Reds. By 1984, the Giants were a better team (although the next two years were to show otherwise), the Dodgers had proven to be the undisputed masters of the West, and now the Padres were ready to kick butt after years of humiliation. Now the Cardinals would open 1984 with a trip to California against three tough teams.

The expected nightmare stemming from a trip west did not come true. The Cardinals went 3–4 before coming home, so the year began on a positive note. Bruce Sutter did not complain of any pain in his arm and began to look like his pre-1983 self. Bob Forsch came down with arm trouble, but Joaquin Andujar took over as the ace of the rotation. The Cardinals took care of the Pirates when they got home, but then a 7-game losing streak began to sink St. Louis. The Cubs had made some big deals in the off-season and in the last days of spring training, and now they were on top. The Mets, too, finally had gotten their act together, and all of a sudden it was as if somebody had turned the entire N.L. East upside down; the Cubs and Mets, two longtime doormats, were at the top while the usually tough Expos and Pirates were at the bottom and the Cardinals and Phillies were in the middle. The division was truly in flux.

The Cardinals plodded on in mediocrity. The Cubs, Mets, and Phillies were all fighting for the top spot while the Cardinals were battling the Pirates and Expos to avoid the cellar. The Cardinals were getting better than expected pitching, but the offense sagged. Andy Van Slyke got off to a weak start and found himself benched. Lonnie Smith also started poorly, and the man who had hit over .300 in his first four years was now struggling to hit .250. David Green was struggling. Power hitter George Hendrick was not doing any power hitting, and the jackrabbits were stranded more often than they were scoring. Nobody was driving in many runs. On top of everything else, Green had to undergo treatment for alcohol abuse when he was getting some RBIs, so the Cardinals were hurting.

At least the pitching was doing a decent job. Joaquin Andujar was heading for his first twenty-win season as the undisputed ace of the starters. Dave LaPoint was not dazzling the world, but he was doing okay and gave Herzog some good starts from the left side. Danny Cox became a member of the rotation and showed flashes of brilliance. Neil Allen was pitching better than the booing fans realized, and Bruce Sutter was on target to break the league's record for most saves by a pitcher in a year (37, tied by Sutter himself when he was with the Cubs in 1979) while having his lowest ERA since he won the Cy Young Award five years earlier.

After the All-Star break, the Cardinals began to play better as Whitey Herzog tinkered with the roster. Ken Oberkfell was sent to the Braves, and third base was now manned by Terry Pendleton. Pendleton made some of the best plays at third seen in St. Louis since the time Ken Boyer was at the hot corner, and the rookie also hit the ball hard, a plus for a team that was having hitting troubles. Rick Horton and Kurt Kepshire were recalled from the minors as well to improve the pitching staff. Both were thrown into the starting rotation, and the two lefties did well. The Cardinals then began to put some distance between themselves and the Pirates and Expos. The Phillies were beginning to fade, and St. Louis had a shot at the first division. In 1983 the Cardinals had a rough time with the Phillies in head-to-head play, but in 1984 they had a far better time against them. The Cubs and Mets seemed out of reach, but at least a third-place finish was a good bet.

Late in the season the Cardinals pushed their way past the Phillies for third place and gave the Mets all kinds of trouble in their quest to knock the Cubs out of first place. The offense began to get going again even though George Hendrick had to leave the team for thyroid surgery. St. Louis was on a pace to break its own club record for most steals in a year, set just one year earlier. Ozzie Smith was hitting better than ever (and since the Cardinals got him, he was outhitting Garry Templeton), and he continued to amaze fans with his brilliant defense and his backflips. Already there was talk of the Hall of Fame for Ozzie because of his defense. On September 28 Joaquin Andujar went 10 innings to down the Cubs 4–1 in Chicago for his twentieth win. Andujar led the league in wins and innings (261) and led the Cardinals in everything. St. Louis won 84 games while finishing third, and the pitching was better than most people thought, but it still could have used some improvement. The offense also needed to be retooled, even though the Cardinals stole 220 bases to lead the majors. The Cardinals had returned to the .500 level, but now it was time to try for another flag.

A shot at the flag in 1985 would prove to be a difficult thing to even envision after the 1984 season was over. St. Louis had managed to avoid messy free agent problems for the most part, but they were now confronted by two very messy free agent worries. Bruce Sutter, the man who saved a league-record 45 games in 1984, had just completed his contract, and there were many offers for the league's top fireman. The Cardinals, conservative when it came to money matters, made a nice offer, but Sutter was getting even nicer offers from other teams like the Braves. Atlanta owner Ted Turner wanted a champion desperately and figured that Bruce Sutter would be the man who could bring it in, so he offered a complex deal that would pay Sutter for the next thirty-five years or so. Sutter took the deal and signed with the Braves. Whitey Herzog then stated, "I'm 25 games more dumber," when talking about the Cardinals' 1985 chances.

The next messy affair was Ozzie Smith. Smith's deal ran through 1985, but the shortstop wanted to talk about a new contract. The Cardinals were in a bind. St. Louis had lost Bruce Sutter to free agency, and the fans were very unhappy. Now the Cardinals faced the prospect of losing the even more popular Ozzie Smith after the 1985 season. Letting Smith get away for nothing was something the Cardinals could not afford, but they could not afford to antagonize him either. People recalled Smith's reaction when the Padres tried to trade him, a reaction that almost killed the Smith-Garry Templeton trade, so St. Louis had to be careful.

Tommy Herr and Joaquin Andujar had been given nice deals after Sutter's departure, so now Ozzie Smith wanted his deal as well. Smith was seeking about $2 million a year plus a few other things (like a beer distributorship), and many people thought that such a figure was too high for a man who never hit over .258 in his career, even if that man was the best defensive shortstop who ever lived. The two sides began to disagree, and trade rumors grew. Ozzie Smith was going to the Yankees for Dave Winfield. Ozzie Smith was going to the Phillies for Mike Schmidt. Ozzie Smith was going to the Dodgers. Ozzie Smith was going to the Mets. Ozzie Smith was seemingly going everywhere except to get a pen and sign a deal with the Cardinals. The fans were split on the Ozzie Smith story. Some felt he was worth the money while others thought his price was too high. Besides, many free agents who signed fat deals had ended up getting hurt or simply never approached their numbers of before the deal was made, so light-hitting Ozzie Smith could prove to be one of the biggest busts in the history of free agency if he was given the deal he sought.

The Smith situation continued right through spring training in 1985. Dal Maxvill was now the new general manager, and nobody knew what he would do. The Cardinals wanted to keep Smith, but they admitted that they might trade him. On April 7, 1985, the Cardinals picked up Phillies shortstop Ivan DeJesus and reliever Bill Campbell, so the chances of Smith leaving were increased greatly. Finally, just after the 1985 season began, Ozzie Smith got his contract and his chance to buy a beer distributorship (in the future) and the fans were pleased. Now Ozzie Smith would have to face the tough task of trying to justify all of that money he would be getting from his new contract. Would he ever!

V

Besides the free agent problems that Bruce Sutter and Ozzie Smith represented, the Cardinals also had to deal with the shortcomings of the 1984 season, a season that had Sutter and Smith both doing well for St. Louis. The Cardinals were lacking batters who could knock in runs. George Hendrick was thirty-five and his bat was getting sluggish even before he left for thyroid surgery late in the season, so getting a power hitter was a must. Andy Van Slyke had a bad year, and even if he had a good one, he was still young and the Cardinals needed a proven slugger who could hit some homers, especially on the road. The Cardinals looked around the majors, and when their eyes turned to San Francisco, they found their man.

In 1984 the Giants had a terrible year, losing 96 games and ending up in the cellar. The pitching staff was in ruins, but the Giants still had a strong lineup. San Francisco had a surplus of outfielders and decided that Jack Clark was expendable. In 1984 Clark missed most of the year with knee trouble, but before getting an operation he hit 11 homers, drove in 44 runs, and batted .320 as he was on target for his best year ever. In the past Clark had complained bitterly about his home park, a wind tunnel called Candlestick Park, where home runs die from the wind swirling around and where fans almost die from arctic wind blasts coming out of San Francisco Bay. Jack Clark for years had been the Giants' top player, and he blasted managers, the press, and just about everything else in town over the years. Again Whitey Herzog gambled when he picked up Clark, hoping his knee would hold out while he would stay content. On February 1, 1985, the Giants sent Clark to the Cardinals for David Green, Dave LaPoint, outfielder Gary Rajsich, and shortstop prospect Jose Uribe.

The trade for Clark was especially important because by the time 1985 arrived George Hendrick was gone. On December 12, 1984, the Cardinals sent their top power hitter to the Pirates with a minor leaguer for utilityman Brian Harper and pitcher John Tudor. Harper was a man who could play many positions, the type of player Whitey Herzog loved, especially since the owners decided to cut back the size of major league rosters to twenty-four players for 1985 in order to save a few bucks. Tudor was a tough-as-nails lefty who not only went 12–11 for a weak-hitting Pirate team that finished last in 1984, but had also posted winning seasons in Boston's Fenway Park for the Red Sox, an alleged graveyard for lefties. Tudor would have easily been the number-two man on the 1984 Cardinals, and that was to be his function for 1985.

With Bruce Sutter out of the picture, Whitey Herzog had to find somebody to close out games, even if the Cardinals were doomed for a last-place finish. Herzog saw nobody who could close a game every other day, but he saw a bullpen full of guys who had good years behind Sutter in the past. With John Tudor arriving, Rick Horton was available for the bullpen and he would join Jeff Lahti (a Cardinal since 1982), Ken Dayley (picked up with first baseman Mike Jorgensen from the Braves in mid-1984 for Ken Oberkfell), and Bill Campbell (picked up with Ivan DeJesus from the Phillies) in forming a "bullpen by committee." Horton and Dayley were lefties and Lahti and Campbell were righties, so the St. Louis bullpen would have excellent balance.

No, Whitey Herzog did *not* invent the bullpen by committee in 1985. Herzog had simply put together a bullpen that was common on many teams in years past. Many teams relied on just one man to close games in the 1970s and 1980s, and it was the near culmination of the development of relief pitching in this century. Once, pitchers who sat in the bullpen were injured pitchers playing out their last days or old guys who were washed up as starters. The first of the great relievers who pitched almost exclusively out of the bullpen was Firpo Marberry of the Senators in the 1920s (prior to Marberry great relievers included *starters* like Christy Mathewson and Three Finger Brown, who would relieve about ten times a year in addition to making about forty starts, and they would save key games for other starters), and he baffled the Giants in the 1924 World Series. In the 1930s Johnny Murphy was the big reliever of the game, pitching for the Yankees, but in the cases of Marberry and Murphy, both men were deemed not good enough to start, so off to the bullpen they went.

In the 1940s Joe Page was the hardest thrower on the Yankees and he was kept in the bullpen, making him the first man capable of starting but kept in the bullpen to provide ninth-inning torture for enemy hitters. In the 1950s more relievers arrived, guys like Jim Konstanty (MVP in 1950 for the Phillies), Hoyt Wilhelm, and Roy Face. In the 1960s the top teams had one man good enough to get twenty saves while the weak teams had to use a collection of poor pitchers to share the workload. Those bad teams helped pioneer the bullpen by committee. The 1970s saw pitchers collect thirty saves for some clubs, and to show how important relievers were becoming, the save became an official statistic in 1969. (Prior to 1969 saves were informally counted, and the definition of the word changed over the years.)

During the 1970s teams like the Dodgers, Yankees, and Reds had guys like Mike Marshall, Sparky Lyle, and Rawley Eastwick to save games, while the other teams lacking these iron men continued to make do with odds and ends. Whitey Herzog's Royals were one of the teams that patched together a bullpen by committee by using guys that could not hack it as either a starter or a closer. In 1978 Herzog's Royals had a bullpen consisting of Al Hrabosky (the closest thing to a genuine closer that Herzog had), Steve Mingori, Marty Pattin, Doug Bird, and for a time Andy Hassler. This crew managed to do a decent enough job as the Royals won their third straight division flag, but nobody jumped for joy or praised Herzog as a genius. In 1979 Herzog's bullpen had Hrabosky, Mingori, Pattin, Eduardo Rodriguez, and Dan Quisenberry, and this group did not do the job well at all, costing the Royals a flag and Herzog his job. Everyone said Herzog lost because his bullpen lacked one stopper, like a Rich Gossage, yet no one pointed out that Herzog won the year before with the same bullpen setup with basically the same relievers. Obviously a bullpen by committee is only as good as the pitchers comprising it. Herzog was always amazed at how people credited him with creating the bullpen by committee setup in 1985 when it was done for years before by others, even by Herzog himself, and yet nobody said boo about it until 1985. Once the Cardinals lost the best reliever in the league and won the pennant a year later with a bunch of "nobodies" in the bullpen, there was much ballyhoo over the genius of Herzog. Herzog always laughed about the ballyhoo, because he did not invent the bullpen by committee; he simply had good pitchers and raised the art of "bullpenning" to a science by lefty-righting everybody to death.

That the bullpen by committee was yet to be "invented" meant that going into 1985 the Cardinals had no bullpen at all after losing Bruce Sutter; therefore, the Cardinals could expect a miserable year spent in the lower confines of the league. Jack Clark, he of the bad knee and the bad attitude from San Francisco, was expected to contribute little but strife to the Cardinals. With Ozzie Smith signing a fat contract, he was expected to do what many other players did after getting the big bucks—fail miserably. The starting rotation was still full of questions concerning young Danny Cox and Kurt Kepshire and if third baseman Terry Pendleton would suffer from the "sophomore jinx." Add to all this that the defending division champion would have Cy Young winner Rick Sutcliffe for a whole year (the Cubs got him from the Indians in June 1984, and he went 16–1, bringing the first flag to Chicago since 1945) and the Mets were heavily favored to win after getting the league's best catcher in Gary Carter to handle their excellent young pitchers. Nineteen-eighty-five loomed as one of the worst years in recent Cardinals history.

The schedule maker was very kind to the Cardinals for 1985—no trip to California to open the season; instead, the Cardinals would get to open the season in New York to take on the overwhelming favorite to win the division. When Opening Day arrived on April 9, it looked like a laughable mismatch. The Mets were solid all over. The Met lineup had Keith Hernandez batting third, Gary Carter hitting fourth, Darryl Strawberry as the number-five man, and George Foster in the sixth slot, and they gave New York one of the top lineups in the league. The Mets were also solid defensively, and in general the nonpitchers were strong. Mookie Wilson and Wally Backman gave the Mets speed at the top of the order, and Ray Knight had been a .300 hitter in the past with the Reds and Astros. Overall, Hernandez at first, Backman at second, Knight at third, Foster in left, Wilson in center, Strawberry in right, and Carter catching made the Mets solid at all positions. Only shortstop, manned by Rafael Santana, remained a question. The Met pitching staff was also great. Dwight Gooden was coming off a great rookie year, and he was one of baseball's best hurlers. Ron Darling, Ed Lynch, and Sid Fernandez were also tough, and they were backed by a fine bullpen led by Jesse Orosco and Doug Sisk.

The Cardinals, on the other hand, entered April 9 with a bunch of questions. At first, Jack Clark was spending this first full year at the position, and he was coming off of knee surgery. At second, Tommy Herr's knees weren't exactly in the best shape either. At short Ozzie Smith had to justify his big new salary and he also had, unknown to most people, a small tear in the right rotator cuff, an injury that would pain Smith and cut down the strength of his usually strong arm. At third Terry Pendleton was in his first full year. In left Lonnie Smith was coming off of his worst year over at .250. In right Andy Van Slyke had to prove that he could play every day. Behind the plate Darrell Porter was slipping offensively and defensively, so he would be platooned with rookie Tom Nieto. Only center field was not a question, thanks to Willie McGee. The pitching, as usual, had more questions. Bob Forsch was coming off arm trouble. Danny Cox and Kurt Kepshire would be spending a whole year in the rotation for the first time. And then there was the bullpen, which was considered to be nonexistent. Yeah, the schedule maker was really merciful to St. Louis.

On April 9, Joaquin Andujar faced "Doctor K," Dwight Gooden, and a pitching duel was expected. Instead, both teams scored liberally and Whitey Herzog found himself going to his "nonexistent" bullpen. In the tenth inning the game was tied 5–5 when Neil Allen was summoned to pitch. New Met Gary Carter came up to the plate and promptly endeared himself to New York by belting a game-winning homer off of Allen. The Cardinals lost 6–5 and the nightmare was now under way. After an off day, the two teams again did battle and again it was a hard fought contest, this time a pitching duel. This time, Andy Hassler got the call, and he gave up the game-winning hit in the eleventh inning. Final score: Mets 2,

Cardinals 1. The bullpen by committee was not doing the job, so it seemed.

Despite these two tough losses, Herzog was optimistic. St. Louis might be 0–2, but at least the team did not bow meekly to the team everyone figured was going to a World Series. The Cardinals played hard in those two defeats, so if they were to finish last, at least they'd go down fighting. St. Louis had 160 games left to put together a decent year, and not every team was as good as the Mets. The Pirates proved that when the Cardinals visited them after leaving New York. Pittsburgh had decayed to the point of rigor mortis by 1985, so every team circled the days on the calendar when they were due to face the Pirates. The Cardinals ran like crazy and took just 1 game while losing 2 more tough games. The Cardinals left Pittsburgh with a dismal 1–4 mark before going home to host the Expos. Montreal had been one of the biggest disappointments in recent history; always picked to win, the Expos always managed to come up a loser. In 1985 the Expos were expected to do nothing, and in the Cardinals' home opener they lost 6–1, then beat the locals twice. At this point, the Cardinals were just 2–6 and they had been beaten by both the mighty and the humble. Disaster was surely forthcoming.

St. Louis finally got its act together by the time April ended. First the Cardinals had a replay of 1982 when an outfielder got hurt. In 1982 David Green got hurt and Willie McGee was recalled. Now, in 1985, lightning struck again. McGee got hurt and the usual outfield replacement in Tito Landrum also was ailing, so a call to the minors was placed and up came Vince Coleman. Coleman had blazing speed and once stole 145 bases in the minors in a season, so he was perfect for the St. Louis attack. Whitey Herzog had known that Coleman would get to town soon, but he didn't expect to recall him that early. Coleman got four hits in his second major league game, and he never looked back.

Next the Cardinals were starting to win some games with consistency. Joaquin Andujar was off to another good start, making sure the Cardinals did not touch last place for too long. Andujar was 4–0 in April, and St. Louis ended the month at 8–11, tied with the Phillies for fourth place. The Mets might have been a tough team, but they were tied with the Cubs for first and both teams were just 1 game ahead of the Expos. The Pirates were already falling out of the picture.

In May the Cardinals began to perform well and they were surprising people by staying in a four-team race with the Mets, Cubs, and Expos. Vince Coleman was doing a terrific job for a rookie. St. Louis had led the league with 200 or more steals for three straight years, but the club lacked an explosive base stealer like Coleman. With "Vincent Van Go" leading the way, the Cardinals were leaving all other teams in the dust when it came to sack stealing. Willie McGee returned and he was mashing the ball all over the lot, going for a batting title while joining the league leaders in RBIs. Tommy Herr really surprised everyone because he too was in the RBI forefront, even though he never had had more than 49 RBIs in a season. Lonnie Smith was off to another weak start, so when McGee returned Smith went to the bench, and he finally was traded to the Royals on May 17. The Cardinals' outfield now had Coleman in left, McGee in center, and Andy Van Slyke in right. Jack Clark was not among the league's RBI men, but he was hitting the long ball and his knee was just fine. Clark quickly became a big favorite of Whitey Herzog's, and the slugger was happy in his new home.

On the pitching side, St. Louis was most surprising. The bullpen was now suddenly "discovered" by everyone as the committee was finally doing its job. Herzog began making several pitching changes in the late innings, even having a pitcher hurl to one man, then depart for another pitcher to take his place. All of these moves dazzled the fans, who began to hail Herzog as a genius in hushed tones. The starters were also doing the job, with the exception of John Tudor. Tudor pitched well enough to win, but bad breaks always seemed to come his way, and he was having a 1–7 season. Joaquin Andujar was the rock of the staff at this time, easily headed for another 20-win season. Danny Cox was turning into one of the best-kept pitching secrets in baseball, and Kurt Kepshire kept the team in most games that he started.

St. Louis continued to stay in the thick of the race, and by the end of May the standings showed the Mets ahead by just half a game over the Cubs, 2 games over the Expos, and 2½ over the Cardinals. The Mets were rolling, but earlier in May disaster struck

302

when Darryl Strawberry tore ligaments in his thumb while diving for a ball against the Phillies in New York. The injury was serious enough to sideline Strawberry for over two months, and it came on top of other problems. Doug Sisk, a tough relief pitcher who tore his rotator cuff in late 1984, still was not recovered from the injury, and he was getting hit hard. Starter Bruce Berenyi, another hard thrower, also hurt his arm earlier in the 1985 season, and he was lost. Kelvin Chapman, a man who had done a great job platooning with Wally Backman at second base in 1984, was doing poorly. Despite all of these injuries, the Mets hung onto the lead as June arrived, and they were still expected to win.

In June the Cardinals sizzled, frying all opponents in the process and moving into first place. Vince Coleman continued to steal bases, and he was on top of the league in that category. Ozzie Smith shocked everyone who had thought he would fail by continuing his great defense (despite a rotator cuff problem) and supplementing that with his best hitting ever. John Tudor was finally getting some support, and he joined Joaquin Andujar and Danny Cox in forming a stellar pitching trio. St. Louis spent most of the month facing Eastern rivals, and they kicked butt. The Cardinals went 2–1 against the Pirates, 3–3 against the Phillies, 6–0 against the Cubs, and 6–1 against the Mets. This stretch against New York was pivotal, since the two teams would have only six head-to-head matches left. On June 7 the Cardinals invaded New York for a 4-game set and a pitching duel that saw a 2–2 tie going into the thirteenth inning broken when St. Louis scored five runs while handing Doug Sisk a loss. The next day John Tudor tossed a masterpiece in winning 1–0. On the ninth, in the first game of a twin bill, Dwight Gooden knocked off Bob Forsch 6–1 as he was taking the world by storm with the best pitching seen since 1968. The Cardinals then came back in the nightcap with an 8–2 beating of the locals. The atmosphere for this series was full of tension, since the Cardinals and Mets did not exactly love one another. The Mets were irking opponents with their style of play and their "we are *the* best" attitude. The Mets also ruffled feathers when they would come out of the dugout after *every* home run and bow to the fans. Gary Carter loved this sort of thing the most after years of playing in sedate Montreal, and any time he popped out of the dugout he would thrust his fist in the air. This sort of display looked "bush" to opponents, and it looked like rubbing salt into wounds as well. Whitey Herzog, being such a straight shooter, pointed these things out, which upset the Mets. This new Cardinal-Met feud continued later in the month when the Mets visited St. Louis. Busch Stadium was packed and the fans were delirious as the mighty Mets were swept by excellent pitching. The Cardinals won 3–2 behind Tudor, 6–0 behind Andujar, and 2–1 in eleven frames behind Ken Dayley on June 28–30. At the end of the month, St. Louis was on top by 2½ games over Montreal, 4 over Chicago, and 5 over New York. The potential nightmare that had awaited the Cardinals for 1985 was turning into a very pleasant dream.

On July 15 baseball took time out for the All-Star break. The Cardinals still had the top perch, but the Mets did not go away despite their poor performance against St. Louis in June. The Mets had moved into second place, 2½ games out. The Expos also had to be taken seriously at this point, amazing people with the fact that they were just 4½ games out this late in the year. The Cubs began to fade as injuries crippled their pitching staff, and they were 7½ games out and sinking fast. At midseason the Cardinals had an impressive crew. Jack Clark was having a fine year as the power man in the lineup. Willie McGee was near or at the top in several offensive categories and was enjoying an MVP type year. Vince Coleman had supplanted Rickey Henderson as baseball's top thief. Ozzie Smith suddenly looked *under*paid at 2 million bucks a year for what he was doing. Terry Pendleton was not hitting, but any time he got on base he was a stealing threat and his glove was being compared favorably to Mike Schmidt's. Tommy Herr continued driving runs home with amazing frequency while batting second. Andy Van Slyke was not having a break-through season, but his defense was solid. The catching situation was still messy, but every team has at least one sore spot. Tudor, Andujar, and Cox were being compared favorably with Dwight Gooden, Ron Darling, and Ed Lynch of the Mets and Fernando Valenzuela, Orel Hershiser, and Bob Welch of the Dodgers as a top starting trio. Everyone raved about that "new invention" known as the bullpen by committee. Bill Campbell, Ken Dayley, Jeff Lahti, and Rick Horton were tormenting the enemy on a nightly basis.

304

Bob Forsch, the longest-serving of Cardinals, was doing a great job as a starter/reliever after coming off of arm trouble. The Cardinals were for real.

The Mets might not have been on top at this point, but they were still going to be heard from. Manager Davey Johnson had done an outstanding job lifting the Mets to their first winning record in eight years in 1984, and despite injuries to Doug Sisk, Darryl Strawberry, Bruce Berenyi, and most recently Mookie Wilson, the pilot still had his team right in the thick of things. Roger McDowell took over Sisk's role, Lenny Dykstra replaced Wilson, and Rick Aguilera substituted for Berenyi, and this trio of rookies was doing great. Strawberry was missed the most, and although Danny Heep did well filling in for him, he was not the potential game breaker that Strawberry was. Dwight Gooden was awesome at this point, owning a 13–3 record and standing atop many pitching categories while putting together a Cy Young-type year. Gooden was also in the middle of a 14-game winning streak, and he was looking as great as Steve Carlton in 1972 and even Bob Gibson in 1968 at this time. The Mets would not fade away, injuries or not.

The season resumed on July 18 and the Cardinals dropped 3 straight in Los Angeles before resuming their winning ways. The Mets were right behind the Cardinals, waiting for the chance to slip into first, and the Expos of Andre Dawson, Tim Raines, Jeff Reardon, and company were still close to both teams. Andujar and Tudor continued to win consistently, and Danny Cox continued to shine, despite getting little ink. Tudor was streaking just like Gooden, only Gooden was overshadowing the pitching of any hurler in 1985. As July closed, the Cardinals were 2 games ahead of the Mets and 6 ahead of the Expos. Hanging onto first place at this point was becoming important, because most contenders were now playing like this was the last week of the season, and there was a good reason for this way of thinking. Yet another strike deadline was approaching.

Once again baseball was fouling itself up with more messy battles between the owners and the players' union. Instead of learning from past mistakes (like 1981) and having somewhat amicable negotiations on a new Basic Agreement way ahead of time, the two sides waited until the old agreement expired before plunging into acrimonious bargaining at the last possible minute. This time, the owners were crying of poverty that came from all of the wild spending over free agents. Teams were going bankrupt, the owners cried. The players were upset that they were not getting enough money from TV deals. Again the "poor" owners and players were crying that they were cash-starved. Fans were getting sick and tired of all of this crying over money that both sides seemed to be getting more than enough of yet again, and now another strike was on the way. This time, a strike would possibly kill the rest of the season, since it was due to occur on August 6, an appropriate date, since it marked the fortieth anniversary of the dropping of the first atomic bomb on Hiroshima. Fans wished someone would drop such a bomb on the players and owners, since they were about to ruin yet another season with their greed.

With August 5 being interpreted as the final day of the season, it was imperative for the Cardinals to hang onto first place on that date, in case a postseason was to take place. St. Louis did not want to be deprived of postseason play again due to a strike, like in 1981. When August 1 came, the Cardinals had 1 game in Chicago and 3 at home with the Phillies before the strike would hit. The Mets had an off day on the first before playing 4 against the fading Cubs in Chicago. The two contenders were getting a break in playing fading and weak teams, but the Cardinals held the upper hand by holding the 2-game lead.

On August 1 the Cardinals and Cubs battled for fourteen innings until the Cubs squeezed across a run to win 9–8. With the Mets off, the Cardinal lead was down to 1½ games. The next day the Cardinals went home and knocked off the Phillies 3–2 while the Cubs shaded the Mets 2–1. On the third, the Cardinals lost another tough game when the Phillies pulled out a 6–4 win in ten innings. In the afternoon the Mets had their own ten-inning battle, but they came up a 5–4 winner, shrinking the St. Louis lead back to 1½ games. On the fourth, Dwight Gooden went out and did what he was expected to do—win—and he did it by a 4–1 score. The Cardinals underwent a shelling that same day as Kevin Gross shut out Joaquin Andujar 6–0. The Cardinals now led by a mere half a game going into the final day before the strike.

306

The Cardinals had to win and the Mets had to lose for St. Louis to stay on top on the day before the strike. Both teams winning or losing would also do the trick, but the way the Mets had handled the Cubs going into August 5 meant that the Cardinals had to think about winning their own game instead of hoping for the almost impossible. In the afternoon at Wrigley Field Darryl Strawberry pronounced himself very much fit for postseason play by blasting three home runs while Ed Lynch cruised to an easy 7–2 win. A few hours later the Cardinals entertained the Phillies under artificial light and hoped that Danny Cox would keep St. Louis in first place. Instead, the Phillies worked Cox over for a 9–1 win. The Cardinals entered the strike with a 61–42 mark, half a game behind the Mets, who owned a 62–42 record. If the season was to end on this date, the Cardinals would become the third team in major league history to finish just half a game out of first. (The 1908 Indians were the first team to do it, because the rules of the day did not force a contender to make up rainouts even if they affected the race. The 1972 Red Sox were the second team to do it because of the season-opening strike and the settlement did not allow canceled games to be made up.)

Fortunately for all fans, the strike did not last long. Commissioner Peter Ueberroth (who replaced Bowie Kuhn late in 1984, much to Gussie Busch's delight) took an active role in trying to settle the affair and both sides got together for a marathon bargaining session. On August 7, both sides announced that the strike was over. Both sides hammered out a new Basic Agreement that would last through 1989, and both sides made concessions. The thing that caused so much grief with the 1981 strike, free agent compensation, was dropped by mutual consent. Thus, the sixty-day strike, a most messy affair, was fought for absolutely nothing. Go figure.

The games canceled due to the strike would be made up as best as possible. The Cardinals began play on August 8 at home against the Cubs, pounding them 8–0. The Mets continued to win, and the race was now becoming a two-team battle, since the Expos were slowly fading. On August 20 the Cardinals were back in second place, trailing the Mets by 1½ games, but St. Louis kept running the bases and pouring runs across the plate. On the twenty-third, Joaquin Andujar became the first Cardinal to win 20 games two straight years since Bob Gibson did it in 1968–70 and was winning more games than even Dwight Gooden. John Tudor was becoming even tougher to hit as the season went on, and his ERA was sinking to the 2.00 level. Tudor was being called a lefty version of Bob Gibson because of his competitiveness and his pitching smarts. Tudor was now upstaging Andujar as the Cardinals' top starter, even though his win total was less.

By the end of the month St. Louis was back on top, leading New York by 2 games. Another showdown was coming in September between the two teams, and the vitriol flowed in the press when players on each team talked about the other club. Despite being behind, the Mets continued to act as if they were on top. The Cardinals, led by Whitey Herzog, kept touting themselves as the team that was fighting the whole world. It was a "them against us" mentality in St. Louis, and this irritated the Mets. Both teams thought that they were not getting proper respect from their chief enemy, and this also upset players on both sides.

The Cardinals were going into the final month with their first major injury, one to the ribs of Jack Clark. Unlike the Mets, the Cardinals enjoyed relatively good health in 1985, and the injury to Clark was most grave, since he was the only real home run threat in the St. Louis attack. In late August, the Cardinals were playing the Reds in Cincinnati when former Cardinal pitcher and now Red pitching coach Jim Kaat chatted with his old manager Whitey Herzog. Kaat told Herzog that the Reds had a surplus of outfielders and Cesar Cedeno was available. Cedeno was having a bad year in Cincinnati and wanted out because he was benched. At one time, Cesar Cedeno was considered a Triple Crown threat and he looked great when the Astros first called him up in 1970. But because the Astros play in one of the worst parks for hitters, Cedeno never reached the heights predicted for him. Still, Cedeno had fine years in Houston and he was doing okay in Cincinnati for a time, but he was now declining. Herzog figured he could use another bat, so on August 29 the Cardinals sent a minor leaguer to the Reds for Cedeno.

Whitey Herzog had no place in the outfield for Cedeno, but with Clark ailing, first base was available. Cedeno was familiar with the position. In 1978 Cesar Cedeno had broken his leg and missed most of the year. The next year, the Astros brought back Cedeno slowly, moving him to first base. Cedeno was no Keith Hernandez at first, but he did well enough before moving back to the outfield, so Herzog put him at first base. It was like striking oil in a backyard. Cedeno began to hit like he never had before, and St. Louis had a new hero.

On September 10 the Cardinals went to New York for a 3-game series. New York was swept by pennant fever, since the Mets were tied with the Cardinals, and memories of past clashes between New York teams and the Cardinals came to mind. The Cardinals had tough battles with the New York Giants in 1927, 1928, 1930, 1934, 1935, and 1936, and the Cardinals had some of the all-time great pennant races with the Brooklyn Dodgers in 1930, 1941, 1942, 1946, 1947, and 1949. Now the Cardinals were facing the New York Mets in the latest of classic battles between the small city and the big city. Mets fans wanted a sweep, and so did Cardinals fans, but in a different way. This St. Louis versus New York battle would be like many of the others—great.

On the tenth, Danny Cox faced Ron Darling. Both pitchers had their stuff, but the Mets and Cardinals managed to scrape nine runs between them. The Mets won the first round 5–4 to move a game ahead of the visitors. The next day was a pitching master-piece between John Tudor and Dwight Gooden. Both pitchers were throwing zeroes for nine frames when Gooden was removed for a pinch hitter. Tudor hung in there, and in the tenth Cesar Cedeno blasted a homer to center field off of Jesse Orosco. Tudor finished off the game and won 1–0. Both teams were tied again. September 12 was a really special day in New York. The Mets faced the Cardinals in the afternoon for a first-place battle while at night the Yankees took on the Blue Jays in the first game of four to decide who belonged in first place in the A.L. East. The day was special because it was one of the few times that both the Mets and Yankees were home on the same day and both were gunning for a title. A "Subway Series" danced in the minds of New York baseball fans. The Mets did their part by rallying against the Cardinals to give Orosco a 7–6 win over Ken Dayley in the late innings. Yes, the Yankees kept pace with a win that night as well.

309

The Cardinals left New York down by 1 game, but on the fourteenth it was tied up again. Two days later, the Cardinals grabbed the lead even though the Mets pounded the Phillies 9–0, because on that day St. Louis swept a twin bill from the lowly Pirates in Pittsburgh to move half a game ahead. Cesar Cedeno was proving to be a godsend, and he was hitting well over .400 and doing a good job at first. Joaquin Andujar was becoming a concern, though, because he started to struggle mightily after getting his twentieth win. Andujar began to worry about his status as John Tudor was starting to get all the ink. Still, the Cardinals carried on, holding first place despite having the Mets dog them.

The Mets were now relatively healthy themselves, so they expected a series in St. Louis on October 1–3 to be the key. The Mets schedule between the time the Cardinals left and the time they would meet again called for the team to face the Expos four times in Montreal, the Phillies twice at home, the Cubs twice at home, the Pirates thrice at home, then 2 in Philadelphia and Chicago, and then 3 in Pittsburgh. Except for the Expos, the Mets were facing the three worst teams in the division, so New York had a good shot at moving into first place by the time the trip to St. Louis came. New York split in Montreal, split with the Phillies, swept the Cubs, then took on the Pirates in New York. Pittsburgh was heading for disaster. The Pirates had gotten rid of every veteran they could in a massive rebuilding effort. They were drawing poorly at home, and there were rumors that the team was bankrupt and about to be moved after being sold. Pittsburgh was the worst team in the majors, and the Mets were expected to easily beat the club senseless.

On September 20 the Mets engaged in a tough battle with the Pirates and lost 7–5 in eleven innings. The Cardinals won, so St. Louis picked up a game on New York. The next day the Mets took revenge with a 12–1 win behind Dwight Gooden (as if he needed so many runs). The Mets should have saved some of those dozen runs, because the next day Bob Kipper hurled a 5–3 win against the locals. What a shock! Instead of picking up ground, the Mets lost 2 games to St. Louis in the three days. The Mets recovered somewhat by sweeping 2 in Philadelphia and splitting 2 in Chicago before going to Pittsburgh. On the twenty-seventh, the Mets blew a lead and went down in flames 8–7. The next two days the Mets won 3–1 and 9–7 in ten innings, and neither game was easy. The second game almost exploded into a major disaster when the Mets blew an early, large lead in the ninth before rallying to win. The Mets now had to go to St. Louis with a 3-game deficit that had been fashioned in large part by the Pirates.

A sweep was needed by New York to get back to the top, and after the Pittsburgh experience, it would not be easy. On October 1 Ron Darling and John Tudor each hurled a masterpiece, but both got a no-decision when they were lifted for pinch hitters. In the tenth, the score was tied at 0–0 when Darryl Strawberry hit a titanic home run off the clock in right field off of Ken Dayley. The fans never saw such a shot hit in spacious Busch Stadium before and were silenced. Earlier in the game the fans booed loudly when Keith Hernandez came out to play, the result of his confession of cocaine use while with the Cardinals at the Pittsburgh drug trial of a former Phillies caterer. Jesse Orosco got credit for the 1–0 win.

The Mets were now 2 games out and people pointed to the damage that the Strawberry homer did to the clock when Dwight Gooden faced Joaquin Andujar in a battle of 20-game winners. Back in April Andujar won the game that resulted in Gooden's first of four losses on the year, so the local fans were hoping for a repeat. Gooden was not his usual awesome self and had to labor to get out of jams. Still, Gooden won the battle by a 5–2 score, moving the Mets to within 1 game of the Cardinals. Andujar did not look sharp in this game and again there was concern by and over the hurler, but most people were more concerned with the final game of the series.

On October 3 the Mets manager made a gutsy move, giving the start against Danny Cox to rookie Rick Aguilera. Dave Johnson was second-guessed right to game time over why he used the rookie instead of hard-throwing sophomore Sid Fernandez or the veteran Ed Lynch. Johnson figured that the two aforementioned hurlers would have trouble holding the St. Louis jackrabbits on base, and Aguilera had not only a better delivery, but also a good year, so the rookie got the ball. Aguilera pitched brilliantly, but the Cardinals ran on him anyway and Cox dodged enough bullets to eke out a tough 4–3 win, pushing the Mets back to 2 games down.

The mighty Mets now needed a miracle to catch the team everyone had picked to finish last, but one was not forthcoming. On October 4 the Mets beat the Expos, but the Cardinals also won, so the magic number was down to one. The next day the Mets were losing when word came that the Cardinals had beaten the Cubs 7–1 to clinch the division title. The Cardinals had a great regular season in 1985, making it one of the greatest in club history. St. Louis won 100 games for the first time since 1967 and had two 20-game winners for the first time since 1942. The Cardinals swiped 314 bases, fourth best total in the twentieth century, and went on to have the MVP in Willie McGee and the Rookie of the Year in Vince Coleman. (The former was the batting champ while the latter led the league in steals.) It was truly a great year for the St. Louis Cardinals all around. Now they would have to face the Los Angeles Dodgers in the newly expanded best of seven league championship series, and the Dodgers were armed with excellent pitchers, as usual.

Unlike the 1982 Braves, the 1985 Dodgers were packed with pitching. Number-five starter Rick Honeycutt went 8–12 with a 3.42 ERA in an injury-plagued season, so that alone tells much. Fernando Valenzuela, Orel Herchiser, Bob Welch, and Jerry Reuss were all backed by Ken Howell and Tom Niedenfuer in the bullpen. The Los Angeles lineup was not especially fearsome, but with guys like Pedro Guerrero, Mike Marshall, Steve Sax, and Mike Scioscia, the Dodgers were capable of some hitting. After all, they didn't go 95–67 solely because of their pitching.

The playoffs opened on October 9 in Los Angeles, and John Tudor faced Fernando Valenzuela in a battle of lefty aces. The Dodgers broke through for a run in the fourth when Bill Madlock was safe on a Terry Pendleton error, then took a page out of the Cardinals' book by stealing second and finally scored on a Pedro Guerrero single. Two frames later the Dodgers put the game away with 3 runs coming from RBI singles by Mike Scioscia and Candy Maldonado and an RBI double by Steve Sax. Tudor, who had a puny 1.93 ERA in the regular season, failed to last six innings after giving up the 4 runs. St. Louis got one run in the seventh when pinch hitter Tito Landrum singled home Pendleton, but in the end the locals won 4–1.

The next day the Dodgers put on their hitting shoes and quickly disposed of the Cardinals' other 20-game winner, Joaquin Andujar. After scoring a run on a wild pitch, St. Louis gave up 3 runs in the bottom of the third when Orel Hershiser singled home Sax, then the pitcher scored on a Ken Landreaux double and finally Bill Madlock's single scored Landreaux. In the next inning Andujar was sent to the showers when Los Angeles launched another rally. Scioscia got a bunt single despite being one of the slowest Dodger runners, and then he scored on a Greg Brock homer. Rick Horton came in to stop the locals for the rest of the frame, but in the fifth he gave up another double to Landreaux and then an RBI single to Mike Marshall. In the sixth Horton was knocked out as Los Angeles scored twice more on RBI singles by Madlock and Guerrero. In the ninth St. Louis scored a run on a Vince Coleman single, but the Cardinals went back home with an 8–2 drubbing to ponder.

On October 12 the playoffs resumed at Busch Stadium and Danny Cox tried to halt the Dodgers against Bob Welch. St. Louis used its speed to force trouble, and it worked well. After Coleman singled in the first, he stole second. Willie McGee drew a walk, and then both runners moved up on Welch's wild pickoff attempt, Coleman scoring in the process. Tommy Herr then walked and stole second, putting two men in scoring position. After Andy Van Slyke drew a walk, Pendleton grounded out, scoring McGee and giving the Cardinals a 2–0 lead. In the second, Coleman walked, then went to third when Scioscia tried to pick him off. Herr then homered, putting St. Louis on top 4–0. Cox, meanwhile, stifled the Dodgers over 6 innings and allowed only 2 runs when Marshall doubled home a run in the fourth and Landreaux singled home a seventh-inning run. The bullpen then took over and Ken Dayley got the save in the 4–2 St. Louis win.

Vince Coleman drove the opposition crazy all year, and he was a great psychological weapon (as the third playoff game proved). On the thirteenth, disaster struck the Cardinals when Vince Coleman was seriously injured in one of the all-time weirdest events. Before the start of the fourth game, Coleman was on the field playing around when someone activated an automatic tarp. The tarp at Busch Stadium lies underground on the first and third base sides, and when a button is pushed the tarp comes out of the ground and rolls across the field. Coleman did not know that the tarp was turned on until it was too late. Coleman fell and the tarp began rolling over his leg. The tarp was stopped before tragedy occurred, but damage was already done. Coleman's left leg was damaged enough to keep him out of the rest of postseason play. As a result, Tito Landrum got the start in left field for the fourth game.

Tudor was asked to even the series against Jerry Reuss. In the second inning the Cardinals set a playoff record by scoring 9 runs, knocking Reuss out before the second frame was even over. St. Louis also scored 3 more runs in the game and went on to crush Los Angeles 12–2. Landrum was sensational as a fill-in, going 4 for 5 with 3 RBIs. The Cardinals lashed four pitchers for 15 hits, yet they stole no bases and got only 2 extra-base hits (doubles by McGee and Cesar Cedeno). The fourth game was one of the biggest routs in playoff history, and it now appeared that the Cardinals had momentum on their side.

Whitey Herzog surprised a few people by selecting Bob Forsch as the starter for the fifth game against Valenzuela, but for a time it looked like Herzog had done it again. In the first McGee and Ozzie Smith drew walks, then both were plated by a Herr double. Forsch held the 2–0 lead until the fourth, when Landreaux singled, then scored on a homer by Madlock. Dayley relieved Forsch and he pitched well. Hard-throwing rookie Todd Worrell (who was added to the bullpen in late August) then took over, and he did well. Jeff Lahti then came on in the ninth and had a perfect inning. Valenzuela also pitched well for eight frames, and the score was tied at two when Tom Niedenfuer was called upon to start the bottom of the ninth. Niedenfuer retired McGee, and then up stepped one Ozzie Smith, he of the $2 million a year contract who was supposed to fail but instead hit a career-high .276. Smith, a switch hitter, was batting from the left side against the righty Niedenfuer. Ozzie had played eight seasons in the majors and had over 4,000 at bats in his career, but not one time did he ever hit a homer from the left side. Then it happened. Niedenfuer went into his windup and threw a fastball that Smith sent right over the right field wall for a game-winning homer. The fans were delirious, as if they had just seen the homer that had clinched a world championship. St. Louis won the game 3–2 and held a 3–2 lead in the series going back to Dodger Stadium.

Despite his late-season problems, Joaquin Andujar was given the ball against Orel Hershiser. Hershiser was a tough cookie who went 19–3 with a 2.03 ERA in the regular season, but he was behind both Dwight Gooden and John Tudor when it came to stats. (The former had a 24–4 season with 268 strikeouts and a 1.53 ERA, while the latter went 21–8 with a 1.93 ERA and 10 shutouts.) Andujar again had his problems, giving up solo runs in the first and second. The Cardinals came back with 1 in the third when Andujar doubled and scored on a Herr single. The Dodgers got 2 more runs in the fifth when Andujar's error allowed Mariano Duncan to get on. Duncan eventually scored on a sac fly by Guerrero, and Los Angeles also got a solo homer from Madlock. St. Louis battled back in the seventh and knocked out Hershiser. Darrell Porter and Landrum both singled; then both advanced a base on a Steve Braun ground out. McGee then singled home the two men. Hershiser was lifted in favor of Niedenfuer, and the Dodgers bullpen ace was again victimized by Smith; this time, the Cardinal tripled, scoring McGee and cutting the Dodger lead to a tie at four apiece. In the eighth Worrell gave up a run when Marshall homered, putting the locals back into the lead. Niedenfuer now tried to close out the game, but he couldn't. With 1 out McGee singled and stole second. Smith walked. Herr grounded out, moving the runners to second and third with 2 out and Jack Clark coming up. Most managers would have walked the lone Cardinal power hitter intentionally, but Tom Lasorda did not. Niedenfuer threw a pitch, and it immediately took off like a rocket for left field. Left fielder Pedro Guerrero slammed down his glove in disgust as the ball easily went into the seats for a three-run homer. The Cardinals had a 7–5 lead, and when Dayley pitched a perfect ninth inning for the save, the Cardinals were National League champions for the second time in four seasons. Tom Niedenfuer joined Ozzie Smith and Jack Clark as the latest names in the lore of the St. Louis Cardinals. Now it was time for the last piece of business of the amazing 1985 campaign: the World Series.

The Cardinals had made themselves league champs through come-from-behind rallies (the sixth playoff game showed that) all

315

year long, and so had their series opponents—the Kansas City Royals. The Royals were behind the Angels in the latter part of the regular season before overtaking them in the final week. The Royals then found themselves down 3–1 in the playoffs, but Kansas City charged back, winning their pennant by bagging the final 2 games in Toronto against the Blue Jays team everyone thought was better. George Brett had an injury-free year, and 1985 was one of his best ever. Bret Saberhagen led a strong starting rotation, and Dan Quisenberry was still the best reliever in the American League. Like the Cardinals, the Royals relied on pitching, speed, and defense to win their pennant, and they also had a fine manager in Dick Howser. Missourians were delighted at the World Series being a local affair, and they called it the "I-70 Series" because of the highway linking St. Louis and Kansas City. Because both teams were heavy on comebacks, the series was considered a toss-up, although many felt the Cardinals were the better team by just a shade. Overall, the two teams seemed to be a perfect match.

The series opened on October 19 in Kansas City with John Tudor facing a tough lefty in Danny Jackson. The Royals scored first when Jim Sundberg walked and eventually scored on a Steve Balboni single. The Cardinals quickly tied it an inning later in the third when Terry Pendleton walked and came around to score on a Willie McGee ground out. In the fourth Tito Landrum doubled with 1 out, then scored on Cesar Cedeno's double, giving St. Louis a 2–1 lead. The Cardinals tacked on 1 more run in the ninth when Tommy Herr singled to open the frame and scored on Jack Clark's double. St. Louis got just 7 hits, but Tudor was stingy and Todd Worrell picked up a save in the 3–1 win over the locals.

The Royals sent out another lefty in Charlie Leibrandt to oppose Danny Cox, but once again the Cardinals were able to handle it. Kansas City took the first lead in the fourth when Willie Wilson singled, then scored on a George Brett double. Frank White then doubled as well, scoring Brett and giving the Royals a 2–0 lead. Leibrandt's junkballing baffled the Cardinals for a while, but in the ninth St. Louis finally solved him. McGee doubled to open the frame, and it looked like the game would end when Leibrandt got 2 quick outs, but Clark singled to bring McGee home. Landrum doubled, putting runners in scoring position. The Royals then issued an intentional walk to Cedeno, loading the sacks. Pendleton then came through with a double, good for 3 RBIs, putting St. Louis on top 4–2. Leibrandt left, but the damage was already done. Jeff Lahti slammed the door in the ninth for a save, and the Cardinals went back to St. Louis with a 2–0 series lead.

On the twenty-second, Kansas City called on its ace, Bret Saberhagen, to halt the Cardinals. The chances of that happening were good, because he would face Joaquin Andujar, once an ace, but now a mystery. Andujar had been beaten with shocking ease since getting his twentieth win in late August, but Herzog liked his guts and stuck with him. In the fourth, Andujar got into a jam, giving up a 2 run double to former teammate Lonnie Smith. In the fifth, Andujar was again in trouble when he was replaced by Bill Campbell, but by then it was too late. Brett singled, then scored on a homer by White, giving the Royals a 4–0 lead. Saberhagen was tough, allowing only a run in the sixth when Clark singled home Ozzie Smith. In the seventh Rick Horton was victimized for an RBI double by White and an RBI single by feeble-hitting Buddy Biancalana. Saberhagen went the distance as he easily won 6–1 on a 6 hitter.

Yet another lefty was sent to face the Cardinals in the fourth game, Bud Black, while Tudor toed the rubber for the locals. Dick Howser's use of so many lefties was simple to figure: lefties tend to have a better move to first base, and that is very important when the opposition likes to steal bases. Black was only 10–15 with a 4.33 ERA in the regular season, so Howser was in danger of getting behind 3–1 in the series just to stop the St. Louis running game. In the second the Cardinals got a rare homer when Tito Landrum hit a 1 out shot into the right field seats. An inning later, McGee hit a homer, and suddenly the team that hit just 87 homers in the regular season (better than only Pittsburgh in the majors) had 2 in a World Series game. To show the Cardinals were not impersonating another team, St. Louis scored a fifth-inning run in their usual manner. Pendleton tripled, then came home when Tom Nieto put down a great squeeze bunt. Black fielded the ball, then threw it away, and Pendleton came home, making it 3–0 St. Louis. Black wasn't battered all over the place (he allowed just 4 of the

Cardinals' 6 hits), but he did lose the game 3–0. St. Louis now had a 3–1 lead in the series.

The Royals sent Danny Jackson out to save them from elimination, and he was opposed by Bob Forsch. The Royals scored first in the first, when Lonnie Smith singled and eventually scored on Frank White's ground out. Tommy Herr hit a ground rule double and then scored on a conventional two-bagger by Jack Clark, tying the game at one after one inning. In the second, Kansas City applied the knockout punch to Forsch when Jim Sundberg doubled, Buddy Biancalana singled (scoring Sundberg), Lonnie Smith walked, and Willie Wilson tripled (good for 2 runs). Rick Horton got St. Louis out of further trouble, but the Royals now had a 4–1 lead. Jackson then went on to throttle the Cardinals on just 5 hits, while he got a run in the eighth and another in the ninth, giving him an easy 6–1 win.

The Cardinals went back to Kansas City on October 26 leading 3–2 in the series, but there were problems. St. Louis wasn't hitting a lick, getting no more than 7 hits in any one of the first 5 games. Joaquin Andujar was pitching poorly in the postseason, so he had to be finally passed over in the rotation. The Cardinals were not running all that well either, as Vince Coleman was being missed despite the great efforts of his replacements. St. Louis might have held the edge in games, but it seemed that Kansas City was more confident of victory.

Danny Cox faced Charlie Liebrandt in a rematch of the second game. Both pitchers were superb—Cox allowing just 7 hits and a walk in 7 innings while Leibrandt gave up 4 hits and 2 walks in almost 8 innings. Leibrandt, though, gave up a run in the eighth when Terry Pendleton singled, moved to second on a walk by Cesar Cedeno, then scored on a pinch single by Brian Harper. Dan Quisenberry came in to shut the door in the remainder of the eighth, so the Cardinals went into the ninth with a 1–0 lead. Todd Worrell came on to preserve the world championship for St. Louis, and his first batter to face was pinch hitter Jorge Orta. Orta hit a shot to the right side of the infield, and Jack Clark fielded it. Worrell covered first and Clark threw to him, but Orta was called safe by umpire Don Denkinger. Whitey Herzog launched a violent argument to get the call changed, but it failed. TV replays showed that

Orta was indeed out, but the call stood. Steve Balboni then popped up a ball in foul territory that Clark failed to catch, so in his next life Balboni singled, putting two men on. Onix Concepcion ran for Balboni and Jim Sundberg tried to bunt, but Worrell threw to third to force out Orta. A passed ball moved both runners into scoring position, so Hal McRae was walked intentionally to load the bases and set up a possible double play. Dane Iorg, a former Cardinal, then hit for Dan Quisenberry (no designated hitter was used in the 1985 World Series) and lashed a 2-run single, scoring Concepcion and Sundberg and giving the Cardinals a 2–1 loss. Herzog seethed with anger and he blasted the umpiring in the series, giving special treatment to Don Denkinger right after the game. The series was now tied at 3 games apiece, and momentum had shifted to the Royals.

The Cardinals were still fuming right up to game time as John Tudor was set to face Bret Saberhagen. The nation had been caught up with "Saberhagen Mania" as his wife was expected to have the family's first child at any time as the series began and on the twenty-sixth delivered a son. The Cardinals had other memories of October 26, and they were very unpleasant and etched in their minds here on the twenty-seventh. Making matters worse, Don Denkinger was the home plate umpire for this game.

Disaster struck almost immediately. In the second the Royals got a 2-run homer from Darryl Motley to take a 2–0 lead. An inning later, the Royals applied the death blow. Lonnie Smith and George Brett executed a Cardinal specialty—the double steal. Frank White then walked, loading the bases. Tudor then clearly showed that he was not himself by walking Jim Sundberg to force in a run. Bill Campbell came in and served a 2-run single to Steve Balboni, giving the Royals a 5–0 lead. The Cardinals, who saw a nightmare turn into a beautiful dream when it came to the regular season and playoffs, now saw the beautiful dream really turn into a nightmare in the last 2 games of 1985. But the worst was yet to come.

Again, St. Louis was being handcuffed at the plate. A beaming Saberhagen was breezing through the game, and it looked like a dull game was in store until the fifth inning came. Kansas City treated the hometown crowd with a 6-run outburst, but it was nothing to compare with the one the Cardinals had at the same time. Bill Campbell began the frame, then left. Jeff Lahti came in next, followed by Rick Horton. Still in the fifth inning, Horton was replaced by Joaquin Andujar. By this time, the game was out of reach for St. Louis and Andujar was not a happy camper. Not only was Andujar not used as a starter after the third series game, but he was totally ignored in the bullpen as well. Now that the game was hopeless, Andujar was brought in to mop up the mess and he faced Jim Sundberg. Andujar threw a 2–2 pitch that was called a ball by Don Denkinger. Whitey Herzog exploded into a rage, storming out of the dugout to give the umpire a piece of his mind. Since a manager can't argue a ball-strike call, he was automatically out of the game. Herzog left and Andujar, who was less than thrilled with the call himself, threw another pitch. Ball four, bases loaded again. Andujar was even more enraged than Herzog at this call, and he looked like he was ready to kill Denkinger. Teammates had to try hard to restrain the pitcher, who managed to bump the umpire while giving him an earful of epithets in two languages. Andujar was ejected and Bob Forsch had to come in to finish the mess that was becoming the last game of the season. Joaquin Andujar's days in St. Louis were now numbered.

For the record, Bret Saberhagen went the distance as he allowed just 5 hits. The Cardinals were beaten, 11–0, in the worst shutout defeat in World Series history, tying the 1934 Tigers' last-game performance (against the Cardinals) for that dubious honor. St. Louis was the most inept-hitting team in series history for a series lasting 7 games. The Cardinals batted just .185 after leading the National League in hitting at .264 and collected no more than 7 hits in a single series game. Dick Howser's strategy of using lefties to cut down on the Cardinals' running game worked well, since St. Louis stole just 2 bases in 7 games after stealing 314 in 162 games.

Despite the bitter disappointments, the blown call, and the tirades of the World Series, the 1985 Cardinals had a far better year than anyone would have expected. St. Louis was everyone's choice for the cellar after Bruce Sutter left, but instead the Cardinals were the winningest team in the majors. Bruce Sutter had a terrible year for the Braves because of rotator cuff trouble and never again was effective, so his loss was actually a plus for the Cardinals. Whitey

Herzog came up with a new ace reliever in hard-throwing Todd Worrell, so he would probably replace the excellent bullpen by committee in 1986. Whitey Herzog would always maintain that the Cardinals should have won the 1985 World Series (he was right on that one, because of the blown call in the sixth game) and Don Denkinger would spend the winter getting death threats and crank calls (luckily he was an American League umpire, so he wouldn't have to work in St. Louis in the regular season) and Vince Coleman was still a question mark concerning his leg, but the 1985 season was finally at an end. It was now time to look at 1986.

VI

Whitey Herzog was just about at the top of the world at the end of the 1985 season, but he was not *at* the top, so it was time to accomplish that in 1986. The catching situation was not at all good in 1985, so it was time to get a catcher. Joaquin Andujar left a bad taste in many people's mouths after the World Series, so much so that even Whitey Herzog had to consider trading him at this time. The Mets could be expected to make moves to get themselves to the top, so the Cardinals had to counter any move the Mets made. In November the Mets picked up lefty Bob Ojeda from the Red Sox, evidently learning from the Royals that lefties can indeed stifle a running game. Besides, Ojeda might turn out to be another John Tudor, so the Mets sent a gaggle of their top prospects to Boston to land the lefty. On December 10, the Cardinals moved to fill in their gap behind the plate by sending Joaquin Andujar to the A's for catcher Mike Heath and pitcher Tim Conroy. Heath had a strong throwing arm, and Conroy was a highly regarded lefty who had struggled in Oakland for the last few years. The trade seemed to have the potential to help both teams, but it turned out to be a bust.

Spring training 1986 came and most people put their money on the Mets to take the division. It was expected that the Mets would win because of their powerful lineup and deep pitching, and everyone praised the front office for putting a probable world champion team together. The Cardinals were expected to contend, but most people did not pick them to win. Whitey Herzog was upset that his team was being lumped in with the rest of the division as an also-ran after winning the pennant the year before. "It's as if the Mets won the pennant instead of us last year," said Herzog. Both teams did not like each other due to their styles. (The Mets: We are the best. The Cardinals: It's us against the world.) Despite the Cardinal-Met rivalry, managers Whitey Herzog and Davey Johnson got along well and they would often fish in Florida together in the winter. Both men respected each other's abilities and made sure that their teams respected one another, even if they hated one another.

The Cardinals entered 1986 with the same old questions concerning their pitching. Joaquin Andujar might have been volatile, but he did win 20 games two straight years while tossing over 220 innings four straight years. Replacing Andujar would not be easy. Kurt Kepshire, a lefty who looked promising as a rookie in 1984 and who started 1985 as part of the rotation, ended 1985 as an ignored hurler because he was getting pounded too often. Tim Conroy had promise, but skeptics did not think he was ready to replace Andujar any time soon. Bob Forsch was coming off of arm trouble and he did not look good in the postseason of 1985, so he was still a big question. Only John Tudor and Danny Cox were not questions, and both had to be healthy for the Cardinals to do anything in 1986. Cox, who won 18 games in 1985, was now the number-two man in the rotation behind Tudor, but who would comprise the rest of the rotation was left to pot luck.

Just before the end of spring training Danny Cox foolishly jumped off a seawall and hurt his ankle, knocking him out of the rotation at the start of 1986. St. Louis began the year at home against the Cubs, and John Tudor outpitched Rick Sutcliffe 2–1. The Cardinals were off to a great start as Whitey Herzog put together a decent rotation that was now backed by fine setup relievers and closer Todd Worrell. On the fourteenth of April the Cardinals went to New York for their first head-to-head meeting with the Mets. As was the case in 1985, the two teams played hard, taking a 2–2 tie into the thirteenth inning until St. Louis scored four runs to give reliever Pat Perry a win. Rain canceled the rest of the series, disappointing New York fans, but that meant some doubleheaders later in the season.

The Cardinals owned a 7–4 record when the Mets came to St. Louis on April 24 for 4 games. The Mets were on a roll themselves, and like the last series between the two clubs at Busch Stadium in 1985, this one was deemed important and attracted packed houses. In the first game it looked like the Cardinals were ready to show the Mets who the boss was when something went wrong. Todd Worrell had a 4–2 lead in the ninth to save when Howard Johnson blasted a 2-run homer to tie the game. In the tenth, George Foster homered, and the Cardinals were 5–4 losers. The next day, Dwight Gooden breezed to a 9–0 beating of the locals with former reliever and now emergency starter Rick Horton taking the loss. In the third game Danny Cox was back and he pitched well, but the Mets hung onto a 4–3 win when St. Louis grounded into a double play in the ninth. The final game saw John Tudor pitch a good game, but Bob Ojeda was better and the Mets completed a sweep by winning 5–3. St. Louis fans were stunned at how their team was beaten. The first game seemed to set the tone for the rest of the season, when the Cardinals looked like they did a year before, but then the 2 late homers just destroyed the fantasy that 1986 was just an extension of 1985. That first-game loss tore the heart out of the Cards, and 1986 looked like a very long year.

The Cardinals suddenly went into a batting slump. Vince Coleman's leg was fine, but his bat was not. Tommy Herr, who shocked everyone with 108 RBIs in 1985 to lead the team, was struggling to his worst year ever. Jack Clark and Willie McGee also were having rough years. Mike Heath, who was supposed to solve the catching problem, was having his worst year ever behind the plate, and his hitting also was poor. Mike Lavalliere was recalled, but his hitting was not much better. Only Ozzie Smith and Andy Van Slyke were doing as well as 1985 or better. The pitching was far better than thought, but the offense was terrible. The league's best-hitting team of 1985 was at the bottom in 1986.

The Mets, meanwhile, were flying. Like a well-oiled machine, New York was grinding up opponents and spitting out the remains while pulling away from the rest of the division. Montreal was the only club to stay somewhat near the Mets, but it was obvious that the Expos were no match for the Mets. New York went 13–3 in April and 18–9 in May, so nobody was about to catch them. That 4-game sweep in St. Louis had done wonders for New York's confidence. In 1985 the Mets were only 8–10 against the Cardinals, but now they showed that they could beat the team expected to bother them in convincing fashion.

As the year wore on, the Cardinals were stricken by a problem that did not touch them too much in the previous year—injuries. Rick Horton went to the disabled list. Ken Dayley ailed. Jeff Lahti, the big man in the 1985 bullpen by committee, missed almost all of 1986 with a career-ending arm injury, and he never returned to the majors after 1986. Willie McGee was nagged by injury to his legs. With the hitting being so poor it looked like the entire lineup was hit by injury, yet it tried to carry on.

The Cardinals endured two awful months in April and May. After the 7–4 start St. Louis posted those 4 straight losses to the Mets, and although they got to .500 again the day after the Mets left, they dropped under that mark for almost the entire rest of the year. An 8–10 April was followed by a poor 9–17 May. A trip to California brought St. Louis back to the bad old times when they went 2–5 against the improving Giants and the slumping Padres and Dodgers. At home for much of May, the Cardinals failed to get the job done against the three California teams, the improved Astros, the always tough Reds, and even the dismal Braves. From May 13 to May 30, St. Louis went just 3–12, and all but 4 of those games were at home. The offense in that stretch produced no more than five runs in any one of the losses, and the fans began to stay home. The expected nightmare for 1985 was a year late in arriving.

With the Cardinals ahead of only the even more inept Pirates in the standings, Whitey Herzog was ready to admit defeat. The Mets were far away and even a .500 season was becoming too much to hope for when Herzog admitted that the Mets would win the division. New York papers blared headlines of the Cardinals conceding defeat as if St. Louis had just forfeited the flag to the Mets. "It's Over Says Herzog" was one such headline, referring to former Mets manager Yogi Berra's saying, "It ain't over 'til it's over." Some players were unhappy at Herzog's concession, but the pilot was simply admitting the truth. The Mets were on a pace that would give them the league's best record since the 1975 Reds went 108–54 en route to a world championship. Whitey Herzog once again told it like it was.

Late in June the Cardinals got more bad news: Jack Clark would miss the rest of the year with a broken thumb. St. Louis was having a rough enough time trying to score runs *with* their power hitter in the lineup, so now they would have to do without the only true home run threat in their lineup. Clark wasn't exactly burning up the league at the time of his injury, with 9 homers and 23 RBIs on a .237 average, but his presence always scared the opposition. St. Louis was 14–10 in June when the news came and it seemed like the team was turning around at the time, but St. Louis went 1–4 the rest of the month. Still, at 15–14 the Cardinals had a great month of June considering their lack of hitting.

By the time the All-Star break arrived on July 14, St. Louis was in fifth place, 24 games out of first. The offense continued to be feeble and the pitching spotty, but there were some good points. Bob Forsch was back to his 1982 form, and he joined John Tudor and Danny Cox in forming a decent, if not great trio. Todd Worrell was among the league leaders in saves even though he had few leads to save while posting a tiny ERA and striking out many batters. Andy Van Slyke was hitting for average and was under-rated defensively in right field. Ozzie Smith's rotator cuff was killing him, and unlike 1985, he could no longer hide that fact, but still he did the job defensively while leading the team in hitting. Rookie Greg Matthews was also doing a nice job as a pitcher, and rookie Mike Lavalliere was fine defensively behind the plate, even though his hitting was not so fine.

In the second half the Cardinals began to regroup and play better baseball. St. Louis won 7 straight and ended July with a 14–12 mark. In August the Cardinals began to play more like they did a year before and put together some consistency. Vince Coleman was stealing bases at a good clip, and Willie McGee began to do some hitting. Tommy Herr also began to drive in runs, and the Cardinals began to put together their first big month of 1986. St. Louis went to New York for 6 games against the mighty Mets and took 4 wins from the best club in baseball on their home turf.

The pitching continued to do a decent job, and St. Louis posted a 19–12 mark for August.

After the extremely poor start of the first two months, it was almost certain that the Cardinals would end up fifth with at least 90 losses, better than only the truly awful Pirates, but as September began there was hope that St. Louis could move into the first division and pull out a .500 season. The Cardinals continued getting clutch hits and good pitching to go with solid defense while playing above .500 for the month. The Phillies seemed a sure bet to bag second place, but the Expos were faltering and third place was becoming available. St. Louis posted a 14–13 mark for September, and going into the last 5 games of the year in early October the Cardinals would face the weak Pirates and Cubs in their quest for a .500 season. But it was not meant to be. The Cardinals had one rainout and 4 losses to conclude 1986 with a 79–82 record, good enough for third place by 1 game over the Expos.

Despite the dismal injury-plagued year, Whitey Herzog figured 1986 to be somewhat a success. In the second half the Cardinals played some good ball, proving they were not completely dead. The pitching staff held out, and if John Tudor did not miss the last couple of weeks with an injury St. Louis might have finished over .500. Bob Forsch was back, as his 14–10, 3.25 year showed. Todd Worrell easily replaced the committee bullpen setup with thirty-six saves to lead the league and captured the Rookie of the Year award. Greg Matthews won 11 games as a rookie, showing hope for the future. Ozzie Smith hit a career-high .280, and Andy Van Slyke hit a career-high .270. So there was hope for a better 1987.

On the negative side St. Louis got only 61 RBIs from Tommy Herr (enough to lead the team with Van Slyke and the lowest team-leading figure since Rogers Hornsby drove in 60 runs to lead the club in 1918), a .256 average out of Willie McGee (down from a league-leading .353 in 1985), and a .232 mark from Vince Coleman (down from .267) as the leadoff man. Mike Heath was a total failure at .205 and was sent to Detroit in August. Terry Pendleton hit just .239, and although that was only one point less than the year before, the Cardinals could not afford such a mark in 1986 with everyone struggling. The Cardinals hit .236 as a team, fourteen points less than the next worst team. St. Louis also hit a paltry 58 homers, making them the only big league team to fail to hit 100 homers in 1986. St. Louis did steal 262 bases, but it was not enough to accomplish much on the year. Andy Van Slyke hit 13 homers to lead the team, the only Cardinal to reach double figures. Not since 1968 had the Cardinals been so bad offensively, and this poor offense came in a year of increased offense around the majors, so outstanding pitching could not be blamed. Something had to be done for 1987.

VII

In 1987 something indeed was going to be done, and it would affect not only the Cardinals, but every team in the majors. Offensive production was low in 1984, but in 1985 hitting improved in both leagues and in 1986 people were beginning to claim that there was an imbalance between the hitting and the pitching, one that was increasing in the former's favor. Seven thousand, eight hundred, and ninety-four runs were scored in the National League in 1984, and two years later 8,096 runs scored. The American League scored 10,027 runs in 1984 and 10,449 runs in 1986, so offense was indeed increasing. But nobody had any idea that 1987 would produce offense that began rivaling the output of 1930, and like 1930, the Cardinals would be in the middle of a tight race.

The Cardinals ended 1986 with a catching situation that looked too much like the situation after 1985, so St. Louis again went looking for a backstop. The Cardinals were hoping that good health and a massive bouncing back of the offense would enable them to contend in 1987, so they made few moves other than to secure a new catcher. During the winter no catchers were available and all of the teams were conspiring to not sign free agents in an attempt to cut costs. In early 1987 the Phillies risked the wrath of the other teams by signing catcher Lance Parrish, and that move left Cardinal fans scratching their heads in amazement. Parrish had been one of the American League's top catchers since 1979, when he took over the position full-time for the Tigers, and he would be just what the Cardinals needed. Instead, St. Louis let a divisional rival get him, and few people understood why. Andre

Dawson was another free agent that was supposed to be up for grabs, but again the Cardinals passed, just like the other teams. Dawson had been a top outfielder since 1977 for the Expos, but his knees were in terrible shape from playing on artificial turf and he wanted out of Montreal. Chicago's Wrigley Field seemed like the perfect place for Dawson, and he offered the Cubs a blank contract, allowing the club to sign him for whatever price they were willing to pay. This was too good to pass up, so the Cubs signed Dawson for $500,000 in 1987, chump change for a player of Dawson's caliber, but the player agreed to the figure and he would prove to be a real bargain.

Spring training was almost over, and still the Cardinals were lacking the catcher that they wanted. The Pirates were still trying to straighten out the mess that they had fallen into a few years before and were looking for young players to build a future on. The Cardinals and Pirates talked trade, and on April 1 Pittsburgh sent catcher Tony Pena to St. Louis for catcher Mike Lavalliere, out-fielder Andy Van Slyke, and pitcher Mike Dunne. The arrival of Pena, long a high-quality backstop, made the Cardinals a legitimate contender for 1987. Pena would handle a pitching staff of youth and experience, youth coming from Greg Matthews and rookie Joe Magrane as well as relief ace Todd Worrell while Bob Forsch, John Tudor, and Danny Cox provided the experience. The Cardinal lineup was expected to bounce back, and it would get a boost from Tony Pena as well, since he had many good years with the Pirates at the plate as well as behind it.

As usual, the Mets were expected to win again. New York had posted a 108–54 record in 1986, finishing over 20 games ahead of the second-place Phillies while launching several come-from-behind wins. The Mets were simply awesome in the regular season, but the postseason was another story. First, the Astros furnished stiff opposition for the Mets in the playoffs after everyone thought the Mets would take care of Houston rather easily. The Astros had enough good pitching to match New York's, and the playoffs featured one hard-fought, gut-wrenching game after another. Mike Scott, once a struggling Met, dominated his old club in two playoff games with his split fingered fastball (the Mets, like other teams, called it a scuffball), and if the Mets did not manage to stage a dramatic comeback late in the sixth game they would have faced Scott in the Astrodome in the seventh game, and most people thought Scott would win that game. The sixth playoff game went extra innings, and it was the guttiest game of the greatest National League championship series ever played to that time, surpassing even the 1980 playoffs between the Astros and Phillies that featured four extra-inning games in the then best of five format. After downing the Astros, the Mets had another stiff battle with the Red Sox in the World Series. Boston looked like the winner of the series when they scored twice in the top of the tenth inning of game 6, but the Mets staged one of the greatest comebacks in series history even though they were down to their last strike of the year on two occasions in that game. The next day the Mets again rallied to defeat the Red Sox and they won one of the all-time great World Series, rivalling even the 1975 Red Sox–Reds Series.

As the Mets' struggles in the postseason proved, even an allegedly great team needs luck and rallies to win all of the marbles, so maybe the Mets were overrated to begin with. Going into 1987 the Mets received a shock with the behavior of Dwight Gooden. First Gooden missed the series victory parade in New York; then he had a scuffle with the law in Florida. Early in 1987 Gooden checked into a drug rehab center for cocaine problems, leaving the Mets without their pitching leader for the next few months. Nineteen-eighty-seven would start rough for New York, especially with ace reliever Roger McDowell recovering from hernia surgery.

The Phillies were expected to be a factor in 1987 as well. In 1986 they surprised everyone by winning 86 games and became the only team to have a winning record against the Mets (10–8). Mike Schmidt was coming off of his third MVP year and Lance Parrish would add another big bat to the Philadelphia attack that had Schmidt, Von Hayes, Juan Samuel, and Glen Wilson. The Phillies were also expected to overcome their questionable pitching by slugging their way to the first division.

The Cubs also were expected to be tough after getting Andre Dawson. Good health was imperative for the Cubs to make progress. In 1985 and 1986 injuries ruined any chance that Chicago had to contend wire to wire, but when healthy the Cubs could be tough. Dawson would join a lineup that had Ryne Sandberg, Leon

Durham, Jody Davis, Keith Moreland, and Shawon Dunston. The pitching was iffy, led by Rick Sutcliffe and backed by Lee Smith in the bullpen, so a healthy lineup was a must. The Pirates were expected to do nothing since they were rebuilding, and the Expos were no longer a favorite after losing Tim Raines for at least a month (the Expos could not resign him due to rules on free agents until May, because they could not come to terms with the player before a deadline) and Andre Dawson forever. Thus the race was expected to be between the Mets, Phillies, Cardinals, and maybe the Cubs, with the Mets expected to win. Good health would determine how far the latter three teams would go; so it was thought.

The Cardinals opened the 1987 season in Chicago on April 7, and they swept a brief 2-game set. The Mets took 2 at home from the Pirates, and the Phillies dropped 2 in a row to the lowly Braves in Atlanta. So far, the Cardinals and Mets were tied for first while the Phillies and Cubs were at the bottom. The season was only two days old, but in a projected tight race every game matters, even the first ones.

On the tenth, the Cardinals went to Pittsburgh and Tony Pena wanted to do well against his old teammates. Instead, Tony Pena was greeted by a foul tip onto his thumb, breaking it and sidelining him for a long time. The injury to Pena was the first of a wave that seemed to continue right from the dismal 1986 season. St. Louis left Pittsburgh with a four-game split as it was becoming obvious that the Pirates were not the same old team that had finished last for three straight years. The Cardinals had gotten a catcher from Pittsburgh who now could not do anything while the Pirates got from St. Louis a catcher doing well and an outfielder who was doing even better. Whitey Herzog was not pleased, but there was nothing he could do about it.

On the seventeenth, the Cardinals were home to face the Mets for the first time and the usual big crowd was on hand to see the locals battle the beasts of New York. John Tudor and Bob Ojeda both pitched well, but Tudor emerged a 4–3 winner, so any thoughts by the Mets to do what they did a year earlier in St. Louis were squashed. The next day both teams engaged in a slugfest, something that was becoming quite common already in 1987. St.

Louis outslugged the Mets by a 12–8 score, warming the hearts of the local fans. On the nineteenth, the Mets and Cardinals closed out their series with Greg Matthews facing Sid Fernandez. St. Louis was winning when disaster struck. Mets catcher Barry Lyons tried to field a pop fly near the Cardinal dugout, and he was charging full speed. (Since any game between these two teams was like war, everyone played their hardest possible.) John Tudor was sitting in the dugout when Lyons came crashing into it, breaking a bone just below Tudor's knee in one of the freakiest accidents ever resulting in an injury. The Cardinals left the game with a 4–2 win and minus their ace starter, who wasn't even on the mound when he was hurt. Some Cardinals grumbled about Lyons's action, but most agreed it was simply a freak accident. Neither team liked each other, but they certainly would not try to cripple one another. Besides, the Cardinals tried to warn Lyons off and break his fall, but it was just one of those things. Tudor was expected to be through for the rest of the year.

Later in the month the Cardinals went to New York and won 2 out of 3, so the 1987 Cardinals were not going to wither and die like the 1986 squad did after the April fiasco in St. Louis of that year. St. Louis ended April by being perched on top with a 12–8 record, 1 game ahead of the Mets and 2 ahead of the Cubs. The Phillies were having problems with their pitching *and* their hitting, and they were already sinking with a 7–13 mark, 5 games out and in the cellar. Philadelphia never did get its act together and fell out of the race for good.

Despite being in first place, the Cardinals were an ailing club. Pena and Tudor were both out, and highly touted Jim Lindeman, who was supposed to replace Andy Van Slyke in right field, was having a bad year due to back problems. Tommy Herr had a groin injury, and he was out for a few weeks. The pitching staff was not enjoying the success of 1986, but then no team was getting pitching that would thrill anybody. Unlike 1986, though, the 1987 Cardinals had a good bench, one that measured favorably with the team's 1985 solid bench. Jose Oquendo was picked up for a song and dance from the Mets, and he became the best utilityman in baseball. Oquendo was originally a shortstop, but Whitey Herzog told him to learn other positions so he could play more. As a result,

331

Oquendo filled in nicely for Herr and suddenly a light hitter also became a good hitter. Steve Lake was also picked up cheaply from the Cubs, and he did a fine job in Tony Pena's absence. John Morris, picked up from the Royals in the 1985 Lonnie Smith trade, became a capable spare outfielder, as did Curt Ford. Rod Booker gave St. Louis another good infield sub, so Whitey Herzog regained the flexibility of 1985 that he had lacked in 1986.

At this time, offense was most definitely on the rise in the majors. Players who were simply mediocre for years suddenly became tough hitters. Wade Boggs of the Red Sox was never known for his power, but he was cracking homers and driving in a ton of runs all over the place. Mike Pagliarulo of the Yankees became a bona fide home run threat after years of disappointing numbers. Jose Oquendo was one of the worst hitters in the game when he first came up in 1983 (.213 says it all), but now he was ripping the ball like never before. Howard Johnson of the Mets had been considered little more than a platoon player, but in his first year as a regular he was crushing the ball. Terry Pendleton was off to a fantastic season after hitting just .240 in the two years he was a regular.

As was the case in 1930, everyone claimed that the ball was juiced up, but as was expected, officials of baseball and the ball maker said that was not so. Pitchers wondered what was going on. Some players were accused of using corked bats after hitting homers that nobody would have expected. Some pitchers tried to compensate by doctoring the ball, and later in the year Joe Niekro of the Twins was caught with an emery board that he tried to discard when the umpires went to search him. Historians began figuring the chances of batting records falling and how 1987 would stack up against 1930, better known as the "Year of the Hitter." Most people laughed when officials said the 1987 ball was no different than the ones used in the last few years, because offense was clearly higher in May 1987 than it was in May of the last few years.

As for the Cardinals, the ball was just fine after the hitting woes of 1986. Pendleton was hitting around .300, and he was driving in several clutch runs. Jack Clark was having his best year ever, ranking among the league leaders in homers and RBIs. Willie

McGee was back on track with his RBI total, and he raised his average into the .290s. Ozzie Smith was the most mystifying of all, batting over .300 and driving in runs. Nobody would have ever envisioned Ozzie Smith hitting .300 unless he was tripping on LSD, and Smith made sure his defensive reputation wasn't ruined by having his usual great year in the field. Vince Coleman became a fearsome leadoff man as his average jumped into the .290s. The 1987 Cardinals looked even more devastating offensively than the fine 1985 club had. St. Louis was hitting more homers, but it was also on top in steals yet again.

In May the Cardinals spent a month facing Western foes. The Dodgers and Padres were again having bad years, and the Cardinals took care of them by going a combined 4–3 against those two teams. The Giants were tough, taking 2 in St. Louis, but the Cardinals were rude guests in San Francisco by returning the favor. The Reds and Astros were expected to be tough, but St. Louis went 9–0 against both teams for the month. The Braves were also dispatched in rather easy fashion, giving the Cardinals a 29–17 record when May was over.

The Mets were still expected to do something, but the loss of Dwight Gooden was tough. The Mets were undergoing an injury wave that was crippling Gary Carter's effectiveness and taking its toll on the pitching staff. Bob Ojeda, the winningest Met of 1986 with 18 wins, had elbow trouble and was out. Sid Fernandez had a balky knee and tried to pitch through it, cutting down his effectiveness. Dave Cone, a rookie picked up early in the year from the Royals, had to pitch in the rotation before he was ready, and he broke a finger late in May. Rick Aguilera hurt his elbow at the same time, and he was done for the next few months. Roger McDowell came back, but he was hit hard in the bullpen. Jesse Orosco also was being hammered often, as the entire Met pitching staff was in disarray. The Mets ended May in fourth place, 5½ games out and just 1 game over .500. The Cubs, who were thus far healthy and riding the booming bat of Andre Dawson, were second, just two games behind the Cardinals.

After spending a month facing Western rivals, the Cardinals were slated to face Eastern opponents in June. On June 4 the Cardinals went to Chicago to face the Cubs in a key 4-game series.

St. Louis was up to the task, winning the first two games 3–1 and 5–1 behind Danny Cox and Greg Matthews before losing 6–5. In the finale, the two teams had a slugfest at tiny Wrigley Field, but the Cardinals emerged with a 13–9 win. The next day, the Cardinals went to Philadelphia and got another poor pitching performance, but again they prevailed, 12–8. The Cardinals took 2 of 3 from the Phillies, then swept 3 from the Cubs in St. Louis to send the Cubs on their way out of the race. The Pirates finally gave the Cardinals some worthy opposition, playing 4 tough games in Busch Stadium and taking 2, the last game lasting ten frames. Next came a team that was starting to get its act together in the Expos.

Montreal was expected to battle Pittsburgh for the cellar after years of disappointment and a bad 1986 season, but the Expos started well despite not having two of their top players in Andre Dawson and Tim Raines. Raines returned in early May, and he was off to a hot start. Tim Wallach was becoming the successor to Mike Schmidt as the league's top third baseman, and young Andres Galarraga joined the two aforementioned stars in forming a potent trio of hitting terrors. Early in June Dennis Martinez was picked up to bolster the rotation, and he started well. The team nobody took seriously was now having a good year.

On June 19 the Expos went to St. Louis for three games and they won the first game 8–7 in a ten-inning battle. The next day the Expos again topped the locals, this time 7–5. The Cardinals won the last game 7–3, but it was not easy. The Expos were proving to be a tough team. Later the Cardinals took 2 of 3 in Montreal, but only after going eleven innings to bag the last game. At the end of the month, the Cardinals had the lead and the Expos had pushed past the Mets for second place, trailing by 6½ games. It looked like the Cardinals would be enjoying a season similar to the one the Mets had in 1986, but the pilot cautioned his team against over-confidence. Whitey Herzog knew that there was plenty of season left.

The Cardinals lost two out of three in New York, but then moved into July with a 9-game winning streak, sweeping 3 from the hapless Braves, taking back-to-back twin bills from the Dodgers, and then winning 2 in a row from the Giants in an acrimonious series that saw the Cardinals pick up a Western enemy that Ozzie

Smith described in his autobiography as "even worse than the Mets." Both teams claimed that the other was using corked bats, throwing scuffballs, and going head-hunting. Both teams had a little fight, and managers Whitey Herzog and Roger Craig had to be restrained from going at each other. After this exchange of unpleasantries, the two teams promised revenge, and both looked like they might see each other in the postseason to continue their feud on national TV. On July 15 the All-Star break came and the Cardinals looked like a runaway winner. St. Louis owned a 56–30 record and led the second place Expos by 9 games. The hitting was excellent, the running was great, the defense was tight, and the pitching was holding up well, given the fact that everyone and his grandmother was hitting homers. It looked like the 1987 Cardinals would be a lot like the 1986 Mets.

At this point the St. Louis offense was one of the best in the league. Although Andre Dawson was putting together a monster year for the Cubs, Jack Clark looked like the future MVP winner as he continued to rank among the leaders in homers and RBIs. Possibly even more valuable was Ozzie Smith. Smith was hitting around .300 and was headed for over 70 RBIs while going for yet another Gold Glove, all of this while batting second. Terry Pendleton and Vince Coleman continued having the best years of their careers. Willie McGee was hitting closer to his 1985 level than his 1986 level. Tommy Herr was driving in runs again. Tony Pena was back, but he was struggling with the bat. The right field spot was manned by many when Jim Lindeman got off to a bad start and Curt Ford was now getting the bulk of the playing time there and he also was hitting. St. Louis also was at the top in steals again, so run scoring was prolific. None of the pitchers were having a great year, but they were getting the job done. The bullpen went from saving games in 1985 to winning many in 1987 when the starters had trouble finishing what they began. Todd Worrell was still bringing heat in saving the victories. Yes, it looked like a Cardinal runaway.

But something went wrong. After the All-Star break the St. Louis attack began to sputter. Montreal began to win with consistency, and now the Expos were making a move to close the gap between themselves and St. Louis. The Expos finished out July with an 11–4 streak that shaved five games off of the Cardinals' lead over them. The Mets also began to get their act together as the pitching staff began to stabilize. The Mets went to St. Louis knowing that they had to sweep the 3-game set in order to stay in the race; anything less would virtually kill them off. On July 28 Howard Johnson belted a long homer and Whitey Herzog moved to impound his bat. Johnson was one of several hitters who, prior to 1987, was little better than mediocre, but he was now having a great year. Tony Pena seized the bat, and a tug of war ensued. The umpires took the bat in order to X-ray it for cork (the X rays turned out to be negative), but the homer counted. The Mets won the game 6–4, and the Mets retaliated for the Johnson bat incident by calling for the checking of Cardinal bats. The next day the Mets pulled out another 6–4 win, this time in ten innings. Dwight Gooden then completed a 3-game sweep with a 5–3 win. The Mets were still alive, but now they had to face the Expos in Montreal. All of a sudden, St. Louis held a 4-game lead over Montreal and a 6½ game lead over New York. A Cardinal rout had turned into a three-team race.

The Mets went to Montreal and took two out of three. Next the Expos faced another test by going to face the Cardinals in head-to-head play at home. Rick Horton beat Bryn Smith in the opener, but the locals came back with a 10–5 win, then a 2–1 victory that lasted thirteen frames. St. Louis got a big boost when John Tudor came back on August 1, but his arrival did not stop the Cardinal slide. Still, the return of the Cardinal ace was unexpected and very much welcomed in St. Louis. Tudor would be needed to stop the slide somewhat. The Expos handled the Cardinals well at home, but on August 10–12 they lost 2 of 3 in New York to the oncoming Mets. The Cardinals had to keep on winning while the Expos and Mets were busy trying to beat each other, and St. Louis did win, holding a 5-game lead over Montreal and a 5½-game lead over New York, as of the middle of August.

The Cardinals' schedule called for one last meeting with Western teams before facing the Mets and Expos in key September showdowns. The Astros were beginning to fade, but they still had good pitching, even in this hitter-happy season. The Astros swept three from the Cardinals in Houston to start off the Cardinals' slate against the West. In Cincinnati the Reds gave the Cardinals a tough time as well, but St. Louis took a 3-game set anyway. The Cardinals returned home and took 2 of 3 from the Astros, swept 3 from the Braves, won 1 of three from the Reds, and took 2 of three from the Padres to end their 1987 battles with the West. After John Tudor downed San Diego 6–4 on September 6, the Cardinals got on a plane and flew to Montreal to begin a month of key battles between the Cardinals and Expos, the Cardinals and Mets, and Mets and Expos. During the Cardinals' fight with the Western teams the Expos and Mets managed to keep pace by also playing Western teams, and going into the Montreal series the Cardinals held a 3½-game lead over the Mets and a 5-game lead over the Expos.

On September 7 Danny Cox got the ball against Pascual Perez. Montreal had slapped together a rotation of odds and ends that other teams didn't want, and Perez was cut loose by the pitching-poor Braves before the Expos took a chance on him. Manager Buck Rodgers had done a brilliant job with Perez and the rest of the "rejects" to get the Expos into a pennant race this late in the season, and now Montreal had a shot to overthrow the Cardinals. The Expos jumped all over Cox, and Perez coasted to a 9–2 win. The next day Bryn Smith outpitched Bob Forsch as the Expos won again 4–1. Dennis Martinez was then supported by a strong attack and he routed rookie Joe Magrane 8–3 as Montreal completed a 3-game sweep to move to just 2 games out. The Mets moved to within 1½ games of the Cardinals by taking 2 out of 3 from the Phillies during the Cardinal-Expo series.

Not only did the Cardinals suffer a 3-game sweep in Montreal, but they also suffered a potentially devastating loss when Jack Clark sprained his ankle going into first base in the last game of the series. Clark had popped 35 homers at the time of his injury and had crossed the 100 RBI line as well, so his loss was critical. Without the top power threat in their lineup, the Cardinals were expected to leave many of their speedsters on the bases. Run scoring had dropped after the All-Star break even with Clark in the lineup, but now the loss of Clark would be coming at a time when St. Louis was facing the two main rivals in hand-to-hand battle. Fans in Montreal and New York sensed doom for the Cardinals and hoped that their teams could take advantage of the Cardinals' misfortune. The Cardinals tried to downplay the injury, saying that Clark could still play if it was very necessary, but the fact of the matter was that Clark was basically through for 1987.

With a three-game sweep and Clark's loss fresh in their minds, the Cardinals flew to New York for another key three-game set. New York's tabloids ran large headlines about the series, and scribes speculated on the Cardinals' chances of winning even one game of this series (they said such chances were poor) and on an inevitable St. Louis slide out of the race. The Cardinals were expected to be demoralized, and a packed Shea Stadium would be filled to capacity with screaming fans taunting the visitors. The Cardinals' prospects for a good end to the year were indeed bleak.

On September 11 the Cardinals took the field against the team all of New York was saying was the best in the league, if not the majors. The Mets finally had their starting rotation mostly together, and they sent out Ron Darling, the only starter not to be lost during the year, to move the Mets to within half a game of the visitors. The Mets jumped out to the lead, and the local crowd was boisterous, sensing victory for their heroes. In the sixth inning, Ron Darling became the last Met starter to be put out of the rotation when he tore up his thumb going for a bunt. No matter; the Mets had a good bullpen, and it quickly took over for Darling. In the ninth, Roger McDowell was cruising. The Cardinals then got their second hit of the game while looking at a 4–1 deficit. Willie McGee singled home a run with one strike left in the game, making it a 4–2 game. Up stepped Terry Pendleton. The crowd anticipated a win by their beloved team, but instead Pendleton sent an 0–1 pitch over the wall in center field, stunning the crowd into silence and tying the game at four. An inning later, it was over. St.Louis scored twice against Jesse Orosco, and the Cardinals pulled out a 6–4 win.

The next day the Cardinals had murder on their mind. Dwight Gooden had joined the chorus of dirge singers who sang about the clear destruction of the Cardinals, and the Cardinals wanted to knock out the Met ace in revenge. Gooden belittled the team and told the scribes what he was going to do to the Cardinals as well as how great the Mets were. Greg Mathews got the ball against Gooden, and it was no contest. St. Louis fell on Gooden like a brick building in an earthquake, and the Cardinals breezed to an 8–1 win. The Mets salvaged a game in the series when Dave Cone beat Danny Cox 4–2 in a long-lasting game marked by bad weather, but the New York dream of another flag was dying. Instead of gaining ground, the Mets actually lost a game in the standings after the much ballyhooed series was over. St. Louis left New York with a 2½-game lead on the Mets and a 3-game lead on the Expos.

The Mets were reeling from their disappointing series against the Cardinals, but they still had a shot at the top. On the sixteenth, the Mets went to Montreal for another key series, this one lasting 2 games. The Cardinals hoped the two teams would split the series so they would not gain ground, and that's what happened. Dwight Gooden shut out the Expos 10–0, and Pascual Perez won the next day 4–1. The Cardinals, though, did lose ground to the Mets, and after the games of the seventeenth were over the Cardinals led the Mets by 1½ games and the Expos by 3. A 2-game set in New York between the Mets and Expos proved more helpful for the Cardinals. On September 23 the Mets shaded the Expos 4–3, but then the Expos returned the favor the next day by shading the Mets 5–4. The Mets and Expos were now through with playing each other for 1987, and each team had a series left to play in St. Louis. By the time the twenty-fourth was over, the Cardinals held a 3½-game lead over the Mets and a 4-game lead on the Expos. Both teams would have to stay no further away in the standings when they went to St. Louis to stay alive.

On September 29 the Expos arrived in St. Louis for their last important series of the year. At this point, a three-way tie for the flag was still possible and the National League worked out a formula where the team with the best home record would win the division if the Cardinals, Mets, and Expos all ended up tied at year's end. If only two teams were tied, then the usual 1-game playoff would be used. Montreal was looking for a sweep, the Mets were basically hoping for a split in the 4-game set, and the Cardinals needed just 3 out of 4 wins to knock both the Expos and Mets out to clinch the flag. On the twenty-ninth Joe Magrane pitched a beautiful game against Dennis Martinez and won 1–0. The next game it was another pitching duel as Greg Mathews shut out Bryn Smith 3–0, making it a sweep of a twin bill. The next day the

Cardinals had a shot to clinch it, but Pascual Perez downed Bob Forsch 6–1. On October 1 the Mets were in town to open a season-ending trio of games the next day. Many Mets sat in the stands rooting for the Expos to win, but Danny Cox breezed to an 8–2 win over Jay Tibbs to clinch the Cardinals' third division title in the last six years. The Cardinals then lost two of three to the Mets in the superfluous year-ending series, but that suited St. Louis just fine. The Cardinals were on top yet again. It was now time for the playoffs against another team that the Cardinals had no love lost for—the San Francisco Giants.

The Giants had won their first title of any kind in sixteen years, and it came just two years after the team lost 100 games for the first time in their history. The Giants were much like the team that they were in the early 1960s, a power-packed bunch that slammed 205 homers, second only to the Cubs in the league. General manager Al Rosen made many fine deals in his two years on the job, and on the Fourth of July he picked up Kevin Mitchell, Dave Dravecky, and Craig Lefferts from the Padres in a trade, and all three men played key roles in the Giants' season. The Giants also got Rick Reuschel and Don Robinson from the Pirates later on in the season, which also helped the Giants to victory. The playoffs were expected to produce fireworks because of the bad blood between the Cardinals and Giants that came from their fight earlier in the year, and St. Louis was favored to win even though Jack Clark was out due to their postseason experience of the past.

The playoffs opened on October 6 in St. Louis, and Rick Reuschel opposed Greg Mathews. The Giants scored once in the first, but the Cardinals tied it in the third. The game was tied at 2 when the Cardinals broke through for 3 runs, knocking out Reuschel. Terry Pendleton got a bloop hit to drive in a run, and then weak-hitting pitcher Greg Mathews singled home 2 runs to give St. Louis a 5–2 lead. The Giants got another run in the eighth, but Todd Worrell and Ken Dayley shut the door and the Cardinals had a 5–3 win.

John Tudor faced Dave Dravecky in the second game, and the Giants were able to handle the Cardinal ace. Will Clark belted a 2-run homer in the second and Jeffrey Leonard hit a solo shot in the fourth to stake the Giants to a 3–0 lead. Dravecky was a tough man to hit, as the Cardinals looked like they had in the 1985 World Series. St. Louis got singles from Tommy Herr and Jim Lindeman, and that was it. In the eighth, Ozzie Smith made an error that let 2 runs score, and the Giants breezed to a 5–0 win.

On October 9 the playoffs moved to San Francisco and Joe Magrane was pitted against Atlee Hammaker. The Giants got 3 runs in the second and then 1 more in the third on Jeffrey Leonard's third homer in as many games. Leonard was an irritant to the Cardinals with his "one flap down" trot after each homer. The Cardinals called the action "bush" and worse; Leonard stated that if the Cardinals did not like it that was just too bad. Many people figured that the Cardinals might retaliate against Leonard, but except for a war of words, nothing happened between the two clubs. Magrane was knocked out and replaced by Bob Forsch, who got out of a fifth-inning jam to keep the visitors in the game. In the sixth, Jim Lindeman popped a 2-run homer to cut the Giants' lead in half. An inning later Hammaker was driven out of the game when the Cardinals launched a 4-run rally. Dan Driessen, a man who spent twelve-plus years in the majors and who had signed a minor league deal with St. Louis before being recalled to replace Jack Clark, began the rally with an RBI single. Vince Coleman got 2 RBIs on a single, and Lindeman drove in a run with a sac fly. Todd Worrell came into the game in the seventh and allowed a ninth-inning run, but he managed to save a 6–5 win for Forsch.

In the fourth game the Cardinals took the first lead when they got 2 runs in the second inning for Danny Cox, but the lead did not hold up. The Giants lashed 3 homers to take the game. Robbie Thompson hit a solo shot in the fourth, and an inning later Leonard hit a 2-run blow, making him the third man in playoff history to hit 4 homers in a series. (The others were Bob Robertson of the 1971 Pirates and Steve Garvey of the 1978 Dodgers.) Bob Brenly ended the scoring for the game with a solo homer in the eighth, making Mike Krukow a 4–2 winner.

Both clubs traded runs in the first and third innings of the fifth game, but then the Giants came through with another rally. Forsch again had to relieve; this time it was Mathews who needed help, and this time Forsch did not have it. Chilli Davis singled off of Forsch and the rally began to pick up steam when Will Clark singled him to third. Brenly walked, loading the bases, and then Jose Uribe banged out a 2-run single. Mike Aldrete hit a sac fly, and Thompson hit a triple. Four runs came home in the fourth and Rick Horton had to bail Forsch out, but it was too late. Joe Price replaced Reuschel, and he got the win in the Giants' 6–3 victory. San Francisco led the series 3–2 as it shifted back to St. Louis, and the hard-hitting Giants looked like they would easily dispose of the Jack Clark–less Cardinals.

John Tudor, winner of many clutch games for the Cardinals in his three years with the club, was called upon to keep St. Louis alive against Dravecky. Tudor again came through with another great effort, and he needed it. Dravecky was again stifling the Cardinals, but this time they caught a break. In the second inning Tony Pena hit a fly ball into the lights in right field. Candy Maldonado lost sight of the ball, and it dropped in and rolled to the wall. Pena chugged his way to third with a triple. One out later Jose Oquendo hit a shot to Maldonado, and although he caught it, Maldonado's throw was not perfect and Pena eluded the tag in scoring a run. That was all Tudor needed to work with, and he left the game in the capable hands of Worrell and Dayley, who went on to preserve Tudor's 1–0 win. The series was now tied at 3 games each.

Danny Cox had missed his start in the first game with a stiff neck, but he was healthy for the seventh game. Atlee Hammaker was a controversial choice for the Giants to try to win the flag, and the lefty just did not have it. In the second, Willie McGee singled home Pena, then Oquendo hit the third home run of his big league career, a 3-run shot that knocked Hammaker out of the game. In the sixth, Tommy Herr swatted a 2-run single, and the hard-hitting Giants were en route to a season-ending loss. For the second straight game San Francisco was shut out, this time by a 6–0 score, and the Cardinals won their third pennant of the 1980s. It was the fourth decade that the Cardinals won at least three pennants (the others were the 1930s, the 1940s, and the 1960s), and it was their fifteenth league title since 1926, more than any other team in baseball in that span except for the New York Yankees. (The Dodgers also won fifteen pennants between 1926 and 1987, but one would have to combine their years in Brooklyn and Los Angeles to do it and since the Dodgers' *real* history dates back only to 1958, that makes the Cardinals the champs in N.L. flags won from 1926 to 1987.)

St. Louis now had to face another hard-hitting team in the Minnesota Twins in the World Series. The Twins of 1987 are a perfect example of the travesty that postseason play can become when it comes to the playoffs. Minnesota was just 85–77, a mark that won the A.L. West, but one that would have put them 2 games behind the Yankees if the Twins played in the East, and the Yankees were only fourth in their division that year. The Twins posted a dismal 29–52 mark away from their unsightly home in the Metrodome, the worst road mark ever for a team appearing in the series. The 1987 Twins also brought the worst record of an American League champion ever to the series, their reward for beating a Detroit Tigers team, which had gone 98–64 (the best in the majors), in the playoffs. The only team with a worse record going to a series was the 1973 Mets, who went 82–79, so now each league had the distinction of contributing a woeful team to a World Series due to being lucky in the playoffs. To make things even luckier for the Twins, the 1987 series would have the American League team as the home team in 4 out of 7 possible games, so Minnesota's 56–25 home record (the best in the majors) would really come in handy. Still, most people put their money on St. Louis to win. After all, the Cardinals got by the hard-hitting Giants, so overcoming the hard-hitting Twins should have presented no problem.

The series began in Minnesota on October 17, and the Cardinals heard ear-splitting noise unlike any they ever heard before. The Cardinals play 6 games every year in the Houston Astrodome but the noise in that big stadium was nothing compared to the racket of the smaller Metrodome. The Metrodome had weird features such as a roof that tended to obscure the ball and a right field wall made of plastic that was dubbed the "trash bag" because that is what it looked like. Since it opened in 1982 the Metrodome was blasted by teams in the American League, and the natives were so sick of all of the rips about their stadium that they put up a big sign saying WE LIKE IT HERE. Making sure TV cameras would not miss it, the fans put the sign in a place where it could be seen any time the pitcher was shown by a camera on the third base side of the field.

The Cardinals did not like it there and the racket must have had some effect, because starter Joe Magrane failed to last four innings. In the fourth inning the Twins overcame a 1–0 deficit by scoring 7 runs, 4 of which came from Dan Gladden's grand slam, the first in a series in seventeen years. Gary Gaetti became the first player in sixteen years to get 2 hits in a series game inning when he singled and doubled in the 7-run outburst, and the Cardinals must have thought they were time-warped back to the seventh game of the 1985 World Series, inning number 5, but at least there was no emotional outburst on the Cardinals' part this time. The Cardinals gave up three more runs, and Frank Viola easily won 10–1.

The next day the Cardinals continued to think they were in the Twilight Zone when Minnesota again scored big in an inning. In the fourth inning the Twins took a 1–0 lead into the frame and left it with a 7–0 lead. Danny Cox was the victim this time, as he failed to get through the fourth and needed help from Lee Tunnell to escape the disaster. The Twins added another run in the sixth, but at least the Cardinals came up with some runs themselves. In the fifth Terry Pendleton singled and eventually scored on a ground out by Tony Pena. In the seventh Curt Ford singled and then scored on a Pena single. In the eighth St. Louis came through with two more runs when Dan Driessen doubled home Vince Coleman and Willie McGee singled home Driessen. Still, the Cardinals could not close the gap enough and they went down to an 8–4 loss.

On October 19 the stock market crashed, dropping over 500 points. The Cardinals looked like they were en route to a similar crash in the World Series after being outscored 18–5 in the first 2 games. The Cardinals were playing at home starting the next day, and John Tudor was asked yet again to right the team. Like Wall Street, the Cardinals were in desperate need of damage control, and John Tudor was the man.

Tudor faced Les Straker, a longtime minor leaguer who finally made it to the big leagues in the pitching-poor year of 1987, and both hurlers did well. The Twins scored once in the sixth on Tom

Brunansky's RBI single that scored Greg Gagne, but the locals came back in the seventh. Juan Berenguer relieved Straker and was greeted by a leadoff single by Jose Oquendo. Tony Pena singled. Terry Pendleton, not starting because of a leg injury he had sustained in the playoffs, hit for Tudor and bunted the runners over. Coleman doubled home both men to put the Cardinals in the lead; then he stole third and scored on Ozzie Smith's single. Todd Worrell came in and saved Tudor's 3–1 win, showing that the Cardinals were not done yet.

In the fourth game the Twins sent their ace, Frank Viola, to the mound to face Greg Mathews. The Twins had Mathews on the ropes in the fourth with the score tied at 1 each, but Bob Forsch came to the rescue and got the Cardinals through without allowing a run. In the bottom of the fourth, St. Louis put together their own big inning. Pena walked and Oquendo singled him to third. Tom Lawless, playing third for the injured Pendleton, lashed his second big league homer, putting the Cardinals on top 4–1. St. Louis scored 3 more runs on Jim Lindeman's RBI single and a 2-run double by Willie McGee, knocking out Viola in the process. Minnesota added a meaningless run in the fifth, but the Cardinals kept the lead and won 7–2, tying up the series.

In the fifth game Danny Cox pitched well and again the Cardinals came through with a rally, this time at Bert Blyleven's expense. In the sixth the game was scoreless when Coleman got a single. Smith singled. One out later, both runners pulled off a double steal. Driessen drew a walk. One out later, Ford ripped a 2-run single, scoring Coleman and Smith, and Driessen and Ford took an extra base on Kirby Puckett's throw. Oquendo hit a shot to Gagne, who made an error, allowing Driessen to score. The Cardinals left the inning with a 3–0 lead, and they scored 1 more run in the seventh when Smith singled home Coleman. In the eighth, the Twins rallied for 2 runs and it looked like they might tie up the game, but Worrell managed to get out of the jam and the Cardinals hung on for a 4–2 win.

Thus far the series had produced a bizarre contrast. In two games at Minnesota, the Twins easily crushed the Cardinals, scoring almost at will. At St. Louis, the Twins looked stifled in a big stadium while the Cardinals stuck to their usual game plan and were successful. Both teams played their brand of baseball in their own ballpark, but once one team visited the other, the visitors looked terribly overmatched, as if they did not even belong in a World Series. This clear contrast was never so evident in previous series, and even though the Cardinals held a 3–2 lead in the series, many felt they were doomed to failure by playing the last 2 games in Minnesota.

John Tudor was sent out against Les Straker, and on paper the Cardinals seemed to have the edge. Going into the last of the fifth St. Louis looked like a winner, holding a 5–2 lead when disaster struck. Puckett singled, then scored on a Gaetti double. Don Baylor then tied it with a homer, and when Brunansky singled, Tudor was removed in favor of Rick Horton. Steve Lombardozzi ended up singling home Brunansky, and the Twins took a 6–5 lead. Within minutes, the Cardinals were reduced from a lead to a deficit. In the sixth, the Twins applied the death blow. Gagne singled and Puckett walked; then both advanced on a passed ball. Baylor was walked intentionally and Ken Dayley came on to face lefty-hitting Kent Hrbek. It took seventeen years for the thirteenth grand slammer to be hit in series history, but it only took one week for number 14 to be hit; Hrbek delivered it against lefty Dayley, and the Cardinals were out of the game. The Twins tacked on another run in the eighth, and the final was Minnesota 11, St. Louis 5.

By now, many people assumed that the Twins would clinch the world championship no matter what the Cardinals did, and that proved to be the case. In the second inning the Cardinals scored twice when Pena doubled home a run and Steve Lake singled home another, but one could sense that doom in the dome was closing in on the Cardinals. In the bottom of the inning Lombardozzi singled home Brunansky, cutting the Cardinal lead in half. In the fifth the locals tied it on Puckett's RBI double that scored Gagne. The Twins loaded the sacks in the sixth and got a run on an infield hit by Gagne. The Twins got 1 more run in the eighth on an RBI double by Gladden that scored Tim Laudner. Jeff Reardon came out for the ninth, retired the side in order, and the Cardinals were beaten. By dint of winning the pennant in a year when the American League got 4 out of 7 home games in the series, the Twins were world champs.

Despite the fact that the Minnesota Twins lucked their way to a world title, the Cardinals had a great year in 1987. There was some buzzing that Jack Clark should have at least tried harder to get back into the lineup for the series, since just having him in the lineup was enough to alter opposing strategy, even if he never even got a hit. Clark did try, but his ankle still bothered him too much, so he never played in the series. Still, the Cardinals did outlast the Mets and Expos in a tight race for the division title and they did get past the hard-hitting Giants in the playoffs, so the year was not a total loss. And if Branch Rickey and Sam Breadon were still alive they would have been mighty pleased with the Cardinals' attendance in 1987. The Cardinals became the second team ever to draw 3 million fans in a season (the Dodgers did it first and in a far larger market), not bad for a team playing in a city containing under 450,000 people. Once people thought one team could simply not survive in St. Louis, let alone prosper, but in 1987 the St. Louis Cardinals not only prospered; they thrived and outdrew every team in the majors, including the Los Angeles Dodgers and the New York Mets, teams that were in huge markets. The Cardinals had certainly come a long way from the days of trying to draw 300,000 in a year.

The Cardinals' offense improved mightily in 1987. Jack Clark hit 35 homers and drove in 106 runs. Willie McGee had 105 RBIs. Terry Pendleton hit .286 with 96 RBIs. Tommy Herr had 83 RBIs. Vince Coleman led the league in steals for the third straight year and hit .289. Ozzie Smith hit second all year but still got 75 RBIs while hitting .303. Again the Cardinals stole over 200 bases. The pitching staff was not great, and it set a record. No team went to the World Series without at least one pitcher winning at least 14 games, but the Cards did it while having no pitcher win more than 11 games (Danny Cox, Bob Forsch, and Greg Mathews) in 1987. The bullpen of Todd Worrell, Ken Dayley, Rick Horton, and Bill Dawley as well as others certainly played a key role in getting the job done.

Besides being unhappy about the Cardinals' not winning the World Series, many of the team's fans were upset when Andre Dawson won the MVP award. The National League was really messed up in 1987 when it had to give the MVP and Cy Young awards to players from a last-place team (Dawson of the Cubs) and

347

a team that finished next to last (Steve Bedrosian of the Phillies). Both teams would have finished out of the race without the award winners, and the fact that both did despite the fine years of Dawson and Bedrosian shows that the writers who voted for them did so without taking into account the fact that such awards should go to players on contenders. The Cardinals got a Cy Young effort from Todd Worrell (8–6, 33 saves, 2.66, compared to Bedrosian's 5–3, 40 saves, 2.83) and an MVP effort from Jack Clark before he got hurt. The biggest piece of robbery came when Dawson (who did have a great year at 49, 137, .287) won the MVP over Ozzie Smith. Smith delivered the season of his life offensively while still playing his usual great defense. Smith was the glue that held the Cardinals together all year, and any time a shortstop on a pennant winner has a great year at bat as well as in the field he should get the MVP award. Even players from the Giants, Mets, and Expos deserved the two awards more than did the two winners. Dawson and Bedrosian should not be put down for their fine years, but the point is their teams would have stunk even if they were not on them, while there was little chance that the Cardinals would have won even their division without Smith and Worrell. MVP and Cy Young awards should go to the players who best kept their teams in contention while having the best year from among all the candidates, not to players who have great years for weak and dismal teams.

VIII

Nineteen-eighty-seven proved to be the last year of gradually increasing offense. Despite claims by magnates that the ball was not juiced up, the numbers showed otherwise. In 1987, 4,458 homers were hit in the majors, compared to 3,813 in 1986 and 3,258 in the last year before the offensive increase, 1984. Higher batting averages, more runs scoring, and an increase in extra-base hits also were found in 1987 compared to 1984 and even the good offense years of 1985 and 1986. Pitching suffered accordingly. Seven National League pitchers had an ERA under 3.40 in 1987 while nineteen hurlers in the same league had an ERA under 3.40

in 1984. Attendance reached record levels, but as in 1930, people came in large numbers not to see 7–6 games day after day, they came to see good baseball, and too much hitting, like too much pitching, is not good baseball if it happens too often. The outcry on all of the increased offense was loud, and it was expected that the hitting-pitching balance would be restored in 1988.

In other developments after the 1987 season the umpires decided to strictly enforce the balk rule in 1988. Whitey Herzog had long complained that teams playing his had their pitchers rush their deliveries, which seemed an attempt to deceive Cardinals runners. Since the Cardinals began to use the steal as a big weapon, opponents had tried to defense against them in every possible way, and the best way seemed to have the pitcher throw the ball quickly. Herzog maintained that "quick pitching" was tantamount to balking and that the umpires should call a balk when the pitcher did not come to a clear stop before delivering the pitch. Most of the time Herzog lost his argument on the balk, but in 1988 the rule would be enforced. People began to call the enforcement of the balk rule the "Herzog rule."

Another big development after 1987 concerned free agency. It seemed that since 1985 the big-name free agents were not even approached by teams other than their old ones, and as a result free agents for the most part signed with their old teams. The Phillies bucked the trend by signing Lance Parrish in early 1987, and the Cubs followed by signing Andre Dawson, but the market was still cold for free agents. The players' union considered the whole free agent flap an act of collusion on the part of the owners, and that would be a breach of the Basic Agreement. The players decided to have the issue submitted to an arbitrator, who would decide if the owners were really acting illegally. In 1987 the players won against the owners on this issue of collusion, and the free agent market after the season was indeed freer. Another arbitrator had to decide what to do about the free agents of the past few years who were forced to go back to their old teams due to collusion, and when the dust settled such players were given another shot at free agency in early 1988. Players who experienced collusion after the 1985 season, like Kirk Gibson, were free to sign new deals, and Gibson moved from the Tigers to the Dodgers when he gained "second-look" free agency. Other victims of collusion would receive the same treatment in the future, and they would also receive monetary compensation.

One player who moved to another team after 1987 (but not as a second-look free agent) via free agency was Jack Clark. Early in 1988 the Yankees offered a fat contract and Clark signed it, leaving the Cardinals without a power hitter. St. Louis moved quickly to replace Clark at first base by signing former Braves slugger Bob Horner. Horner was considered a likely Hall of Famer when he first came up to Atlanta in 1978 after hitting 23 homers in half a year. Horner was good for 30 homers a year, but he always had weight trouble and was getting hurt. In 1983 his wrist was so badly damaged that it looked like he was through, but Horner came back and on July 6, 1986, he became only the eighth player in National League history to hit 4 homers in a game. After the 1986 season Horner signed a one-year contract to play in Japan, and after a good year there Horner decided to accept a deal from St. Louis.

Despite losing Clark, the Cardinals were expected to contend, with Horner as his replacement. Again the Mets were picked by many to win, although the Cardinals had their adherents. Everyone expected pitching to improve around the majors in 1988, so the Cardinals would be expected to have a good pitching staff after coming off of a year where they didn't have a twelve-game winner. The running game was expected to be helped by the "Herzog rule," so enemy pitchers would now balk a runner to second before the runner would steal third and score on virtually anything. People thought the Cardinals would now find scoring runs easier than ever. Wrong.

The 1988 season proved to be a tougher year than even 1986 was. The Cardinals got off to a twelve-inning loss in Cincinnati on the first day of the season, and the wave of injuries began again when Ken Dayley tore a muscle in his back. The Cardinals looked flat in dropping three straight in New York and in losing two of three at home to the Mets in April. Bob Horner was not hitting the long ball, but he was driving in runs. Still, it was not enough. The offense across the board was sputtering like in 1986, and all of the balks being called in record numbers were not helping the Cardinals. The lack of a power hitter who could break the game open was hurting the Cardinals, so they sent Tommy Herr to the Twins for slugger Tom Brunansky. Brunansky gave the Cardinals some sock, and the trade of Herr allowed the Cardinals to make Jose Oquendo the everyday second baseman. Oquendo played the position as if he had played it all his life and he continued to hit well, even though the ball seemed to be back to normal.

In May the Cardinals started to right themselves after an 8–14 April. Overall, the offense still had trouble. Vince Coleman was not on pace to steal 100 bases for the fourth straight year, and his batting average was down from 1987. Terry Pendleton was hitting like he did before 1987 as well, and Willie McGee's RBI production was way down. Bob Horner was still not hitting homers. Only Ozzie Smith and Jose Oquendo were matching or exceeding expectations that were set from the previous year. The pitching was decent, and the Cardinals began to move back into the race.

Then came June. The injuries piled up and the losses followed easily. Bob Horner hurt his shoulder and was done for the year. Joe Magrane was hit by injury. Danny Cox and Greg Mathews both were hurting. John Tudor, who had knee surgery after the 1987 season, was slow in recovering, and he had already missed much of April. The offense continued to struggle. In the middle of June the Cardinals visited New York, Pittsburgh, and Montreal, and they went 2–7 against these three contenders. The June swoon that produced an 11–16 mark continued into July. From July 1 to July 19 the Cardinals were just 2–12 against the three teams from California, and in that dismal stretch the Cardinals scored as many as five runs just twice. Rumor had it that the Cardinals were going to clean house, just like they did after the 1969 season. John Tudor, the man who had won several key games for St. Louis, was on the trading block for a slugger. Jack Clark and Tommy Herr were gone, so was Joaquin Andujar, so the key men who made the Cardinals a National League force in the 1980s were already on their way out.

The dreary 1988 season dragged on. St. Louis posted a weak 8–19 record in July, and on August 1 the team owned a wretched 45–59 record and was wallowing in the second division with the Cubs and Phillies for company. The Mets and Expos were contending as expected, and the Pirates were surprising everyone with a great year, staying close to the Mets all year to that point. On the

Cardinals, the hitting situation was becoming acute, as Terry Pendleton was out with an injury and Tom Brunansky was now struggling. St. Louis had to act, and on August 16 John Tudor was sent to the Dodgers for Pedro Guerrero. Guerrero was unhappy in Los Angeles after having many fine years there, and he wanted out. The Cardinals needed a slugger to make up for Brunansky's slump, and Guerrero was the man for the job. The Cardinals began to play better as the offense came to life with Guerrero revitalized. Tony Pena was hitting far better than the year before (he hit .214 in 1987), and Vince Coleman, Ozzie Smith, and Jose Oquendo all were producing consistently. During August the Cardinals began to look like their old selves and posted a 17–12 month.

The Cardinals opened September missing Bob Forsch, who had been the longest-lasting member of the team (going back to 1974), after sending him to the Astros for Denny Walling, but St. Louis was ready to finish respectably. St. Louis began the month with an 8–2 streak, but then another batting slump hit and the Cardinals were back to skidding along against the better teams. The Mets were rough all year on the Cardinals (St. Louis went just 4–14 against them), and so were the Pirates (11–7 against the Cardinals) as the Cardinals faltered. St. Louis concluded a poor 1988 season with 3 straight losses in New York. The pitching staff did a decent job in 1988 with a 3.47 ERA that was only 2 points above the league average, but the offense was bad. Jose DeLeon, picked up from the White Sox after 1987, was the ace with a 13–10 record and Todd Worrell again had over 30 saves, but the hitting was just too much to overcome. St. Louis outscored only the Braves in finishing the year in fifth place, 25 games behind the first-place Mets.

The Cardinals left 1988 behind showing the baseball world that they were a streaky team. In 1983, 1986, and 1988 the Cardinals offered an inept defense of their National League crowns, and nobody knew what to expect from them from one year to the next. It seems that during much of their history the Cardinals have failed miserably when they were expected to contend or win while they have surprised people by either winning or at least contending in years where they were expected to do nothing. In 1983, 1986, and 1988 the Cardinals were expected to at least contend, but they failed miserably. In 1985 few people picked St. Louis to finish anywhere except last, yet the Cardinals almost won the whole pie that year. Other years that the Cardinals were expected to do little but instead did much included 1967 and 1926, among others, so maybe the 1989 Cardinals would be able to surprise people.

St. Louis picked up outfielder Milt Thompson from the Phillies as their main move for 1989, and many people expected another mediocre year from them. The Mets again topped everyone's list as the team to beat, with challenges coming from the Pirates and Expos. Once 1989 began, the Pirates got off to a rough start due to injuries and the Cardinals began their year with two games in New York. St. Louis split the series and then took 2 of 3 from the Mets at Busch Stadium. The Cardinals were getting good hitting from Pedro Guerrero, who many people thought was washed up when the Dodgers traded him, but he was proving to be anything but washed up. St. Louis wanted to get off to as good a start as possible, because Danny Cox and Greg Mathews were not ready for the year due to injury, so a quick start would soften inevitable pitching slumps. The Cardinals indeed did start well and ended April on top with a 13–9 mark.

Another injury was coming when Willie McGee was hobbling around with a bad pair of legs. Milt Thompson, who was expected to play little beyond giving rests to McGee, Vince Coleman, and Tom Brunansky, suddenly got plenty of playing time when McGee was more out of the lineup than in. In May the Cardinals began to slump and the Mets and Expos joined them in a race. The Cubs also began to rise, and Whitey Herzog tried to hold his under-strength team in contention. Unlike past years, the bench was weak, so St. Louis had to play its regulars day after day. Guerrero continued to hit well while playing first base, but Vince Coleman continued to see his batting average shrink. St. Louis posted a losing record in May, but after that they began to play consistently.

In June the Cardinals took on the Expos and surprising Cubs in hand-to-hand play. Chicago took 2 of 3 in St. Louis to open the month, but then the Cardinals went to Montreal and took 3 of 4 from the locals. The Expos had failed for years to deliver a legitimate division title to their fans (they won one in the strike-tainted 1981 season even though St. Louis had the best overall

353

record), and just before the Cardinals arrived they made a big deal with the Seattle Mariners to land their ace in Mark Langston. Langston cost Montreal four fine prospects, but the fans figured that the fine lefty would pitch their team to a flag before leaving as a free agent at the end of the year. Rookie Ken Hill managed to outpitch Langston 5–2 on June 7, and the Cardinals completed their good series the next day with another win.

The Cardinals next went to Chicago and took 3 out of 4 there. Jose DeLeon and Joe Magrane (the 1988 ERA king with a 2.18 mark despite a 5–9 record, the fewest wins by an ERA champ ever) opened the series by throwing shutouts before Cris Carpenter won a slugfest in the third game 10–7. The Cubs took the final game 10–3 against Scott Terry, but the 6 wins in 8 games on the road trip put St. Louis into the lead. The Cardinals then returned home and took 2 of 3 from the Expos, putting a dent in that team's pennant hopes, Langston or no Langston.

Despite the Cardinals' success against the Expos and Cubs, those two teams were not simply going away, and neither were the Mets. The Mets were trying to make a transition from fading stars like Gary Carter and Keith Hernandez to players deemed the superstars of tomorrow like Gregg Jeffries and Dave Magadan, and they were still in the race. In 1988 the Expos were rough on the Cardinals, but in 1989 St. Louis was having no problem handling them. St. Louis had an even worse time with the Mets in 1988, and the season still contained thirteen head-to-head meetings between the two teams as June was ending, so the race could be perceived at the time as being up for grabs until those contests were over.

At the All-Star break on July 10, the Cardinals owned a 44–39 record, good enough for fourth place, 3 games behind the Expos and right in the hunt with the Mets and Cubs. Many people expected the Cardinals to put on another strong second-half performance to take the division, like they did in 1982, 1985, and 1987, and many people also thought the Expos would put on their usual second-half fade. The Cubs were also expected to fail, and that would leave only the Mets to battle the Cardinals for the division title. The Cardinals were getting great years out of Joe Magrane and Jose DeLeon, another solid year from Todd Worrell in the bullpen, and, in general, decent pitching, even though Danny Cox

354

and Greg Mathews were lost for the year. Pedro Guerrero continued to power the attack, and Jose Oquendo and Ozzie Smith both were hitting well and turning double plays. Terry Pendleton was hitting with the power of 1987 (but not the average of that year) and Milt Thompson was having an outstanding year in center as Willie McGee's year was being ruined by all sorts of injuries. Tom Brunansky was hitting the long ball as well, and although Vince Coleman was not hitting for a good average and was striking out too much, he was still going for yet another stolen base title. St. Louis seemed poised to get the job done.

Right after the All-Star break the Cardinals went to California and had a decent trip before going home to play 3 games against the Cubs. The Cardinals lost the first 2 games in tough fashion, 3–2 and 4–2, before pulling out a 2–0 shutout behind Jose DeLeon. Chicago was not fading as expected, since they took 2 of 3 from the Cardinals in St. Louis, then swept 3 from the Mets at home. If any team was fading it was the Mets, who closed July with a 7-game losing streak. The Expos were still playing well enough to stay in the race, and going into August the race still contained four teams.

The Cardinals faced the Mets at St. Louis for 4 games in a pivotal series that many thought would set the tone for the rest of the year. On July 31 DeLeon shut out the Mets for most of the way and ended up a 3–2 winner over Ron Darling. The next day the Mets bombed Scott Terry 11–0 as Sid Fernandez got the easy win. On August 2 New York sent newly acquired Frank Viola to the mound and he came out of a tough game with a 4–3 win. Both teams played another 1-run game, and this time the Cardinals prevailed in a battle of bullpens by a 6–5 score. The Mets went back home and swept 3 from the Expos, triggering Montreal's slide out of the race, while the Cardinals took care of the Phillies at home. A week later the Mets hosted the Cardinals for a big 5-game set. On the tenth the Cardinals dropped a twin bill by 5–1 and 6–4; then they came back to win 3–0 against Frank Viola. The Cardinals then dropped the last two contests by tough 3–1 and 3–2 scores. Suddenly the Mets looked like the team to beat and it looked like the Cardinals would follow the Expos right out of the race.

St. Louis, however, had no intention of fading away meekly. The hapless Braves visited the Cardinals for 4 games, and they were swept easily. The Cardinals then made a trip to Cincinnati, Atlanta, and Houston and went 6–4, keeping themselves in the hunt. The Mets went 3–6 in that span of games while the Cubs went 2–7, so the Cardinals were not about to fade. St. Louis still had 4 games left with New York and 6 with Chicago, including a season-ending series at home against the Cubs left for September–October.

On September 3 the Cardinals finished playing Western teams by taking 2 of 3 from the Astros at home. The fading Expos came to town next and split 2 games with the locals before the Cardinals went to New York for 2 games. The Cubs were struggling and so were the Mets, so all signs pointed to the flag going to St. Louis. The Mets managed to split the 2 games, but they were now playing very sluggishly. A 5–4 loss late in a game against the Dodgers in New York a few weeks earlier seemed to trouble the Mets greatly, and the Cardinal-Met series lacked the usual electricity. The Cardinals next had a big series in Chicago, and 2 wins out of 3 could have given the Cardinals the momentum needed to bag the flag.

On September 8 the Cardinals and Cubs engaged in a slugfest, but the visitors managed to outlast the locals 11–8. St. Louis was down 7–1 at one point, but the Cardinals fought back and won when Pedro Guerrero blasted a 3-run homer late in the game. The Cubs were in first place when the series began, but the tough loss cut their lead to just half a game. The next day, both teams were having another tough game. St. Louis held a 2–1 lead late in the game, but with Todd Worrell having elbow trouble the task of saving the game fell to Ken Dayley. Dwight Smith singled and took an extra base when Tom Brunansky hesitated in fielding the ball. A base hit fetched him home, and the game was tied. In the tenth the Cubs scored another run, and they were 3–2 winners. The game seemed to deflate the Cardinal balloon. The next day Scott Sanderson downed Ken Hill 4–1 and the Cardinals left Chicago trailing by 2½ games.

St. Louis returned home and played poorly against the Pirates, dropping 3 straight. The Cubs, revitalized by their win against the Cardinals on the ninth, kept playing well. The Cardinals tried to play well enough to make the season-ending series at home against the Cubs mean something, but they had problems and hope was

356

fading. The Cubs played well enough to put distance between themselves and the Cardinals and Mets, and that last series in St. Louis meant nothing. The Cardinals ended up third, 7 games behind the Cubs and 1 game behind the Mets for second place.

Despite having no bench and having had another year full of injury, the Cardinals surprised many people and had a solid year, contending from wire to wire. Willie McGee missed most of the year, but Milt Thompson did a great job in his stead, batting .290 and playing well in center. Vince Coleman hit only .254, but he did lead the league in steals with 65. Tom Brunansky hit only .239 but had 20 homers and 85 RBIs. Pedro Guerrero proved his critics wrong with a .311 average, 17 homers, and 117 RBIs. Ozzie Smith hit .273 while doing his usual great thing with the glove. Jose Oquendo batted .291, and Terry Pendleton hit .264 with 13 homers and 74 RBIs. Tony Pena hit .260. Obviously, the Cardinal offense improved tremendously over 1988. Joe Magrane won 18 and Jose DeLeon went 16–12 as the top two pitchers. Ken Hill was only 7–15 in his rookie year, but he showed promise. Scott Terry was 8–10 as a starter/reliever, and the bullpen did well again despite the loss of Todd Worrell in the last month of the season. All in all, 1989 was a good year for the Cardinals.

As the Cardinals looked forward to the new decade of the 1990s, they did so without the man who had saved the team from leaving town. On September 29, 1989, Gussie Busch died, at age ninety. Busch got along famously with White Herzog, and questions were raised about the direction the Cardinals were going to take now that big baseball fan Busch was gone. August Busch III took control of the Cardinals on his father's death and announced that past policy would be maintained. Herzog probably wondered what effect Busch's death would have on his status. Although Herzog had given up the post of general manager years earlier, he still had input in trade-making decisions and he would always shoot the breeze with the Cardinal boss. The Cardinals would now be run by people who were businessmen first and foremost and baseball fans second, so they might not like the idea of an employee telling them what they should do to improve their assets. As 1989 ended, though, nothing had changed concerning Herzog and the Cardinals.

The Cardinals spent most of the 1989 off-season signing their own players who were free agents. Danny Cox missed all of the 1989 season, and he was given a contract and was expected to bounce back. Rick Horton and Frank DiPino, two other free-agent Cardinals from the bullpen, were also retained. The Cardinals also moved to improve their rotation by signing free-agent Bryn Smith from the Expos and John Tudor from the Dodgers. St. Louis also picked up outfielder Dave Collins to shore up their bench and made a minor deal with the Phillies that sent Jim Lindeman, once a highly touted prospect, over to Philadelphia. The Cardinals made no alterations to their lineup, figuring that Willie McGee would bounce back from his injury-ruined 1989 campaign.

The Cardinals were expected to be tough in 1990, and they were also expected to give the Mets (yeah, they were picked by many yet again to win it) and Cubs as well as the Expos trouble. St. Louis hosted the Expos to open 1990, and the Cardinals won the first game of the new decade 6–5 in eleven innings. The next day, Bryn Smith downed his old team 4–2, and it looked like the Cardinals were off to a good start. St. Louis failed to steal 200 bases in 1989 for the first time since 1981, but everyone expected that to be changed in 1990. The Cardinals relied heavily on the power of Pedro Guerrero and Tom Brunansky in 1989, so in 1990 it would be back to basics. People were right about the Cardinals' relying too much on the big guns and not enough on running in 1989, and that situation would indeed change in 1990, but only because of problems.

Tom Brunansky got off to a miserable start, and after the 2–0 start the Cardinals began to struggle mightily. Milt Thompson also was hitting poorly, and right field was in disarray. Vince Coleman and Willie McGee were off to good starts, but Pedro Guerrero was not and the two big guns were leaving too many men on base. Even worse was the loss of ace reliever Todd Worrell, whose 1989 elbow injury was more severe than thought at first. Whitey Herzog had to go back to a bullpen by committee setup, but this time he did not have the capable men to get by and his bullpen looked more like the 1979 Royals bullpen than the 1985 Cardinals bullpen that Herzog had both managed.

The offense struggled throughout the first month and St. Louis began unloading players who were deemed disappointing. Tony Pena was sent to the Red Sox, and so was Tom Brunansky. Lee Smith, a flamethrowing reliever who was no longer needed by Boston after they picked up Jeff Reardon, promptly plugged the Cardinals' hole in the bullpen, but the team continued to struggle. The pitching rotation was in disarray as Danny Cox again failed to throw a pitch all year. Greg Mathews was still injured. Jose DeLeon, considered to have the stuff of a 20-game winner, was having a year that might produce 20 losses. Scott Terry struggled. Bryn Smith was having a good year and John Tudor was having a great year, but two starters don't carry a rotation.

St. Louis plunged into the cellar by June, and the team was en route to its worst year in a long time. Whitey Herzog was upset over the lackluster play of the team as the season was going down the drain. The situation was worsening in St. Louis because Willie McGee, Vince Coleman, and Terry Pendleton were all going to be free agents after the season, and the new bosses of the Cardinals were less than happy about that prospect. The Cardinals tried to talk trade with other teams over the three players, but the players offered were not to the liking of St. Louis. With three regulars heading for free agency, no team can keep its focus on winning for long, and the Cardinals were now in a rebuilding phase. Todd Zeile and Tom Pagnozzi shared the catching duties, but Zeile was struggling at the plate and behind it as well. Other players were auditioned for outfield jobs in right field, since Milt Thompson continued to struggle.

Whitey Herzog was increasingly agitated over what he perceived to be a lack of hustle and the will to win, and with Gussie Busch no longer around to talk with, Herzog was tired of the grind of managing. St. Louis was enduring a nightmare season as the All-Star break approached. On July 2 the Giants beat the Cardinals in San Francisco 3–2. The next day the Giants won again 4–0. Herzog was seeing enough. When the Giants completed a sweep with a 9–2 drubbing of the Cardinals on July 4, St. Louis owned a disastrous 34–47 mark and Herzog had had enough. After the game, Whitey Herzog announced that he was resigning as manager of the Cardinals. After ten years, the Whitey Herzog era in St. Louis was over. Coach Red Schoendienst took the helm for the third time in Cardinals history while a permanent manager was sought.

Under Schoendienst the Cardinals continued to slump while a new manager was being sought. Don Baylor was considered a top candidate, and so was former Cardinal Joe Torre. The Cardinals interviewed several candidates for the job in almost a month. Finally the Cardinals announced that Joe Torre was the man for the job. Torre had managed the Mets when they struggled in 1977–81, but he did a great job with the Braves in 1982–84. Torre took over on August 2, and he conducted experiments such as putting Todd Zeile at third base and looking at young pitchers like Omar Olivares. Ray Lankford and Bernard Gilkey were also tried out in right field and looked good.

On August 29, the Cardinals traded Willie McGee to the A's even though he was leading the league in hitting at .335. Oakland sent top outfield prospect Felix Jose to St. Louis with two minor leaguers. Torre placed Jose in right field, and he hit .271 while showing speed and power. St. Louis continued to struggle in the last month, but the youngsters were proving themselves as Torre presided over a youth movement. The Cardinals concluded 1990 with a weak 70–92 record and finished last for the first time since 1918, but at least there was hope for the future. Joe Torre would now preside over the start of the Cardinals' second century.

Part VIII

The Next Century (1990–   )

The Cardinals did indeed lose Terry Pendleton and Vince Coleman to free agency after the 1990 season, but they would be replaced by Todd Zeile and Felix Jose. The Cardinals went into 1991 expecting to be a last-place team as they continued to rebuild. The outfield would now feature Jose, Ray Lankford, Bernard Gilkey, and even Milt Thompson. The infield would have Zeile at third, Ozzie Smith at short, Jose Oquendo at second, and Pedro Guerrero at first. Tom Pagnozzi would do the bulk of the catching after being a backup for the last three years. John Tudor retired after a great last year, but the rotation would be anchored by Bryn Smith, Joe Magrane, and Jose DeLeon. Lee Smith was going to be the workhorse in the bullpen. Joe Torre was going to have to lead the Cardinals to another surprising season to start their second century in the National League.

The Cardinals did start well in 1991, staying ahead of the weak Phillies, the disappointing Cubs, and the even more disappointing Expos for much of the early going. The Cubs finally were the favorite to win instead of the Mets, but it was the Mets who challenged the Pirates, while the Cubs had pitching problems. Bernard Gilkey and Ray Lankford struggled, but Felix Jose was sensational in his first full year, going for a batting title for much of the year. Lee Smith was having the best season of his great career, leading the league in saves. Ozzie Smith was in the last year of his contract and there were rumors that he would be traded to the Dodgers, but Smith had his usual fine year all around and finished out the year in St. Louis. The pitching staff held up well, and in the second half the Cardinals left the Expos and Phillies behind for good while edging past the Cubs for third place. In August, the Cardinals dealt their old pals the Mets a few crippling losses, sending them out of the race and moving themselves into the second place position. As September came the Cardinals were still stealing bases, and with the Mets fading badly, the Cardinals were the only team to get close to the powerful Pirates. The Pirates, though, took off, and the Cardinals had to settle for second place. After everyone figured the Cardinals would finish last, St. Louis was the only club other than Pittsburgh to finish with a winning record and easily took second place.

So Joe Torre did a great job in his first full year as the manager of the Cardinals. St. Louis has plenty of speed and youth that will make them a tough team to beat in the years to come. The Cardinals of 1991 were simply the latest of a long line of surprising Cardinal clubs that surpassed expectations, and they will be a force to reckon with in the future. At least the St. Louis Cardinals will begin their second century in the National League on a far better footing than they started their first one hundred years.

Appendixes

Appendix A

National League Standings of the Cardinals

Year	Won-Lost	Pct.	GB	Pos	Year	Won-Lost	Pct.	GB	Pos
1892	31–42*	.425	22¼	9th	1920	75–79	.487	18	5th**
	25–52+	.325	28½	11th	1921	87–66	.569	7	3d
	56–94‡	.373	46	11th	1922	85–69	.552	8	3d**
1893	57–75	.432	30½	10th	1923	79–74	.516	16	5th
1894	56–76	.424	35	9th	1924	65–89	.422	28½	6th
1895	39–92	.298	48½	11th	1925	77–76	.503	18	4th
1896	40–90	.308	50½	11th	1926	89–65	.578	—	1st
1897	29–102	.221	63½	12th	1927	92–61	.601	1½	2d
1898	39–111	.260	63½	12th	1928	95–59	.617	—	1st
1899	84–67	.556	18½	5th	1929	78–74	.513	20	4th
1900	65–75	.464	19	5th**	1930	92–62	.597	—	1st
1901	76–64	.543	14½	4th	1931	101–53	.656	—	1st
1902	56–78	.418	44½	6th	1932	72–82	.468	18	6th**
1903	43–94	.314	46½	8th	1933	82–71	.536	9½	5th
1904	75–79	.487	31½	5th	1934	95–58	.621	—	1st
1905	58–96	.377	47½	6th	1935	96–58	.623	4	2d
1906	52–98	.347	63	7th	1936	87–67	.565	5	2d**
1907	52–101	.340	55½	8th	1937	81–73	.526	15	4th
1908	49–105	.318	50	8th	1938	71–80	.470	17½	6th
1909	54–98	.355	56	7th	1939	92–61	.601	4½	2d
1910	63–90	.412	40½	7th	1940	84–69	.549	16	3d
1911	75–74	.503	22	5th	1941	97–56	.634	2½	2d
1912	63–90	.412	41	6th	1942	106–48	.688	—	1st
1913	51–99	.340	49	8th	1943	105–49	.682	—	1st
1914	81–72	.529	13	3d	1944	105–49	.682	—	1st
1915	72–81	.471	18½	6th	1945	95–59	.617	3	2d
1916	60–93	.392	33½	7th**	1946	98–58	.628	—	1st++
1917	82–70	.539	15	3d	1947	89–65	.578	5	2d
1918	51–78	.395	33	8th	1948	85–69	.552	6½	2d
1919	54–83	.394	40½	7th	1949	96–58	.623	1	2d

Year	Won-Lost	Pct.	GB	P
1950	78–75	.510	12½	5th
1951	81–73	.526	15½	3d
1952	88–66	.571	8½	3d
1953	83–71	.539	22	3d**
1954	72–82	.468	25	6th
1955	68–86	.442	30½	7th
1956	76–78	.494	17	4th
1957	87–67	.565	8	2d
1958	72–82	.468	20	5th**
1959	71–83	.461	16	7th
1960	86–68	.558	9	3d
1961	80–74	.519	13	5th
1962	84–78	.519	17½	6th
1963	93–69	.574	6	2d
1964	93–69	.574	—	1st
1965	80–81	.497	16½	7th
1966	83–79	.512	12	6th
1967	101–60	.627	—	1st
1968	97–65	.599	—	1st
1969	87–75	.537	13	4th
1970	76–86	.469	13	4th
1971	90–72	.556	7	2d
1972	75–81	.481	21½	4th
1973	81–81	.500	1½	2d
1974	86–75	.534	1½	2d
1975	82–80	.506	10½	3d*
1976	72–90	.444	29	5th
1977	83–79	.512	18	3d
1978	69–93	.426	21	5th
1979	86–76	.531	12	3d

Year	Won-Lost	Pct.	GB	P
1980	74–88	.457	17	4th
1981	30–20*	.600	1½	2d
	29–23+	.558	½	2d
	59–43‡	.578	—	1st
1982	92–70	.568	—	1st
1983	79–83	.488	11	4th
1984	84–78	.519	12½	3d
1985	101–61	.623	—	1st
1986	79–82	.491	28½	3d
1987	95–67	.586	—	1st
1988	76–86	.469	25	5th
1989	86–76	.531	7	3d
1990	70–92	.432	25	6th
1991	84–78	.519	14	2d

*First half.
**Tied for position.
+Second half.
‡Overall record.
++Defeated Brooklyn two games to none in pennant playoff.
Note: Standings for 1892–99 are for a twelve-team league. Standings for 1900–61 are for an eight-team league. Standings for 1962–68 are for a ten-team league. Standings for 1969–91 are for a six-team Eastern Division. Eighteen-ninety-two standings reflect split-season format used that year. Nineteen-eighty-one standings reflect split season due to strike.

Appendix B
The All-time Cardinal Roster (1892–1991)

Ody Abbott, 1910
Ted Abernathy, 1970
Babe Adams, 1906
Buster Adams, 1939, 1943,
   1945–46
Joe Adams, 1902
Sparky Adams, 1930–33
Jim Aducci, 1983
Henry Adkinson, 1895
Tommie Agee, 1973
Juan Agosto, 1991–
Eddie Ainsmith, 1921–23
Gibson Alba, 1988
Cy Alberts, 1910
Grover Alexander,* 1926–29
Luis Alicea, 1988, 1991–
Dick Allen, 1970
Ethan Allen, 1933
Neil Allen, 1983–85
Ron Allen, 1972
Matty Alou, 1971–2, 1973
Tom Alston, 1954–57
Walt Alston,* 1936
George Altman, 1963
Luis Alvarado, 1974, 1976
Brant Alyea, 1972
Ruben Amaro, 1958
Red Ames, 1915–18
Craig Anderson, 1961
Dwain Anderson, 1972–73
Ferrell Anderson, 1953
George Anderson, 1918

John Anderson, 1962
Mike Anderson, 1976–77
John Andrews, 1973
Nate Andrews, 1937, 1939
Joaquin Andujar, 1981–85
Pat Ankenman, 1936
John Antonelli, 1944–45
Harry Arndt, 1905–7
Scott Arnold, 1988
Luis Arroyo, 1955
Rudy Arroyo, 1971
Dennis Aust, 1965–66
Benny Ayala, 1977
Les Backman, 1909–10
Bill Bailey, 1921–22
Doug Bair, 1981–83, 1985
Doug Baird, 1917–18, 1919
Dave Balenhaster, 1964
Bill Baker, 1948–49
Steve Baker, 1983
Ollie Baldwin, 1908
Art Ball, 1894
Jimmy Bannon, 1893
Jap Barbeau, 1909–10
George Barclay, 1902–4
Ray Bare, 1972, 1974
Clyde Barfoot, 1922–23
Greg Bargar, 1986
Mike Barlow, 1975
Frank Barnes, 1957–58, 1960
Skeeter Barnes, 1987
Frank Barrett, 1939

369

Red Barrett, 1945–46
Shad Barry, 1906–8
Dave Bartosch, 1945
Frank Bates, 1899
Ed Bauta, 1960–63
John Baxter, 1907
Johnny Beall, 1918
Ralph Beard, 1954
Jim Beauchamp, 1963, 1970–71
Johnny Beazley, 1941–42, 1946
Zinn Beck, 1913–16
Jake Beckley,* 1904–7
Bill Beckmann, 1942
Fred Beebe, 1906–9
Ed Beecher, 1897
Clarence Beers, 1948
Hi Bell, 1924, 1926–30
Les Bell, 1923–27
Joe Benes, 1931
Pug Bennett, 1906–7
Vern Benson, 1951–53
Sid Benton, 1922
Augie Bergamo, 1944–45
Jack Berly, 1924
Joe Bernard, 1909
Frank Bertaina, 1970
Harry Berte, 1903
Bob Bescher, 1915–17
Frank Betcher, 1910
Hal Betts, 1903
Bruno Betzel, 1914–18
Jim Bibby, 1972–73
Louis Bierbauer, 1897–98
Steve Bilko, 1949–54
Dick Billings, 1974–75
Frank Bird, 1892
Ray Blades, 1922–28, 1930–32
Harry Blake, 1899
Sheriff Blake, 1937
Coonie Blank, 1909
Don Blasingame, 1955–59
Johnny Blatnik, 1950

Buddy Blattner, 1942
Bob Blaylock, 1956, 1959
John Bliss, 1908–12
Clyde Bloomfield, 1963
Charlie Boardman, 1915
Joe Boever, 1985–86
Sammy Bohne, 1916
Dick Bokelmann, 1951–53
Bill Bolden, 1919
Don Bollweg, 1950–51
Bobby Bonds, 1980
Frank Bonner, 1895
Rod Booker, 1987–89
Pedro Borbon, 1980
Frenchy Bordagaray, 1937–38
Rick Bosetti, 1977
Jim Bottomley,* 1922–32
Bob Bowman, 1939–40
Cloyd Boyer, 1949–52
Ken Boyer, 1955–65
Buddy Bradford, 1975
Dave Brain, 1903–5
Harvey Branch, 1962
Jackie Brandt, 1956
Kitty Brashear, 1902
Joe Bratcher, 1924
Steve Braun, 1981–85
Al Brazle, 1943, 1946–54
Harry Brecheen, 1940, 1943–52
Ted Breitenstein, 1892–96, 1901
Herb Bremer, 1937–39
Roger Bresnahan,* 1909–12
Rube Bressler, 1932
Ed Bressoud, 1967
Rod Brewer, 1990–
Marshall Bridges, 1959–60
Rocky Bridges, 1960
Grant Briggs, 1892
Nellie Briles, 1965–70
Ed Brinkman, 1975
John Brock, 1917–18
Lou Brock,* 1964–79

Steve Brodie, 1892–93
Ernie Broglio, 1959–64
Herman Bronkie, 1918
Jim Brosnan, 1958–59
Tony Brottem, 1916, 1918
Buster Brown, 1905–7
Don Brown, 1915
Jimmy Brown, 1937–43
Three Finger Brown, 1903
Tom Brown, 1895
Willard Brown, 1894
Byron Browne, 1969
Cal Browning, 1960
Pete Browning, 1894
Glenn Brummer, 1981–84
Tom Brunansky, 1988–90
George Brunet, 1971
Tom Bruno, 1978–79
Ron Bryant, 1975
Johnny Bucha, 1948, 1950
Jerry Buchek, 1961, 1963–66
Jim Bucher, 1938
Dick Buckley, 1892–94
Fritz Buelow, 1899–1900
Nels Burbrink, 1955
Al Burch, 1906–7
Bob Burda, 1962, 1971
Lew Burdette, 1963–64
Tom Burgess, 1954
Sandy Burk, 1912–13
Jimmy Burke, 1903–5
John Burke, 1899
Leo Burke, 1963
Jesse Burkett,* 1899–1901
Ken Burkhart, 1945–48
Jack Burnett, 1907
Ed Burns, 1912
Farmer Burns, 1901
Ray Burris, 1986
Ellis Burton, 1958, 1960
Guy Bush, 1938
Ray Busse, 1973

Art Butler, 1914–16
John Butler, 1904
Johnny Butler, 1929
Bud Byerly, 1943–45
Bill Byers, 1904
Al Cabrera, 1913
John Calhoun, 1902
Jim Callahan, 1898
Wes Callahan, 1913
Harry Camnitz, 1911
Llewellan Camp, 1892
Bill Campbell, 1985
Billy Campbell, 1905
Dave Campbell, 1973
Jim Campbell, 1970
Sal Campisi, 1969–70
Chris Cannizzaro, 1960–61
Doug Capilla, 1976–77
Bernie Carbo, 1972–73, 1979–80
Jose Cardenal, 1970–71
Tex Carlton, 1932–34
Steve Carlton, 1965–71
Duke Carmel, 1959–60, 1963
Cris Carpenter, 1988–
Hick Carpenter, 1892
Clay Carroll, 1977
Cliff Carroll, 1892
Kid Carsey, 1897–98
Bob Caruthers, 1892
Pete Castiglione, 1953–54
Danny Cater, 1975
Ted Cather, 1912–14
Cesar Cedeno, 1985
Orlando Cepeda, 1966–68
Bill Chambers, 1910
Cliff Chambers, 1951–53
John Chambers, 1937
Charlie Chant, 1976
Chappy Charles, 1908–9
Tom Cheney, 1957, 1959
Cupid Childs, 1899
Pete Childs, 1901

371

Nels Chittum, 1958
Bob Chlupsa, 1970–71
Larry Ciaffone, 1951
Al Cicotte, 1961
Gino Cimoli, 1959
Ralph Citarella, 1983–84
Doug Clarey, 1976
Danny Clark, 1927
Jack Clark, 1985–87
Jim Clark, 1911–12
Mark Clark, 1991–
Mike Clark, 1952–53
Phil Clark, 1958–59
Josh Clarke, 1905
Dad Clarkson, 1893–95
Doug Clemens, 1960–64
Jack Clements, 1898
Lance Clemons, 1972
Verne Clemons, 1919–24
Donn Clendenon, 1972
Reggie Cleveland, 1969–73
Tony Cloninger, 1972
Ed Clough, 1924–26
Dick Cole, 1951
John Coleman, 1895
Percy Coleman, 1897
Vince Coleman, 1985–90
Dave Collins, 1990
Phil Collins, 1935
Ripper Collins, 1931–36
Jackie Collum, 1951–53, 1956
Bob Coluccio, 1978
Joseph Connor, 1895
Roger Connor,* 1894–97
Tim Conroy, 1986–87
Ed Conwell, 1911
Duff Cooley, 1893–96
Jimmy Cooney, 1924–25
Mort Cooper, 1938–45
Walker Cooper, 1940–45, 1956–57
Mays Copeland, 1935
Joe Corbett, 1904

Roy Corhan, 1916
Rheal Cormier, 1991–
Pat Corrales, 1966
Frank Corridon, 1910
Jim Cosman, 1966–67
John Costello, 1988–89
Tom Coulter, 1969
John Coveney, 1903
Bill Cox, 1936
Danny Cox, 1983–88
Estel Crabtree, 1933, 1941–42
Roger Craig, 1964
Doc Crandall, 1913
Forrest Crawford, 1906–7
Glenn Crawford, 1945
Pat Crawford, 1933–34
Willie Crawford, 1976
Jack Creel, 1945
Bernie Creger, 1947
Creepy Crespi, 1938–42
Lou Criger, 1899–1900
Jack Crimian, 1951–52
Jack Crooks, 1892–93, 1898
Ed Crosby, 1970, 1972–73
Jeff Cross, 1942, 1946–48
Lave Cross, 1898, 1899–1900
Monte Cross, 1896–97
Bill Crouch, 1941, 1945
George Crowe, 1959–61
Walt Cruise, 1914, 1916–19
Gene Crumling, 1945
Hector Cruz, 1973, 1975–77
Jose Cruz, 1970–74
Tommy Cruz, 1973
Mike Cuellar, 1964
George Culver, 1970
John Cumberland, 1972
Joe Cunningham, 1954, 1956–61
Ray Cunningham, 1931–32
Nig Cuppy, 1899
Clarence Currie, 1902–3
Murphy Currie, 1916

John Curtis, 1974–76
John D'Acquisto, 1977
Gene Dale, 1911–12
Jack Damaska, 1963
Pete Daniels, 1898
Rolla Daringer, 1914–15
Alvin Dark, 1956–58
Vic Davalillo, 1969–70
Jerry DaVanon, 1969–70, 1974, 1977
Curt Davis, 1938–40
Jim Davis, 1957
Kiddo Davis, 1934
Ron Davis, 1968
Spud Davis, 1928, 1934–36
Willie Davis, 1975
Bill Dawley, 1987
Boots Day, 1969
Pea Ridge Day, 1924–25
Ken Dayley, 1984–90
Cot Deal, 1950, 1954
Dizzy Dean,* 1930, 1932–37
Paul Dean, 1934–39
Doug DeCinces, 1987
George Decker, 1898
Tony DeFate, 1917
Rube DeGroff, 1905–6
Ivan DeJesus, 1985
Bobby Del Greco, 1956
Joe Delahanty, 1907–9
Bill DeLancey, 1932, 1934–35, 1940
Art Delaney, 1924
Jose DeLeon, 1989–
Luis DeLeon, 1981
Eddie Delker,1929, 1931–32
Wheezer Dell, 1912
Frank Demaree, 1943
Lee DeMontreville, 1903
Don Dennis, 1965–66
John Denny, 1974–79
Paul Derringer, 1931–33

Russ Derry, 1949
Joe DeSa, 1980
Leo Dickerman, 1924–25
Murry Dickson, 1939–40, 1942–43, 1946–48, 1956–57
Chuck Diering, 1947–51
Larry Dierker, 1977
Pat Dillard, 1900
Pickles Dillhoefer, 1919–21
Mike Dimmel, 1979
Frank DiPino, 1989–90
Dutch Distel, 1918
Bill Doak, 1913–24, 1929
George Dockins, 1945
Cozy Dolan, 1914–15
John Dolan, 1893
Red Donahue, 1895–97
She Donahue, 1904
Mike Donlin, 1899–1900
Blix Donnelly, 1944–46
Jim Donnelly, 1898
Patsy Donovan, 1900–1903
Klondike Douglass, 1896—97
Taylor Douthit, 1923–31
Tommy Dowd, 1893–97, 1898
Dave Dowling, 1964
Carl Doyle, 1940
Jeff Doyle, 1983
Moe Drabowsky, 1971–72
Lee Dressen, 1914
Rob Dressler, 1978
Dan Driessen, 1987
Carl Druhot, 1906–7
Bob Duliba, 1959–60, 1962
Taylor Duncan, 1977
Wiley Dunham, 1902
Grant Dunlap, 1953
Jack Dunleavy, 1903–5
Don Durham, 1972
Joe Durham, 1959
Leon Durham, 1980, 1989
Leo Durocher, 1933–37

Erv Dusak, 1941–42, 1946–51
Jim Dwyer, 1973–75, 1977–78
Eddie Dyer, 1922–27
Bill Earley, 1986
George Earnshaw, 1936
John Easton, 1892
Rawley Eastwick, 1977
Johnny Echols, 1939
Al Eckert, 1935
Joe Edelen, 1981
Johnny Edwards, 1968
Wish Egan, 1905–6
Red Ehret, 1895
Harry Elliott, 1953, 1955
Jim Ellis, 1969
Rube Ellis, 1909–12
Bones Ely, 1893–95
Bill Endicott, 1946
Del Ennis, 1957–58
Charlie Enwright, 1909
Hal Epps, 1938, 1940
Eddie Erautt, 1953
Duke Esper, 1897–98
Chuck Essegian, 1959
Roy Evans, 1897
Steve Evans, 1909–13
Bob Ewing, 1912
Reuben Ewing, 1921
Ron Fairly, 1975–76
Pete Falcone, 1976–78
George Fallon, 1943–45
Harry Fanok, 1963–64
Doc Farrell, 1930
John Farrell, 1902–5
Bobby Fenwick, 1973
Joe Ferguson, 1976
Don Ferrarese, 1962
Neil Fiala, 1981
Mike Fiore, 1972
Sam Fishburn, 1919
Bob Fisher, 1918–19
Mike Fitzgerald, 1988

Max Flack, 1922–25
Tom Flanigan, 1958
Curt Flood, 1958–69
Tim Flood, 1899
Ben Flowers, 1955–56
Jake Flowers, 1923, 1926,
  1931–32
Rick Folkers, 1972–74
Curt Ford, 1985–88
Hod Ford, 1932
Bob Forsch, 1974–88
Alan Foster, 1973–74
Jack Fournier, 1920–22
Jesse Fowler, 1924
Earl Francis, 1965
Tito Francona, 1965–66
Charlie Frank, 1893–94
Fred Frankhouse, 1927–30
Herman Franks, 1939
Willie Fraser, 1991–
George Frazier, 1978–80
Joe Frazier, 1954–56
Roger Freed, 1977–79
Gene Freese, 1958
Howard Freigau, 1922–25
Benny Frey, 1932
Frankie Frisch,* 1927–37
Danny Frisella, 1976
Art Fromme, 1906–8
John Fulgham, 1979–80
Chick Fullis, 1934–35
Les Fusselman, 1952–53
Phil Gagliano, 1963–70
Del Gainor, 1922
Fred Gaiser, 1908
Bad News Galloway, 1912
Pud Galvin,* 1892
Bill Gannon, 1898
Joe Garagiola, 1946–51
Danny Gardella, 1950
Glenn Gardner, 1945
Art Garibaldi, 1936

Mike Garman, 1974–75
Debs Garms, 1943–45
Wayne Garrett, 1978
Rich Gedman, 1991–
Charley Gelbert, 1929–32, 1935–36
Frank Genins, 1892
Al Gettel, 1955
Charlie Getzien, 1892
Rube Geyer, 1910–13
Bob Gibson,* 1959–75
Billy Gilbert, 1908–9
George Gilham, 1920–21
Frank Gilhooley, 1911–12
Bernard Gilkey, 1990–
Carden Gillenwater, 1940
George Gillpatrick, 1898
Hal Gilson, 1968
Dave Giusti, 1969
Jack Glasscock, 1892–93
Tommy Glaviano, 1949–52
Kid Gleason, 1892–94
Bob Glenn, 1920
Harry Glenn, 1915
John Glenn, 1960
Danny Godby, 1974
Roy Golden, 1910–11
HaL Goldsmith, 1929
Julio Gonzalez, 1981–82
Mike Gonzalez, 1915–18, 1924–25, 1931–32
Bill Goodenough, 1893
Marv Goodwin, 1917, 1919–22
George Gore, 1892
Herb Gorman, 1952
Hank Gornicki, 1941
Julio Gotay, 1960–62
Al Grabowski, 1929–30
Mike Grady, 1897, 1904–6
Alex Grammas, 1954–56, 1959–62
Wayne Granger, 1968, 1973
Mudcat Grant, 1969

Mark Grater, 1991–
Dick Gray, 1959–60
Bill Greason, 1954
David Green, 1981–84, 1987
Gene Green, 1957–59
Bill Greif, 1976
Tim Griesenbeck, 1920
Tom Grieve, 1979
Sandy Griffin, 1893
Bob Grim, 1960
Burleigh Grimes,* 1930–31, 1933–34
John Grimes, 1897
Charlie Grimm, 1918
Dan Griner, 1912–16
Marv Grissom, 1959
Dick Groat, 1963–65
Johnny Grodzicki, 1941, 1946–47
Joe Grzenda, 1972
Mario Guerrero, 1975
Pedro Guerrero, 1988–
Harry Gumbert, 1941–44
Joe Gunson, 1893
Don Gutteridge, 1936–40
Santiago Guzman, 1969–72
Bob Habenicht, 1951
Jim Hackett, 1902–3
Harvey Haddix, 1952–56
Chick Hafey,* 1924–31
Casey Hageman, 1914
Kevin Hagen, 1983–84
Joe Hague, 1968–72
Don Hahn, 1975
Fred Hahn, 1952
Hal Haid, 1928–30
Ed Haigh, 1892
Pop Haines,* 1920–37
Charley Hall, 1916
Russ Hall, 1898
Bill Hallahan, 1925–25, 1929–36
Bill Hallman, 1897
Dave Hamilton, 1978

Fred Haney, 1929
Larry Haney, 1973
Dick Harley, 1897–98
Bob Harmon, 1909–13
Chuck Harmon, 1956–57
Brian Harper, 1985
George Harper, 1928
Jack Harper, 1900–1901
Vic Harris, 1976
Bill Hart, 1896–7
Chuck Hartenstein, 1970
Fred Hartman, 1897, 1902
Andy Hassler, 1984–85
Grady Hatton, 1956
Arnold Hauser, 1910–13
Bill Hawke,1892–93
Pink Hawley, 1892–94
Doc Hazleton, 1902
Francis Healy, 1934
Bunny Hearn, 1910–11
Jim Hearn, 1947–50
Mike Heath, 1986
Cliff Heathcote, 1918–22
Jack Heidemann, 1974
Emmet Heidrick, 1899–1901
Don Heinkel, 1989
Tom Heintzelman, 1973–74
Bob Heise, 1974
Clarence Heise, 1934
Charlie Hemphill, 1899
Solly Hemus, 1949–56, 1959
George Hendrick, 1978–84
Harvey Hendrick, 1932
Roy Henshaw, 1938
Keith Hernandez, 1974–83
Larry Herndon, 1974
Tommy Herr, 1979–88
Neal Hertweck, 1952
Ed Heusser, 1935–36
Mike Heydon, 1901
Jim Hickman, 1974
Jim Hicks, 1969

Irv Higginbotham, 1906, 1908–9
Dennis Higgins, 1909–10
Andy High, 1928–31
Palmer Hildebrand, 1913
Tom Hilgendorf, 1969–70
Carmen Hill, 1929–30
Hugh Hill, 1904
Ken Hill, 1988–
Marc Hill, 1973–74
Jack Himes, 1905–6
Bruce Hitt, 1917
Glen Hobbie, 1964
Ed Hock, 1920
Art Hoelskoetter, 1905–8
Joe Hoerner, 1966–69
Marty Hogan, 1894–95
Mul Holland, 1929
Ed Holly, 1906–7
Wattie Holm, 1924–29, 1932
Ducky (Howard Elbert) Holmes,
   1906
Ducky (James William) Holmes,
   1898
Don Hood, 1980
Sis Hopkins, 1907
Johnny Hopp, 1939–45
Bill Hopper, 1913–14
Bob Horner, 1988
Rogers Hornsby,* 1915–26, 1933
Oscar Horstmann, 1917–19
Rick Horton, 1984–87, 1989–90
Paul Householder, 1984
John Houseman, 1897
Doug Howard, 1975
Earl Howard, 1918
Art Howe, 1984–85
Roland Howell, 1912
Bill Howerton, 1949–51
Al Hrabosky, 1970–77
Jimmy Hudgens, 1923
Rex Hudler, 1990–
Charles Hudson, 1972

Frank Huelsman, 1897
Miller Huggins,* 1910–16
Dick Hughes, 1966–68
Terry Hughes, 1973
Tom Hughes, 1959
Jim Hughey, 1898, 1900
Rudy Hulswitt, 1909–10
Bob Humphreys, 1963–64
Ben Hunt, 1913
Joel Hunt, 1931–32
Randy Hunt, 1985
Ron Hunt, 1974
Herb Hunter, 1921
Steve Huntz, 1967, 1969
Walter Huntzinger, 1926
Clint Hurdle, 1986
Bill Hutchinson, 1897
Ira Hutchinson, 1940–41
Ham Hyatt, 1915
Pat Hynes, 1903
Dane Iorg, 1977–84
Walt Irwin, 1921
Ray Jablonski, 1953–54, 1959
Al Jackson, 1966–67
Larry Jackson, 1955–62
Mike Jackson, 1971
Elmer Jacobs, 1919–20
Bert James, 1909
Charlie James, 1960–64
Hal Janvrin, 1919–21
Hi Jasper, 1916
Larry Jaster, 1965–68
Julian Javier, 1960–71
Hal Jeffcoat, 1959
Adam Johnson, 1918
Alex Johnson, 1966–67
Billy Johnson, 1951–53
Bob Johnson, 1969
Darrell Johnson, 1960
Jerry Johnson, 1970
Ken Johnson, 1947–50
Lance Johnson, 1987

Si Johnson, 1936–38
Syl Johnson, 1926–33
Cowboy Jones, 1899–1901
Gordon Jones, 1954–56
Howie Jones, 1921
Nippy Jones, 1946–51
Red Jones, 1940
Sam Jones, 1957–58, 1963
Tim Jones, 1988–
Bubber Jonnard, 1929
Mike Jorgensen, 1984–85
Felix Jose, 1990–
Lyle Judy, 1935
Al Jurisch, 1944–45
Skip Jutze, 1972
Jim Kaat, 1980–83
Ed Karger, 1906–8
Eddie Kasko, 1957–58
Ray Katt, 1956, 1958–59
Tony Kaufman, 1927–28,
   1930–31, 1935
Marty Kavanagh, 1918
Eddie Kazak, 1948–52
Bob Keely, 1944–45
Vic Keen, 1926–27
Jeff Keener, 1982–83
Bill Keister, 1900
John Kelleher, 1912
Mick Kelleher, 1972–73, 1975
Al Kellner, 1959
Win Kellum, 1905
Bill Kelly, 1910
John Kelly, 1907
Jim Kennedy, 1970
Terry Kennedy, 1978–80
Matt Keough, 1985
Kurt Kepshire, 1984–86
George Kernek, 1965–66
Don Kessinger, 1976–77
Newt Kimball, 1940
Hal Kime, 1920
Wally Kimmick, 1919

Ellis Kinder, 1956
Charlie King, 1959
Jim King, 1957
Lynn King, 1935–36, 1939
Walt Kinlock, 1895
Tom Kinslow, 1898
Matt Kinzer, 1989
Mike Kircher, 1920–21
Bill Kissinger, 1895–97
Lou Klein, 1943, 1945–46, 1949
Nub Kleinke, 1935–37
Ron Kline, 1960
Rudy Kling, 1902
Clyde Kluttz, 1946
Alan Knicely, 1986
Jack Knight, 1922
Mike Knode, 1920
Darold Knowles, 1979–80
Will Koenigsmark, 1919
Gary Kolb, 1960, 1962–63
Ed Konetchy, 1907–13
Jim Konstanty, 1956
George Kopshaw, 1923
Ernie Koy, 1940–41
Lew Krausse, 1973
Kurt Krieger, 1949, 1951
Howie Krist, 1937–38, 1941–43,
    1946
Otto Krueger, 1900–1902
Ted Kubiak, 1971
Willie Kuehne, 1892
Ryan Kurosaki, 1975
Whitey Kurowski, 1941–49
Bob Kuzava, 1957
Mike Laga, 1986–88
Lerrin LaGrow, 1976
Jeff Lahti, 1982–86
Eddie Lake,1939–41
Steve Lake, 1986–88
Bud Lally, 1897
Jack Lamabe, 1967
Fred Lamline, 1915

Hobie Landrith, 1957–58
Don Landrum, 1960–62
Tito Landrum, 1980–83, 1984–87
Don Lang, 1948
Max Lanier, 1938–46, 1949–51
Ray Lankford, 1990–
Paul LaPalme, 1955–56
Dave LaPoint, 1981–84, 1987
Ralph LaPointe, 1948
Bob Larmore, 1918
Lyn Lary, 1939
Don Lassetter, 1957
Arlie Latham, 1896
Mike LaValliere, 1985–86
Doc Lavan, 1919–24
Tom Lawless, 1985–88
Brooks Lawrence, 1954–55
Tom Leahy, 1905
Leron Lee, 1969–71
Jim Lentine, 1978–80
Barry Lersch, 1974
Roy Leslie, 1919
Dan Lewandowski, 1951
Bill Lewis, 1933
Johnny Lewis, 1964
Sixto Lezcano, 1981
Don Liddle, 1956
Gene Lillard, 1940
Bob Lillis, 1961
Johnny Lindell, 1950
Jim Lindeman, 1986–89
Jim Lindsey, 1929–33, 1934
Royce Lint, 1954
Larry Lintz, 1975
Frank Linzy, 1970–71
Mark Littell, 1978–82
Jeff Little, 1980
Dick Littlefield, 1953
John Littlefield, 1980
Carlisle Littlejohn, 1927–28
Danny Litwhiler, 1943–44, 1946
Paddy Livingston, 1917

Larry Locke, 1962
Whitey Lockman, 1956
Bill Lohrman, 1942
Jeoff Long, 1963–64
Tommy Long, 1915–17
Art Lopatka, 1945
Aurelio Lopez, 1978
Joe Lotz, 1916
Lynn Lovenguth, 1957
John Lovett, 1903
Grover Lowdermilk, 1909, 1911
Lou Lowdermilk, 1911–12
Peanuts Lowery, 1950–54
Con Lucid, 1897
Bill Ludwig, 1908
Memo Luna, 1954
Ernie Lush, 1910
Johnny Lush, 1907–10
Bill Lyons, 1983–84
Denny Lyons, 1895
George Lyons, 1920
Hersh Lyons, 1941
Bob Mabe, 1958
Ken MacKenzie, 1963
Johnny Mackinson, 1955
Max Macon, 1938
Bill Magee, 1901
Lee Magee, 1911–14
Sal Maglie, 1958
Joe Magrane, 1987–90
Art Mahaffey, 1966
Mike Mahoney, 1898
Duster Mails, 1925–26
Jim Mallory, 1945
Gus Mancuso, 1928, 1930–32,
    1941–42
Les Mann, 1921–23
Fred Manrique, 1986
Rabbit Maranville,* 1927–28
Walt Marbet, 1913
Marty Marion, 1940–50
Roger Maris, 1967–68

Fred Marolewski, 1953
Charlie Marshall, 1941
Doc Marshall, 1906–8
Joe Marshall, 1906
Freddie Martin, 1946, 1949–50
John Martin, 1980–83
Morrie Martin, 1957–58
Pepper Martin, 1928, 1930–40,
    1944
Stu Martin, 1936–40
Marty Martinez, 1972
Silvio Martinez, 1978–81
Teddy Martinez, 1975
Ernie Mason, 1894
Greg Mathews, 1986–88, 1990
Wally Mattick, 1918
Gene Mauch, 1952
Harry Maupin, 1898
Dal Maxvill, 1962–72
Jakie May, 1917–21
Jack McAdams, 1911
Ike McAuley, 1917
Bake McBride, 1973–77
George McBride, 1905–6
Joe McCarthy, 1906
Lew McCarty, 1920–21
Tim McCarver, 1959–61, 1963–69,
    1973–74
Pat McCauley, 1893
Bob McClure, 1991–
Billy McCool, 1970
Jim McCormick, 1892
Harry McCurdy, 1922–23
Lindy McDaniel, 1955–62
Von McDaniel, 1957–58
Mickey McDermott, 1961
John McDougal, 1895–96
John (Sandy) McDougal, 1905
Will McEnaney, 1979
Guy McFadden, 1895
Chappie McFarland, 1902–6
Ed McFarland, 1896–97

Dan McGann, 1900–1901
Bill McGee, 1935–41
Willie McGee, 1982–90
Dan McGeehan, 1911
Jim McGinley, 1904–5
Lynn McGlothen, 1974–76
Stoney McGlynn, 1906–8
Bob McGraw, 1927
John McGraw,* 1900
Mark McGrillis, 1892
Austin McHenry, 1918–22
Ed McKean, 1899
Larry McLean, 1904, 1913
Jerry McNertney, 1971–72
Larry McWilliams, 1988
Lee Meadows, 1915–19
Joe Medwick,* 1932–40, 1947–48
Sam Mejias, 1976
Luis Melendez, 1970–76
Steve Melter, 1909
Ted Menze, 1918
John Mercer, 1912
Lloyd Merritt, 1957
Sam Mertes, 1906
Steve Mesner, 1941
Butch Metzger, 1977
Ed Mickelson, 1950
Ed Mierkowicz, 1950
Pete Mikkelson, 1968
Larry Miggins, 1948, 1952
Eddie Miksis, 1957
Bob Miller, 1957, 1959–61
Charlie Miller, 1913–14
Doggie Miller, 1894–95
Dots Miller, 1914–17, 1919
Dusty Miller, 1899
Eddie Miller, 1950
Elmer Miller, 1912
Kohly Miller, 1892
Stu Miller, 1952–54, 1956
Buster Mills, 1934
Larry Milton, 1903

Minnie Minoso, 1962
Clarence Mitchell, 1928–30
Johnny Mize,* 1936–41
Vinegar Bend Mizell, 1952–53, 1956–60
Herb Moford, 1955
Fritz Mollwitz, 1919
Wally Moon, 1954–58
Jim Mooney, 1933–34
Donnie Moore, 1980
Gene Moore, 1933–35
Randy Moore,1937
Terry Moore, 1935–42, 1946–48
Tommy Moore, 1975
Whitey Moore, 1942
Jerry Morales, 1978
Bill Moran, 1892
Charley Moran, 1903, 1908
Forrest More, 1909
Bobby Morgan, 1956
Eddie Morgan, 1936
Joe Morgan, 1964
Gene Moriarty, 1892
John Morris, 1986–90
Walter Morris, 1908
Hap Morse, 1911
Walt Moryn, 1960–61
Mike Mowrey, 1909–13
Jamie Moyer, 1991–
Heinie Mueller, 1920–26
Billy Muffett, 1957–58
Jerry Mumphrey, 1974–79
George Munger, 1943–44, 1946–52
Les Munns, 1936
Steve Mura, 1982
Simmy Murch, 1904–5
Tim Murchison, 1917
Wilbur Murdock, 1908
Ed Murphy, 1901–3
Howard Murphy, 1909
Morg Murphy, 1896–97

Soldier Boy Murphy, 1902
Tom Murphy, 1973
Red Murray, 1906–8
Stan Musial,* 1941–44, 1946–63
Bert Myers, 1896
Hy Myers, 1923–25
Lynn Myers, 1938–39
Mike Nagy, 1973
Sam Nahem, 1941
Sam Narron, 1935, 1942–43
Ken Nash, 1914
Mike Naymick, 1944
Mel Nelson, 1960, 1968–69
Rocky Nelson, 1949–51, 1956
Art Nichols, 1901–3
Kid Nichols,* 1904–5
Charlie Niebergall, 1921, 1923–24
Tom Niedenfuer, 1990
Dick Niehaus, 1913–15
Bert Niehoff, 1918
Bob Nieman, 1960–61
Tom Nieto, 1984–85
Tom Niland, 1896
Pete Noonan, 1906–7
Irv Noren, 1957–59
Fred Norman, 1970–71
Lou North, 1917, 1920–24
Ron Northey, 1947–49
Jose Nossek, 1969–70
Howie Nunn, 1959
Rich Nye, 1970
Rebel Oakes, 1910–13
Ken Oberkfell, 1977–84
Dan O'Brien, 1978–79
Johnny O'Brien, 1958
Jack O'Connor, 1899–1900
Paddy O'Connor, 1914
Ken O'Dea, 1942–46
Bob O'Farrell, 1925–28, 1933, 1935
Brusie Ogrodowski, 1936–37
Bill O'Hara, 1910

Tom O'Hara, 1906–7
Charley O'Leary, 1913
Ed Olivares, 1960–61
Omar Olivares, 1990–
Gene Oliver, 1959, 1961–63
Diomedes Olivo, 1963
Al Olmsted, 1980
Randy O'Neal, 1987–88
Dennie O'Neil, 1893
Jack O'Neill, 1902–3
Mike O'Neill, 1901–4
Jose Oquendo, 1986–
Joe Orengo, 1939–40
Charlie O'Rourke, 1959
Patsy O'Rourke, 1908
Tim O'Rourke, 1894
Ernie Orsatti, 1927–35
Champ Osteen, 1908–9
Claude Osteen, 1974
Jim Otten, 1980–81
Joe Otten, 1895
Mickey Owen, 1937–40
Rick Ownbey, 1984, 1986
Gene Packard, 1917–18
Dick Padden, 1901
Don Padgett, 1937–41
Tom Pagnozzi, 1987–
Phil Paine, 1958
Lowell Palmer, 1972
Al Papai, 1948, 1950
Stan Papi, 1974
Freddy Parent, 1899
Kelly Paris, 1982
Harry Parker, 1970–71, 1975
Roy Parker, 1919
Roy Parmalee, 1936
Tom Parrott, 1896
Stan Partenheimer, 1945
Mike Pasquariello, 1919
Daryl Patterson, 1971
Harry Patton, 1910
Gene Paulette, 1917–19

Gil Paulsen, 1925
George Paynter, 1894
George Pearce, 1917
Frank Pears, 1893
Alex Pearson, 1902
Homer Peel, 1927, 1930
Charlie Peete, 1956
Heinie Peitz, 1894
Joe Peitz, 1894
Geronimo Pena, 1991–
Orlando Pena, 1973–74
Tony Pena, 1987–90
Terry Pendleton, 1984–90
Ray Pepper, 1932–33
Hub Perdue, 1914–15
Mike Perez, 1991–
Pol Perritt, 1912–14
Gerald Perry, 1991–
Pat Perry, 1985–87
Bill Pertica, 1921–23
Steve Peters, 1987–88
Jeff Pfeffer, 1921–24
Ed Phelps, 1909–10
Ed Phillips, 1953
Mike Phillips, 1977–80
Bill Phyle, 1906
Ron Piche, 1966
Charlie Pickett, 1910
George Pinckney, 1892
Vada Pinson, 1969
Cotton Pippen, 1936
Tim Plodinecd, 1972
Tom Poholsky, 1950–51, 1954–56
Howie Pollet, 1941–43, 1946–51
Bill Popp, 1902
Darrell Porter, 1981–85
J. W. Porter, 1959
Mike Potter, 1976–77
Nelson Potter, 1936
Jack Powell, 1899–1901
Ted Power, 1989
Joe Presko, 1951–54

Mike Proly, 1976
George Puccinelli, 1930, 1932
Bob Purkey, 1965
Ambrose Puttmann, 1906
Finners Quinlan, 1913
Joe Quinn, 1893–96, 1898, 1900
Jamie Quirk, 1983
Dan Quisenberry, 1988–89
Roy Radebaugh, 1911
Dave Rader, 1977
Ken Raffensberger, 1939
Gary Rajsich, 1984
John Raleigh, 1909–10
Milt Ramirez, 1970–71
Mike Ramsey, 1978, 1980–84
Dick Rand, 1953, 1955
Vic Raschi, 1954–55
Eric Rasmussen, 1975–78,
    1982–83
Tommy Raub, 1906
Jack Rothrock, 1934–35
Stan Royer, 1991–
Dave Rucker, 1983–84
Ken Rudolph, 1975–76
Jack Russell, 1940
Paul Russell, 1894
John (Jack) Ryan, 1901–3
John Ryan, 1895
Mike Ryba, 1935–38
Ray Sadecki, 1960–66, 1975
Bob Sadowski, 1960
Mark Salas, 1984
Slim Sallee, 1908–16
Ike Samuls, 1895
Orlando Sanchez, 1981–83
Ray Sanders, 1942–45
War Sanders, 1903–4
Rafael Santana, 1983
Al Santorini, 1971–73
Bill Sarni, 1951–52, 1954–56
Ed Sauer, 1949
Hank Sauer, 1956

Ted Savage, 1965–67
Carl Sawatski, 1960–63
Jimmie Schaffer, 1961–62
Bobby Schang, 1927
Bob Scheffing, 1951
Carl Scheib, 1954
Richie Scheinblum, 1974
Bill Schindler, 1920
Freddy Schmidt, 1944, 1946–47
Walter Schmidt, 1925
Willard Schmidt, 1952–53,
    1955–57
Red Schoendienst,* 1945–56,
    1961–63
Dick Schofield, 1953–58, 1968,
    1971
Ossee Schreckengost, 1899
Pop Schriver, 1901
Heine Schuble, 1927, 1936
Johnny Schulte, 1927
Barney Schultz, 1955, 1963–65
Buddy Schultz, 1977–79
Joe Schultz, 1919–24
Walt Schultz, 1920
Ferdie Schupp, 1919–21
Lou Scoffic, 1936
George Scott, 1920
Tony Scott, 1977–81
Kim Seaman, 1979–80
Diego Segui, 1972–73
Epp Sell, 1922–23
Carey Selph, 1929
Walter Sessi, 1941, 1946
Jimmy Sexton, 1983
Mike Shannon, 1962–70
Spike Shannon, 1904–6
Wally Shannon, 1959–60
Bobby Shantz, 1962–64
Al Shaw, 1907–9
Don Shaw, 1971–72
Danny Shay, 1904–5
Gerry Shea, 1905

Jimmy Sheckard, 1913
Biff Sheehan, 1895–96
Ray Sheperdson, 1924
Bill Sherdel, 1918–30, 1932
Tim Sherrill, 1991–
Charlie Shields, 1907
Vince Shields, 1924
Ralph Shinners, 1925
Bob Shirley, 1981
Burt Shotton, 1919–23
Clyde Shoun, 1938–42
Frank Shugart, 1893–94
Dick Siebert, 1937–38
Curt Simmons, 1960–66
Ted Simmons, 1968–80
Dick Simpson, 1968
Dick Sisler, 1946–47, 1952–53
Ted Sizemore, 1971–75
Bob Skinner, 1964–66
Gordon Slade, 1933
Jack Slattery, 1906
Enos Slaughter,* 1938–42,
    1946–53
Bill Smith, 1958–59
Bob Smith, 1957
Bobby Gene Smith, 1957–59, 1962
Bryn Smith, 1990–
Charley Smith, 1966
Earl Smith, 1928–30
Frank Smith, 1955
Fred Smith, 1917
Germany Smith, 1898
Hal Smith, 1956–61
Jack Smith, 1915–26
Jud Smith, 1893
Keith Smith, 1979–80
Lee Smith, 1990–
Lonnie Smith, 1982–85
Ozzie Smith, 1982–
Reggie Smith, 1974–76
Tom Smith, 1898
Wally Smith, 1911–12

Homer Smoot, 1902–6
Red Smyth, 1917–18
Frank Snyder, 1912–19, 1927
Ray Soff, 1986–87
Eddie Solomon, 1976
Kid Somers, 1893
Lary Sorensen, 1981
Elias Sosa, 1975
Allen Sothoron, 1924–26
Billy Southworth, 1926–27, 1929
Bob Spade, 1910
Chris Speier, 1984
Daryl Spencer, 1960–61
Ed Spiezio, 1964–68
Scipio Spinks, 1972–73
Ed Sprague, 1973
Jack Spring, 1964
Joe Sprinz, 1933
Tuck Stainback, 1938
Gerry Staley, 1947–54
Harry Staley, 1895
Tracy Stallard, 1965–66
Virgil Stallcup, 1952–53
Pete Standridge, 1911
Eddie Stanky, 1952–53
Harry Stanton, 1900
Ray Starr, 1932
Bill Steele, 1910–14
Bob Steele, 1916–17
Bill Stein, 1972–73
Jake Stenzel, 1898–99
Ray Stephens, 1990–
Bobby Stephenson, 1955
Stuffy Stewart, 1916–17
Bob Stinson, 1971
Chuck Stobbs, 1958
Milt Stock, 1919–23
Dean Stone, 1959
Tige Stone, 1923
Alan Storke, 1909
Allyn Stout, 1931–32
Cub Stricker, 1892

Joe Stripp, 1938
Johnny Stuart, 1922–25
John Stuper, 1982–84
Willie Sudhoff, 1897–98,
    1899–1901
Joe Sugden, 1898
Harry Sullivan, 1909
Joe Sullivan, 1896
Suter Sullivan, 1898
Tom Sunkel, 1937, 1939
Max Surkont, 1956
Gary Sutherland, 1978
Bruce Sutter, 1981–84
Jack Sutthoff, 1899
Johnny Sutton, 1977
Charlie Swindells, 1904
Steve Swisher, 1978–80
Bob Sykes, 1979–81
John Tamargo, 1976–78
Lee Tate, 1958–59
Don Taussig, 1961
Carl Taylor, 1970
Chuck Taylor, 1969–71
Jack Taylor, 1904–6
Jack (Brewery Jack) Taylor, 1898
Joe Taylor, 1958
Ron Taylor, 1963–65
Rube Taylor, 1903
Bud Teachout, 1932
Patsy Tebeau, 1899–1900
Garry Templeton, 1976–81
Gene Tenace, 1981–82
Greg Terlecky, 1975
Scott Terry, 1987–
Dick Terwiliger, 1932
Bob Tewksbury, 1989–
Moe Thacker, 1963
Tommy Thevenow, 1924–28
Jake Thielman, 1905–6
Roy Thomas, 1978–80
Tom Thomas, 1899–1900
Gus Thompson, 1906

384

Mike Thompson, 1973–74
Milt Thompson, 1989–
Bob Tiefenauer, 1952, 1955, 1961
Bud Tinning, 1935
Bobby Tolan, 1965–68
Fred Toney, 1923
Specs Toporcer, 1921–28
Joe Torre, 1969–74
Mike Torrez, 1967–71
Paul Toth, 1962
Harry Trekell, 1913
Coaker Triplett, 1941–43
Bill Trotter, 1944
Tommy Tucker, 1898
John Tudor, 1985–88, 1990
Oscar Tuero, 1918–20
Lee Tunnell, 1987
Tuck Turner, 1896–98
Old Hose Twineham, 1893–94
Mike Tyson, 1972–79
Bob Uecker, 1964–65
Tom Underwood, 1977
Jack Urdan, 1959
Jose Uribe, 1984
John Urrea, 1977–80
Lou Ury, 1903
Benny Valenzuela, 1958
Bill Van Dyke, 1892
Andy Van Slyke, 1983–86
Dazzy Vance,* 1933–34
John Vann, 1913
Emil Verban, 1944–46
Johnny Vergez, 1936
Ernie Vick, 1922, 1924–26
Bob Vines, 1924
Bill Virdon, 1955–56
Dave Von Ohlen, 1983–84
Bill Voss, 1972
Pete Vuckovich, 1978–80
Ben Wade, 1954
Leon Wagner, 1960
Bill Walker, 1933–36

Duane Walker, 1988
Harry Walker, 1940–43, 1946–47,
  1950–51, 1955
Joe Walker, 1923
Roy Walker, 1921–22
Tom Walker, 1976
Bobby Wallace,* 1899–1901
Mike Wallace, 1975–76
Ty Waller, 1980
Denny Walling, 1988–90
Dick Ward, 1935
Cy Warmoth, 1916
Lon Warneke, 1937–42
Jack Warner, 1905
Bill Warwick, 1925–26
Carl Warwick, 1961–62, 1964–65
Ray Washburn, 1961–69
Gary Waslewski, 1969
Steve Waterbury, 1976
George Watkins, 1930–33
Milt Watson, 1916–17
Art Weaver, 1902–3
Skeeter Webb, 1932
Herm Wehmeier, 1956–58
Bob Weiland, 1937–40
Perry Werden, 1892–93
Bill Werle, 1952
Wally Westlake, 1951–52
Gus Weyhing, 1900
Dick Wheeler, 1918
Jim Whelan, 1913
Pete Whisenant, 1955
Lew Whistler, 1893
Ade White, 1937
Bill White, 1959–65
Ernie White, 1940–43
Hal White, 1953–54
Jerry White, 1986
Burgess Whitehead, 1933–35
Fred Whitfield, 1962
Possum Whitted, 1912–14
Bob Wicker, 1901–3

Floyd Wicker, 1968
Bill Wight, 1958
Fred Wigington, 1923
Del Wilbur, 1946–49
Hoyt Wilhelm,* 1957
Denney Wilie, 1911–12
Ted Wilks, 1944–51
Jimy Williams, 1966–67
Otto Williams, 1902–3
Stan Williams, 1971
Steamboat Williams, 1914, 1916
Howie Williamson, 1928
Joe Willis, 1911–13
Ron Willis, 1966–69
Vic Willis, 1910
Charlie Wilson, 1932–33, 1935
Craig Wilson, 1989–
Jimmie Wilson, 1928–33
Owen Wilson, 1914–16
Zeke Wilson, 1899
Ivy Wingo, 1911–14
Jim Winford, 1932, 1934–37
Tom Winsett, 1935
Rick Wise, 1972–73
Corky Withrow, 1963
Chicken Wolf, 1892

Harry Wolter, 1907
John Wood, 1896
Gene Woodburn, 1911–12
Hal Woodeschick, 1965–67
Frank Woodward, 1919
Floyd Wooldridge, 1955
Todd Worrell, 1985–89
Red Worthington, 1934
Mel Wright, 1954–55
Stan Yerkes, 1901–3
Ray Yochim, 1948–49
Babe Young, 1948
Cy Young,* 1899–1900
Joe Young 1892
Pep Young, 1941, 1945
Joel Youngblood, 1977
Eddie Yuhas, 1952–53
Sal Yvars, 1953–54
Chris Zachary, 1971
Elmer Zacher, 1910
George Zackert, 1911–12
Dave Zearfoss, 1904–5
Todd Zeile, 1989–
Bart Zeller, 1970
Eddie Zimmerman, 1906
Ed Zmich, 1910–11

Player Totals by Letter

A = 44
B = 151
C = 122
D = 83
E = 25
F = 48
G = 74
H = 119
I = 2
J = 35
K = 59
L = 71
M = 149
N = 24

O = 33
P = 65
Q = 4
R = 69
S = 153
T = 44
U = 6
V = 13
W = 79
X = 0
Y = 9
Z = 8
Total = 1489

*Hall of Famer.

Note: Including the above listed players that are marked with an asterisk, Branch Rickey and Bill McKechnie are also in the Hall of Fame (for off-the-field accomplishments). Walt Alston and Miller Huggins are also in the Hall of Fame primarily for off-the-field accomplishments.

Appendix C
Managers of the Cardinals

Chris Von Der Ahe, 1892
Bill Watkins, 1893
George Miller, 1894
Al Buckenberger, 1895
Joe Quinn, 1895
Lew Phelan, 1895
Chris Von Der Ahe, 1895
Harry Diddlebock, 1896
Arlie Latham, 1896
Chris Von Der Ahe, 1896
Roger Connor,* 1896
Tommy Dowd, 1896–97
Hugh Nicol, 1897
Bill Hallman, 1897
Chris Von Der Ahe, 1897
Tim Hurst, 1898
Patsy Tebeau, 1899–1900
Louis Heilbroner, 1900
Patsy Donovan, 1901–3
Kid Nichols,* 1904–5
Jimmy Burke, 1905
Matthew Stanley Robison, 1905
John McCloskey, 1906–8
Roger Bresnahan,* 1909–12
Miller Huggins,* 1913–17
Jack Hendricks, 1918
Branch Rickey,* 1919–25
Rogers Hornsby,* 1925–26
Bob O'Farrell, 1927
Bill McKechnie,* 1928

Billy Southworth, 1929
Bill McKechnie, 1929
Gabby Street, 1930–33
Frankie Frisch,* 1933–38
Mike Gonzales, 1938
Ray Blades, 1939–40
Mike Gonzalez, 1940
Billy Southworth, 1940–45
Eddie Dyer, 1946–50
Marty Marion, 1951
Eddie Stanky, 1952–55
Harry Walker, 1955
Fred Hutchinson, 1956–58
Stan Hack, 1958
Solly Hemus, 1959–61
Johnny Keane, 1961–64
Red Schoendienst,* 1965–76
Vern Rapp, 1977–78
Ken Boyer, 1978–80
Jack Krol, 1980
Whitey Herzog, 1980
Red Schoendienst, 1980
Whitey Herzog, 1981–90
Red Schoendienst, 1990
Joe Torre, 1990–

*Hall of Famer.
Note: Forty-six different men have managed the Cardinals in fifty-five moves since 1892.

Appendix D

Cardinal Players Who Also Managed (77)

Walt Alston (Bkn [N] 1954–57; LA [N] 1958–76)
Ray Blades (StL [N] 1939–40)
Jim Bottomley (StL [A] 1937)
Ken Boyer (StL [N] 1978–80)
Roger Bresnahan (StL [N] 1909–12; Chi [N] 1915)
Tom Brown (Was [N] 1897–98)
Jimmy Burke (StL [N] 1905; StL [A] 1918–20)
Roger Connor (StL [N] 1896)
Pat Corrales (Tex [A] 1979–80; Phi [N] 1982–83; Cle [A] 1983–87)
Roger Craig (SD [N] 1978–79; SF [N] 1985–)
Lave Cross (Cle [N] 1899)
Alvin Dark (SF [N] 1961–64; KC [A] 1966–67; Cle [A] 1968–71; Oak [A] 1974–75; SD [N] 1977)
Spud Davis (Pit [N] 1946)
Patsy Donovan (Pit [N] 1897, 1899; StL [N] 1901–3; Was [A] 1904; Bkn [N] 1906–8; Bos [A] 1910–11)
Tommy Dowd (StL [N] 1896–97)
Leo Durocher (Bkn [N] 1939–46; 1948; NY [N] 1948–55; Chi [N] 1966–72; Hou [N] 1972–73)
Eddie Dyer (StL [N] 1946–50)
Herman Franks (SF [N] 1965–68; Chi [N] 1977–79)
Joe Frazier (NY [N] 1976–77)
Frankie Frisch (StL [N] 1933–38; Pit [N] 1940–46; Chi [N] 1949–51)
Kid Gleason (Chi [A] 1919–23)
Mike Gonzalez (StL [N] 1938, 1940)
Alex Grammas (Pit [N] 1969; Mil [A] 1976–77)
Sandy Griffin (Was [AA] 1891)
Burleigh Grimes (Bkn [N] 1937–38)
Charlie Grimm (Chi [N] 1932–38, 1944–49, 1960; Bos [N] 1952; Mil [N] 1953–56)
Don Guttereidge (Chi [A] 1969–70)
Bill Hallman (StL [N] 1897)

Fred Haney (StL [A] 1939–41; Pit [N] 1953–55; Mil [N] 1956–59)
Grady Hatton (Hou [N] 1966–68)
Solly Hemus (StL [N] 1959–61)
Rogers Hornsby (StL [N] 1925–26; Bos [N] 1928; Chi [N] 1930–32; StL [A] 1933–37, 1952; Cin [N] 1952–53)
Art Howe (Hou [N] 1989–)
Miller Huggins (StL [N] 1913–17; NY [A] 1918–29)
Darrell Johnson (Bos [A] 1974–76; Sea [A] 1977–80; Tex [A] 1981–82)
Eddie Kasko (Bos [A] 1970–73)
Don Kessinger (Chi [A] 1979)
Lou Klein (Chi [N] 1961–62, 1965)
Arlie Latham (StL [N] 1896)
Bob Lillis (Hou [N] 1982–85)
Whitey Lockman (Chi [N] 1972–74)
Rabbit Maranville (Chi [N] 1925)
Marty Marion (StL [N] 1951; StL [A] 1952–53; Chi [A] 1954–56)
Gene Mauch (Phi [N] 1960–68; Mon [N] 1969–75; Min [A] 1976–80; Cal [A] 1981–82, 1985–87)
George McBride (Was [A] 1921)
Jim McCormick (Cle [N] 1879–80)
John McGraw (Bal [N] 1899; Bal [A] 1901–2; NY [N] 1902–32)
Buster Mills (Cin [N] 1953)
Terry Moore (Phi [N] 1954)
Joe Morgan (Bos [A] 1988–91)
Kid Nichols (StL [N] 1904–5)
Jack O'Connor (StL [A] 1910)
Bob O'Farrell (StL [N] 1927; Cin [N] 1934)
Joe Quinn (StL [N] 1895; Cle [N] 1899)
Del Rice (Cal [A] 1972)
Wilbert Robinson (Bal [A] 1902; Bkn [N] 1914–31)
Cookie Rojas (Cal [A] 1988)
Bob Scheffing (Chi [N] 1957–59; Det [A] 1961–63)
Red Schoendienst (StL [N] 1965–76, 1980, 1990)
Burt Shotton (Phi [N] 1928–33; Cin [N] 1934; Bkn [N] 1947, 1948–50)
Dick Sisler (Cin [N] 1964–65)
Bob Skinner (Phi [N] 1968–69; SD [N] 1977)
Jack Slattery (Bos [N] 1928)
Allen Sothoron (StL [A] 1933)
Billy Southworth (StL [N] 1929, 1940–45; Bos [N] 1946–51)
Eddie Stanky (StL [N] 1952–55; Chi [A] 1966–68; Tex [A] 1977)
Patsy Tebeau (Cle [P] 1890; Cle [N] 1892–98; StL [N] 1899–1900)
Joe Torre (NY [N] 1977–81; Atl [N] 1982–84; StL [N] 1990–)

Bill Virdon (Pit [N] 1972–73; NY [A] 1974–75; Hou [N] 1975–82; Mon [N] 1983–84)
Harry Walker (StL [N] 1955; Pit [N] 1965–67; Hou [N] 1968–72)
Bobby Wallace (StL [A] 1911–12; Cin [N] 1937)
Del Wilbur (Tex [A] 1973)
Jimy Williams (Tor [A] 1986–89)
Jimmie Wilson (Phi [N] 1934–38; Chi [N] 1941–44)
Ivy Wingo (Cin [N] 1916)
Chicken Wolf (Lou [AA] 1889)
Cy Young (Bos [A] 1907)

Note: N = National League; A = American League; P = Players League; AA = American Association.

Appendix E
Cardinals Who Won Awards

<u>Most Valuable Player</u>
1925—Rogers Hornsby
1926—Bob O'Farrell
1928—Jim Bottomley
1931—Frankie Frisch
1934—Dizzy Dean
1937—Ducky Medwick
1942—Mort Cooper
1943—Stan Musial
1944—Marty Marion
1946—Stan Musial
1948—Stan Musial
1964—Ken Boyer
1967—Orlando Cepeda
1968—Bob Gibson
1971—Joe Torre
1979—Keith Hernandez (cowinner)
1985—Willie McGee

<u>Gold Gloves</u>
Ken Boyer 1958–61, 1963
Bill White 1960–65
Bobby Shantz 1962–63
Curt Flood 1963–69
Bob Gibson 1965–73
Dal Maxvill 1968
Ken Reitz 1975
Keith Hernandez 1978–82
Ozzie Smith 1982–

Willie McGee 1983, 1985–86
Joaquin Andujar 1984
Terry Pendleton 1987, 1989

<u>Cy Young</u>
1968—Bob Gibson

<u>Rookie of the Year</u>
1954—Wally Moon
1955—Bill Virdon
1974—Bake McBride
1985—Vince Coleman
1986—Todd Worrell

<u>Triple Crown</u>
1922—Rogers Hornsby (42 HRs,
    152 RBIs, .401 AVG)
1925—Rogers Hornsby (39 HRs,
    143 RBIs, .403 AVG)
1937—Ducky Medwick (31 HRs,
    154 RBIs, .374 AVG)

Note: MVPs prior to 1931 were selected
by the league; since 1931 they have
been picked by writers. The Cy Young
Award was not issued before 1956, the
Rookie award not issued before 1947,
Gold Gloves not awarded before 1957.

Appendix F
Cardinals Who Led the National League

Batting Averages
1901—Jesse Burkett (.382)
1920—Rogers Hornsby (.370)
1921—Rogers Hornsby (.397)
1922—Rogers Hornsby (.401)
1923—Rogers Hornsby (.384)
1925—Rogers Hornsby (.403)
1931—Chick Hafey (.349)
1937—Ducky Medwick (.374)
1939—Johnny Mize (.349)
1943—Stan Musial (.357)
1946—Stan Musial (.365)
1948—Stan Musial (.376)
1950—Stan Musial (.346)
1951—Stan Musial (.355)
1952—Stan Musial (.336)
1957—Stan Musial (.351)
1971—Joe Torre (.363)
1979—Keith Hernandez (.344)
1985—Willie McGee (.353)
1990—Willie McGee (.335)*

Home Runs
1922—Rogers Hornsby (42)
1925—Rogers Hornsby (39)
1928—Jim Bottomley (31)+
1934—Ripper Collins (35)+
1937—Ducky Medwick (31)+
1939—Johnny Mize (28)
1940—Johnny Mize (43)

Runs Batted In (since 1907)
1920—Rogers Hornsby (94)+
1921—Rogers Hornsby (126)

1922—Rogers Hornsby (152)
1925—Rogers Hornsby (143)
1926—Jim Bottomley (120)
1928—Jim Bottomley (136)
1936—Ducky Medwick (138)
1937—Ducky Medwick (154)
1938—Ducky Medwick (122)
1940—Johnny Mize (137)
1946—Enos Slaughter (130)
1948—Stan Musial (131)
1956—Stan Musial (109)
1964—Ken Boyer (119)
1967—Orlando Cepeda (111)
1971—Joe Torre (137)

Runs Scored
1901—Jesse Burkett (139)
1921—Rogers Hornsby (131)
1922—Rogers Hornsby (141)
1924—Rogers Hornsby (121)+
1933—Pepper Martin (122)
1937—Ducky Medwick (111)
1946—Stan Musial (135)
1948—Stan Musial (135)
1951—Stan Musial (124)+
1952—Stan Musial (105)+
     —Solly Hemus (105)+
1954—Stan Musial (120)+
1967—Lou Brock (113)+
1971—Lou Brock (126)
1979—Keith Hernandez (116)
1980—Keith Hernandez (111)
1982—Lonnie Smith (120)

Hits
1910—Jesse Burkett (228)
1920—Rogers Hornsby (218)
1921—Rogers Hornsby (235)
1922—Rogers Hornsby (250)
1924—Rogers Hornsby (227)
1925—Jim Bottomley (227)
1936—Ducky Medwick (223)
1937—Ducky Medwick (237)
1942—Enos Slaughter (188)
1943—Stan Musial (220)
1944—Stan Musial (197)
1946—Stan Musial (228)
1948—Stan Musial (230)
1949—Stan Musial (207)
1952—Stan Musial (194)
1964—Curt Flood (211)+
1971—Joe Torre (230)
1979—Garry Templeton (211)
1985—Willie McGee (216)

Walks
1892—Jack Crooks (136)
1893—Jack Crooks (121)
1910—Miller Huggins (116)
1914—Miller Huggins (105)
1924—Rogers Hornsby (89)
1953—Stan Musial (105)
1987—Jack Clark (136)

Doubles
1911—Ed Konetchy (38)
1920—Rogers Hornsby (44)
1921—Rogers Hornsby (44)
1922—Rogers Hornsby (46)
1924—Rogers Hornsby (43)
1925—Jim Bottomley (44)
1926—Jim Bottomley (40)
1931—Sparky Adams (46)
1936—Ducky Medwick (64)
1937—Ducky Medwick (56)
1938—Ducky Medwick (47)

1939—Enos Slaughter (52)
1941—Johnny Mize (39)+
1942—Marty Marion (38)
1943—Stan Musial (48)
1944—Stan Musial (51)
1946—Stan Musial (50)
1948—Stan Musial (46)
1949—Stan Musial (49)
1950—Red Schoendienst (43)
1952—Stan Musial (42)
1953—Stan Musial (53)
1954—Stan Musial (41)
1963—Dick Groat (43)
1968—Lou Brock (46)
1979—Keith Hernandez (48)
1989—Pedro Guerrero (42)+

Triples
1893—Perry Werden (29)
1915—Tommy Long (25)
1917—Rogers Hornsby (17)
1921—Rogers Hornsby (18)
1928—Jim Bottomley (20)
1934—Ducky Medwick (18)
1938—Johnny Mize (16)
1942—Enos Slaughter (17)
1943—Stan Musial (20)
1946—Stan Musial (20)
1948—Stan Musial (18)
1949—Stan Musial (13)+
     —Enos Slaughter (13)+
1951—Stan Musial (12)+
1966—Tim McCarver (13)
1968—Lou Brock (14)
1977—Garry Templeton (18)
1978—Garry Templeton (13)
1979—Garry Templeton (19)
1985—Willie McGee (18)
1991—Ray Lankford (15)

Total Bases
1901—Jesse Burkett (313)

394

1917—Rogers Hornsby (253)
1920—Rogers Hornsby (329)
1921—Rogers Hornsby (378)
1922—Rogers Hornsby (450)
1924—Rogers Hornsby (373)
1925—Rogers Hornsby (381)
1926—Jim Bottomley (305)
1928—Jim Bottomley (363)
1934—Ripper Collins (369)
1935—Ducky Medwick (365)
1936—Ducky Medwick (367)
1937—Ducky Medwick (406)
1938—Johnny Mize (326)
1939—Johnny Mize (353)
1940—Johnny Mize (368)
1942—Enos Slaughter (292)
1943—Stan Musial (347)
1946—Stan Musial (366)
1948—Stan Musial (429)
1949—Stan Musial (382)
1951—Stan Musial (355)
1952—Stan Musial (311)
1971—Joe Torre (352)

Slugging Percentage
1917—Rogers Hornsby (.484)
1920—Rogers Hornsby (.559)
1921—Rogers Hornsby (.639)
1922—Rogers Hornsby (.722)
1923—Rogers Hornsby (.627)
1924—Rogers Hornsby (.696)
1925—Rogers Hornsby (.756)
1927—Chick Hafey (.590)
1934—Ripper Collins (.615)
1937—Ducky Medwick (.641)
1939—Johnny Mize (.626)
1940—Johnny Mize (.636)
1943—Stan Musial (.562)
1944—Stan Musial (.549)
1946—Stan Musial (.587)
1948—Stan Musial (.702)
1950—Stan Musial (.596)

1952—Stan Musial (.538)
1987—Jack Clark (.597)

Wins
1926—Flint Rhem (20)+
1931—Bill Hallahan (19)+
1934—Dizzy Dean (30)
1935—Dizzy Dean (28)
1942—Mort Cooper (22)
1943—Mort Cooper (21)+
1945—Red Barrett (23)‡
1946—Howie Pollet (21)
1960—Ernie Broglio (21)+
1970—Bob Gibson (23)+
1984—Joaquin Andujar (20)

Stolen Bases
1900—Patsy Donovan (45)
1927—Frankie Frisch (48)
1931—Frankie Frisch (28)
1933—Pepper Martin (26)
1934—Pepper Martin (23)
1936—Pepper Martin (23)
1945—Red Schoendienst (26)
1966—Lou Brock (74)
1967—Lou Brock (52)
1968—Lou Brock (62)
1969—Lou Brock (53)
1971—Lou Brock (64)
1972—Lou Brock (63)
1973—Lou Brock (70)
1974—Lou Brock (118)
1985—Vince Coleman (110)
1986—Vince Coleman (107)
1987—Vince Coleman (109)
1988—Vince Coleman (81)
1989—Vince Coleman (65)
1990—Vince Coleman (77)

Strikeouts
1906—Fred Beebe (171)**
1930—Bill Hallahan (177)

1931—Bill Hallahan (159)
1932—Dizzy Dean (191)
1933—Dizzy Dean (199)
1934—Dizzy Dean (195)
1935—Dizzy Dean (182)
1948—Harry Brecheen (149)
1958—Sam Jones (225)
1968—Bob Gibson (268)
1989—Jose DeLeon (201)

Earned Run Average (since 1913)
1914—Bill Doak (1.72)
1921—Bill Doak (2.59)
1942—Mort Cooper (1.78)
1943—Howie Pollet (1.75)
1946—Howie Pollet (2.10)
1948—Harry Brecheen (2.24)
1968—Bob Gibson (1.12)
1976—John Denny (2.52)
1988—Joe Magrane (2.18)

Innings Pitched
1894—Ted Breitenstein (447)
1898—Jack Taylor (397)
1907—Stoney McGlynn (352)
1932—Dizzy Dean (286)
1935—Dizzy Dean (324)
1936—Dizzy Dean (315)
1945—Red Barrett (285)‡
1946—Howie Pollet (266)
1960—Larry Jackson (282)
1984—Joaquin Andujar (261)+

Saves (since 1969)
1975—Al Hrabosky (22)+
1981—Bruce Sutter (25)
1982—Bruce Sutter (36)
1984—Bruce Sutter (45)
1986—Todd Worrell (36)
1991—Lee Smith (47)

Complete Games
1894—Ted Breitenstein (46)
1897—Red Donohue (38)+
1898—Jack Taylor (42)
1899—Cy Young (40)+
    —Jack Powell (40)+
1901—Jack Powell (45)
1904—Jack Powell (39)
1907—Stoney McGlynn (33)
1927—Pop Haines (25)+
1933—Dizzy Dean (26)+
1934—Dizzy Dean (24)
1935—Dizzy Dean (29)
1936—Dizzy Dean (28)
1945—Red Barrett (24)‡
1969—Bob Gibson (28)

Shutouts
1900—Cy Young (4)
1924—Allen Sothoron (4)+
1927—Pop Haines (6)
1932—Dizzy Dean (4)+
1934—Dizzy Dean (7)
1942—Mort Cooper (10)
1944—Mort Cooper (7)
1948—Harry Brecheen (7)
1949—Howie Pollet (5)+
1953—Harvey Haddix (6)
1962—Bob Gibson (5)+
1966—Bob Gibson (5)+
    —Larry Jaster (5)+
1968—Bob Gibson (13)
1971—Bob Gibson (5)
1984—Joaquin Andujar (4)+
1985—John Tudor (10)

*Ended year in Oakland (AL).
+Tied.
‡Started year in Philadelphia (NL).
**Started year in Chicago (NL).

Bibliography

Aaron, Hank, and Lonnie Wheeler. *I Had a Hammer*. New York: Harper-Collins, 1991.

Alexander, Charles C. *John McGraw*. New York: Penguin, 1988.

Boswell, Thomas. *Why Time Begins on Opening Day*. New York: Penguin, 1984.

Complete Baseball Record Book. St. Louis: Sporting News Publishing, 1989.

Fleming, G. H. *The Dizziest Season*. New York: William Morrow, 1984.

———. *The Unforgettable Season*. New York: Fireside, 1981.

Frommer, Harvey. *Primitive Baseball*. New York: Atheneum, 1988.

Golenbock, Peter. *Bums: An Oral History of the Brooklyn Dodgers*. New York: Pocket Books, 1984.

Herzog, Whitey, and Kevin Harrigan. *White Rat*. New York: Harper & Row, 1987.

Honig, Donald. *The National League*, rev. ed. New York: Crown, 1987.

Hood, Robert E. *The Gashouse Gang*. New York: William Morrow & Co., 1976.

Kahn, Roger. *The Boys of Summer*. New York: Perennial Library, 1987.

Kiner, Ralph, and Joe Gergen. *Kiner's Korner*. New York: Arbor House, 1987.

Kuhn, Bowie. *Hardball*. New York: Times Books, 1987.

MacFarlane, Paul, ed. *Hall of Fame Fact Book*. St. Louis: Sporting News Publishing, 1982.

Mead, William B. *Two Spectacular Seasons*. New York: Macmillan, 1990.

Miller, James Edward. *The Baseball Business*. Chapel Hill, NC: University of North Carolina Press, 1990.

Musial, Stan, and Bob Broeg. *Stan Musial*. Garden City, NY: Doubleday, 1964.

Nash, Bruce, and Allan Zullo. *The Baseball Hall of Shame*. New York: Pocket Books, 1985.

Neft, David S., and Richard M. Cohen. *The Sports Encyclopedia: Baseball*, 7th ed. New York: St. Martin's Press, 1989.

Nemec, David. *Great Baseball Feats, Facts, and Firsts*. New York: New American Library, 1989.

Official Baseball Dope Book. St. Louis: Sporting News Publishing, 1981.

Official Baseball Guide, 1980–91. St. Louis: Sporting News Publishing, 1991.

Official World Series Record Book. St. Louis: Sporting News Publishing, 1979.

Reichler, Joseph L. ed. *The Baseball Encyclopedia*, 7th ed. New York: Macmillan, 1988.

Reidenbaugh, Lowell. *Baseball's 25 Greatest Pennant Races.* St. Louis: Sporting News Publishing, 1987.

Ritter, Lawrence S. *The Glory of Their Times.* New York: Vintage Books, 1985.

Robinson, George, and Charles Salzberg. *Baseball's Worst Teams.* New York: Bantam Doubleday Dell Publishing Group, 1991.

Schaap, Dick. *Steinbrenner.* New York: Avon Books, 1982.

Seymour, Harold. *Baseball*, 2 vols. New York: Oxford University Press, 1989.

Smith, Ozzie, and Rob Rains. *Wizard.* Chicago: Contemporary Books, 1988.

Talley, Rick. *The Cubs of '69.* Chicago: Contemporary Books, 1989.

Veeck, Bill, and Ed Linn. *Veeck—As in Wreck.* New York: Bantam Books, 1962.

Will, George F. *Men at Work.* New York: HarperCollins, 1990.